DANGER CLOSE!

A Vietnam Memoir

Phil Gioia

STACKPOLE
BOOKS
Essex, Connecticut

STACKPOLE BOOKS

An imprint of Globe Pequot, the trade division of The Rowman & Littlefield
Publishing Group, Inc.
4501 Forbes Blvd., Ste. 200
Lanham, MD 20706
www.rowman.com

Distributed by NATIONAL BOOK NETWORK

British Library Cataloguing in Publication Information available

Library of Congress Cataloging-in-Publication Data

Names: Gioia, Philip J., 1946- author.
Title: Danger close! : a Vietnam memoir / Phil Gioia.
Description: Guilford, Connecticut : Stackpole Books, [2022] | Summary: "Danger
    Close! recounts the Vietnam War from the unique boots-on-the-ground perspective
    of a young officer who served two tours in two different divisions. He tells his story
    thoughtfully, straightforwardly, and vividly, from the raw emotions of unearthing
    massacred human beings to the terrors of fighting in the dark, with tracers slicing
    the air"— Provided by publisher.
Identifiers: LCCN 2021048907 (print) | LCCN 2021048908 (ebook) | ISBN
    9780811771207 (cloth) | ISBN 9780811771214 (ebook)
Subjects: LCSH: Gioia, Philip J., 1946- | Vietnam War, 1961-1975—Personal
    narratives, American. | Vietnam War, 1961-1975—Biography. | LCGFT:
    Biographies. | Personal narratives.
Classification: LCC DS559.5 .G57 2022 (print) | LCC DS559.5 (ebook) | DDC
    959.704/3092 [B—dc23/eng/20211012
LC record available at https://lccn.loc.gov/2021048907
LC ebook record available at https://lccn.loc.gov/2021048908

♾️™ The paper used in this publication meets the minimum requirements of
American National Standard for Information Sciences—Permanence of Paper
for Printed Library Materials, ANSI/NISO Z39.48-1992.

This memoir is a window into a life begun seventy-five years ago, in a very different America. It is of growing up in an Army family during the Cold War, and of combat as a young infantry officer, in a war fought long ago, and far away.

Phil Gioia
Marin County, California
2022

To my mother and father, with eternal gratitude.

CONTENTS

CONTENTS

INTRODUCTION:
FLIGHT TO PHU BAI

February 1968

Somewhere over the mountains we punched into a dark, violent storm front. An hour earlier we baked in oven-like heat at Chu Lai as other troop serials boarded boxy, twin-engine C-123s painted in sand-green camouflage. Angular-snouted F-4 Phantoms taxied past, canopies raised, oxygen masks dangling from the crews' helmets. A few fighter jocks looked over at us, raising a gloved-hand thumbs-up. Some troops waved; a few cheered. Most sat motionless, weapons across their knees.

So new in-country that we were still in jump boots and stateside fatigues, we watched the bedlam, bludgeoned by shrill turboprops and earsplitting roars of jets climbing out in full afterburner.

Now in the iron grip of the storm, the plane bucketed up and down, dropping with a lurch, men rising weightless off the seats. Across the compartment a few tried sleeping, slumped on nylon-and-tubing seats. Others stared into their thoughts. A pair shouted to each other, barely heard above the roaring engines ten feet away beyond the thin aluminum skin.

Blue-white lightning cracked past the view ports. We sank in a sickening sideways slide. I wondered if the plane could fly on one engine. The troops seemed unconcerned; most had been here before, a few twice.

As we howled down through the storm, I reflected on volunteering. Whatever was going to be was on the way. The plane leveled; I stood, turning to the door's view port. What I saw remains flickering, badly lit—a film detailed now as fifty years ago.

We raced through purplish light under immense dark clouds fat with rain. Water sheeted past the port. As far as I could see were dark marshes, silver paddies, long lines of trees swaying in high wind, lit by strobes of lightning.

Descent brought more into focus: rice fields, a fast glimpse of a figure in a paddy astride an animal—a buffalo?—then a dirt road, rows of barbed-wire fencing, another road, and WHAM! We were down, braking hard, props reversing, equipment straining to break loose.

Taxiing past rows of helicopters, fuel bowsers, jeeps, and trucks, we turned, slowed, and stopped. The engines wound down. The whine of the tail ramp motor brought hot, wet air stinking of kerosene-based JP-4, rotting vegetation, and swamp mud. We gathered gear to deplane.

Turning in to a sandbagged revetment across from us, a twin-rotor Marine CH-46 helicopter lowered its tail ramp. It had flown from the combat base at Khe Sanh, under siege on the Laotian border. We looked straight into its troop compartment filled with haggard, helmeted men in flak jackets.

Three humped, gray-green bags lay on the deck at their feet. Four to each, the men carried the sagging bags down the ramp in the rain. A truck idled, its tailgate lowered. With care they lifted their burdens, sliding them onto the truck bed.

A Marine captain appeared. Rain poured off the brim of his utility cap. "What outfit you people with?"

"82nd Airborne, Sir."

He looked at the streaming sky, communing with some unseen Marine god. "Paratroopers. All we need."

I looked at my platoon sergeant. He grinned like a Cheshire cat.

How did I get here? What was to come? I always wanted to lead American soldiers in action. I volunteered for hazardous duty; I trained for combat. The path I followed was a long one; it began immediately after the greatest war the world had ever known. This is that story.

WHO WE WERE

In the 1950s and 1960s, children in Army families were frequently referred to as "Army brats." A colorful term, though it misses the mark. Most military children of that era were anything but "brats." Due to the challenges posed by their military environment and frequent moves to new assignments, they had to be adaptive, perceptive, reactive, and creative. Far more than in civilian life, a military child's behavior could reflect directly on his or her parents' careers.

In my generation as an Army child in the 1950s, you belonged to an extended tribe, with an inherited, carefully guarded culture, handed down with its own myths, stories, legends, and rituals.

Sounds were unique. Drums and bugles, military bands; the boom of the evening gun; the music of "Retreat" as the flag was slowly lowered every evening. Everyone—walking, driving, running—stopped and faced the flag, or the music if they couldn't see the flag, with their hand on their heart; the men in uniform saluting. It was done naturally and silently, a tableau that froze everyone for a minute or two, then they went on their way.

Sounds of helicopters, truck convoys, tanks, and armored vehicles. The strident, urgent braying of the alert horn, hoarse and imperative. The signature sound of the Cold War.

Smells and tastes. On the seagoing transports that took us abroad and brought us home, machine oil, a whiff of the day's entrée, and fresh paint. On Army posts, the smell of sun on hot canvas treated with water repellent. The chemical taste of water from "Lister" bags. Tropical chocolate from old C-rations; hard as brown crayons, with a waxy undertaste.

Freshly buffed floor wax in the hospital corridors. Hoppe's Number 10 gun oil, when your father shot for record every year and cleaned his weapon on the back porch.

Mogas exhaust, from jeeps and trucks. Cigarette, cigar, and pipe smoke, in all the buildings. And coffee brewing; the Army ran on it.

Never-ending activities: blood drives and bond drives, Cub Scouts, Boy Scouts, and Girl Scouts. The moms volunteered as "Gray Ladies" at the hospital, and were in constant rounds of coffees, civic or relief projects, and bridge games.

Slack times: weekend dinners with the family at the Officers Club. Summers at the post swimming pool. Rainy days, nestled in a comfy armchair at the post library. My first library card, from the Old Cadet Library at West Point: a replica of the Army Engineers' castle insignia, with stone turrets, creaky stacks, and wood floors worn down by generations of cadets.

Army medicine: the dispensaries were open 24-7. Aches, pains, and fevers under 105? The remedy was a big, white all-purpose capsule, an APC. The three main ingredients were aspirin, phenacetin, and caffeine. Phenacetin is a painkiller; it boosts the aspirin. With caffeine? Just the thing to prescribe to kids; it's a wonder we survived.

Coughs? The solution was "elixir turpinhydrate." Likely the most effective cough suppressant ever, and for good reason. The medical dictionary defines it as "a preparation of the expectorant terpin hydrate, with sweet orange peel tincture, benzaldehyde, glycerin, alcohol, syrup, water, and the antitussive opiate codeine." Alcohol? Codeine? No wonder it was known as "GI gin." It was prescribed to kids as well.

If the West Point hospital had given out "frequent customer" cards, mine would have been the platinum version. I fell off bikes, out of trees, and once from a cliff behind the Catholic chapel. No wonder I became a paratrooper; I worked through all that "fear of falling" stuff.

When I showed up at the emergency room or the dispensary, the medics would get out the suture kits. To this day the smell of rubbing alcohol brings memories of medics and nurses in starched whites, and Army doctors in the old TW, "tropical weight," short-sleeved tan uniforms.

Recovering from a really bad bike accident in 1955, I watched the first H-bomb test on a black-and-white TV set in the solarium of the old West Point hospital. Several nurses in starched whites, an old sergeant, and me in a blue Army hospital bathrobe. As the countdown ended and the bomb went off, the cameras overloaded, turning the TV screen white in the glare. The sergeant said, "Jay-zus! Kid, I don't envy you the future!" At which, one of the nurses bopped him on the head with a folded magazine.

We grew up under the specter of the Bomb. I don't recall anyone being neurotic about it. We trusted our parents to do the right thing, whatever that was. We trusted in the government.

Sure, there were "duck-and-cover" drills, where we dropped off our desk chairs in school and rolled up in a ball on the floor until the teacher told us it was OK to come up. My classmate Herky giggled so much we all started giggling. The teacher told us to cut it out; this was serious stuff. But we all knew there wasn't much that ducking and covering was going to do to save us.

It was called the Cold War; our fathers were in the Army because of it. Their jobs were about shielding the nation from communist aggression. That sounded pretty noble, but it meant we were military nomads, shifted from one place to another to fulfill "the needs of the service."

Like any town, every Army post had housing developments, a general store and a food market, churches, a gym and a swimming pool, and a library. But they weren't by any means "ordinary" towns. You could bicycle past acres of troop barracks, airfields full of airplanes and helicopters, or tank parks, artillery ranges, motor pools, demolition ranges, or firing ranges. And at nights, far off, depending on the post, there were the flash and WHUMP! of explosions, the hammering bark of automatic weapons, and parachute flares hanging in the sky.

Army architecture could be historic, as at West Point or the Presidio of San Francisco. Or brutally utilitarian, as at any one of the posts that expanded in World War II. Thirty thousand two-story, wooden-framed barracks and other buildings, intended to last only through the war, were still in use when we went off to college. We grew up with them as part of our landscape. Many survived, some designated today as national heritage structures.

Ours was a life lived on many stage sets, among a scratch crew of actors, all of whom were just passing through. Some stayed a bit longer than others, but in the end all departed, for yet another stage set.

If you were a kid, you had to adapt. You were always leaving one set of friends and dropping into a new place full of strangers. Your dad came home one day; there would be a hushed conversation with Mom in the kitchen. Then at dinner he would announce, "Boys, the movers will be here in two weeks. We're going to . . . ," and you were off on the next leg of the adventure.

Being an Army child was like that, but in spite of the challenges, it was a great way to grow up. It informed my future character with three traits I may not have developed otherwise: flexibility, volunteerism, and leadership.

We bagged groceries in the commissary, bought model kits at the PX, went to dinners and holiday parties with our parents at the Officers Clubs. We used military scrip or MPCs as money instead of greenbacks. We knew the exchange rates between the dollar and the lira, the deutschmark, and the franc. We knew that Frankfurters and Hamburgers were citizens of German cities.

Many of us didn't see TV until our families were reassigned to the States. Our Army quarters were assigned according to Dad's rank; the interiors were flat white; holes in the walls were not permitted.

We ate a few Thanksgiving or Christmas dinners in unit mess halls, while our dads, in dress blues, traditionally manned the serving line for the soldiers. At Christmas, Santa usually arrived at the post children's Christmas party in a helicopter, jeep, or tank.

We learned early that no task was too great; responsibility came early. Shifting a family halfway around the world was a team effort, in some cases a contact sport. Everyone bore a hand, even the youngest, and someone, for God's sake, made sure the movers didn't pack the cat.

There was a common set of social skills. You were taught to look adults in the eye, shake hands like you meant it, and speak when spoken to. If your parents were out, you answered the phone, "Major Smith's quarters. This is Major Smith's son speaking. May I help you?" It didn't matter if it was a friend of your parents' calling, or the president of the United States. You answered that way and were prepared to write down the message and repeat it back to the caller. Every time.

In Italy, the villa we lived in near the sea had poor heating. My dad rigged a better system that kept the house toasty, and needed a tank of kerosene outside kept filled from World War II–era five-gallon jerry cans. Every Army kid knew them; they had a bronze screw plug that had to be knocked loose and tightened with a small sledge, and a flexible metal spout that had to be snap-fitted securely. They weighed a ton. They had to be lifted up above the kerosene tank and the spout fitted into the aperture. In the grip of an Italian winter, in sleet and rain, with kerosene all over your hands and raw knuckles? No problem; if that heater went out, it got cold in the house. Suck it up.

Those days were long before the internet or social media. When you left for a new assignment, your friends disappeared. In every new place, you were hit with a flood of information: new people, acceptable practices, taboos. Almost everyone was new themselves, would be there two years, or three, then off to a new assignment.

Networking? We didn't have a name for it, but everyone did it; it was social survival. Friends were valuable; good friends were priceless. In the changing mix of kids around you, a friend who shared your interests and watched your back was rare. When I later read about how fighter pilots relied on their wingmen, I got the concept right away.

To some the world was immense. To Army kids, a lot smaller. Paris, Aschaffenburg, Hohenfels, Rome, Yokohama, Heidelberg, Tokyo, Vienna, Aviano—all were potential assignments, or places where other kids had lived. We told each other all about it. We cruised to Naples, Tripoli, Piraeus, and Istanbul. We walked the streets of Pompeii, climbed the Acropolis, and watched the sun rise on the Bosporus and set in the Tyrrhenian Sea. We rode in gondolas down the Grand Canal in Venice, swapped worked-silver "puzzle rings" from the bazaar in Istanbul.

Our Japanese rattan living room set had plush cushions on curved bamboo frames; indestructibly comfy. Other families' quarters sported carved German furniture, French antiques, Moroccan leather hassocks. There were Libyan camel saddles, brass Turkish trays, Italian dinnerware, and Thai porcelain elephants. Christmas ornaments spoke to an assortment of countries; our celluloid Santa had "Made in Occupied Japan" stamped on its base.

We bounced off on family summer car trips to Carcasonne, Marseille, Barcelona, Madrid, or Toledo; all marked off on big, foldout Michelin maps. No television? No problem. The Grundig shortwave in the living room pulled in stations from all around the world.

Flexibility and resilience. My first two years of high school were in Alabama. Because my father's next assignment to Korea was "unaccompanied," we moved to New York for a year. Dad returned just as the Cuban Missile Crisis developed. Because of that turbulence I attended four high schools in four years.

You kept your fears to yourself. Your father was in the Army; he'd taken the oath; it wasn't without risk. Dad was gone on short notice several times and never discussed, at least with us kids, where he was or what he did. In Italy in 1957 and 1958, it was in the far north in winter; he brought back Italian Alpini mountain infantry hats for my brother and me. We learned by scuttlebutt later that a planeload of other officers had hit a mountain; no survivors. At Fort Rucker in 1961, another Army family down our street lost their father, shot down by a Cuban jet during the Bay of Pigs while flying for the CIA in support of the botched invasion.

When I entered Virginia Military Institute in summer 1963, the war in Vietnam was a far-off affair, with American advisers. By the time I graduated in 1967 as a commissioned Army lieutenant, it was an American war, roaring like a jet engine, sucking thousands of young men, masses of matériel, and oceans of money into its maw—with a large piece of the American national psyche with them.

In 1949 all of that was far in the future. I had a few hoops to get through beforehand. The first was shaped like a Japanese Torii gate.

YOKOHAMA

1949–1952

I was born in Greenwich Village, New York City, in April 1946—in the front ranks of the postwar Baby Boom. The Village then was a bastion of the bohemian lifestyle; who could imagine a native son of the Village was destined for the soldier's life?

My earliest memory is of Fort Dix, New Jersey, where Dad was in the 9th Infantry Division. We lived in a converted wooden World War II troop barracks. In the postwar housing shortage, they rated as officer's family quarters. The former upper and lower platoon bays had been converted into apartments. Mom said when the family downstairs slammed their door, the beaverboard walls flexed.

Before we were able to move onto Dix, we lived in a cottage off-post in the small town of Browns Mills. It was short on amenities. There is a photo of me getting a bath in a giant stew pot. I think it was a bath—no carrots or greens are visible in the water. I have a hazy memory of being carried by my father along a line of white picket fences and a pond with ducks. Mom said that had to be at six months old.

ACROSS THE PACIFIC

In 1949, Mom and I went to Japan to join my father, who had preceded us by six months. We left New York in January, three days cross-country by train to Seattle, then by ship to Yokohama.

I remember fluorescent lights over the platforms at Penn Station, the growling of giant, idling electric engines. Our compartment had a sofa with pillows on one side, a table under the window. Each evening the porter switched the sofa to a bed and lowered the bunk above, which was folded into the wall during the day. Bundled in the covers with Mom reading a story, I went to sleep to the rhythm of the rails.

From the observation dome we saw unending snow on the plains, the purple shadows of twilight in the Rockies. In the dining car, I'm told I serenaded our fellow passengers with a singing performance. I wish there were some way to apologize.

In those postwar years, most overseas travel was by ship. It was the height of the great passenger liners of the American Export and United States Lines on Atlantic runs, and American President and Matson Navigation on the Pacific.

Military air travel was by priority and seldom included families. To carry Army personnel, their families, and cargo on both oceans, MSTS, the Military Sea Transport Service ran a fleet of very large ships converted from World War II P-2 class troop transports.

From the late 1940s through the 1970s, they sailed between Seattle and San Francisco to points in the Pacific, and from New York and Norfolk to Europe. Crewed by civilians, they were designated USNS since they were naval vessels, not warships. Named for generals, to Army children of my era, they were as familiar as the makes of American cars or the names of Major League baseball teams: the *Patch*, *Gaffey*, *Sultan*, *Buckner*, *Patrick*, *Walker*, *Rose*, and *Darby*.

The *Buckner* might carry families from New York to Bremerhaven. After a three-year stay in Germany, the *Darby* could take them back to New York. In our case, the *Gaffey* took Mom and me from Seattle to Yokohama; three years later, we sailed on the *Patrick* from Yokohama to San Francisco.

Like her sister ships, the *Gaffey* was a very big, gray, two-funnel transport. On our voyage to Yokohama, she was loaded with servicemen, officers with their families, and wives and children traveling to join their husbands and fathers. Mom and I had a cabin with two bunks, a porthole above a small metal desk, a steel sink, and a tiny bathroom. Looking out of that porthole was my first view of the deep blue Pacific, rolling away to the far horizon.

Everywhere we went on the ship Mom kept me on a leash, clipped to a harness; it saved my life. There was a test of the watertight doors with no warning. I was scampering along ahead of Mom on the end of that tether. Seeing the enormous steel door just ahead begin to slam shut on me, she hauled back on the leash so hard I landed on my tail and started to cry.

In a few moments the door swung open revealing two of the ship's officers, ashen faced, staring, expecting to see a mangled little tyke's body. Whatever Mom said to them, it was clear she was very, very unhappy. I'm sure they got the message.

After a week at sea, we entered Yokohama, passing the big black-and-white-striped lighthouse at the harbor entrance. In the postwar years, much of American commercial and military logistic shipping was landed at Yokohama; as an officer in the Army's Transportation Corps, my father was stationed there.

YOKOHAMA *SAIKEN*

In 1948, the Marshall Plan sent enormous American financial aid, foodstuffs, and agricultural equipment to European countries impoverished by the war. The program was intended to assist in their rebuilding and to stabilize their economies so that they might resist turning to communism.

No such program existed for Japan, which was as thoroughly devastated by the war as Europe. Every Japanese city of significant size had been systematically bombed with high explosives, incendiaries, or both. Many were literally leveled.

Though General Douglas MacArthur had undertaken the task of establishing a new Japanese constitution and supporting the rebuilding of the country, very little immediate postwar financial or economic aid was provided by the United States.

In 1950, Yokohama still showed the effects of the firebombing raids of March 1945, which had destroyed huge areas of the city. With characteristic Japanese determination and effort, the city was *saiken*: rebuilding.

Streetcars ran on overhead electric wires. Building construction was by manual labor. There were no machine tools; the sound of hammers and saws was constant. People bustled about in not very colorful crowds. Gasoline and machine oil were limited; trucks and buses ran on wartime wood-gas generators, converting wood and charcoal into a gaseous fuel. The big, black "gasifier" boilers mounted on the backs of vehicles emitted clouds of noxious smoke.

AREA X

At Yokohama, we lived in Army quarters at Negishi Heights, known as Area X. The land had been cleared and quarters built only a year or so before we arrived. Ours was half a two-story duplex, with living room, dining room, and kitchen downstairs and three bedrooms and a bathroom above—a big step up from the converted barracks at Dix.

American forces and civilian agencies in Japan provided jobs for Japanese, welcome opportunities in those economically challenged years. One program in Yokohama provided young Japanese women as housemaids for Army officers' homes. The girls in the program lived in a separate dormitory in the Army family housing area reporting to their employers' quarters every morning.

We had two maids; for an American family on a captain's pay, it was a fabulous luxury. Yuriko was from Yokohama. Fumiko was a blue-eyed Ainu from the Kuril Islands far to the north, occupied by the Russians at the end of the war.

Anthropologists define the Ainu as one of the original indigenous people of Japan. To the Japanese, the Ainu were a minority, marginalized and discriminated against for many years.

I wish I knew the circumstances of how Fumiko came to be living in Yokohama. Was her family displaced by the war? Did she somehow travel from the far north of the islands by herself? None of it seemed to affect her or Yuriko; they were both happy and did a lot of giggling.

Our quarters were functional, anything but stylish. Summers were hot, humid, and rainy. There was no air-conditioning. Each duplex had a metal laundry pole in the backyard. Moms and housemaids kept a weather eye out; impending rain sent them scurrying to retrieve clothes, regardless of their dryness.

One day at noon we were at the kitchen table; the house began swaying, dishes falling off the shelves. The maids scooped me up and ran outside, setting me down on the lawn, which was rising and falling as an earthquake swept the area. As Japanese, they were used to it. I wasn't. I thought it was like a rollercoaster ride.

Except for occasional earthquakes, which Japan experiences more than any other highly populated region of the world, life for American military families in postwar Japan was better than in the States, which was struggling at that time to provide housing, medical care, and education for millions of returning servicemen and women. Many of the amenities of life were provided by the military, with medical care and housing provided at no cost.

With the benefit of our maids, my mother, like a lot of other officers' wives, participated in rounds of bridge games, wives' club functions, charity work, volunteering as a "Gray Lady" at the hospital, and overseeing the children.

Mom went to flower-arranging classes and demonstrations of ritualistic Japanese tea ceremonies, and she collected very good-quality teak and rattan furniture that endured all our many subsequent moves.

With a few other wives, Mom learned of Paul Jacoulet, a French artist born in Paris who moved to Japan with his family at age ten. Jacoulet became wholly immersed in Japanese culture and art, remaining in Japan his entire life. Mom and her friends visited Jacoulet's studio in Karuizawa, acquiring a number of his prints of Japanese and Koreans in traditional costume. In that, they unknowingly joined General MacArthur and Queen Elizabeth II as collectors of Jacoulet's art.

Until I left for college, several of Jacoulet's beautiful prints were on the walls of our homes wherever we lived. Decades later I was pleased to see an entire gallery of his work in the Museum of Art in Honolulu, including a few of the same prints that had hung on our family's walls.

One of the earliest military conversations I can recall is my father talking to our neighbor, another Army officer, about the fighting then ongoing in Greece. A civil war was underway as Greek communists, supported by the Soviet Union, fought Greek nationalists, supported by the United States and Britain.

My father and our neighbor were sitting on the porch of our quarters. I was down on the walkway with a piece of chalk. I had no idea why anyone would fight about something called "grease." I assumed the dads knew what they were talking about and went on drawing airplanes in chalk on the sidewalk.

One memorable escapade of my early years in Yokohama involved my getting the urge to travel like the grown-ups. Perhaps I had seen something in downtown Yokohama and thought it would be a good idea to revisit. I walked down to the corner of our housing area and boarded the Army shuttle bus, riding along until something looked interesting, then exiting and wandering around downtown Yokohama. My freedom continued until an American mom saw me alone, gathered me up, and eventually determined whom I belonged to.

Why the Japanese bus driver, working for the Army, let an unescorted four-year-old on the bus remains a mystery. Why he let me off is another. But it was interesting to be in the crowd with no one paying attention to me—until I was collared by that American mom. Rats.

SAINT JOSEPH COLLEGE

There was an American elementary school in Yokohama with Army civilian-contract teachers. My parents instead enrolled me at Saint Joseph College, a Catholic prep providing kindergarten through high school for Japanese students and children from US Army and "expat" foreign families.

Established in 1901 by the Swiss brothers of the Marianist order, Saint Joseph, due to Switzerland's neutrality, remained open during World War II. Brother Leo, the headmaster, ran the school with tight Swiss efficiency.

Saint Joseph was located on the Bluff, a high area overlooking downtown Yokohama and the harbor. Japanese families sent their children to be acclimated to Western culture and to learn English. The school had hosted Japan's first Boy Scout troop, established in 1911.

A number of prominent future leaders in the Japanese government would be Saint Joseph alumni. Decades later, when I was a student in the graduate business school at Stanford, a classmate who had worked for *Asahi Shimbun*, Japan's most respected newspaper, was a fellow Saint Joseph alumnus.

OTHER *GAIJIN* KIDS

There were a number of non-Japanese *gaijin* kids at Saint Joseph who weren't expatriates or Americans. They were Russians. Their presence was the kind of anomaly of history that washed people up in odd places. They were "White Russians" whose families had been loyal to the tsar. The Whites fought against the Bolsheviks during the Revolution. Defeated, they fled first to Harbin in Manchuria, then to Japan, where they settled in Yokohama.

During World War II they were closely watched by the Kempetai, the Japanese secret police. George was one of the Russian kids at Saint Joseph who spoke fluent English, Japanese, and Russian. Tragically, his brother was killed in the American B-29 air raids that leveled most of Yokohama in March 1945. A truly charismatic fellow, in later life George went on to a highly successful career in California, in international commercial insurance.

My friend Robin was an American classmate at Saint Joseph. His father worked for an international oil company. Their home was in the expatriate residential enclave on the Bluff. I remember visiting him there several times. I don't recall the circumstances; there was no such thing as "play dates" then. I assume my mother took me or had some other reason to visit.

At about age five, it was the first time I was aware of a difference between our level of living and others'. Our quarters were our home; we had comfortable furniture, books, a record player, and framed prints on the walls. I liked it a lot. Robin's home was very different—bigger by far than ours, surrounded by towering pine trees and gardens. It had a koi pond and a very spacious patio. I didn't think about it much at the time, but I've remembered it.

The houses in Area X were built just a few years after the war's end; we were one of the first families to occupy them. In 1951 the area's management was turned over to the Navy, which kept it as family housing until 2015. Several generations of service children were raised at Negishi.

SHOGUN OR *DAIMYO*?

In 1949, Japan was a defeated, occupied nation, the only time in its long history it has been under control of a foreign power. With the weighty title of Supreme Commander for the Allied Powers, or SCAP, General Douglas MacArthur headed the US occupation forces in Japan. As a conquering warrior, he could easily have assumed the role of *shogun*, a military dictator. In that role, he would have been perfectly recognizable to any Japanese. Instead, though he was "as inaccessible as the Wizard of Oz," as one observer put it, MacArthur ruled as a remarkable humanitarian, more like a *daimyo*, a feudal landowner.

His impact on Japan was immense. Though politically conservative, he set about liberalizing all aspects of Japan's society, government, and economy. Japan's constitution was written by MacArthur's staff and adopted by the Japanese government in 1947. It established the emperor as the head of state and permanently renounced war. It established individual rights for all Japanese, including first-ever rights for women. It remains the oldest unamended constitution in the world.

JAPAN AND THE WEST

Japan's interaction with the West began with the arrival of Portuguese traders in the sixteenth century. Followed by the arrival of the Spanish and Dutch, trade developed until a series of imperial edicts in the 1630s closed Japan off from the world. For two centuries thereafter, Japan remained under self-imposed isolation.

In the early nineteenth century, America established profitable trading interests in China and wanted to extend them to Japan. In 1853, President Millard Fillmore ordered US Navy commodore Matthew Perry to proceed to Japan. Perry arrived unannounced in the bay at Edo (present-day Tokyo) with a letter for the emperor offering to open diplomatic and trading relations. He was commanded to leave, and did so.

In 1854 Perry returned at the head of a squadron of eight warships. This time the message was clear; the result was the Treaty of Kanagawa, granting limited concessions to the Americans. Perry's expeditions opened the door; the Meiji Restoration of 1868 fully ended Japan's isolation from the West.

As Westerners of various nationalities arrived, a commercial community grew. Cultural differences led inevitably to confrontations, one of the most notorious of which was the "Richardson incident" of 1862. Two men and a woman, all British subjects, were riding their horses in the Yokohama area. They came upon a procession escorting a litter carrying a *samurai* chief. The road was narrow. Japanese custom required all travelers to yield to *samurai*. Richardson refused to give way, attempting to ride between the litter carrying the chief and his bodyguards. That action wasn't only insulting to the Japanese; it displayed an unacceptable lack of *wa*, the quality of harmony within a group over one's own interests.

The chief's bodyguards attacked Richardson with their long, razor-sharp *wakizashi* swords. His autopsy later recorded no less than ten mortal wounds. The other man and woman riding with Richardson were unharmed.

Queen Victoria's representative in Japan demanded compensation for Richardson's death; the *samurai* clan refused. In the first recognized act of war against Japan by a Western power, British gunboats bombarded the center of the clan's territory near Yokohama. The clan paid £25,000 in compensation.

Following their brief show of successful force, British troops were stationed in Yokohama to protect British subjects and businesses. They also introduced cricket and rugby to Japan. Ironically neither caught on; in contemporary Japan, baseball is one of the most popular sports.

The first European-style horse races in Japan were held at Negishi, at a track built on drained marshland. For many years the Negishi races pitted the finest horses in Japan against each other, ridden by jockeys in colorful costumes. From our quarters on the Heights, we looked down at the huge, four-story racetrack grandstand built by Emperor Meiji in 1866. It had three massive towers, each with a pair of enormous round windows.

Horse racing continued at Negishi until the war closed it in 1942. The grandstand remains abandoned today, overgrown with ivy, looming over the surrounding residential area like some colossus from an ancient culture. If you ever meet an American who lived in Yokohama as a military child, just say, "Remember the grandstand?" and you're in the club. It's the magic Negishi-memory word.

I WIND UP "IN IT"

Japanese farmers have fertilized their crops for centuries with liquid human waste, stored in open cistern pits. In the farm fields on the land behind our quarters, I tried to rescue a puppy that had fallen into one of these "honey bucket wells."

It was clear the puppy was about to die a miserable death. Reaching for the dog, I lost my balance and fell in. Thankfully it wasn't deep. I pushed the puppy out and made my way home.

Yuriko and Fumiko kept me outside, holding their noses and giggling while they hosed me off. Mom came home during this process, hit the ceiling, and rushed me down to the Army dispensary. After a medical examination, doses of truly vile medicine, and a series of inoculations, all turned out well. I think I've blanked out a good part of the rest of that story. Yuck.

That episode of "volunteerism" became family lore; there would be times in the future when more than puppies were at risk.

NO SMOKING, EVER

My dad had a civilian driver, a Japanese man who wore an odd cap. I know now it was a Japanese Army forage cap from the war. Very likely he had been a soldier. He never smiled. He smoked nonstop. Everybody smoked.

One morning the driver was standing by the jeep. My father was inside the house. I must have pointed to his cigarette. He handed it to me. I took a big puff. My reaction was immediate, and in various colors. He doubled up laughing so loudly that my dad came out to see what was causing the ruckus. He began laughing as well. Whatever his name was, that man did me a favor. I never smoked again.

A SUNDAY IN JUNE

We went to Kamakura to see the *daibutsu*, the huge statue of Buddha. It was hollow and big enough to walk inside. There is a photo of me in jacket and shorts with a pennant on a bamboo stick. The great statue looms in the background.

Arriving back at Area X, groups were out on the lawns in front of the quarters. Grown-ups were talking in clusters, children running around them. It was the first time I recall seeing parents unsure, unsettled. News had broken that North Korea had invaded the South.

Change came quickly. Yokohama became a hub for military matériel arriving in Japan for the war in Korea. Long truck convoys growled day and night past our housing area and down to the harbor.

We listened to Armed Forces Radio from Tokyo. Our soldiers were fighting; I didn't know much more. At the beginning it seemed very bad. Then our soldiers landed at Inchon, and Seoul was captured.

My father had seen action in the OSS in World War II. After the war, he became an expert in keeping troops and supplies moving. He was told he would remain in Japan to ensure that nothing held that up. I'm sure Mom was relieved.

Dad took us to the harbor to see General Ridgway's arrival. He was to command all the United Nations forces in Korea. An Army band on the pier beside the transport played marches; soldiers were in formation. The general stood on a stand with many flags. He spoke to a big crowd. Very impressive, for a small boy.

Families came and went through the war years. Transport departures at Yokohama were big affairs. Passengers lined the rails; streamers and confetti were thrown between crowd and ship. The lines cast off, the gap between ship and pier grew. Against the deep baritone booming of the ship's horn, the pier-side band played "Auld Lang Syne": good-bye, God bless, safe voyage home.

The war in Korea radically changed America's perception of Japan. From a defeated, occupied nation, it became a major support base for the American and UN forces in Korea, and a bulwark against communist expansion in the region. American war procurement fueled Japan's recovery. It was one reason for Japan's development as a future economic giant. The other was Japanese cultural unity, powerful when applied to national objectives.

Pan American introduced its "Stratocruiser" service from San Francisco to Tokyo. Huge, four-engine propeller airliners, the Stratocruisers were built on modified B-29 bomber designs. When the first of the giant new planes arrived at Tokyo's Haneda airport, the American community turned out en masse to visit. It must have been summer; there is a photo of me in white T-shirt and shorts on one of the station's baggage tugs with the Pan Am logo. The gleaming silver airplane looms in the background.

I remember American military parades in downtown Yokohama. Marching bands, soldiers, trucks towing trailers with "floats" of various themes. One parade had a float bearing a giant Mount Fuji the enormous, symbolic volcano that dominates the skyline and can be seen, on a day when the air is clear, from downtown Tokyo.

Another had a big model of a silver C-119 Flying Boxcar twin-engine aircraft, suspended over a diorama of a snow-covered Korean battlefield. Spewing from the open cargo doors at the rear of the plane, between its twin tail booms, was a line of scale parachutes, suspended from which were various scale-model pieces of military equipment.

Wow! I wanted that model airplane! I imagined it hanging in my room. I asked my father if he could get it for me. He said it probably belonged to whoever made it. But in kid logic, that explanation cut about zero ice. I wanted it, and that was it—end of message.

I'm still waiting for it.

THE "FORGOTTEN WAR"

American soldiers in Japan in the late 1940s were occupiers in a defeated country. Military readiness and training occasionally took second place to the easy life. When war exploded across the Sea of Japan in June 1950, the first US units sent to Korea from Japan were badly mauled. President Truman's decision to commit significant US forces turned the war into a United Nations effort. The first months were a litany of US defeats, until MacArthur's bold landing on the west coast of the Korean Peninsula at Inchon regained the initiative. The war eventually settled into a vicious static fight, with both sides dug into forbidding mountainous terrain.

The armistice effected in 1953 put a formal end to the fighting, but armistices don't end wars. North Korea never surrendered or signed a peace agreement; the armistice merely put combat in abeyance.

The Korean War killed forty thousand American soldiers in three years. The Vietnam War killed fifty-eight thousand in ten years. Yet the Korean War was scrupulously referred to by the US government and media at the time as a "police action," and is now referred to as "the forgotten war."

I MEET THE AMERICAN *DAIMYO*

My father bundled me into our car, a surplus jeep, and drove to Tokyo. We stood outside the main entrance to the huge Dai Ichi building. It had been the headquarters of a major Japanese insurance company but was requisitioned as General MacArthur's headquarters. Every day at noon General MacArthur emerged, to be driven to his home at the American embassy for lunch. Whatever passed in those few moments between my dad and the general is lost. I only remember it was raining; a very tall man reached down, smiling, and shook my hand.

My father was an admirer of the general. That did not extend to a few other World War II generals. Mark Clark had commanded 5th US Army in Italy during World War II. Dad was in the OSS in Italy with Italian partisans fighting German forces, far behind the lines of defense the Germans had built across the Italian Peninsula. He believed many Allied soldiers died needlessly due to Clark's generalship. From what I have studied of the Italian campaign, my assessment comes down on my father's side.

FUJI AND CICADAS

Mount Fuji was referred to by Americans as Fujiyama but correctly by the Japanese as Fuji-san. On the wall of my office is the beautiful woodblock print of Fuji-san that hung in my room in Yokohama: a dreamscape of the snow-clad mountain etched clearly against a cloudless sky, at its base a tranquil lake on which a single white sail appears.

Winters were cold in Yokohama, but we rarely had snow. The hot, wet months came in June and July, with heat, humidity, and the racket of emerging cicadas. The hundred-decibel squeaking of the large insects is actually the males' mating call. Cicadas don't have a lot of time for subtlety.

There are over a hundred species of Japanese cicadas. The Japanese mark official summer when the racket of many millions of them begins. A few cicadas are annoying; millions are disorienting. Sleeping during cicada season can be a challenge.

They die in vast numbers, but they can be deceptively alive while remaining perfectly motionless. If you step near them, they explode into motion, racing off at high speed. The Japanese call them *bakudan*, "cicada bombs."

Japanese kids hunt cicadas, keeping them in their houses in small bamboo cages. No thanks. On the other hand, crickets represent good luck and good fortune. The chirping of a house cricket in a bamboo cage is a good thing.

DAD

My father had many engaging traits. He laughed a lot. He whistled. He called everyone "laddie." Years later I learned that term, and "righty-O," were from his service in England before going to Italy in the OSS during the war.

He worked on "secret projects" in the spare bedroom. Until the arrival of my brother in 1950, he used it as a study and workroom. He built a beautiful model of a Navy Corsair fighter from a balsa wood kit. It was painted a deep navy blue. I wish I still had it.

Dad built a play structure: two four-by-eight sheets of plywood nailed to a frame for a floor, surrounded by a wooden fence with a gate. Colorfully striped fabric covered a raised, peaked frame above, open at the sides. It kept me and my friends corralled in the shade, observable by Mom and the maids from the kitchen window.

One afternoon Dad dropped a bundle on the back lawn, unrolling it with a foot-operated air pump. A yellow Air Force life raft emerged. Filled to the top with water, it was a great swimming pool. We jumped off from the bow, which rose at an angle to the rest of the raft. We learned there was no deep end the hard way.

Dad had an affinity for geraniums. Wherever we lived, they were with us. He potted them in porcelain, crockery, fired clay, and at times in GI coffee cans. I remember him whenever I see their cheery red.

MOM

Her father came from Italy in the early twentieth century and apprenticed as a stonemason. The mosaic frieze below the altar at the Cathedral of Saint Thomas in Manhattan is partly his work. Branching out, he built a sizable business in architectural cast stone, prospering in the boom years of the 1920s, when almost every new building in New York City sported it. They lived in New Rochelle, a then fashionable suburb of New York City; she was driven to school in a Duesenberg.

All that changed in the market crash of 1929 and the Great Depression, but it didn't affect Mom. Relentlessly upbeat, she went to Hunter College in New York City, did modeling, worked as a secretary, and married my father, an artillery second lieutenant, in 1943.

She told me of moving to Fayetteville, North Carolina, with Dad on his first assignment. They lived, literally, in a converted chicken coop; wartime housing was that scarce. He came home one evening with the side of his head scorched by fire; he had been that close to an exploding pile of artillery fuses.

When Dad went to Europe in the OSS, she was visited by a Military Intelligence officer; he told her she might not be hearing from Dad for a while. He cautioned her to be aware of suspicious people around her and to stay away from the edge of the station platforms in the New York City subway. *That* got her attention.

Mom may have been raised an Italian American "princess," but she was tough as chrome steel when the situation required. Yet I don't recall her ever speaking ill of anyone. She was invariably cheerful, smiling, and able to conjure goodies and treats seemingly out of thin air.

She made close friends wherever we were stationed. She was my den mother in Cub Scouts, and she was avidly interested in my scouting progression to Eagle.

She had everything it took to back Dad in his Army career, seemingly effortlessly able to shift the family every several years to some new place, new chapter. She outlived him by forty-five years and never remarried. I miss her and Dad very much.

TYPHOON

September was tropical storm season. They were called typhoons then, not hurricanes. There was a very big one in 1950. The day before it hit, soldiers nailed plywood over the window in the kitchen door. They left a thin space between the wood sheets so we could see out.

The sky turned greenish gray. Torrents of rain came first, then wind building steadily. Just before dark the power failed. Dad lit a lantern on the dining room table. We sat listening to the howling of the storm. My father checked the doors and windows. I slept in my parents' room; the storm roared all night long.

Just before dawn, Dad woke me, motioning for me to follow. In the kitchen he put me on a stool so I could see out through the gap between the boards. A warehouse was down the service alley behind our quarters. The wind had gotten under the edge of the roof. It worked the frame loose, lifting a bit more as the nails holding it slowly gave. Suddenly the entire roof ripped right off, sailing away like a giant black bat.

Sometime after the typhoon, I learned I was "going to have a new brother or sister." In those days before ultrasound, the way that question was answered was "on delivery." On a rainy day in March, my brother David was carried in by Mom and Dad, bundled up in a basket. Life from then on was going to be a team sport.

THE *PATRICK*

In 1952 we sailed home on the USNS *Patrick*. All Mom and Dad's friends came to the pier to see us off. Many times we had stood down there, looking up at good friends leaving. Now it was our turn. The people on the pier weren't just my parents' friends. They were fellow officers and their wives, members of a family difficult to explain to those on the outside. The memories of shared experiences would be related over and over through the years.

We all threw streamers and confetti. As the ship's horn sounded, the band broke into "Auld Lang Syne." It was one of the few times I saw Mom cry.

Somewhere in mid-Pacific, the ship held "man overboard" and lifeboat drills. It was a military transport; they ran it by the numbers. The crew threw a buoy with a pennant overboard. The ship's horn sounded several blasts; the *Patrick* slowed and stopped. The crew swung out one of the motor lifeboats and lowered it to the water. We watched the boat power over, and the crew retrieved the marker buoy.

Dad's 8mm color film shows military families gathered all along the boat deck at their assigned boat stations. Everyone wore gray, big-collared kapok life jackets that tied across the front. Dad picked me and my brother up by the backs of our jackets and held us off the ground like a pair of salmon.

The morning we arrived in San Francisco was sunny and windy. Dad said we had to "pick up a pilot" first. I thought he meant a plane had crashed. Good thing we'd had that lifeboat drill and seen the crew do their stuff.

Again, the ship slowed and stopped. A big sailing vessel was some way off, its sails loosely flapping. It looked like it wasn't going anywhere. Dad said it was the pilot boat; the pilot would be coming to the ship to guide us into San Francisco.

We watched two men in a small metal skiff about ten feet long with an outboard motor leave the side of the sailing ship. Riding up and down on the swells, it headed for the *Patrick*. Our crew opened a hatch in the side of the ship. They lowered a "Jacob's ladder" that hung straight down the steel side.

The fellow in the back of the boat steered using the outboard. A heavyset man in a heavy gray overcoat sat on the front bench seat smoking a cigar. In my father's film he is wearing a stylish snap-brim fedora, and no lifejacket.

As the boat came up against the bottom of the ladder, the man timed the rise and fall of the swells, stood up, reached out, and grabbed a rung. The little boat swayed out a bit. It looked like he might fall into the sea. But with a perfectly timed hop, and with a briefcase in his other hand, he jumped onto the ladder and climbed straight up the side of the ship and in through the hatch. Impressive. If he had missed, in that outfit he would have gone straight down, the fedora floating as a marker.

UNDER THE GOLDEN GATE

We entered San Francisco Bay on the first day of March 1952, brother Dave's second birthday. The forward well deck of the ship was filled with soldiers returning from Korea. They wore the insignia of the 2nd Infantry Division: an "Indian chief" in profile in full war bonnet.

They were silent as the ship passed under the enormous Golden Gate Bridge, its huge shadow sweeping over us. We could hear the sound of the traffic far above. Then they erupted in cheers and whistles, throwing their hats in the air. They had survived Korea.

The *Patrick* tied up to the Army transport docks at Fort Mason. A big sign was painted on the end of one of the pier sheds: "Welcome Home, US Army." It looked old and faded. Dad said it had been put there to welcome men coming home from World War II.

In the processing office at the pier side, which has since become a very chic vegan restaurant, I saw my first television set. It was black and white, running a commercial for some kind of candy, and cartoons. Magic!

2

WILLIAMSBURG

1952–1953

Like pieces on a chessboard, the Army moved its soldiers to satisfy "the needs of the service." Like little tribes of military nomads, their families moved right along with them.

How we eventually got to Virginia in 1952 had roundabout beginnings in 1943. At that time, my father was a newly commissioned second lieutenant in a field artillery battery at Camp Roberts, California. His unit, the 27th Infantry Division, was on its way to the Pacific theater.

OSS: THE OFFICE OF STRATEGIC SERVICE

In the heat of that California summer, my father was summoned to an interview by a US Navy officer who addressed him in fluent Italian. The meeting came without explanation as to why or what the next steps might be. After some time discussing various topics, all in Italian, Dad was told to wait for further instructions.

As my father related it years later, the Navy officer told him that volunteers were needed for hazardous duty, but specifics could not be revealed. He said it was fairly clear that whatever the Navy officer was referring to, it had to do with either Italy or areas where Italian forces were deployed. One thing was clear: it had little chance of having anything to do with duty in the Pacific theater.

Shortly afterward, orders assigned my father to OSS. The Office of Strategic Service was a very secret "cloak and dagger" organization then, the forerunner of the future Central Intelligence Agency and the Army's Special Forces.

My father once said that, years after his OSS service, he saw a copy of the recommendation forwarded by the Navy officer. It stated, "This officer is an excellent candidate. He speaks a perfectly acceptable New York Italian."

At a reception in Washington, DC, in the early 1970s, I met a very senior CIA officer; he had been in the OSS during the war and assured me he could get my father's records for me. A few weeks later he called. "We have them, but they're classified," he said. "They can't be released. You can put in a FOIA [Freedom of Information Act] request, but the formal response will be we don't have them. Sorry."

In the mid-1990s, I finally received my father's OSS file from the CIA. Heavily redacted, it arrived without notice or return address, in a brown envelope with no other communication. His assignments to OSS's "SO" in England and Italy were cataloged. There were no other reports, statements, or discussion.

During World War II, the OSS fielded operational groups (OGs), "Jedburgh" teams (Jeds), special operations (SO), and secret intelligence (SI) agents and radio operators. OGs were teams of American soldiers in US uniform fluent in the language of their target country. They were forerunners of modern Special Forces "A" detachments. "Jedburghs" were three-man teams of an American officer, a British or French officer, and a radio operator. "Jed" teams were parachuted into France during or immediately after the Normandy invasion in June 1944 to organize and lead French resistance fighters.

In early 1944 after OSS training in Maryland, my father was sent to England, assigned to a secret base known as Area H. Located near the village of Holme in the British Midlands, Area H supported resistance and OSS units, teams and agents in German-occupied France and the "low countries" of Holland, Belgium, and Luxembourg.

A wide range of items were stored at Area H: weapons, ammunition, clothing, food, medical supplies, radio sets, maps printed on paper or silk, escape and survival equipment, codes, and a variety of highly imaginative "dirty trick" devices.

"Dirty trick" devices included explosives concealed inside perfectly crafted lumps of false coal or sewn into the dried bodies of dead rats. Air-dropped to resistance units on the Continent, they could be tossed into the coal tenders of railway locomotives. Shoveled by unsuspecting train crews into the fireboxes of their engines, the results were highly destructive.

Equipment was assembled and packed according to coded requests that were transmitted by radio operators attached to resistance groups or by OSS agents or units on the Continent. Compartmented cylindrical "C" containers, each with its own parachute, were dropped by the "Carpetbaggers," a unique, dedicated squadron of matte-black four-engine B-24 Liberator bombers.

On nights with no moon or minimal light, risking enemy antiaircraft and night fighters, Carpetbagger aircraft flew hundreds of miles across blacked-out Europe. They dropped their supply containers, often accompanied by clandestine SO and SI agents, onto pinpoints of shaded light or small fires lit by resistance groups on the ground.

Following the liberation of France in 1944, my father flew to the OSS base at Bari in southeastern Italy. His fluency in Italian was key to developing strong relationships with Italian partisan groups. Several were far to the north of the Allied forces that were slowly advancing against heavily defended German defensive fortification lines.

There is a brief video in an OSS film of my father in the winter of 1944–45. He was jumpmastering an OG team in American uniforms, parachuting from a twin-engine C-47 over mountains somewhere in northern Italy. The film is silent. The plane's wide port-side cargo door was removed; snow lay thick on the mountains seen below. Everyone was in layers of winter gear. Some men chewed gum; others smoked. When they shouted to one another, their breath came in bursts of steam.

It must have been well below zero in that plane. They would be jumping into the unknown, far from any other American forces. It was also known at that time that an entire OSS OG team on a different mission had been betrayed by Italian collaborators and captured by the Germans, every man executed still in American uniform.

When OSS was deactivated after the war, the Army intended to reassign him to field artillery. Instead, he decided he'd "had enough of loud noises" and transferred to the Army's Transportation Corps. There he became a logistician, a specialist in providing fighting forces with the transport and supplies required to sustain operations.

"AMATEURS TALK TACTICS"

There is an oft-quoted phrase that "amateurs talk tactics; professionals study logistics." Though its attribution is murky, its meaning is clear. Strategists or tacticians who ignore or underestimate the importance of logistics do so at their peril.

Alexander the Great moved his army from Greece to India and back, defeating numerous adversaries in the Middle East, Africa, and Europe. He could not have achieved that operational tempo or success in battle without timely and consistent supply for his forces, along with their equipment and draft animals. He is reputed to have said, "Those ensuring my supply are humorless; they know they will be the first to be executed if my campaigns fail for want of anything."

In his treatise *On War*, the famous military theoretician Carl von Clausewitz states, "The essence of supplying, training, and transporting the soldier to the right place at the right time is of paramount importance."

The term "logistics" made its way into the US Army's glossary in the late 1930s; at the Infantry School at Fort Benning, it was emphasized as a critical component of future military operations.

So much so that when the United States entered World War II, Admiral Earnest King, chief of naval operations, said, "I don't know what the hell this 'logistics' is that General Marshall is always talking about, but I want some of it!"

Dad's specialty meant we would live in interesting places. One was Williamsburg in Virginia for the two years he was stationed at nearby Fort Eustis, the Army's Transportation Center.

Compared to the combat forces fighting "out at the sharp edge," the transportation resources and logistics services of armies have generally been undercelebrated. But they have been critical to all army commanders from the time technology provided better means to move men and supplies than by manpower alone.

In the Civil War, railroads enabled Union and Confederate commanders to rapidly move troops, equipment, and supplies. The US Military Railroad was created by the Union, with authority to seize railroads and telegraphs for military use. It provided support in every Civil War theater and major campaign, and was a major factor in enabling the ultimate Union victory.

During the war, the Ohio, Mississippi, Tennessee, Cumberland, and other rivers provided "avenues of approach" into the heart of Confederate territories. The Union Army built over ninety river steamers and chartered or impressed hundreds of others. The waterborne mobility those vessels afforded the Union was another major factor in its victory. By today's standards, those rail and water efforts may seem crude, but the Army was learning.

By the Spanish-American War in 1898, the lessons had been all but forgotten. Transport and logistics in getting the American expeditionary force to Cuba were a disaster. A single rail line ran down the Florida peninsula to the embarkation port at Tampa. Trains and freight backed up in a line many miles long. There was no system to loading the trains according to the units needing their supplies.

Little thought or organization was given to loading the chartered civilian ocean transports. Landed on Cuba in a disorganized melee, troops were supplied with spoiled canned beef, unroasted coffee beans, and hardtack. Between the incompetence of the quartermasters, tropical diseases, and the enemy, it's a wonder so many soldiers survived that brief but deadly campaign.

America's entry into the "Great War" in 1917 proved it to be as unprepared then as it was two decades earlier. Logistics and shipment had improved, but America could not provide combat equipment adequate to the demands of the twentieth-century war being fought in France and Belgium. The American Expeditionary Force was equipped with American rifles but had to fight with French and British machine guns. Most American artillery was of French design; American pilots also flew British and French aircraft.

World War II brought radical improvements. Beginning in 1942, America developed Franklin Roosevelt's "arsenal of democracy," producing an ever-increasing flow of trucks, tanks, ships, planes, and weapons and equipment of every kind. America equipped its fighting forces and Allies alike, in every theater of the global war.

Though every bomb, bullet, and bean had to be transported across two great oceans, one of them infested with German submarines, a high percentage were successfully delivered. So critical was the transatlantic ocean supply line between the United States and Britain in World War II that Winston Churchill said afterward that the threat posed by German submarines was the only issue that kept him awake at nights.

Military food and food service also became a science. Rations designated A, B, C, D, and K were created to sustain specific numbers of men in specific theaters of operation in specific jobs. The ubiquitous C-ration, designed to sustain one man in combat for one day, was still issued until the last few years of the Vietnam War.

My father's assignment to Fort Eustis brought him, and us, into the fold of the Transportation Corps, or "TC," as I heard it referred to hundreds of times growing up. The TC was a tight clan within the larger Army family. Many TC officers and men had served together in previous postings or knew each other by reputation. There was a lot of pride in what they were doing.

My father's fellow TC officers were an eclectic lot, specialists in rail, truck, air, and sea transport. TC postings overseas could be to some interesting places. Of course there were TC assignments to places like Fort Leonard Wood, Missouri, or Fort Polk, Louisiana, but my father's assignments to Japan, West Point, and later Italy were due to his unique specialty needed in those places. We were very fortunate; we saw much more of the world.

COLONIAL WILLIAMSBURG

In 1952, instead of applying for quarters on the post at Fort Eustis, Mom and Dad bought a three-bedroom ranch-style house on the outskirts of Williamsburg, backed by a deep pine forest. Unlike our Army quarters in Japan, it was our first real home. I loved it; the woods were right across the backyard. There were deer, rabbits, box turtles, cardinals, robins, blue jays, and ponds full of frogs and pollywogs. The burring sound of woodpeckers sounded constantly from the woods.

We lived on the outskirts of Colonial Williamsburg, the restoration of the capital of the eighteenth-century British colony of Virginia. It was fascinating, a completely new experience for a boy whose early, formative years were in Japan. A "living lesson" in American history, the colonial restoration at Williamsburg very likely triggered my lifelong interest in history. It was the first step along my path to becoming a future historian.

In the eighteenth century, Williamsburg was the focus of government power and colonial grace. Later, it was the seat of fiery revolutionary rhetoric. By the early twentieth century, it was gently decaying and was well along to becoming just another ordinary Virginia town.

Williamsburg's history might have wound up buried under parking lots, service stations, fast-food franchises, and a few inns and motel chains. It was instead rescued from the historical dustbin by a man with imagination and foresight, and by his patron with immense wealth.

When Dr. William Goodwin became pastor of Bruton Parish Church in Williamsburg in 1903, the old town was in sad condition. Most of the eighteenth-century structures were gone from fire, neglect, or wrecking and scavenging for other construction. The few remaining original eighteenth-century structures were rotting away, roofs sagging, porches separating. Some streets were unpaved; every rain produced fresh mud. Chickens scavenged in the ruts.

Dr. Goodwin saw past all that. In his mind, George Washington still rode down Duke of Gloucester Street, and Thomas Jefferson held forth at the Raleigh Tavern.

Goodwin wanted to bring Williamsburg back to life. His vision of restoring the colonial capital of Virginia to its eighteenth-century appearance found a willing patron in David Rockefeller, possibly then the only man in America with the wealth and conviction to underwrite the task.

Goodwin's vision and Rockefeller's backing produced as close a copy of the original Williamsburg as could be made. Because of their collaboration, you can walk the streets of the town today. Actors in the dress of the late 1700s might speak with you of tobacco harvests at plantations on the James River, the latest ships arriving from England, and debates in the meetings of the burgesses, the advisory board to the governor.

A single original document details Williamsburg as it appeared in the last days of the Revolutionary War. In 1782, French troops were billeted in the town, following the surrender the previous year of British forces at nearby York-town. Drawn by an anonymous French military engineer, it is known as the "Frenchman's Map."

On it the locations of the town's buildings are shown as they existed at that time. The Governor's Palace, the Capitol, the Raleigh Tavern, commercial buildings along Duke of Gloucester Street, and dwellings large and small—all are rendered in their outlines to scale. In some cases, outbuildings like kitchens, stables, and smokehouses are also shown.

The Frenchman's Map has been used as a guide for decades of archaeological exploration, revealing foundations, postholes, fence lines, and refuse pits. Accurate reproductions of the structures that stood on those sites resulted.

Today, Williamsburg as a full-sized, detailed replica of a functioning eighteenth-century colonial capital and town attracts visitors from all over the world. It is said to have served as an inspiration to Walt Disney, as an example he could look to with confidence, that a grand fantasy park of his own imagination could be created.

FORT EUSTIS

In contrast to Williamsburg's beautiful restored colonial appearance, Fort Eustis in the early 1950s was one of the least visually inspiring, most utilitarian of Army posts. But, like Williamsburg, it also sits on historic ground, with its own history.

Mulberry Island is a few miles down the James River from Williamsburg. In 1610, having suffered three seasons of starvation and malaria, the surviving settlers of Jamestown, the original English colony in Virginia, decided to abandon the New World. Aboard ship and determined to return to England, they were intercepted at Mulberry Island in the nick of time by their patron, Lord Delaware, leading a relief supply fleet newly arrived from England.

Delaware stood to lose a fortune if the colony failed. He convinced the fleeing colonists to return to Jamestown for one last try. His coercive action at Mulberry Island ensured that Jamestown would survive. By so doing, he also unknowingly ensured that Williamsburg would emerge as Virginia's future capital.

During the Civil War, the Confederacy built a fort on Mulberry Island. Afterward it dozed for a half century until the US Army bought it in 1918, establishing Camp Eustis as an artillery training center and balloon observation school.

Between the wars, Camp Eustis served as a government prison for bootleggers and a Depression-era camp for the Civilian Conservation Corps (CCC). In World War II it again became an artillery training center. In 1946, Fort Eustis was designated as the home of the Army's Transportation Corps.

WALSINGHAM ACADEMY

Soon after we arrived in Williamsburg, Mom took me to Walsingham Academy, a small K–12 prep school on Jamestown Road. Run by the Sisters of Mercy, in 1952 it had two hundred students.

Coming from Saint Joseph Academy in Yokohama, I must have been in the secret parochial school admissions pipeline: the petite mother superior asked me to tell her a bit about Japan, had me do a few math problems and some spelling, and I was enrolled.

The sisters wore the full black habit and cowl over white collar and headpiece. As they glided along the corridors, they looked a bit like regal penguins. Strict but not overly so, they were great teachers. There was little doubt they expected you to perform your best.

Walsingham was a day school for girls and boys and a boarding school for girls. There were a few Army kids. I liked being in school there for the two years my dad was stationed at Fort Eustis. I made friends who would still be at Walsingham when we returned a decade later.

Most of my classmates were from Williamsburg and a few towns on its outskirts with names like Croaker, Norge, Lightfoot, and Bottom's Bridge. One classmate's father was senior silversmith for the colonial restoration; another's was master gardener at the restored Governor's Palace and the colonial Capitol. Mom sent me off to Walsingham every day with my own lunch. My favorite TV show was *Tom Corbett, Space Cadet*, so I had an official "Space Cadet" lunch box, the tin kind with the plastic handle, with rocket ships on it. Mom would put in a peanut butter and jelly sandwich on Wonder Bread, with an apple, an Oreo, and milk in the Space Cadet thermos. I'm not saying my lunchbox scored me any social points, but the boys thought it was neat. We hadn't figured girls out yet, so their opinions didn't register.

A CONFEDERATE FORT

In the early 1950s, moms were perfectly OK with their kids being outside un-supervised during summer months. We were expected to enjoy ourselves, not blow up the world, and be home for lunch or supper.

We had a spaniel named Buffer, possibly the world's doziest dog. He wouldn't pay attention to commands or instruction, but he showed up pronto at mealtimes. We would go on long walks together in the woods. There was poison ivy, poison oak, and copperhead snakes. Buffer may have been in his own world, but in the woods he stayed right beside me, which assured him as much as he did me.

Buffer and I discovered a long, high, overgrown mound deep in the forest behind the house. It ran off in both directions for quite a way, then turned a corner at each end and continued. It was very big; I never explored the whole thing. It had a wide, shallow ditch in front of it that was partially filled with brush and other plants. The pines in the forest were very tall; it was impossible to envision the whole thing.

During the Civil War, those mounds were Fort Magruder, a major Confed-erate "earthworks" defensive position. It sat astride an important junction on the road to Richmond, then the capital of the Confederacy. Packed with can-non and infantry, surrounded by a huge moat filled with sharpened wooden spikes, the fort played a major role in the Battle of Williamsburg in 1862. It was attacked by Union forces under Union general George McClellan but was never taken.

On my explorations I found bits of that Civil War fight lying right on the ground. The earth in the area was sandy; many things that were buried or cov-ered over "percolated" up to the surface over the years. I brought home lead musket balls, "minié" shot, and a corroded belt buckle. I still have some of the minié shot.

LIGHTER-THAN-AIR

I had the chance to see a few things in Virginia that are no longer part of Ameri-can life. On one ramble in the forest, Buffer and I emerged into a very large clearing. A voice called, "Hey, kid!" I looked around; no one was in sight. The voice came again: "Hey, kid! Up here!"

Hanging above the clearing was a huge airship, a "blimp," absolutely enor-mous, shining silver-gray in the clear blue sky, with "US NAVY" in big black capital letters on its side. A man leaned out of a window in the side of the gondola under its belly.

The blimp's motors were stopped; it silently drifted in the breeze. It was so big it blocked the sun as it crossed the clearing. The man laughed and waved. I waved back. "So long, kid!" he called. I remember that airship; it impressed me. I think it impressed Buffer too.

Decades later in California, my neighbor was a retired admiral who flew on the Navy's truly giant airships as a young officer. In the 1930s he had served aboard USS *Macon*, an enormous dirigible, much larger than blimps.

He said the crew of the blimp I had seen were "free-ballooning," practiced by all "lighter-than-air" crews in case their motors failed. They would "trim the ship" so that it maintained height, letting the wind move it along. They enjoyed watching the expressions of people on the ground, who had no idea they were overhead until they looked up or the crew shouted down to them.

The *Macon*'s sister dirigible, the equally enormous USS *Akron*, went down at sea off the East Coast in 1933. Of the seventy-six men on the ship that midnight, only three survived.

My neighbor was transferred to other duty just before *Macon* herself was lost at sea in a storm off the California coast in 1935. Eighty-five men rode the ship into the ocean on a February evening in 1935; all but two survived.

Sure, there were risks, he said, but there was no duty equal to serving on the great airships. "Those were the days of 'stand-up aviation'"; the officers and the helmsman at their stations in the control gondola, the same as on the bridge of a ship at sea, as they "sailed the skies."

NORFOLK & WESTERN

One morning Buffer and I were deep in the forest, near the railroad line that ran southeast to Newport News. From far off in the pines came the throaty moan of a steam whistle. We both sat on a hummock to watch.

You could feel the rhythmic vibration through the ground coming from far off. Suddenly a giant black Norfolk & Western locomotive pounded past, hauling a line of freight, drive wheels and connecting rods flying, huge clouds of smoke and steam pouring off the engine. The engineer in blue coveralls and billed hat waved a gauntleted hand to us, flashing a big grin as he pulled the whistle cord.

Steam engines and airships may be long gone, but they're very much alive in my memory.

COLOR BLIND

Virginia was segregated then; the Army wasn't. A lot of the soldiers who manned the Transportation units were African American.

Sometime during our stay in Williamsburg, on a visit to my grandparents in New York City, Mom made an appointment for me with her family's doctor. His office was in Morningside Heights on the upper west side of Manhattan, near Harlem. As we were setting off, my grandmother said, "You'll get to see all the colored people!" I thought that sounded great and looked forward to it.

When we returned that evening, my grandmother asked if I'd seen the colored people. Nope. I expected to see blue people, perhaps green or purple, but no luck; everyone looked normal. I said so. It became family lore.

THE KEY WEST AGREEMENT

The Transportation Corps units at Fort Eustis at that time were truck and rail, with maritime units like Army tugs and landing craft on the neighboring James River. TC also owned the Army's aircraft.

A 1948 conference of the armed services with the secretary of defense at Key West, Florida, defined the aviation roles of the Army, Navy, and Air Force. The Army was limited to helicopters and light, fixed-wing aircraft for liaison, reconnaissance, and air evacuation.

The Key West Agreement would get in the way of the Army's attempt to develop its own tactical close air support aircraft a few years later. I would have the chance as a teenager to see a bit of that effort.

MY FATHER'S ARMY

Though as kids our contact with soldiers was occasional, we saw them and heard them up close. Their language was "colorful." They still wore the World War II, faintly canvas smelling heavy twill fatigues with the anodized black metal buttons with thirteen embossed stars. They wore brown combat boots. If you passed downwind, their distinctive aroma was usually tobacco smoke and aftershave.

Officers wore the short, wool serge "Eisenhower" jacket over khaki shirt and black tie, or the "pinks and greens," a dark olive-drab gabardine wool coat with a sewn-on cloth belt over khaki shirt and black tie and light-shade drab trousers.

With the fatigue uniform, they were just beginning to wear the ridiculous "Ridgway" cap, a rigid brimmed pillbox that could neither be folded nor easily stowed. The Army had also developed the M1951 patrol cap, resembling the Marine Corps's utility cap. It was soft and foldable and could be worn under the helmet. But the Ridgeway cap was required for all duties when wearing the fatigue uniform. Later in the 1950s, the Ridgeway cap became infamous after its adoption by Fidel Castro and his Cuban communist colleagues.

As pretentious as it might seem today, officers at that time often carried swagger sticks. Since they were nonregulation, they came in a variety of creative materials, finishes, and *accoutrements*. A particularly popular version was an empty, polished .50 caliber cartridge casing, into which a highly lacquered or painted wooden shaft was inserted, tipped by the bullet portion of the .50 caliber round.

For officers and noncommissioned officers (NCOs) whose jobs warranted it, desktop name-and-rank blocks were also de rigueur. The bulkier and more ostentatious the better. Those who had served in the Far East might display jade or inlaid mother of pearl, while those "stateside" or in Europe might have blocks fashioned of any variation of local materials. The owner's name was usually rendered in block letters but could also be in Gothic or Old English script.

In spite of all that trivia, the Army in the early 1950s was a deadly serious business. Many officers and soldiers were veterans of hard combat during the Second World War. Men were being killed and wounded in Korea.

The Soviet Union was a growing, dedicated enemy. It detonated its first atomic bomb in 1948 and was building additional nuclear weapons. The Russian Army occupied Eastern Europe and a buffer zone of captive communist countries. In a few years, those nations would join an alliance against the West under the Warsaw Pact.

WE LIKED IKE

At home in the United States, a "Red Scare" was underway. Wisconsin senator Joseph McCarthy claimed that communist agents and "sympathizers" had infiltrated the Department of State, the Truman administration, and the US Army. Hearings in Congress sought to root out communist sympathizers and disloyal Americans.

In spite of domestic and international tensions, life in America in the early 1950s was a time of great economic expansion and industrial production. The postwar housing shortage was addressed by huge nationwide suburban developments like Levittown in New York and Westlake in San Francisco, with related schools, churches, and shopping centers. Young families bought their first homes, filling them with televisions, appliances, and children. Automobile sales soared.

General Dwight Eisenhower had retired; he was president of Columbia University. He decided to run for the presidency with a promise to visit Korea and seek an end to the war. He declared himself a Republican, won the election, and went to Korea. His efforts and diplomacy resulted in an armistice in 1953.

A TIDEWATER GHOST TOWN

We lived on Penniman Road in Williamsburg, named for a genuine Virginia ghost town. In 1916, America hadn't yet entered the Great War raging in Europe. Though America was neutral, American companies were busily manufacturing and selling great amounts of war matériel to Britain and France.

In 1916 the DuPont Corporation built an ammunition plant and town on farmland along the nearby York River. Both were named Penniman, after the DuPont chemist who invented a safer dynamite than the nitroglycerin version. As a result, the Old Williamsburg Road was changed to Penniman Road.

At the height of the war, the Penniman plant employed fifteen thousand workers. Most of the workforce were women, from all levels of Virginia society. It was highly dangerous; they sewed and filled powder bags and inserted booster charges in artillery shells. Escape chutes sprouted from all levels of the shell-loading buildings, enabling workers to abandon quickly in case of fires, which could lead to explosion.

There were both. Women were killed and maimed, but they stayed at it. Eventually the Army sent soldiers to replace them. The women refused; it was their opportunity, they said, to serve the war effort.

Industrial safety standards were minimal; chemicals turned the women's skin and hair yellow. They jokingly called themselves "canaries," but illness and other effects from chemical exposure followed, lasting long after the war.

Penniman was a company town, with a post office, a hospital, a school for workers' children, and a library, all built by DuPont to the company's blueprints. Homes were simple, built in four residence patterns, assembled on-site from prefab kits shipped to Penniman by rail.

Just as the war ended in 1918, the global influenza pandemic struck Penniman. Women workers died in the overcrowded hospital and the library, converted for the emergency. Some were buried at Penniman; the bodies of others were shipped by rail to their families.

The plant closed. The buildings were disassembled and hauled away. Some of the DuPont pattern homes were transported by barge to other towns on the peninsula and are occupied as residences today. In a few years, all traces of Penniman disappeared. Penniman Road is its only legacy.

TIDEWATER IN THE 1950S

Tidewater Virginia had one thing in common with Yokohama: summers were very hot and equally humid. Dad took us to nearby Yorktown to swim in the York River. It was just right for kids; the shallows stretched out a long way. The coast guardsmen at the Yorktown station gave families at the beach rides in their DUKWs, big amphibious trucks that drove right into the water and shifted to propellers at the back. They would plow along, down past the York River bridge and back. It was great to feel the wind and get the spray on us. Afterward, Dad took us all to Nick's restaurant by the bridge for milkshakes.

In the summer of 1952, Dad decided to build an addition onto the back of our house. His friend Art, another Army officer, helped. They had met when they were assigned to the 9th Division at Fort Dix. Born in Poland, Art came to America as a teen. Like many immigrants at that time, his hard-to-pronounce Polish name was changed to a more "Americanized" one.

During the war he fought as an infantry officer. He saw Italy, he said, the hard way, as a platoon leader and company commander. Art and Dad were such good friends I would call him "Uncle" Art. As a brigadier general, he would reappear in my later Army life.

On supply runs for the project, Dad and Art took me to a hardware store in Williamsburg. Sharp smells of fresh-cut lumber and paint; kegs of nails, tools on shelves, wheelbarrows, and shovels—it was homey and crowded and had been there many years. Small-town American, something out of a Norman Rockwell painting. You can't find them anymore.

Dad and Art built the addition from the ground up. They knocked out the wall, dug the trenching, put in the foundation, and erected the upright studs and framing, all with handsaws, hammers, and nails. They put up the shiplap outside wall and knotty-pine interior.

They worked so quickly that a lighter my father carried from the war, engraved with British and American parachute wings, was walled in. Dad discovered it missing just as they put in the last pine paneling. He didn't know where it was—inside the wall—and they weren't about to try to find it, unwinding all that work. He and Art had a good laugh; someone in the future might discover it, if they ever took the house apart.

As the last part of the project, Dad and Art built a new porch for the kitchen door. They poured cement into the molds for the steps, waited a bit, then picked me and my brother up and plunked our feet down in the cement. Our footprints may still be there.

There is a snapshot of Mom and Dad the evening the project was finished, Mom in a party dress, Dad in white shirt and bow tie, martinis on the table. That photo is the 1950s to me. My parents were young, and they had weathered the war. Raising their family, their lives stretched out ahead.

ADMIRABLE PEOPLE

I've always been greatly impressed by my parents' generation. Born in the boom years after the First World War, their childhoods were in the Great Depression. Coming of age as the German Army smashed into Poland, they were called to serve as part of an unprepared nation.

The Army was small, the fifteenth largest in the world. It grew to over nine million men and women, operating on every continent, in every hemisphere. It took on the German Reich, Imperial Japan, and Fascist Italy. When it was over, the dictators' armies were smashed, their air fleets were swept from the skies, and their navies were at the bottom of the world's oceans.

They returned home, packed their uniforms and memories in boxes, and put them on the shelf. Some went to school on the GI Bill, others into the workforce. A few, like my dad, manned the remaining Army.

They married their sweethearts and went forward, populating the nation with a new generation, raising us on vitamin-enriched milk, Wonder Bread, Wheaties, and John Wayne.

They watched us become Boy or Girl Scouts, play Little League ball, and take tap or ballet. They signed us up for cotillion and piano lessons and got us braces for our teeth. They worked with us on stamp collections, insect collections, and science projects. They taught us to look people in the eye when we greeted them and shake hands like we meant it. They took us to church.

They smoked, played bridge, and ate steaks and baked potatoes without a thought. They drank their martinis dry or with a twist and didn't give a damn if they were shaken or stirred. They didn't worry about whether they were low-brow, middlebrow, or highbrow.

They wanted us to have everything, better than they did. As far as they could, they gave us exactly that.

3

WEST POINT

1953–1956

One summer morning in 1953 my parents handed the keys of the Williamsburg house to new owners. We set off for my father's new assignment at the United States Military Academy at West Point, New York.

TILLMAN PLACE

At West Point we were back in government quarters, assigned according to rank. Lots of captains were there as instructors, tactical officers, and staff. Most married captains' quarters were brick row houses. Majors rated slightly bigger brick row houses. Lieutenant colonels lived in even bigger duplexes, also brick. Colonels, department heads, and professors lived in big, semi-Gothic stone houses set on lawns under huge oaks, many overlooking the Hudson River.

Every quarters, no matter the size, had a small sign with the occupant's rank and last name. In the Army in the 1950s, no matter your rank, you could have the inside of your quarters painted any color, as long as it was flat white.

Early 1950s Army quarters were elemental by today's standards. The kitchen had a sink, stove, and refrigerator. No garbage disposal, microwave, or dishwasher. No air-conditioning. The post engineers, as on every Army installation, were responsible for roads, sidewalks, electric and telephone poles, snow clearing, and maintenance of hundreds of buildings and quarters, including painting the interiors flat white.

GEORGE AND JOANNE

We lived at 511B Tillman Place. Our next-door neighbors at 511C were George and Joanne Patton. George came to West Point in the early 1950s from commanding a tank company in the Korean War. The son of General George S. Patton of World War II fame, he was a "tactical officer," responsible for the training, discipline, and performance of a company of cadets.

A cadet company's "Tac" could make the cadets' lives endurable or miserable, depending on their personalities and how strictly they oversaw the cadets' discipline. George was tall, handsome, athletic, and square jawed—every inch an Army officer. His speech could be gentle or "colorful," an adjective interpreted as you like.

Joanne, herself a former Army child and daughter of a general, was beautiful, resembling the film star Grace Kelly. Because of their heritage, George and Joanne were the next best thing to American military royalty.

Graduated from West Point in the class of 1946, George was commissioned in Armor, the tank branch. His father, the famous World War II general, had been a cavalryman in the "Old" Army, and was largely responsible for the development of the Army's tank combat capability in World War II.

George's basset hound Flanker was always wandering "off the patch." George often drove to some place like Thayer Gate, at the southern limit of the Academy reservation, where the Military Police intercepted the dog, on his way into the neighboring town of Highland Falls. Though possessed of an independent spirit, Flanker was lovable and cartoonish in appearance. George's language could become extremely colorful in episodes like this; we could hear Joanne admonish him, "Now *really*, George."

George and Joanne invited us several times to weekend at their family's estate in Hamilton, Massachusetts. The visits were high points of my memories of West Point.

George's father was born and raised in Pasadena, California. On a family summer trip to Catalina Island in 1902, he met Beatrice Ayer from a wealthy Boston family that owned the island. George and Beatrice married. In the 1920s they bought an estate in Hamilton, naming it Green Meadows. It was a big, white clapboard eighteenth-century house surrounded by green lawns sloping down to the Ipswich River. Barns and stables completed the property.

The main house and surrounds were a museum of artifacts collected by General Patton during his military career. Many were captured German items sent home from his World War II campaigns in North Africa and Europe. The lofty, raftered "great room" was filled with regimental flags, banners, sabers, lances, models of soldiers and tanks, and floor-to-ceiling bookcases. A six-foot model of the German battleship *Scharnhorst* in a glass case flanked one wall of the dining room.

Outside, on the rear wall of the house, a metal German eagle spread its wings, its talons clutching a circular wreath containing a Nazi swastika. A large bronze bust of Adolf Hitler stood on the paving stones in a corner of the patio.

Willie, General Patton's white bull terrier, still very much alive in his last years at the farm, was fond of urinating against Hitler's bust; a streak of bright orange scored its greenish patina. My father and George thought this was first rate and encouraged Willie each time he lifted a leg.

Though Willie couldn't run very fast, he loved to chase the local school bus. The driver would see Willie making for the bus, slow down, and stop to let him bite the tires. Willie would gnaw on one for a bit, then the driver would gradually move the bus off, the children cheering and a satisfied Willie trotting to the house.

George was a great soldier, charismatic and colorful. He kept those characteristics through his Army career, retiring as a major general. In all his assignments, George cared deeply for his soldiers. After he left the Army, George turned Green Meadows into a farm, producing berries and vegetables. They were sold at the farm and at fairs and other community events. He named various plots on which the farm's fruits and produce were grown after soldiers killed in action in Vietnam, in the 11th Armored Cavalry Regiment. As a colonel, George commanded the 11th in 1968.

Years later, an Army friend who left active service after Vietnam and remained in the Army Reserve told me a story. It highlighted George's love of the Army and its soldiers. It occurred years after George had retired to Green Meadows.

As a Reserve lieutenant colonel, my friend commanded an armored cavalry squadron in Massachusetts. His unit would occasionally send a few vehicles to various county fairs and other events to "show the flag." At one of the monthly Reserve meetings, one of his troop commanders, a captain, reported on a recent fair.

He had taken a few of his soldiers and their tracked armored vehicles. They set up, with displays of equipment. There was a good turnout of grown-ups and kids. All were very interested in the vehicles and displays.

An elderly fellow in a straw hat came over from a farm stand where he and a few much younger helpers were selling fruits and vegetables. The man looked the captain's vehicles over, talked to his sergeants, patted one or two of them on the back, and returned to the stand. He did not speak to the captain.

A bit later the captain asked his sergeants what the old man had talked about. They told him he had made some comments that indicated he sure knew a lot about armored vehicles. But, they said, he was a little nuts; he claimed to be George Patton.

JOE AND MARY PHARR

Our other neighbors at West Point were Joe and Mary Pharr Love. Joe came from Mississippi. He'd been a lieutenant in the Army Air Force during the war. When the war ended, he resigned his Reserve commission and applied to West Point. On graduating in 1950, he was commissioned in infantry.

Immediately after graduating, Joe and many of the young officers in his class were given only the basics of tactical training, and then were almost immediately sent to Korea. Joe was a platoon leader and company commander in the 5th Infantry Regiment, earning the Combat Infantryman's Badge and the Silver Star. So many were killed and wounded in Joe's West Point class, it was afterward known as "Bloody '50."

Joe's assignment at West Point in 1954 was as aide-de-camp to the Academy's superintendent, General "Babe" Bryan. A general's aide is the military equivalent of an executive assistant to a corporate CEO. He keeps the general's schedule, screens his calls, maintains his correspondence, and acts as gatekeeper on visitors' access. He arranges the general's transportation, billeting, and dining as necessary and performs other duties as the general requires.

The aide also supervises the receiving line at receptions, standing to the immediate left rear of his general and the general's lady, murmuring a few words of information about the next person or couple about to be introduced.

Aides are personally chosen by their generals. They are privy to a rarified stratum of the Army that few other junior officers see. They are entrusted with highly confidential and classified information.

When on the general's official business, aides are regarded as speaking with the authority of their general. In dealings with others of all ranks, a general's aide is wise to act at all times as diplomatically as possible. While duty as an aide is considered a step toward possible advancement to senior rank, it can be a two-edged sword. The cross-currents and politics of advancement in the Army are no different from those in the corporate world. There may be competing personalities with long memories and sharp knives.

George, Joe, and my father became lifelong friends. Mom, Mary Pharr Love, and Joanne Patton did likewise. Our families visited each other on future assignments. The Loves' daughter Mary Bland became my unofficial Army sister; we've been good friends ever since.

THE MISSION OF THE AIR FORCE

Before the Loves became our neighbors, an Air Force captain and his family lived next door. He was assigned to the Academy as an instructor in the Department of Foreign Languages. Flying the F-86 Saber jet in Korea, he shot down two enemy MiG-15 fighters.

There was a lot of backyard socializing at West Point among officers and their families. One evening, as my father was poking steaks on the barbecue and George Patton was passing around glasses of adult beverages, our Air Force neighbor, who likely had already had a couple, said, "Phil, do you know what the mission of the Air Force is?"

I was seven at the time; I must have replied something about shooting down enemy airplanes, to which he said, "Naw. Always remember, it's to fly, fight, and fuck!" My father and George thought that was hilarious. My first introduction to a real fighter pilot.

A BOY'S LIFE

West Point was great for boys. Our row of quarters backed up to steeply hilled woods of oak, cedar, and spruce. During the Revolution, West Point was established as a fortified set of heights. Cannon covered twin enormous chains stretched across the Hudson to Constitution Island. The double chains, covered by the artillery at West Point, were intended to prevent British warships from sailing up or down the Hudson. It worked; they never did.

The forts at West Point, and the outposts that protected them, were on bluffs and hills. We climbed into the forests near Fort Putnam and played in the remains of stone redoubts built by Washington's Continentals. We sat on green-tinged enemy cannon displayed at Trophy Point. We climbed on coast artillery six-inch "disappearing" guns at Battery Meigs, looking over the Hudson below Battle Monument. History at West Point was there to be touched.

I went to West Point Elementary School. Our classes were with kids from Army families of all ranks. I walked both ways to school in all weather; the stream beside the road ran swift and clear in spring, summer, and fall, with tiny crayfish immobile under the ice in winter. How they survived those Hudson Valley winters remains a mystery.

On the school playing fields, it was teamwork and more teamwork. Coach Poness was everywhere with his cry of "Play up! Play up and *drive!*" We stood beside our desks at 11:00 a.m. each November 11 for a minute of silence, in remembrance.

I suppose it's no surprise that whenever a teacher would ask what we wanted to be when we grew up, my answer was always the same: an Army officer, like my father. Not a lawyer or a dentist or doctor. Not even a Space Cadet like Tom Corbett. The term "astronaut" was far off in the future.

When I turned seven, my father took me to the Old Cadet Library to get my library card. A gray Gothic stone castle with twin towers, the library had gloss-black wooden arched doors flanked by old cannon barrels in the walls, set vertically with muzzle upright.

The librarian sat at a big raised desk in the reading room. She typed out my card: *thwock-thwock-ding!* Zowie! I could check out books!

The kids' collection was in one of the castle's towers. My first two selections were *Yankee Ships and Yankee Skippers* and *The Complete Book of Outer Space* by Willy Ley. The one on Yankee whaling ships was heavy going, but Willy's book fascinated me with space travel.

The library's enormous reading room was three floors high. Oil portraits of stiff-looking "Old Army" officers in high-collared blue uniforms with gold buttons, "shoulder boards," and bushy beards frowned down. In their day, with straight razors as the only option, daily shaving must have been pretty risky. It was likely less of a chore, and a lot safer, to grow a beard.

Spiral iron stairs stood in each corner of the reading room, leading up to cast-iron, wood-floored walkways supported by wrought-iron braces. Each balcony ran along high bookshelves. It was a *very* old library; the balcony floorboards creaked and groaned as cadets walked on them.

Facing the library from across the street was a larger-than-life statue of General George Patton in fleece-collared jacket, combat boots, and steel helmet, holding field glasses. Legend had it that a pair of "Buffalo" nickels were embedded in the statue's hands.

Behind Patton were several clay-surfaced tennis courts on which, years later as a high school student, I chased tennis balls for Lieutenant Arthur Ashe, who coached the cadet tennis team. Ashe was a real gentleman, with a lethal serve.

Across from one flank of the library was an enormous, empty four-story granite-walled structure. It was the old Cadet Riding Hall, where generations of cadets were required to master horsemanship. Mounting and dismounting, riding appropriately at walk, trot, canter, and full gallop—all were graded exercises required before a cadet could graduate.

Starting in 1955, the Riding Hall was gutted, reinforced, and converted to an academic building, renamed Thayer Hall after West Point's first superintendent. When completed, it would hold several floors of classrooms and the future home of the Academy Museum, with a parking lot on the roof.

My father took me there one summer day, just after work had begun on the cavernous, vacant interior. The compacted dirt floor was being excavated. The odor of dirt mixed with a huge amount of ancient horse manure was stunning. Before America entered World War II, my father was in a horse-drawn artillery unit in the New York National Guard. For him, that smell must have brought back a lot of memories. Whenever I think of the old horse cavalry, I recall that pungent odor, long gone by the time I became a soldier.

I spent hours in the old Academy Museum. It was across from the hospital, through a dressed-granite "sallyport." A shield-shaped gray sign edged in black, bearing an Athenian helmet and scabbarded sword, pointed the way with a golden arrow. Left, up stone steps to a switchback landing, up again past a set of heavy, studded wooden doors with big, black wrought-iron straps and rings.

A vaulted, two-story hall ran the length of the building, packed like a historian's attic with memorabilia of American military arms. All in one huge, cluttered space, it was nothing like the orderly, multifloored museum that would be installed in Thayer Hall in the 1960s.

A French-built Renault *tankette* and a 75mm field gun sat side by side. The gun had fired the first shot by American artillery in World War I. American industry was unable to provide such weapons in 1917–18: both the *tankette* and field gun were of French manufacture. That would change radically in World War II.

There were artifacts from Chippewa, the Wilderness, the Army of the West, the Indian Campaigns, captured banners from the Civil War, the Boxer expedition of 1900, and both World Wars. Ranked around the walls, rising to the ceiling, were American regimental flags, national colors, faded guidons, streamers, and pennants. Shot with holes, torn, mended, and patched, they were inscribed with homespun stitching or hand-painted honors: Malvern Hill, Petersburg, Seven Pines, Atlanta, Chickamauga.

When school wasn't in session at West Point, Mom would boot us out in the mornings. We rode our bikes everywhere, often to Delafield Pond, a deep lake fed by a mountain spring. The diving platform had boards at the fifteen- and thirty-six-foot levels. I didn't go off the high dive until years later, before going to parachute school in the Army.

I didn't know until much later that my parents were split on allowing us to go swimming due to the polio scare sweeping the country. It inflicted almost immediate paralysis on its victims, which included thousands of children. LIFE and other weekly magazines had photos of children in "iron lung" machines, literally keeping them alive.

Polio's cause was unknown; there was no known cure. Doctors advised mothers to keep their children from becoming overheated, bathe them frequently, and keep them away from crowds. When two children further down Tillman Place were stricken, the moms doubled down on preventing our exposure.

My brother and I had to be home by noon, took baths every day after lunch, and were banished to our rooms to rest for two hours. I did a lot of reading that summer, including every copy of my *Boy's Life* magazines and *Classics Illustrated* collections until they fell apart.

Dr. Jonas Salk's development of a vaccine for polio in 1955 and its distribution in 1956 saved countless children's lives. The Nobel Prize he was awarded didn't come close to matching the gratitude of millions of moms.

THE WIZARD'S CASTLE?

Across the Hudson, a turreted castle rose above the far forest skyline. Legend had it that the castle scenes in the 1939 hit film *The Wizard of Oz* had been filmed there.

I imagined the Witch in one of those towers, looking into her crystal ball, plotting doom for Dorothy and her crew: the Lion, Tin Man, Scarecrow, and Toto, Dorothy's little black dog. All very coolly spooky.

Many years later I learned the castle, known as Dick's Folly, had been built around 1903, had no resemblance to the castle in the film, and worse, was never occupied by a witch. Drat.

THE ARMY TEAM

Athletics were a major part of life for the cadets at West Point. Coached by "Red" Blake, Army's star football team was quarterbacked by Pat Uebel. We went to a lot of the cadet rallies, usually at night, with the cadets around a huge bonfire chanting, "Beat Colgate!" "Beat Penn!" and names of other college opponents. Loudest of all each year was "BEAT NAVY!"

Home game days at Michie Stadium saw the cadets marching onto the field and filling the stands on one side, while the visiting team's supporters filled the other. The West Point band pounded out loud, inspiring music. The cadets sang "On Brave Old Army Team," the Academy fight song, and rendered a number of thunderous cheers and whistles for the Army players. It could get pretty cold up in those concrete stands, but no one seemed to mind much. If the sun was shining, it was a great spectacle.

In the 1950s, the Corps of Cadets at West Point was just over two thousand, all male. When the Corps marched onto the enormous parade ground known as the Plain, with colors and guidons snapping in the breeze, it was a sight that impressed visitors from around the world.

There was a neat trick of optics at play in those spectacles. The Corps was organized into cadet battalions and companies. The cadet companies were filled by men ranked by size. On the day new cadets entered, they were lined up in a random file. Upperclassmen barked, "If you're taller than the man in front of you, move up!"

That enabled them to carve out blocks of men in similar height groups. So, when the Corps was arrayed on the parade ground, the companies at each end had the tallest men, descending in height, company by company, toward the center. When the Corps was viewed from either end, the trick of perspective made it appear that every man was exactly the same height.

One June, President Eisenhower, himself a West Point graduate, came to review the Corps at parade. My father somehow arranged to bring me right up onto the reviewing stand and introduced me to the president. He did the same when Queen Frederica of Greece visited the Corps one very cold winter. I found myself being smiled at by a real queen. My father was beaming just as much.

"THE LONG GRAY LINE"

John Ford, the famous film director, and his Hollywood crew filmed *The Long Gray Line* at West Point. Again, my father walked me through the cordon separating the many onlookers and introduced me to Ford. They had met during the war when they were both in England in OSS. We met Tyrone Power, who was being costumed for a scene on the parade ground, and Maureen O'Hara, who was watching from a folding chair set beneath a huge umbrella.

My father introduced me to Roy Rogers at a rodeo at Madison Square Garden in New York City. In my eight- or nine-year-old mind at the time, Roy

Rogers was as big magic as the president. I'm certain his ability to effortlessly get behind the scenes practically everywhere must have been an attribute that served him well in the OSS during the war. I would meet a lot of his former OSS colleagues as I grew up; like him, they were unique.

CUB SCOUTS

My parents enrolled me at West Point as a Cub Scout in Pack 23. Mom was my den mother. I still have my Bobcat pin. My first Cub Scout campout was at Round Pond, on the West Point reservation. That started me on the Scouting road that led eventually to Eagle Scout; I have always been thankful for it.

For Boy Scout and Cub Scout troops on Army posts in the 1950s, the Army was effectively the world's biggest camping equipment store; there were warehouses full of gear left over from World War II: tents, sleeping bags, rucksacks, stoves. Whatever you needed, they had it.

The Cub Scout fathers at West Point, who had "roughed it" through World War II, intended on going first class where camping was concerned. So on that first campout we slept on army cots with nice mattresses, blankets and sheets, and soft pillows, in a big army wall tent with a wooden floor.

Our fathers cooked us pancakes, eggs, and orange juice in the mornings and hamburgers in the evening. We took little nature walks and did some crafts. At night we watched cartoons shown by a projector running off a small Army generator.

In 1969, as a company commander in Vietnam, my unit had a "stand-down" in a rear base area after weeks in the jungle, cutting our way through bamboo and vines and living like forest creatures.

After a couple of beers with the troops, I told them about that first Scout campout. I said something like, "So that's what I expected the Army to be like."

There was silence. Then one of the men said, "Sir, if that's what you thought being in the Army was all about and you volunteered for the infantry, you are one dumb shit." There followed a general roar of approval as the men fell off their chairs laughing, me right along with them.

TV IN THE EARLY 1950S

Television was a major part of home life. Our TV was black and white, the pictures grainy by today's crisp standards. If there was color TV in the early 1950s, no one we knew had one. Cable television was far off in the future; everyone had an antenna on their roof, or a set of "rabbit ears" on top of the TV set. The picture clarity depended on how the antenna was adjusted, and there was a lot of finesse and "body English" required to get the rabbit ears adjusted just right to best capture the TV signal.

In the mid-1950s, the entire national television news was fifteen minutes, at 6:00 p.m. The rest of the day was taken up with a variety of scheduled programming on only three networks: CBS, NBC, and ABC.

The day's program schedule was published in the newspapers. The daily schedule, week by week, was also published in *TV Guide*, a small magazine. There was no way to record programs. If you weren't sitting in front of the TV at the time a program was aired, you missed it, period.

Daytime TV began with the original *Today* show, emceed by a bow-tied Dave Garroway who wore horn-rimmed glasses. Though hard to believe given today's programming focus, *Today* at that time was pitched at kids and their parents, with a little news, some toy demonstrations, and occasional readings of children's stories.

Today's ratings began to slump. Garroway was "assisted" by the show's official mascot, J. Fred Muggs, a chimpanzee with more poise than many of the current crop of television commentators. J. Fred was a big hit, saving the show from decline. Garroway would sign off each day by holding up his hand, palm out, while intoning, "Peace."

SATURDAY MORNINGS ON POST

There was a two-hour matinee of cartoons and cowboy movies for the West Point kids. It was in a large formal theater with a stage, where real shows were held and each year the graduating cadet class put on the annual "Hundredth Night Show," celebrating one hundred days to graduation.

Plenty of popcorn flew through the air at those matinees. On one occasion, a couple of boys released a jar full of moths; they flew up into the projector beam, dancing around, creating enormous splotchy shadows on the screen. I wouldn't be surprised if in later life those boys went into Special Forces or worked for the CIA.

TABLETS, TABLETS

Whoever had the contract for supplying bronze tablets all over West Point likely retired early. They were everywhere, commemorating achievements, events, and persons. Two that I remember were over the entry to the cadet gymnasium. One read:

> *Upon the fields of friendly strife are sown the seeds that on other fields and other days, shall bear the fruits of victory.*
>
> —Douglas MacArthur

The other:

> *I have a secret and dangerous mission. Send me a West Point football player.*
>
> —George C. Marshall

The first quote is vintage MacArthur, who served as superintendent of West Point and restructured its antiquated nineteenth-century curriculum.

The second is more than likely fiction. Marshall was a graduate of the Virginia Military Institute and first captain of its Corps of Cadets. He had captained the VMI football team. He was extremely taciturn; a statement like that was not in his character.

But it made for great public relations. The quote, I suspect, is the product of Colonel Russell "Red" Reeder, a member of the Army Athletic Department in the early 1950s. A brave soldier who lost a leg at Normandy, Reeder also wrote a series of popular children's books about the adventures of Clint Lane, a fictional West Point cadet.

Reeder's sister Nardi authored a biography of Marty Maher, an Irish immigrant who began in the Army as a waiter in the West Point cadet dining hall. Maher witnessed generations of cadets passing through, many to become famous generals, others to die in action. Her book on Maher later became the basis of the very popular film *The Long Gray Line*.

HUDSON CRUISE

Major General "Babe" Bryan was superintendent of the Academy from 1953 to 1956. A large, steel Army power yacht on the Hudson River, captained by

"Swede" Larsen, a senior warrant officer, was available for river outings for the superintendent. It also provided occasional cruises for West Point's Army families.

As General Bryan's aide, our next-door neighbor, Joe Love, arranged a trip for several families. We left the Academy dock on a late September morning, the trees an autumn palette of bright orange, yellow, and red on both banks. Passing the town of Cold Spring with its main street running down to its river docks on the eastern shore, we sailed close to Constitution Island, where the chains across the river had been anchored in the Revolutionary War.

As we sailed north, the ruins of an old gray castle, overgrown with ivy and moss, passed on our right on "Bannerman's Isle." Frank Bannerman of New York City built it in the early twentieth century to store US military equipment after the Civil War, bought on a sealed bid to the US government. Years later, Bannerman also bought 90 percent of the cannon, artillery ammunition, and gunpowder captured during the Spanish-American War.

From his showrooms in New York City, Bannerman built a worldwide military surplus business, selling the equipment, ordnance, and munitions stored in the castle. In 1920, a fire caused the artillery shells and powder charges to detonate with enormous force, tearing the structure apart. By the 1950s, the castle was an overgrown, deserted shell, a memory to Frank Bannerman, the true "father" of the Army-Navy surplus business.

As we cruised upriver, trains on the New York Central's twin tracks zipped through tunnels cut into the solid rock of the hills along the eastern shore. We passed beneath the looming mass of Storm King Mountain and, leaving Cornwall-on-Hudson on our left, sailed up under the Newburgh–Beacon Bridge.

Turning, our southbound journey took us past West Point and the place where in 1780 General Benedict Arnold, his attempt to turn the fortress at West Point over to the British discovered, was picked up by HMS *Vulture*, a Royal Navy sloop of war. During the remainder of the Revolution, Arnold went on to fight as a British general in the American South.

Under the Bear Mountain Bridge, we were passed by the northbound *Alexander Hamilton*, one of the Hudson River Day Line's long, slender, three-deck riverboats. A side-wheeler painted white over a black hull, she was a throwback to the Hudson River traffic of the late nineteenth and early twentieth centuries, appearing as something out of a Currier & Ives lithograph.

When the *Hamilton* sounded her whistle passing the Bear Mountain Bridge, it could be heard well above West Point. She swept majestically past us, the huge "rocking beam" on her upper deck driving her enormous covered sidewheels.

South past Bear Mountain Park, we turned again in the river opposite Stony Point. In July 1779, American general Anthony Wayne led a night assault on the British fortifications there, which commanded the river. Wayne's plan of attack used three columns of infantrymen. He instructed his soldiers to approach silently, attacking only with their bayonets. The resulting fierce night fight was a success; the Americans seized the position. Wayne's consistent daring and audacious performance as a combat commander earned him the nickname "Mad Anthony."

With sandwiches and sodas for the kids, and frequent narration from our skipper, Mister Larsen, on the sights and history of the points along the river, the cruise on the Hudson was a memorable day.

"SECOND STAR TO THE RIGHT"

Sunday evening television entertainment in those years featured the *Ed Sullivan Show*, with variety acts and famous performers. Kate Smith was a frequent guest to sing "God Bless America." Other great performers with their own television shows were Steve Allen, Dinah Shore, Jackie Gleason, Jack Benny, and Phil Silvers.

Two of my favorite programs in the "grown-up" category were *Twentieth Century* and *You Are There*, both hosted by Walter Cronkite. *You Are There* was written in such a way that viewers felt as though they were actually on-scene during great events in history. Cronkite would sign off each episode with, "What sort of a day was it? A day like all days, filled with the events that alter and illuminate our time, and you were there."

My father and I watched every one of the World War II *Victory at Sea* series; Richard Rogers's soaring musical themes for the show's segments remain some of my favorites. Watching those programs further boosted my interest in military history.

One evening in March 1955, along with an estimated sixty-five million others across the country, we watched a broadcast from New York City of Mary Martin, live on-stage, in *Peter Pan*. The pixie-like actress, playing the role of an enchanted boy, soared through the air, fought with pirates, and rescued Tinker Bell.

We laughed at Cyril Ritchard as Captain Hook, trying to elude the crocodile that had eaten his alarm clock and emitted a "tick-tock" sound. Mary Martin's directions to Never-Never Land, "Second star to the right, and straight on 'til morning!" became a treasured family phrase for decades.

Hosted by Alistair Cooke, *Omnibus* was an unusual, educational television show airing on Sunday afternoons. In the 1950s, its programming was known as "highbrow," with serious discussions on architecture, music, art, archaeology, and travel. My parents watched it every week.

Much of it was over my head, but it prompted a lot of questions. *Omnibus* had interviews with guests like Frank Lloyd Wright, Leonard Bernstein, and Orson Welles. It also showcased an occasional comedian, like the zany Jonathan Winters.

Sitting on a cushion on the Persian carpet in our living room, with snow on the ground outside and a winter's late Sunday afternoon darkening to night, watching *Omnibus* with my parents, is a distinct and happy memory.

"YOU MAY NOT BE INTERESTED IN WAR"

West Point might have seemed isolated on its rocky ledge beside the Hudson, but events of the Cold War were an occasional subject of dinner table conversation.

One of my father's OSS friends helped defeat the communist forces in the civil war in Greece in the late 1940s. President Truman sent military aid to both Greece and Turkey to help defeat communist insurgencies. Dad's friend was a US adviser to the Greek Army. By this time I knew they weren't talking about a war in "grease," as I had assumed when I heard talk about it in Japan.

In 1954, a communist-led rebellion in the Philippines finally ended. The communist "Huk" guerrillas fought the Japanese during their occupation of the islands in World War II. After the war, the Huks turned against the Philippine government. President Truman sent US military aid and advisers, among whom was Ed Lansdale, a former OSS officer.

Lansdale would play a strong future role as the US supported the creation of the Republic of South Vietnam. I would meet him during my studies in the graduate Foreign Service School at Georgetown in the early 1970s.

Of the defeated communist Huks in the Philippines, my father said the irony was that many of the Italian partisan groups he had worked with against the Germans during the war in Italy were also communists; war creates unlikely alliances against greater enemies.

Joe Love, George Patton, and our fighter-pilot French-language instructor had seen combat in Korea. By 1954 the war had ceased, as the result of the negotiated armistice. An armistice is technically a mutually agreed cessation of fighting, so technically the United States has been at war with North Korea ever since.

In the early 1950s, the French had been fighting a war in Indochina against Vietminh communist guerrillas and their leader, Ho Chi Minh since 1946. French Indochina then included Cambodia, Laos, and Vietnam. Ironically, during World War II, the American OSS had supported Ho Chi Minh and his Vietminh against the occupying Japanese.

One evening at dinner in the spring of 1954, my father said the French had lost a big battle in Indochina. It was the first time I heard the odd name of Dienbienphu.

The preceding fall, the French had parachuted and air-landed troops in a valley, far out on the Laotian border of Vietnam. Naming their heavily fortified positions Dienbienphu for a small colonial post that had been there, they intended to draw the majority of the Vietminh forces to the valley and defeat them there.

Fatally, the French command believed the Vietminh would not be able to position artillery on the surrounding mountains; their heights dominated the fortified French "hedgehog" on the valley floor. In a Herculean effort, the communists did just that, camouflaging their guns. Their artillery pounded the French mercilessly; Dienbienphu fell in May 1954.

My father knew a lot about unconventional or "guerrilla" war. I remember him saying that evening, "I wouldn't be surprised if we get sucked into this Indochina situation."

At that time, President Eisenhower had stated that if the communists were victorious in Vietnam, the remaining Southeast Asian nations would fall to communism "like a row of dominos." Few then knew that Eisenhower believed the French would lose their war in Indochina. To "save" the region from communism, he was considering committing US air and land forces. The plan was to be called "United Action." To sell it to Congress, he needed a partner. He instructed John Foster Dulles, US secretary of state, to approach Britain. The British did not see the situation as justifying commitment of their forces, so "United Action" died. Even so, eventual commitment of US combat forces to Vietnam would be only a decade away.

Immediately after the French lost the Battle of Dienbienphu, there was an international conference at Geneva in Switzerland to decide what to do about Korea and the divided city of Berlin. The issue of Vietnam was also taken up. The conference produced a series of resolutions, among them one suggesting a national vote be taken so the people could select which form of government they preferred The resolutions were known as the Geneva Accords.

France withdrew its forces from Indochina in 1954. The United States ignored the Accords and instead helped set up the independent Republic of South Vietnam, under Ngo Dinh Diem. Ed Lansdale would play a major role as advisor to Diem.

I didn't know much about Indochina or Vietnam then, but it would be waiting for me down the road, a demonstration of Lenin's statement: "You may not be interested in war, but war is interested in you."

SUMMER CAMP

In the summers at West Point, a lot of us kids were packed off for a month to Youth Camp, held at Round Pond, the site of my famous first Cub Scout campout.

It wasn't exactly like being in the Army, but a bit closer than summer camps in civilian life. There was morning flag raising, and in the evening before dinner, we gathered and watched it lowered. There was a headquarters building and a dining hall. We lived in the same Army wall tents as in the Cub Scout campout, on wood floors, with the same cots. The sides of the tents were rolled up during the day and down at night. We made our beds every morning. No one inspected; we did it anyway.

There was rowing and canoeing and archery, foot races, tug-of-war, capture the flag, and other summer pursuits. We learned a bit how to use a compass, had lectures on poison ivy and poison oak, and were told to watch out for snakes. We caught frogs and box turtles, and let them go. At night, fireflies glowed in jars beside our cots. We let them go too.

Grandpa Joe, my dad's father, came for a Sunday visit. I took him out on the lake in a rowboat. A small, dapper man, he wore a dark suit and didn't say much, but he had a twinkle in his dark brown eyes. I think he may have enjoyed my chattering on about the animals that lived in and around the lake.

One afternoon about halfway through the month, an Army helicopter flew over. A few minutes later I was surprised to hear my name over the camp's address system: report to the headquarters building. I found a big box on the chief counselor's table with a parachute still attached to it.

The chief handed me a note in the box, which was full of Hershey chocolate bars. The note was from my dad, who had tossed the box from the helicopter. The chief asked me what I wanted to do with the candy. I said we ought to share it out among our camp mates. That seemed to be the right decision; I suddenly became a very popular camper.

FIRST FLIGHT

One summer afternoon, my father took me down to the North Athletic Field at West Point. There was a two-seat H-13 Iroquois helicopter, with the big plastic bubble up front; the same type that much later became the signature of the TV series *M.A.S.H.*

I was buckled into the seat beside the pilot, who wore a khaki baseball cap and black earphones. As he flipped switches and the rotor blades began to turn, he smiled and said, "Enjoy the view, kid, and don't touch a thing." No problem on that!

We took off, flying north up the Hudson River past Storm King Mountain, then along the river south to the Bear Mountain Bridge, and back to West Point. It was the same route as the afternoon on the supe's launch, but like a magic carpet! Just plopping your kid in an Army helicopter for a ride is impossible today, but in so many ways it was a different, less restrictive Army in those years.

Summers in the Hudson Valley were very hot and muggy; Delafield Pond was always there for a swim. To relieve the heat, at about 4:30 every afternoon in summer we got what Dad referred to as the "duty thunderstorm"; you could almost set your watch by it.

The thunder and lightning were ferocious. Washington Irving, the eighteenth-century storyteller, who lived in Tarrytown down the river, used the storms as the basis for "Rip Van Winkle," in which the thunderous *Donner und Blitzen* in the skies was really the sound of enchanted dwarves rolling balls at ten-pins. Irving also wrote "The Legend of Sleepy Hollow," a tale about a terrible ghost, a mercenary Hessian cavalryman of the Revolutionary War whose head was carried away by an American cannonball.

WILLIE PUTS ONE AWAY

That same summer, Dad took Dave and me to Doubleday Field, the cadet baseball diamond just east of Trophy Point. The New York Giants played an "exhibition game" against Army, the cadet baseball team.

The height of the game was Willie Mays stepping into the batter's box. Willie took a couple of slow swings, hunkered down, cocked the bat over his shoulder, and stared up the forty feet between him and the mound.

The Army pitcher gave a quick signal to the catcher, wound up, and sent a fast ball blistering over the plate. The crack of Willie's bat against that ball meant business. We watched it soar up, up, and out, over the right field line, all the way across the Plain, to land with a CLANK! on the copper-sheathed roof of Cullum Hall, the Officers Club. The stands went wild.

THE HEADLESS HORSEMAN

Halloween was greatly anticipated. In the more relaxed environment of that time, kids roamed the post in a variety of costumes, filling their goody bags with candy at each door. I don't recall any of the homes being near as lavishly decorated as some are today, but the treats were number one.

Each year the Academy would put on an enormous Halloween party at the Field House by the river, an enormous structure enabling athletic events in winter and other "inclement weather." The Hudson Valley had a *lot* of inclement weather.

The West Point Band played, there were hot chocolate and games, and a costume contest in which all the post kids competed. For two years running, my father's costume concoctions won first prize. Year one was a space robot modeled on the then popular film *Forbidden Planet*, with clawlike hands and flashing red eyes. Year two was the "Headless Horseman" from Washington Irving's story. I wore both costumes; my brother Dave carried the Horseman's "head," with its tricorn hat and, yes, flashing red eyes.

BUSTED!

My friend Jay was a classmate in fifth grade at the West Point School. On weekends we would explore on our bikes, all over the post and far out onto the military reservation. On one of these forays we pedaled past a log cabin, much older than any structures we'd seen.

On the way back we decided to explore it. It appeared deserted, and more than a little neglected. The door wasn't locked. Being audacious nine-year-olds, we decided to look around.

In we went. It was vacant, with no furnishings. And very, *very* old. The floors were rough, uneven planks, the huge rock fireplace was soot blackened, and the window glass was so old the trees seen through it were distorted. Spiderwebs were everywhere. It was eerie; we were appropriately spooked.

Coming out the front door, we were greeted by two smiling Military Policemen. They had seen our bikes propped against a tree in front. That got us a ride to the provost marshal's office, West Point's police station.

Calls were made to our fathers to come pick us up. I remember the look the desk sergeant gave us two crew-cut miscreants as we sat on chairs in front of him. It could be translated as, "If you two clowns feel uncomfortable now, you haven't seen anything yet."

He was right; our fathers got a severe talking-to by the provost marshal, who outranked them. They had to sign for us, like a pair of prisoners of war. When we got home, the least of my problems was that I was grounded for a month.

I still feel bad about that. Remember what I said about how whatever an Army kid might do could have an effect on his father's career? What we had done wasn't fatal, but it wasn't a happy episode.

WHITEY AND FRANK

When we lived at West Point, a program called "Plebe Sponsor" enabled officers' families to "adopt" freshman-year cadets, called "Plebes," enabling them to come for Sunday dinner. It was an opportunity for the cadets to have a break from the rigid discipline and pressure, to have a look at an Army officer's family at home, and for families to get to know the cadets.

We sponsored two Plebes, Whitey and Frank. I remember them both in their "dress gray": black-trimmed gray tunics with black stand-up collars. Each time they came to our quarters, Dad told them to relax; they loosened their collars and looked a lot happier.

The "Hundredth Night" show is a gala theatrical, staged annually by the cadet seniors, or First Classmen, when there are one hundred days left until graduation in June. It's a very big thing at West Point; all the officers and wives attend. It happened that my father was off at Fort Leavenworth, Kansas, at the Command and General Staff course, so he arranged for Whitey to escort Mom to the show.

Mom was a knockout, which didn't go unnoticed. At dinner on a Sunday after my father returned from Leavenworth, Whitey related the tale. He was standing in ranks just before supper formation a few days after Hundredth Night, at a "brace," at attention with his chin pulled in, looking straight ahead. He heard footsteps approach then stop behind him. "You were dragging pretty 'pro' at Hundredth Night, Mister. Who was that very attractive woman?" The voice was right behind his ear.

In cadet slang, "dragging" meant to escort; "pro" meant top notch. Whitey must have hesitated; the voice continued, "Well, who was she, Mister?"

Whitey responded, "Sir! The lady I escorted is the wife of my Plebe Sponsor!"

Whitey said there was a pause while the upperclassman digested that data. Then, "Do you recognize my voice, mister?"

"Sir, I do not!" replied Whitey.

"Good." There was the sound of footsteps retreating. Whitey never knew who it was.

Years later, when my father passed away, Frank somehow learned of it. Out of the Army then and in business elsewhere in the country, he nonetheless came all the way to New York to pay his respects to our family. He and Whitey were great.

THE FUTURE IS NOW

In the autumn of our last year at West Point, the long-awaited New York State Thruway system's segment from New York City to Albany was opened to traffic. Dad piled us into our '55 Chevrolet Bel Air, and off we went, down to New York City to visit my grandparents, in half the time it used to take. It was like the future. Actually, it *was* the future: a smooth, divided road with three lanes in each direction. Amazing. I half expected to see rocket ships in the sky.

When you're a child, you take a lot of things for granted, but I was fascinated by that interstate highway. How had it happened? Why had it happened? Who had the idea?

My father explained it had something to do with the Army, and a lot to do with Presidents Roosevelt and Eisenhower. He said President Roosevelt was interested in building a network of toll highways across America to provide jobs during the Depression of the 1930s. In Germany, a similar program was proposed at the same time, resulting in a system of smooth, divided highways known as the Autobahn.

While the German road-building effort proceeded, the ongoing economic crises in America prevented the concept from being realized. In 1944, with military victory a high probability, the Roosevelt administration funded the start of work on the interstate highways. But by the time Dwight Eisenhower became president in 1953, not much had been accomplished. That would change.

Eisenhower wanted to go to France to fight during the First World War, but the Army, recognizing his organizational talents, assigned him to the Tank Corps at Camp Colt, near Gettysburg, in Pennsylvania. There, he trained tank crews and mechanics to be sent to the fighting in France.

With the war over in the summer of 1919 and then a lieutenant colonel, Eisenhower decided to go along as an observer on the "Transcontinental Motor Convoy," an Army "mobility experiment." A collection of eighty-one motorized Army vehicles, the convoy's mission was to cross the United States, from Washington, DC, to San Francisco.

If that doesn't sound like much of a challenge today, in 1919 there were very few reliable roads, none of which traversed the entire country. The first bits of the future transcontinental "Lincoln Highway" had been dedicated in 1913, but in 1919 it was incomplete and an "advisory route" only.

Composed of trucks with a variety of drive systems, the convoy also carried a trailer-mounted tractor, which proved invaluable in pulling vehicles out of ditches and gullies.

The convoy was augmented by a truckload of bandsmen supplied by the Goodyear Rubber Company. Harvey Firestone's tire company supplied two trucks fitted with pneumatic tires; they proved very durable. The other Army trucks had solid rubber tires.

In that long-ago summer, the convoy navigated plains, mountains, and rivers, pausing at towns and cities, which went all out to organize picnics, dances, and other celebrations.

It wasn't all play; dust choked the carburetors, and the unrelenting, bleak terrain was hard on the men. "The intensely dry air, absence of green trees and vegetation, and parched appearance of the landscape," noted the official "after-action" report in its description of the stretch between Point of Rocks and Medicine Bow, Wyoming, "exerted a depressing influence on personnel."

Arriving in San Francisco sixty-two days after departing Washington, and traveling 3,250 miles, along the way the men of the convoy had repaired or rebuilt eighty-eight wooden bridges. To find a passage in several places, the soldiers enlisted the support of trappers and native guides.

The memory of the two months needed to transit the country in 1919 motivated Eisenhower, as did his experience during World War II, during which he had seen the superb German Autobahn system. His armies used it as high-speed routes of advance, hastening their drive into Germany.

In 1956, after much debate and several failed attempts, the National Interstate and Defense Highway Act was passed by Congress and signed into law by Eisenhower.

Sometimes when I drive today on an interstate highway, I think back to those dusty soldiers with their trucks, slowly grinding their way across a nation with no real network of roads.

DARK AGES

Hudson Valley winters were grim; the cadets called them the "Dark Ages." The river froze solid; icebreakers kept a ship passage open. Snow was often two to three feet deep. But it was great for kids.

We had one-person sleds and would spend whole Saturday mornings on a nearby hill, coming home at lunch with our rubber galoshes half full of icy slush to bowls of hot chicken noodle or tomato soup fixed by Mom, then off again for more sledding. Sundays were church in the morning, lunch, more sledding, then *Omnibus* on TV, and off to bed.

On some weekends we would go to Smith Rink, a huge wooden indoor ice-skating structure. Amplified waltzes played as skaters swept round and round or performed pirouettes. The cocoa at the snack counter was hot enough to do serious damage, but it was great just to hold a cup to warm your hands.

My upstairs room at West Point overlooked the woods. Dad decided the windows needed curtains and disappeared into his "wizard workshop" in the basement. Eventually he reappeared with perfectly cut and sewn curtains, stenciled with figures of cowboys and Indians. The cloth material he used was the type used on the big wooden-framed targets at the rifle ranges. It had been treated with pungent waterproofing, which took a while to air out and go away.

DAD BAGS A DEER

In one of those winters, George Patton convinced my father that they needed to go deer hunting. I'm not sure Dad was enthusiastic about the idea; he had never hunted anything but Germans. But on a clear, sunny Saturday morning with fresh snow on the ground, my dad appeared with a bolt-action German Wehrmacht Kar-98 Mauser, with a telescopic sight. Years later I had it reconditioned and the scope realigned, but that morning at West Point, it was "Where did *that* come from?"

They set off in George's car. Late that afternoon they returned with a dead deer tied to the roof. Dad and George decided they would dress it hung by its antlers from a swing set. A bunch of kids and parents gathered around to watch. If this sounds at odds with what's acceptable today, let's remember, "the past is a foreign land."

George said something about how this "wasn't going to be pretty" for the kids. There was a little shuffling among the parents, but nobody left. My father

produced a very big knife and cut the deer open. We'll pass on the details; I
didn't know anything about field-dressing a deer then, so the fine points are
kind of blurred. The deer's insides slithered out onto a tarp Dad had put on the
snow: SPLAT! When they did, two little girl twins who lived up the street fainted.
Plop! Plop! Good thing there was deep snow to break their fall.

CHANGE OF ORDERS

In our last spring at West Point, my father came home one evening with great
news: his next assignment was to France, to the NATO headquarters at Fontainebleau, outside Paris.

Mom was delighted and began perusing French fashions. But not for long.
At dinner a week later, Dad said there was news; his assignment to France was
changed. Mom was crestfallen. She later said she was preparing to hear we were
going to Fort Polk, Louisiana, or Fort Chaffee, Arkansas. Then Dad said, "Do
you think you'd be able to put up with three years in Tuscany, instead?"

4

ITALY

1956–1959

CONSTITUTION

June 1956. Flocks of pigeons flew in and out of the enormous open door-ways. In the huge four-story pier shed on Manhattan's west side, the air carried the tang of salt.

Organized bustle was everywhere. Family groups stood at the foot of the covered gangway leading up to double steel doors opened in the ship's side. Uniformed ship's stewards waited at the gangway's foot, stamping sheaves of tickets. New York "beat cops" strolled by twirling their batons. Porters pushed carts loaded with bags, suitcases, and trunks, layered with stickers from travels to exotic destinations.

Seen through the shed doors, the huge, black wall of the ship's hull stretched left and right, soaring up to a band of white topped with railings, against which colorful clusters of passengers gathered.

It was sailing day for the SS *Constitution*, the American Export Line's sleek transatlantic liner. She was taking us to Italy—six days from New York to Genoa. Launched in 1951, the *Constitution* and her sister ship the SS *Independence* were as different from the Army transports we had sailed to and from Japan on as possible. At twenty-three knots, she was fast, comfortably carrying one thousand passengers each way in first, cabin, and tourist classes.

Laid down and launched at Newport News, Virginia, in the early 1950s, the builder's costs for the *Constitution* and her sister were subsidized by the US government. In time of war, they would be converted to high-speed troop transports. In return for the subsidies, in peacetime her owners provided spaces on each voyage for military families. We were among the fortunate handful on this passage.

The *Constitution* also had a dusting of romantic sparkle; on her previous voyage eastbound from New York, she had carried former actress Grace Kelly to Monaco to be married to Prince Rainier.

Atlantic liner travel in those days was referred to as "crossing." In summer it was a relaxed, enjoyable experience—days of sunshine; mealtimes announced by stewards walking the corridors ringing chimes; an onboard theater with first-run films; a swimming pool on the "Lido" deck, its water gently sloshing back and forth with the roll of the ship.

Eastbound, a few days out from New York, from the ship's address system: "We will be meeting *Independence*, westbound, in one hour." Everyone lined the rails, the two great liners passing within a few hundred yards of each other, horns blowing, everyone cheering and waving. The closing speed of both big ships was above forty miles an hour—very impressive.

Late on day five, we were overflown by a big gray, four-engine prop aircraft with twin tails and red, white, and blue British insignia. It droned in a wide circle around us, its signal light blinking to the ship in rapid Morse code. Dad said it was a patrol bomber based at Gibraltar guarding the entrance to the Mediterranean—a "Shackleton," named for the famous British explorer.

Early next morning we passed Gibraltar. At the end of the last bit of land before the Atlantic, the giant gray-and-green Rock loomed hundreds of feet high, lit by the rising sun. Dad said it looked solid but was honeycombed with miles and miles of tunnels. Inside were cannon, a hospital, headquarters, barracks, and roads.

The Rock was also home to Barbary apes, specially cared for by the British Army. Legend had it that if the apes ever left the Rock or perished, it would fall into enemy hands. That sounded pretty neat to a ten-year-old; I figured the British Army took very good care of them.

LIVORNO, DARBY, AND SETAF

We landed at Genoa on an overcast morning with light rain. Unlike Manhattan, a flat city between two rivers, Genoa's harbor was a huge bowl, surrounded by hills with thousands of buildings in various pastel shades.

At the main railway station, we boarded an express to Livorno on the *Ferrovie dello Stato*, the Italian national rail service. Running on electrified lines, the trains were very comfortable, quiet, and fast. The scenery streaming past was fields, plane trees in serried vertical rows, livestock, sheep, pastel buildings, and towns.

During those Cold War years, most American forces in Europe were in West Germany and France. The Southern European Task Force, or SETAF, pronounced "SEE-taff," were the US forces in Italy. SETAF's insignia was the winged Venetian lion of Saint Mark on a background shield of red, white, and blue. One paw held a gold shield inscribed PAX, "peace" in Latin; the other held an upright gold sword.

SETAF's headquarters was in Verona, famed for Shakespeare's love story of Romeo and Juliet. Its access to the sea was at Livorno, anglicized to "Leghorn." The American military port facilities at Livorno were the reason for Dad's assignment.

The US Army post at Camp Darby was in farmland about six miles inland from Livorno, accessible by highway and canal. A description of Darby at that time was, "a small, remote installation located in the Tuscan region of central Italy, situated between the cities of Livorno and Pisa." That neatly sums it up.

In the mid-1950s, one of SETAF's missions was to stockpile and maintain military equipment in case US forces needed to be moved to the Mediterranean area from Germany or shipped and flown from the States.

Its other mission, which I never heard my father speak of, and didn't learn of until years later, was to support a unique, first-of-its-kind US Army unit. The First Missile Command was built around two nuclear weapons: the "Honest John" free-flight rocket was launched from an inclined rail on a truck; the "Corporal" guided missile was launched vertically from a portable, quickly erected platform.

The Honest John rocket was solid-fueled, with a range of fifteen miles. Its elevation and direction were set before launch. In military terms, it was a "free-flight over ground" weapon, colloquially known as "fire and forget." The Corporal was liquid-fueled. Guided by telemetry from the ground, it could reach out to seventy-five miles. Though the rockets and missiles were positioned in far northern Italy, hundreds of miles from Livorno, their logistics and support came from the American military port at Livorno, and Camp Darby.

This never-discussed "secondary" mission may explain an anomaly that was a demonstration of the term "hidden in plain sight." For several miles along the highway leading to Camp Darby from the coast, a high, chain-link fence topped with barbed wire bordered the road. A parallel access road ran along the other side of the fence. At intervals of several hundred feet, other roads branched off the access into dense pine forest, on either side of which could be seen the concrete faces of huge, mounded bunkers.

For three years, buses taking us to and from school at Camp Darby passed that enormous complex of bunkers in the forest. Yet I don't remember any of my classmates ever mentioning them or being at all curious. My parents never did. I never did. It was as though they didn't exist.

Camp Darby's location was an example of the army adage, "The farther from the flagpole, the happier the soldier." Darby was 150 miles from SETAF headquarters in Verona, which was itself 440 miles from the headquarters of all US forces in Europe, in Heidelberg, Germany. We were very happy at Darby.

TIRRENIA

For a week or so after we arrived in Livorno we lived in a hotel downtown: a great place with high ceilings, marble floors, and potted palms. My dad scouted around, found a newly constructed villa a block from the beach in Tirrenia, and rented it on a three-year lease. The owner was a professor at the University of Cagliari on the island of Sardinia.

With solid walls, high ceilings, and marble floors, the villa was cool in summer but freezing in winter. Dad pronounced the heating system "medieval" and set to work converting it. The new system fed the furnace by drip kerosene from an outside tank under the porch." It was my job to keep the tank topped up. I've described it elsewhere in this story.

Camp Darby was in the heart of Tuscany, close to the sea, with pleasant weather and easy access to some of the great cities of Italy: Pisa, Florence, and Lucca. We understood how fortunate we were in this assignment.

It's difficult not to lapse into the idyllic in describing our life as Americans in Tirrenia in the 1950s, but here goes. We lived in a tile-roofed, pastel villa beneath umbrella pines, located in a beach town suburb of Pisa on a stretch of coast that each summer attracted hordes of vacationers from all over Europe. The weather combined the same moderate temperatures and lack of humidity as in central and northern coastal California, with the same clear sunlight.

Our villa was one of only two at the time on Via di Salici, a street that was still sandy aggregate, not yet asphalted. Every morning a carabiniere, the Italian police officer assigned to our neighborhood, would bicycle down our street, a twin-barreled shotgun slung muzzle down diagonally across his back, his dog trotting behind. Sometime in the afternoon, he would cycle slowly by with the dog, a brace of birds hanging from his belt.

A block of undeveloped pine forest separated our street from the Via Aurelia, Italy's west coast equivalent of California's coastal Highway 1. Originally completed in 241 BC, beneath the bustle of the Fiats, Lancias, and Vespas of the 1950s lay the stones of the original Roman military road, along which the empire's legions had marched, shaded by the ancestors of the umbrella pines that cast their blue shadows on the modern highway.

Summer days were long, fragrant with the aroma of flowers. Air tinged with the tang of pine and sap. Humming of bees. Distant rattle of the *trainino*, the rail trolley between Livorno and Pisa. Droning Vespa scooters, or three-wheeled Piaggio Api, named for their busy-bee buzzing. And "Volare," a song that grew to be a worldwide hit, floated from every *trattoria* and pizzeria.

Beneath that idyll, though, was some unusual history. Our villa backed up onto woods with odd terrain—deep holes overgrown with low foliage and new pine. One day I crossed the road fronting our house, into the woods on the far side. Not far into the new growth, I was standing on the edge of a big, deep hole, its bottom filled with water.

That night I mentioned it to my dad. He said, "It's a bomb crater. The Germans gave this area a good pounding during the war. At least that one went off." He grinned. "There are probably still a few unexploded ones around here."

He went on to explain that after the Allied forces captured the nearby port of Livorno in the war, it became a key logistics and support base for the American advance up the Italian west coast. The German air force, the Luftwaffe, came every night, trying to bomb the port.

That is, bombing where they *thought* the port was. To fool the Luftwaffe, the Americans laid out a network of lights in the pine forest north of the port, right where our neighborhood would be in 1956. They blacked out everything in the real port at night and switched on just a few dim lights in the "dummy" port to let the Germans think it was their real target. It worked; the Luftwaffe bombed the dummy.

Very clever. But for days after, as I cycled down those roads in Tirrenia, I wondered if there might be a sleeping bomb or two, just waiting for the right moment.

FUTBOL

Our neighbors on Via Dei Salici, in the only other house on the street, were a minor Italian *contessa* and her teenage sons, Flavio and Sergio. The boys owned really neat motorbikes. Frequently they would bring out a *futbol*, which to Americans is a black and white soccer ball, and kick it around in the road. Their footwork was truly impressive.

My brother Dave and I were pretty inept at their version of *futbol*; they laughed at us a bit. I said, "OK, wait here a minute," and went inside. Emerging with an ovoid, leather American football, I said to Dave, "Go out for a pass." I threw the football with the right spin; it sailed perfectly into Dave's arms.

Next I gave the ball to one of the brothers and said, "Go ahead; throw to me." His throw was as inept as my *futbol* kick; the ball sailed off, wobbling crazily. That was the end of the ribbing, in either direction.

MORE HISTORY

We went to school on-post at Camp Darby. The teachers and school staff were all Department of the Army civilians. In the 1950s, the academic curriculum in all Army schools on posts worldwide was based on the California state system. At that time, California had the highest educational standards in the country.

My lasting interest in history is due to a gifted teacher who made it come alive through the way she made us feel that the people we read about were more than just names on a page. She told us, "'History is made by people like you and me; everything else is geography and weather." Pretty neat.

JULIA

As in Japan, we had a maid in Tirrenia. Julia was a middle-aged lady from Marina di Pisa. She was thorough, hummed to herself all the time, and didn't put up with any nonsense from boys.

Julia told my father that just before the Americans captured Pisa in August 1944, there was a lot of artillery, shooting from both sides of the Arno River, and lots of airplanes overhead. All the civilians went down into their cellars to hide from the combat, which raged through the night.

In the morning, it seemed quiet. Julia's father went upstairs and looked out. He hurried back and said, "The Japanese are here!" He thought they were fighting on the German side; after all, weren't the Japanese the enemy in the Pacific?

When Julia and her family finally ventured out, they found that the soldiers were indeed Japanese; many were asleep up and down the street, evidently exhausted. But they were in American Army uniforms! Pisa had been captured by the US Army's 442nd Regimental Combat Team, made up of Japanese Americans from Hawaii and California. The 442nd was the most highly decorated regimental combat unit in the US Army in World War II.

Julia also demonstrated some cultural differences. Mom once encouraged her to try some buttered roast corn, a specialty of Dad's. Julia turned her nose up. "Signora," she sniffed, "cibo per bestiale" (Madam, that is food for animals). She was right; in Italy they fed corn to pigs and cattle.

But a few weeks later, my brother's snail collection went missing. He kept them in a pail beside the kitchen door with a bit of screen over it. Julia smiled; she had cleaned them and sautéed them in butter. "Deliziosa."

MOM AND THE TRAFFIC COP

Dad's Italian was fluent; he was frequently assumed to be a native, one big reason he served in the OSS. Mom could hardly speak a word of the language. Though her maiden name was Belladonna and she could pass for an Italian fashion model, she was raised by her Italian American parents in New York to be "more American than the Americans."

Her inability to speak Italian got her into an interesting situation. One afternoon while driving the *contessa*'s borrowed car, she was pulled over by an Italian motorcycle traffic cop. He walked up to her rolled-down window. She flashed him a dazzling smile.

"Signora, sai quanto stavi andando veloce?" he began. He had asked her, "Lady, do you know how fast you were going?" Mom smiled, shook her head, shrugged her shoulders.

He said, "Signora! Mi capisci? Stavi accelerando!" He had said, "Lady! Do you understand me? You were speeding!"

Mom smiled and shook her head again. The policeman was getting agitated, but then it registered.

"Ah! Non se Italiana?" (Ah! You're not Italian?) Mom shook her head again.

"Sei Francese?" (You're French?)

Another smile and head shake.

Then he got it. "Americani?" Mom recognized that and nodded. He shifted to English and in what Mom remembered as a great accent said, "OK! Dammeet'a, lady, don't'a speed!" and walked back to his bike laughing.

NO PHONE, NO TV

During the three years we lived in Italy, we had no telephone or television; I can't remember missing either. Our news came from *Stars and Stripes*, the

American military newspaper. We also took the daily English-language *Rome Daily American* and the Paris edition of the *New York Herald Tribune*. The *Trib'* was our family go-to newspaper when we lived in the States; its Paris edition was like a voice from home.

I looked forward to a comic strip the *Stars and Stripes* had just begun running called *Peanuts*, about a bunch of little kids and a dog, and a one-panel, minimalist brain-teaser cartoon called "Droodles."

The American community in Tirrenia was a pretty tight bunch. With no TV, the adults played a lot of bridge, and the children learned chess early. There was a lot of informal family visiting back and forth on weekends. Mom and Dad and their Army friends would frequently meet, with their children, for long family lunches at *Lanterne Verde*, the Green Lantern, a restaurant in Livorno, or at one of the seaside restaurants in Marina di Pisa. Many of the restaurants offered dining outside under the pines and *bocce* courts. I learned the game.

THE IMPERIALE

The American Officers Club on the town center in Tirrenia was a beautiful 1930s art deco building. Built in the 1930s by Mussolini as a resort for senior members of the Italian fascist party, it retained its original name, the Imperiale. A huge tiled courtyard and fountain led to enormous windowed doors. The club backed up to a beautiful stretch of beach, today still known as the "American Beach."

The Imperiale was the grown-ups' watering hole, and the scene of stage plays written, directed, and performed by the officers and their wives, with a few kids playing bit parts. In 1958 Dad wrote and directed *Transporama*, a comedy that poked fun at practically every aspect of Army life at Darby. Rounds of standing applause after every act brought the house down.

The Imperiale was also the go-to for children's birthdays, holiday parties, and family dinners. I have many fond memories of the club, like the evening a Spanish Air Force officer, a guest of my parents, showed me how to fashion a rabbit hand puppet, with big ears, from a dinner napkin. I've often demonstrated that little puppet to distressed children and am grateful to him for the lesson. It's amazing how that white rabbit hand puppet calms them right down.

MOLESWORTH

The library at Camp Darby was a dowdy, one-story rectangular building; it couldn't have looked more mundane compared to the Gothic splendor of its fortress-like counterpart at West Point. But its book collection was fascinating: top-heavy in British and other European works, and subjects not ordinarily found in libraries in the United States.

For example, I devoured the tales of Nigel Molesworth, a fictional schoolboy at St. Custard's, a highly dysfunctional British prep school. The structure of the school system and the customs of the student body seemed odd, very much unlike our American schools.

Molesworth was illustrated by Ronald Searle, whose whimsical artwork populated *Punch*, the *New Yorker*, *LIFE*, and other top magazines of the 1950s. The Molesworth stories were a glimpse into British culture, in which parents packed their children off to boarding schools at a very early age to be raised and educated by others.

I had no way of knowing then, but I would recognize some of the customs of cadet life at the Virginia Military Institute in the mid-1960s as modeled on those of English "public" schools like Rugby, Eton, Harrow, and yes, Molesworth's own St. Custard's.

At age eleven I also read the first of a series of very grown-up novels about Agent 007, a suave, deadly British intelligence operative who was licensed to kill, and his enemies in SMERSH, the secret Soviet counterintelligence organization. *Very* cool.

ITALY REBUILDS

Italy in the mid-1950s was still recovering from World War II. Electricity and water were occasionally shut off without warning.

On returning from a long summer car trip to Spain and France, we found that the water service was off. It had been a very long day of travel on two-lane Italian roads, with huge trucks, buses, motor scooters, and other traffic. We were hot and tired. We had no stored water in the house and no idea when the water service would resume. What to do?

Fortunately, there was a hand water pump in the corner of the front yard. It had originally provided on-site water during the villa's construction, but hadn't been used since. Identical to the lever-action "pitcher pumps" found on many

American farms, it was cast iron and required "priming" with water to provide suction.

Dad thought for a few moments, then went into the house, emerging with a bottle of champagne, the only liquid we had, and several glasses. "You can survive a long time without food," he said, "but you can't live long without water."

He poured some of the champagne into the top of the pump to wet the pump's valve. I worked the handle, priming the pump; in a few strokes we had water. Dad saved enough champagne for a small amount to share with Mom, and a sip for my brother and me to celebrate. We pumped water until it ran clear and dosed it with halazone tablets before drinking. The problem was solved until our water service resumed.

THE HUNGARIAN REVOLT

The big Grundig shortwave radio in our living room pulled in stations from all over Europe and around the world. In late October, a revolution broke out against the Soviet-backed government in Hungary. University students occupying the Magyar radio station in Budapest broadcast appeals in English for help.

The revolt in Hungary went on for several weeks before being ruthlessly crushed by Russian troops and tanks. Thousands of Hungarians were killed. It may be difficult for some today to appreciate what the Cold War meant, but I remember the sound of desperation in those voices calling for help in the night.

BOY SCOUTS

Scouting was a very big thing in the American community at Darby; many of my friends and their dads were involved. My father served for a time as our scoutmaster. He taught us map and compass, skills I would later use in the Army.

Our Scout troop went on long hikes and overnight camping trips. One evening we were hiking past a farm when the door of the farmhouse opened and a man appeared with a shotgun. He yelled something, to which my father replied in Italian. The farmer laughed, and a lively conversation ensued. It was clear that both my dad and the farmer were having a good time. The farmer waved and closed the door.

As we started off again, I said, "Dad, what did he say?"

"You're leading a bunch of Boy Scouts?" Dad repeated. "Are you crazy, out here at night?" So I told him we were just looking at nature. And he said, "If you guys are so good at nature, have your junior commandos do something about the foxes that are stealing my chickens!"

All the American Scout troops in Europe were part of the Transatlantic Council. Every summer our Troop 76 from Livorno (our Scout uniform shoulder tab said LEGHORN) traveled by rail overnight to the American Scout camp near Lake Como, in northern Italy.

A beautiful spot, it had a timbered lodge as the camp's headquarters, a huge lake with rowboats, and a tent area for the Scout troops from Livorno, Verona, and Vicenza. Like almost everywhere else Boy Scouts from US Army posts gathered, there were the same "GP Medium" wall tents on wooden platforms.

As our scoutmaster, my dad had a separate tent. A circular, conical-roofed affair with vertical walls on a wooden platform, its tall center pole held it up. One evening after supper while my dad was visiting with some of the other dads, a couple of my buddies and I went over to the barn area and untethered a donkey. We led it to Dad's tent and, with one of us leading the way with a carrot, that little guy stepped right in. We tied his halter to the center post, dropped the flaps, and retired to our tent. There we watched for the fun.

Night fell. We waited. Eventually along came Dad with a flashlight, whistling and humming. He opened the flap to his tent and went in. We waited. Nothing. No exclamation, no sound. The flashlight went out. We waited. Nothing. Eventually we went to sleep. Next morning the donkey was back at the barn.

At summer camp, I decided I was going to go for Eagle Scout. It was going to be a lot of work, but I was determined. Four years later in Alabama, I would get that Eagle badge.

CAPTAIN GALLANT OF THE FOREIGN LEGION

An American TV series was being filmed at Cinecitta, an Italian film production complex in Tirrenia. The series was set in French North Africa at the time, when the Foreign Legion outposted some pretty remote forts and oases.

The star of *Captain Gallant of the Foreign Legion* was Buster Crabbe, a former US Olympic swimmer who also starred in *Flash Gordon*, an earlier science-fiction television series.

Our school class visited the movie set on a field trip; it was fun to see camels and goats being led around, prop men tossing hollow "boulders" to each other, and scenes being filmed.

"HARRY" AND "BESS"

Dad bought a rooster and a hen and built a pen for them in the side yard. He named them Harry and Bess, after President and Mrs. Truman. Dad said the rooster strutted around just like President Truman did on his daily "constitutionals" in the streets around the White House, and the hen, well, she looked just like Bess. He would laugh, watching the rooster strut, and say, "Give 'em hell, Harry!" a popular phrase when Truman was president.

THE FRENCH ARMY MUTINIES

What was happening at the same time in French North Africa was not at all amusing. A guerrilla war was underway; Algerian insurgents attacked French civilians and military alike. The French army waged a fierce, no-quarters fight against the rebels. I read the coverage in the papers; we heard about it from our teachers during "current events" at school.

Charles de Gaulle, president of France, decided to grant Algeria its independence. During the Second World War, he had led the Free French forces from England against the German occupation of France. He was tall and pompous, at times overbearingly so, but as the man who kept the flame of France's independence alive in those darkest days of the war, he was a national hero.

The French Army had experienced the surrender of its country to Germany in 1940, then occupation by Germany for almost five years. It had fought a long, ultimately losing war in Indochina, departing in 1954. After another long, brutal war in Algeria, it was being ordered to leave that country as well, abandoning generations of French citizens and pro-French Algerians who had built prosperous businesses and farms.

De Gaulle's decision resulted in a revolt by several French senior generals and a few French military units in Algeria, among them the famed 1st Parachute Regiment of the Foreign Legion. The revolt also spawned the OAS, a secret anti–De Gaulle, "keep Algeria French" organization. The OAS carried out assassinations and terrorist attacks against its perceived enemies in metropolitan France and Algeria.

Dad said there was a danger that mutinous French Foreign Legion parachute units from Algeria might attempt to land in Paris. The airports in and around Paris were closed. I wondered how closing airports would stop parachutists, but I didn't understand much about military tactics then.

In August 1962 after the French left Algeria, the OAS carried out an assassination attempt on De Gaulle's motorcade in Paris. Spraying his car with machine-gun fire as it passed, they killed two of the motorcycle escort and shot out all four tires of the black Citroen DS 19 De Gaulle and his wife were riding in. Shot-out tires or no, the driver managed to maintain control and sped the De Gaulles, unharmed, to safety. A wicker basket of live (and doubtless traumatized) chickens in the trunk of the car was untouched. Afterward, De Gaulle, brushing glass splinters from his coat and comforting Madame De Gaulle, is reported to have snorted, "Amateurs! They could not even hit a *chicken*!"

THE RIF

In 1957, word spread that the US Army would be conducting a "reduction in force," or RIF (pronounced "riff"). The Army had grown rapidly during the Korean War; after the armistice, "downsizing" became necessary.

Then as now, Regular officers were the professional core of the Army; they were always on active service. Reserve officers could be on active service for extended periods but were always vulnerable to having their duty status reverted to inactive, or to being released from the Army altogether, on short notice. While on active duty, Reserve officers, like their Regular counterparts, received full pay and allowances, with access to the post exchange (PX), commissary, and the medical system. Their active service also accrued toward retirement, the first benchmark for which, for Regulars and Reservists alike, was twenty years' service.

During a RIF, many Reserve officers, with only a few years to go to twenty years, could be "separated." A few might be given the opportunity to remain on active duty at a reduction in commissioned rank, or as a noncommissioned officer, for as long as it took for them to reach retirement. They would then be retired at the pay grade of their former officer's rank.

Dad was a Reserve officer. He had been "in grade" as a captain for nine years, not unusual in the 1950s. As weeks went by, Mom and Dad learned of Reserve officers, friends, who were being separated. They must have been extremely anxious, but they never said a word.

One evening Dad came home with a bottle of champagne and flowers for Mom. He had learned he was being released from the Reserves and commissioned in the Regular Army. At the same time, he was promoted from captain to major. A great day.

TRAVELS IN EUROPE

Our Camp Darby school groups made field trips to the marble quarries at Carrara, Leonardo's birthplace and a museum of his inventions at Vinci; to the Palazzo Pitti in Florence; and to Pisa and Lucca. I found the models of Da Vinci's inventions fascinating. He was far ahead of his era, experimenting with the outside borders of the technology of the time, as he knew it.

My father's specialty in maritime logistics and his fluency in Italian attracted the interest of one of the biggest Italian shipping firms. An offer was extended to visit the firm's headquarters in Venice. During the visit, we were guests in a hotel on the Grand Canal. The firm's beautifully varnished, crewed motor launch was at our disposal. We cruised to Murano and Burano, outlying islands in the huge Lagoon of Venice, and to the Lido, the barrier island between the lagoon and the sea. Venice was once one of the greatest powers of Europe. Known as La Serenissima, her ships and galleys ranged the Mediterranean, her fortresses populating major ports and headlands up and down both sides of the Adriatic seacoast.

My memories of that trip are bells sounding in the *campanile*, the tall tower beside the Piazza San Marco; enormous flocks of pigeons; and the fabulous series of canals and bridges for foot traffic.

I learned afterward that the shipping firm offered Dad the position of their principal agent in New York. He would have to resign from the Army to do so. My father considered it but decided the Army was where he wanted to be.

During one summer, an extended car trip to the south of Italy took us down the coast to Rome, Naples, Pompeii, and Herculaneum, then over to the east side of the peninsula and up the beautiful Adriatic coast. Crossing the Appenines, the mountain range that runs right up the Italian spine, the views were amazing.

A trip to Germany late that same summer to visit the Pattons in Heidelberg triggered a desire to learn German, which I have done. We visited the Mercedes corporate headquarters in Stuttgart; I got to sit in the sleekly beautiful "Silver Arrow" Formula One racer, once driven for the Mercedes team by the famous Argentinian, Juan Fangio.

We were late returning to Italy through the Brenner Pass. We were told the snows had begun at the higher altitudes; the pass might closed. Dad decided we would make the run; we set off in our '55 Chevrolet Bel Air in the early evening. At the border checkpoint, a grim, gray-overcoated *Grenzpolizist* held a huge, leashed German shepherd. "You will be on your own!" he said. "We cannot provide assistance!"

My father smiled and nodded; off we went. As we climbed higher, the snow began and intensified. The road was barely passable; fortunately we were behind a huge truck and followed its lights. As we crested the pass, the snows were heaviest; for a few minutes it was nip and tuck, Dad following the dim lights ahead and guiding on the blue reflectors at intervals beside the narrow road.

We crested the pass and broke out into a starry night; the downslope run to the Italian border control point was easy going. At the striped barrier across the road, a jovial border policeman looked at our passports and saw the SETAF sticker on the bumper of our car. He grinned. "Ma! Americani! Ben tornato!" (Hey! Americans! Welcome back!)

DAD BUYS "INSURANCE"

One weekend, my father and I went to Pisa to look around. In those days you could park on the Campo dei Miracoli, the "Field of Miracles", directly beneath the stark white Leaning Tower, which, miraculously enough, defied the laws of gravity.

As we parked the car, Dad was approached by a man in civilian clothes. He was in some semiofficial capacity: he wore a blue, short-visored cap similar to that known today as "Greek fisherman's" style and a white plastic waist belt and strap that went diagonally over one shoulder, like kids in America used to wear then, on safety patrol on school yards. On his belt was a white plastic pouch.

He and Dad spoke in Italian for a few moments. Dad smiled, reached into his pocket, and came up with a few hundred-lira coins. The man took a pad of forms from his pouch and a small rubber stamp. Stamping the form, he tore it off, accepting the coins.

We climbed up the tower's spiral stone stairs inside. We were careful on the downslope side of the spiral to stay well away from the archways leading out onto the circular ledges. For some reason, there were railings on the ledges opposite the uphill archways, but none on the downslopes. You could literally step out and slide off the edge into space.

The view from the top of the tower, above the belfry, was spectacular. With the huge dome of the cathedral behind us, we could see up the coast to Viareggio and south to Livorno. As we stood gazing, I said, "Dad, what did that man downstairs want?"

My father smiled. "Well, he was a soldier in the war, Flip, in the Italian Army. He was wounded. The Italian government gave him that job so he can make some money. He gets to keep whatever he makes."

I thought about that. "So, what did you give him the money for?"

Dad grinned. "He sold me insurance, in case the Leaning Tower of Pisa falls on our car."

We still have the receipt.'

THE "MED CRUISE" AND ELBA

The Navy ran a transport on a regular schedule to ports in the Mediterranean; passenger spaces were available for military families. Departing Livorno aboard the USNS *Geiger*, we called at Naples, Tripoli, Piraeus, and Izmir, then on to Venice and Bari, back around the toe of Italy, and home again. Our visits to Hagia Sophia and the Blue Mosque in Istanbul and the Acropolis in Athens are particularly memorable.

In late fall we took the ferry to Elba, where Napoleon was briefly exiled in 1814. Ten months later he escaped, threatened Europe again, and was finally defeated in an enormous battle at Waterloo, in Belgium. He was as great a terror to Europe in his time as Hitler was in the mid-twentieth century.

Defeated a second time and again captured, Napoleon was banished to St. Helena, a lonely rock in the far South Atlantic, where he lived in a country house, kept under constant watch by British soldiers. He died there six years later.

Napoleon's imperial "N" was on almost every building on Elba; in his palace, the rooms were kept as though he had walked out the day before. The ferry ride from the Italian mainland took no more than an hour. I wondered who had thought that with Elba so close to the mainland, Napoleon would stay there. It was a critical error in judgment.

In the spring of 1959, Dad came home one evening with news of his next assignment. "Do you like airplanes and helicopters?" he asked David and me at dinner.

"You bet!" we chorused.

"Good! We're going to Fort Rucker, Alabama. It's the Army's Aviation Center."

Dad looked happy, but Mom seemed thoughtful. I would learn later she had more concerns about going to Alabama in 1959 than when we went to Japan during the Occupation immediately after the war.

5

ALABAMA

1959–1961

In the summer of 1959, we boarded the SS *Independence* at Genoa for the return to the States. We'd had a run of great postings so far; Alabama was going to be very different.

FORT RUCKER

In the southeastern corner of Alabama, Fort Rucker sits between the towns of Ozark, Daleville, and Enterprise, about twenty-five miles north of the Florida state line. Opened during World War II as then Camp Rucker, the post was a training base for several Infantry divisions and smaller units for combat duty overseas.

In 1949, Hollywood came to Camp Rucker to shoot scenes for *Twelve O'Clock High*, a film starring Gregory Peck about combat stress among the 8th Air Force's B-17 bomber crews in World War II. The filming was done on the then partly overgrown concrete runways at nearby Ozark Army Airfield. They were ideal for the opening and ending scenes at "Archbury," a fictional 1942 American heavy bomber base in England in this classic film.

Like Fort Benning, Fort Rucker was named for a Confederate general. It was located on "submarginal farmland" in an area known as the "Alabama Wiregrass," a region once the ancestral home of the Creek tribe. At congressional direction, the Army moved the Creeks westward off their homeland in the 1830s, as part of the exodus known as the "Trail of Tears."

There were no on-post quarters available when we arrived at Rucker. Dad leased a house in nearby Ozark for a year. A one-story "Alabama four-square" with a floor plan divided into quarters, it was supposedly designed for the hot, humid climate. A wide, high hallway ran straight through from front to back, off which were kitchen, living room, and two bedrooms with baths. High ceilings with fans and a veranda were intended as defenses against the heat of summer. There was no air-conditioning. Despite the design, the house was uncomfortably hot. But as practiced nomads, we endured and made it our home.

Fort Rucker was the US Army's Aviation Center. In 1949 an agreement between the Army and the Air Force signed at Key West restricted Army aviation to "fixed-wing" aircraft for light observation, medical evacuation, and liaison duties, and to helicopters, referred to officially as "rotary wing" aircraft, for the same purposes.

There were several varieties of Army aircraft at Rucker. The naming convention was an "H" prefix for helicopters, followed by Native American tribal names; "U" for Utility aircraft; "L" for Liaison; and "OV" for Observation.

The H-13 Iroquois, for example, manufactured by Bell, was the two-seater helicopter with the big Plexiglas bubble in front, famous from the TV series *M.A.S.H.* It was the aircraft Dad popped me into one day at West Point when I took my first flight. The H-34 Choctaw was a big, tadpole-shaped troop-carrying helicopter I would see in Vietnam; the Marines used it extensively at Hué during the 1968 Tet Offensive.

Fixed-wing Army aircraft were the single-engine U-1 Otter and U-6 Beaver, both built by De Havilland in Canada, and the twin-engine L-23 Seminole, for transporting senior officers.

The powerful, triple-tail, twin-engine turboprop OV-1 Mohawk was a reconnaissance aircraft that carried cameras, infrared equipment, and other classified electronic "snooper" gear. The pilot and copilot sat side by side in the Mohawk. It was so fast it was fitted with ejection seats.

An exception to the above naming convention was the single-engine Cessna L-19 Bird Dog, to become famous as flown in Vietnam by forward air controllers (FACs), directing Air Force fighter-bomber strikes onto ground targets.

ARMY AVIATION EXPERIMENTS

I was fortunate to be present at two moments that are now merely footnotes in the history of Army aviation but at the time I thought were pretty cool.

For the first, Dad mysteriously told me I wouldn't be going to school the next day and I was not to discuss what I would see with anyone. Suspense was pretty high next morning; Dad drove us out into the far reaches of the pine-forested Fort Rucker reservation.

We arrived at a firing range for small arms: rifles and machine guns, with two rows of shooting positions and a set of bleachers between them. A range control tower stood behind the bleachers, atop which flew a red flag. I knew the flag meant live ammunition would be in use, but I didn't see any weapons or shooters.

At various distances downrange were earthen berms. Behind them were trenches. Big, square wooden frames holding cloth targets with concentric rings on them would rise up from the trenches when the range was in use.

A box-bodied, olive-drab ambulance with a big red cross against a white disk on both sides was parked at the end of one of the rows of shooting positions. A pair of medics in fatigues and boots stood beside it.

The bleachers were full of Army officers, chatting and smoking. A few called greetings to my father; no one seemed to take notice of me. As we sat down, an amplified voice from the tower asked for our attention, then said we were about to witness an in-process experiment of the Army's Aviation Board.

A few moments later, an H-13 Iroquois helicopter clattered over the range, circled, and hovered down in profile, well out in front of the bleachers. We could see that a black .30 caliber air-cooled machine gun was mounted along one side. The helicopter revolved so that we could see an identical machine gun on the opposite side. Then it turned and pointed its bubble canopy downrange. As it did so, target frames rose up from behind the berms at various distances.

Firing twin lines of red tracers, the helicopter turned left and right, the pilot methodically "walking" the tracers back and forth in bursts, chewing up the targets. Then it turned and flew off. The announcer said what we had seen was part of an effort to determine if the idea of "armed helicopters" had merit.

Years later in Vietnam, I would remember that day. The Army's sleek, shark-like AH-1 Cobra attack helicopters by then carried rockets, machine guns, and 40mm chin-mounted grenade launchers. They were formidable flying combat machines, and I had been there at one of the tests at the very beginning.

On the second occasion, Dad took me out to Cairns Army Airfield on a Saturday morning. A sleek, olive-drab jet fighter sat on tricycle landing gear in front of a hangar. It looked like a smaller cousin to the North American F-86 Saber jet. It was a G-91, built by Fiat, the Italian automobile giant. The Army was testing the idea of getting its own aircraft for close air support, like the Marines. I thought the jet looked super, but Dad believed the Air Force would fight it. He was right; the Air Force squawked, citing the Key West Agreement. The Army never got their jet.

EARLY ENTREPRENEUR

In the summer of 1960, we moved to lieutenant colonels' quarters on-post, a ranch-style duplex backed up to pine woods, like Williamsburg, but no Confederate fort this time. My brother and I had our own bedrooms. The house also had air-conditioning—*very* welcome.

Living on-post at Rucker provided a summer job opportunity. Residents in all the family housing areas were required to keep their yards "maintained in good order." With that incredible Alabama heat and humidity, I guessed a lot of people would pay to have their lawns taken care of, like gardeners do today. I popped the idea to my dad; he thought it was great. I did some rudimentary market research, walking a number of streets, knocking on doors. I proposed doing the lawns for a flat fee, plus one cent per foot to edge the walkways, sidewalks, and driveways. Zero turndowns!

I needed a mower and an edger. Dad said he would scout around for a used Vespa scooter and helped me build a trailer for it. I could use our mower; he would get a hand edger in Ozark. I could pay for them from the earnings from my lawn business. Sweet!

In later life when I went to graduate business school at Stanford University, I knew all about it when we studied the "loss leader" sales concept. I pitched the lawn mowing at $1.50, low but still real money in those days, and found that the cent-a-foot edging was the real moneymaker. I paid off the scooter, trailer, and edger and put the rest in the bank.

CIVIL RIGHTS, CIVIL STRIFE

Our years in Alabama were at the height of the civil rights movement. Segregation by race was an ugly aspect of life in America, especially in the South, where it was the law. Restrooms and water fountains were signed "for whites only" or "colored only." Schools were segregated, as were restaurants and coffee shops. Even hospital waiting rooms were segregated, where whites were often given preference in treatment.

Until we arrived in Alabama, I had grown up on posts in the Army, integrated since 1947, or Japan and Italy, where there were no such distinctions. On-post at Fort Rucker, there were no color barriers. Army kids played on the same Little League team and were in the same Scout troops. It was only off-post that segregation laws applied. We referred to off-post as "Occupied Alabama."

Fort Rucker had no on-post schools. "White" kids went to school in Ozark, "colored" kids in Enterprise. In the weird lens of discrimination in the South in those years, only those we know as "African Americans" today were considered "colored." Children from Asian, Hispanic, or any other background were "white." It was surreal.

TRAILING THE EAGLE

I completed the qualifications for Eagle Scout while we were at Fort Rucker. It was a lot of fun. I pursued twenty-seven different projects to earn the various "merit badges" that attaining Eagle Scout required. I was awarded my Eagle Scout badge at summer camp at Eglin Air Force Base in Florida, where I was a counselor, teaching swimming and lifesaving to the younger scouts. I didn't learn until long afterward that only 4 percent of all Scouts made it to Eagle.

At Eglin I was also inducted into the Order of the Arrow, the Scouts' national honor society. Before becoming a member of the order, we candidates went through a twenty-four-hour "ordeal" of silence, during which we had little food and performed various chores. Ironically, sixteen year later, as an Army Ranger student, I would be back at Eglin, experiencing what a real ordeal was like.

MONUMENT TO A PEST

Nearby Enterprise, Alabama, had a monument giving thanks to an agricultural pest. A circular fountain in the center of town held a statue of a woman in a Grecian gown, bearing aloft a huge, greatly expanded boll weevil. Entirely painted silver, the statue commemorated the early twentieth-century devastation of the local cotton crop by the boll weevil.

The disaster prompted area farmers to experiment with planting alternative crops like peanuts, which proved to be impervious to the weevil. The peanut business became astonishingly prosperous. In gratitude, citizens erected the weevil monument, a great example of the adage, "If God gives you lemons, make lemonade."

BAY OF PIGS

In April 1961, news broke of a sudden invasion of Cuba, ostensibly by anti-Castro revolutionaries. First reports were confusing. At the United Nations, US ambassador Adlai Stevenson denied US involvement, but very quickly it was revealed as a United States-sponsored, CIA-planned operation.

Castro's forces killed many of the invaders; several Alabama men from the Ozark area were among the dead. As part of a ruse to support the invasion, they had flown twin-engine B-26 bombers painted in Cuban Air Force insignia. They were shot down by Cuban jet fighters. From the Alabama Air National Guard, the men had been clandestinely "transferred" to the CIA for the invasion. In those days military men who were transferred for clandestine CIA projects were referred to as being "sheep dipped."

CARROL HIGH

The high school in Ozark was a 1950s brick behemoth with a columned facade. The classes were pretty dull, except, curiously, Latin. Our teacher said, "Latin is considered a 'dead language.' But imagine if, one day, there was a real Roman, sitting just there, on the other side of the door to the classroom. What could we say to him? What did the 'street Latin' he knew sound like?" *That* was inspiring.

Otherwise I was reading what I liked, building model airplanes, and trying to comprehend the female creatures that cohabited the classrooms. Likely little different from boys my age, I was definitely in my own world. Academic distinction would come later; I would make up for that squandered time, and then some.

PEOPLE OF THE "WIREGRASS"

My English literature teacher comes to mind; it was said she was the great-granddaughter of Raphael Semmes, the captain of the CSS *Alabama*, the Confederate Navy's famous Civil War commerce raider.

The statue of a Confederate soldier stood in the courthouse square at Ozark. During the Civil War, on the second ferocious day of fighting at Gettysburg, the 20th Maine, a Union Army Infantry regiment, held the summit of Little Round Top. The hill was key to the defense of the Union fighting line. If Southern troops took Little Round Top, they could "roll up" the Union lines in a flanking attack.

Confederates of the 15th Alabama regiment, largely recruited from Dale County, launched several fierce attacks. Their losses were severe; the Union soldiers held the hill.

By 1959 the demographics of southeastern Alabama had not yet changed as rapidly as they would in the latter decades of the twentieth century. The people of the region were descendants of eighteenth- and nineteenth-century settlers. Mostly yeomen farmers, many came directly from England and Ireland, with a goodly number from up-country South Carolina and Georgia. There was something of the thunderbolt in their makeup, a folk not to be crossed without consequence.

Early in 1961, Dad was notified he would be going to Korea for an "unaccompanied" one-year assignment in October. He would command a transportation battalion of about eight hundred soldiers. Mom and Dad decided we would sit out the year in Highland Falls, near West Point and close to mom's mother and father in New York City.

6

NEW YORK, FORT EUSTIS

1962–1963

KOREA

Though an armistice had been negotiated between UN forces and North Korea in 1953, US forces remained in South Korea as a legacy of that unresolved ending. In 1960 South Korea was on its way to becoming a regional economic miracle, while North Korea remained a heavily armed, total-communist dictatorship. Border incidents occasionally flared along the Demilitarized Zone at the 38th parallel, many resulting in dead and wounded on both sides.

In midsummer 1962 we rented a house in Highland Falls, New York, near West Point, with a view of the Hudson River. I prepared for junior year at the local high school.

Dad seemed different in the last months in Alabama, not his ebullient, cheery self. In mid-August, we were in the yard in Highland Falls, looking at the river. In Berlin, with no forewarning, the East Germans were building a wall across the city. Tension was high; US forces in Europe were alerted. President Kennedy called up Reserve and National Guard units. I asked Dad what he thought. Though usually well informed on world events, he was oddly disinterested and ambivalent. It was foreboding.

He left for Korea in early October. Through the grim winter that followed, we eagerly awaited his letters and tapes. From halfway around the world, his voice seemed occasionally irresolute, diffident. We counted the months until his return.

DECISIONS

Junior year in high school was unsettling. I was adrift. Though I liked my classmates, I was indifferent in math and science, excelling in literature and history. I considered applying to West Point, but its curriculum at that time was very heavy in mathematics and engineering-related sciences. Years later I learned that the calculus instruction alone was six seventy-five-minute sessions a week. My hat is off to anyone who made it through the Military Academy in those years.

I had always intended to go into the Army after college as an officer. I knew I could be commissioned through ROTC at a college or university, but partly for the structure, partly for the challenge, and partly for the tradition, I decided to go to a military college. The commission would mean that much more. In deciding to go for that challenge, if I was going into the Army as an officer, I would also do it as a Regular officer, a professional.

It was Joe Love who suggested the Virginia Military Institute. I didn't know much about it. Joe, southern gentleman, West Point grad, combat veteran, steered me toward it. "They have a first-class Department of History," he said. "If you score high enough, there's your opportunity for a Regular commission."

Founded in 1839, VMI is in the picturesque Shenandoah Valley. Though much smaller than West Point, in the early 1960s it offered over twelve different majors. Its History Department was indeed first class.

Stonewall Jackson had been an instructor in math and physics at VMI in the 1850s, before rising to fame as a Confederate general in the Civil War. During that terrible war, VMI's Corps of Cadets fought as a combat unit in an 1864 battle in the Shenandoah Valley. George Marshall was one of the most distinguished of VMI's many noted graduates. The school had contributed many general officers in World War II. And yes, there was the opportunity for a Regular Army commission.

RETURN TO FORT EUSTIS

In the spring of 1962 we learned that Dad's new assignment would be a return to Fort Eustis. Closing out the Highland Falls house in June, we moved to my grandparents' in New York City. I would do the fall term of my 1962–63 senior year at Mount Saint Michael, a private prep in the farthest northern portion of New York City. The instructors at "the Mount" were inspiring; the fog in math and science dissipated. I almost maxed trigonometry and began to actually enjoy physics.

COUNTDOWN TO WORLD WAR III

Dad returned from Korea in late September. He was changed, periodically distant, as though hearing far-off music. As he was on leave until reporting in Virginia, we stayed at my grandparents' for a few weeks.

One midnight in early October the phone rang. Outside, it was raining. "An hour? Yes. I'll be ready." Dad hung up. Mom made coffee in the kitchen. Dad came downstairs in uniform, with a small bag. He and Mom talked in low voices. An Army car arrived. Hugs, then he was gone.

No word for a few days. I was at school when the news broke: the president would address the nation that night. I sensed Dad's sudden departure was somehow connected. Knots of students stood in the halls talking, making wild speculations. Outside, the crisp, sun-washed sky, the trees in beautiful fall colors.

The rotary dial and vacuum tubes of Grandma's DuMont television gave off a hot, glass-and-electronics smell. In the dim room we faced the black-and-white screen. Our president was calm, firm. Russian nuclear missiles, he said, had been discovered in Cuba. Our Navy would "quarantine" the island, surrounding it with a blockade of patrolling warships. An attack by Russian forces anywhere in the Western Hemisphere, the president continued, would be regarded as an act of war. In such case, we would launch a massive counterstrike. War glided silently into the room.

The world stayed tethered to the media. Walter Cronkite, the voice of CBS, the same voice as in *You Are There*—now we were all there together. Warships patrolled off Cuba; Russian ships were en route. Would they stop? What if they didn't? No one in or near New York City had illusions; New York was one of the first and biggest nuclear targets.

A US invasion of Cuba was planned, this one no small CIA affair. Airborne divisions, Marine landings, attacks by sea and air. Massive troop movements to ports in the southeastern United States. Rail and highway nets jammed with troop trains, convoys. The Strategic Air Command's ready-alert, nuclear-armed B-47 and B-52 jet bombers were even dispersed to civilian airports across the country.

The Russian ships reached the blockade. Time stood still. The ships turned back. Moscow signaled it would negotiate. The world resumed breathing.

Dad flew home. He had been at Homestead Air Force Base in Tampa, one of the planners for the invasion. He looked haggard. All he would say was, "It was damn close."

In the late 1990s, I was invited to New York City to be interviewed on camera by the History Channel as a commentator on an aspect of the Cuban Missile Crisis. At the studios I met an elderly Russian gentleman who was also to be interviewed. He had been commander of the Soviet rocket forces in Cuba in 1962. Unknown to American intelligence then, there were Russian short-range tactical nuclear weapons on the island, under his command. "Would you have used them if we invaded?" I asked.

"Certainly," he replied. "I was a soldier."

ONE YEAR, TWO HIGH SCHOOLS

I stayed in New York to finish the fall school term at Mount Saint Michael. I would do the spring term of senior year at Walsingham Academy, my fourth high school in four years. Many of my fourth-grade classmates at Walsingham were still there, now seniors. I wondered what it was like to live a life with that degree of stability.

The Virginia spring of 1963 was beautiful; the sisters at Walsingham were motivating. My senior year was an academic success.

Then Dad collapsed at work. A nervous breakdown, the Army doctors said. He was in the Army hospital at Fort Eustis. A visiting medical specialist from Walter Reed Army Medical Center in Washington happened to be on rounds with the hospital's staff. He examined my father and said he suspected a brain tumor. Dad was taken to Walter Reed; an operation removed most of the malignancy, but not all. The doctors told Mom he might live a year or two before the tumor succeeded in its work.

The man who came home from that operation was a shell of the happy, outgoing, whistling man who had been my father. It was devastating to see the change.

7

THE INSTITUTE

1963–1967

While there is no way to fully relate my experiences over four years at the Virginia Military Institute, what follows might serve to describe a bit about the school, its uniqueness as an institution, and a few events from my cadet years in the mid-1900s.

"WAR IS INTERESTED IN YOU"

The year 1963 began with a major battlefield defeat for the Army of South Vietnam. At the village of Ap Bac in the Mekong Delta, a communist Vietcong battalion stood fast against a combined task force of several battalions of ARVN (pronounced "AR-vin") infantry, armor, and paratroop soldiers. The enemy inflicted a severe mauling on the ARVN forces before successfully slipping away at nightfall.

During the battle at Ap Bac, Major John Paul Vann, one of the ARVN's American advisers, repeatedly urged the ARVN commander to attack; he would not do it. Vann was convinced he had let the enemy slip away intentionally, rather than bring them to decisive combat.

It was a recurring problem. A low-intensity guerrilla war had been smoldering in southern Vietnam since the late 1950s, following the withdrawal of French forces and the establishment of the Republic of South Vietnam. The fight at Ap Bac would be a turning point in that war. The enemy had demonstrated he was willing and able to stand up to the best the ARVN could throw at him. That didn't bode well for the prospects of success in eliminating communist activity in the South.

Three Americans were killed and eight wounded at Ap Bac. Of fifteen American H-21 helicopters ferrying ARVN troops into the battle, five were shot down. Only one helicopter escaped battle damage. The fight at Ap Bac took place when the official US position was that no Americans were involved in combat in South Vietnam. To Vann and other Americans in the field advising the ARVN, the South Vietnamese often repeated the same mistakes, appearing increasingly unable to prevail against the communists.

The American advisers reported each incident of ARVN inability or unwillingness to come to grips with Vietcong units to the headquarters of the US Military Advisory Command Vietnam (referred to as MACV and pronounced "Mack-Vee") in Saigon. Their pessimistic reports were shelved. Instead of forwarding their actual assessments to Washington, MACV, headed by General Paul Harkins, forwarded consistently optimistic reports.

A group of young American newspaper correspondents in South Vietnam gradually grew dubious of MACV's "official" claims of ARVN progress. Tiring of the same optimistic reports given in the daily MACV press briefings in Saigon, they eventually sought firsthand information from the American advisers to ARVN.

John Paul Vann and other US advisers were open in their discussions with David Halberstam of the *New York Times*, Neil Sheehan of UPI, and Malcolm Browne of the Associated Press. Vann and his colleagues realized their frankly stated concerns about the inability of ARVN to successfully prosecute the war could damage their military careers. Yet they were determined the truth should find its way out, despite the artificially positive "headway reports" sent to Washington by MACV.

Halberstam, Sheehan, Browne, and others began to file increasingly pessimistic dispatches, published in the *New York Times, Washington Post*, and other major newspapers in the United States. Angry senior officers accused them of disloyalty, even of cooperation with the enemy. Though the military had no authority over them, they were strongly encouraged by senior US commanders and American diplomats alike to "get on the team."

Their reports initially generated concern, then growing anger among senior members of the Kennedy administration and the Joint Chiefs of Staff. General Harkins relieved Vann and several other advisers, transferring them out of South Vietnam. Their Army careers were effectively over.

But as the authenticity of the American reporters' dispatches became more evident, Kennedy himself began to have serious doubt in the ability of the Diem government in Saigon to pursue the war capably. In addition, there was grave concern that Diem, an autocratic Catholic in an overwhelmingly Buddhist population, had lost the confidence of the people of South Vietnam.

In March 1963, apparently concluding that continued US involvement in Vietnam was a losing proposition, Kennedy is recorded as privately remarking to Senator Mike Mansfield his intention to eventually withdraw US advisers from Vietnam. "I can't do it until I'm reelected," he said, referring to the upcoming presidential election of 1964, "so we'd better make damn sure I *am* reelected."

The situation worsened. Vietnam's Buddhist monks had been protesting the Diem government's repression of their freedom of religious expression. Meanwhile Diem continued to confer favoritism on fellow Vietnamese Catholics.

In June, a Buddhist monk burned himself alive in protest in a major Saigon intersection. Malcolm Browne had been alerted that "something" was going to happen; he was present to capture the photo of a monk being drenched in gasoline, then dying in a column of fire. The shocking photo accompanied his dispatch titled "Suicide in Saigon," which was flashed around the world.

As referenced in the coda at the end of this book, in October 1963 Kennedy issued a top-secret National Security Action Memorandum (NSAM 263) directing that the first one thousand US advisers be withdrawn from Vietnam by the end of the year, with all US advisers to be withdrawn by 1965.

Of course, none of us knew at the time that Kennedy was considering withdrawal from Vietnam. He had many other issues to deal with, among which was the upcoming 1964 election. He agreed with Lyndon Johnson that Texas would be a key state in the math of the Electoral College. He scheduled a visit there in November 1963. It was a fatal decision.

NO ORDINARY COLLEGE

VMI did have a great Department of History. The department head was a grandson of the engineer who converted the USS *Merrimack* to the CSS *Virginia*, the Confederate ironclad that battled with the Union Navy's USS *Monitor* at Hampton Roads in 1862. Two of the department's professors were authorities on aspects of the Civil War, and FDR's New Deal in the 1930s. All were veterans of military service in World War II.

The PhD-to-student ratio at VMI was 1:12. We didn't have teaching assistants or instructors with master's degrees; ours were full professors. Several of the faculty held doctorates from Harvard, Oxford, or Ivy League universities.

All held commissions in the Virginia Militia, which predates the United States Army. When George Washington accepted Congress's nomination in June 1775 to head what would become the Continental Army, he did so in the uniform of a colonel in the Virginia Militia.

Though VMI is an ROTC school, with few exceptions it is as different from ROTC programs at colleges elsewhere as night is from day. The system at VMI was 24-7 military, with a regimen that was damned Spartan, and a culture more heavily influenced by the Marine Corps than the Army.

Why did young men of my era self-select to endure four years of military life at VMI? Challenge, tradition, and the desire for structure, to name a few reasons. Some of my classmates were from families that had sent their sons to VMI for generations. Some were directly related to cadets who had fought in VMI's cadet battalion at the battle of New Market in 1864.

In the 1960s, the Institute offered academic majors in English literature, history, foreign languages, biology, chemistry, mathematics, physics, civil and electrical engineering, and several other fields.

On graduation, VMI offered commissions in the Army, Air Force, and Marine Corps. In World War II, VMI had fielded over sixty general officers, in all the service branches. To date, VMI has provided more general officers for the US Army than any other ROTC institution. It provided many Marine Corps generals, two of whom served as commandants of the Marine Corps.

In World War II, five VMI alumni, led by General George S. Marshall, occupied the key positions at the Washington Command Post of the War Department, making worldwide, strategic decisions for the entire nine-and-a-half-million-man US Army.

SOUND OFF!

In the first few minutes after entering the VMI barracks as a freshman, or "Rat," I stood in Jackson Arch with many hapless classmates-to-be. Beside me, just outside the commandant's office, was a then unknown cadet with whom I would later become a lifelong friend. We were in that exaggerated posture known as a "brace": chin pulled way in, body at rigid attention, eyes front.

Several upperclassmen were screaming in our ears to "SOUND OFF! SOUND OFF!" Others were screaming "GET IT IN! GET IT IN!" In later years, Kip, my classmate next to me, explained that an upperclassman was yelling in one of his ears to "GET IT IN!" while another was yelling in the other to "SOUND OFF!"

He said he was "getting it in," but no one had explained to him what he needed to do to "sound off." So he decided to improvise. He took a deep breath and, "AIEEEEEEEEEEEEEEEEEEYAAAAAAAAAH!"

At that erupting primal scream, the upperclassmen around him vanished. In the leaden silence that followed, the commandant's door beside us opened with the slight squeak of an unoiled hinge. The commandant, a colonel, looked out at Kip and said, "You all right, son?"

"Yes, Sir!"

"Good. Good." With a squeak, the commandant closed the door. Upperclassmen instantly reappeared and frog-marched Kip off.

HAYRACKS

To say VMI wasn't an ordinary college environment is an understatement. The cadet rooms in the barracks, built in the early nineteenth century, didn't have space for beds. We slept on mattresses laid on wooden bed frames with folding legs. During the day the frames were stacked against a wall, with mattresses rolled and strapped into cylinders, stacked on end in pairs. Red wool blankets with yellow stripes at either end and thick red comforters were folded and squared, their corners aligned, atop the rolled mattresses.

In the nineteenth century, the mattresses had been stuffed with hay; in the 1960s the bed frames were still referred to as "hayracks," the mattresses as "hays" or "hayrolls." Every evening, as the bugle sounded "Release from Quarters," hayracks came down, hayrolls were laid on them, and blankets and "red boy" comforters were laid out.

The big diamond-paned casement windows in every cadet room were required to be cracked an inch for ventilation, secured by metal hooks. In winter, the man sleeping nearest the windows might wake up mornings to find a dusting of snow on his comforter.

HONOR AND TRADITION

Cadets found guilty of violating the Honor Code at VMI were drummed out of the school in midnight ceremonies. The first, in my freshman year, was on a freezing night in midwinter. We woke to the "long roll" of drums: the "call to arms" in the Old Army, or "action stations" aboard ship. At 2 a.m., it gets your attention. The ceremony, witnessed a number of times over the next four years, never varied.

The "Old Barracks" at VMI dates from before the Civil War. Shelled and burned in 1864 by Union general David Hunter's (USMA, 1822) forces, it was rebuilt after the war exactly as before. It formed a giant, crenelated, four-story square. There were no hallways; all cadet rooms opened out directly onto continuous porches, or "stoops," at each of the four levels. A stone sentry box stood in the center of the immense courtyard below.

On nights when drumming-outs occurred, the overhead lights along the stoops were switched off. Awakened by the rolling of the drums, the entire Corps gathered in motley nocturnal attire, filling the stoops on all four levels, crowding the railings, observing the proceedings below.

The rolling drums ceased. In the cold, starry night, the sudden silence was stark. All was in darkness except for a bright shaft of light spilling into the courtyard from Jackson Arch, the huge, main sally port through the barracks to the parade ground. It was the perfect setting for the drama that ensued.

In a column of twos, the cadet representatives to the Honor Court marched into the courtyard from Jackson Arch. They wore the gray, short-waisted, tailcoated, brass-buttoned "coatee" over gray trousers in winter, or over starched "white duck" trousers in spring and fall.

The court halted. The president of the Honor Court walked in a circle around the sentry box, intoning an address that never varied in the four years I was at VMI. In the acoustics of that space and silence, his voice echoed eerily. "Tonight, the Honor Court has met to try the case of Cadet Smith. Cadet Smith has been found guilty of [here he would name the offense: cheating, stealing, making a false official statement]. Cadet Smith will be banished from the Institute, never to return. His name will never be mentioned at VMI again."

It wasn't.

CADET LIFE

Fourth Class, or freshman year, at VMI was referred to as "Rat" year. Then came sophomore or Third Class, junior or Second Class, and at last senior or First Class. If you survived your Rat year, filled with harassment, discipline, academics, and military duties, you became an upperclassman. From there, it was a matter of staying on top of academics and military duties.

Each class earned a number of "privileges" as they moved up the seniority pecking order. As only one of many examples, Rats were required to double-time in the mess hall, going directly to and from their tables. If they were temporarily halted by crowding as everyone entered, they would jog in place. All upperclassmen could walk in the mess hall, but Third and Second were required to walk directly to their tables and walk directly out later; no loitering. Only Firsts could loiter or "visit" among the tables during meals.

In 1839 the founders of VMI were all Virginians of note, many with English or Scots-Irish heritage. They were very much Anglophiles. Accordingly, VMI was founded on the same social, traditional, and disciplinary codes as existed at the elite English "public" schools of that time.

"Canings," or physical punishment, meted out in nineteenth-century English "public" schools and those meted out by cadets in the 1960s weren't a coincidence. Cadet life at VMI in the 1960s eerily resembled that found in *Tom Brown's School Days*, a novel of student life at England's Rugby school from 1832 to 1842.

First Classmen at VMI could inflict physical punishment on any Rat for a number of unwritten but then understood and accepted reasons. Punishment could be delivered to the Rat's bottom only, and usually with a twisted wire coat hanger. The number of strokes was determined by the Rat himself, who randomly opened the copy of the Institute's regulations kept in every cadet room. The number of strokes was determined by the right-hand digit of the right-hand page number. Fortunate were Rats who turned up zeroes.

The "old boy/new boy" relationship that existed at Rugby and other English public schools in the nineteenth century was also mirrored at VMI in the 1960s. As one of their class privileges, Firsts selected a Rat to serve as an informal personal servant. The Rat reported to the First's room every morning, five minutes before the bugle sounded First Call for morning formation. He put away the First's hayrack, hayroll, and bedding. He could be required to shine the First's shoes and run menial errands for him when he wasn't in class, at authorized study, or on military duty. He helped his First dress out for parade.

In return, the First kept an eye out for his Rat, performed a few favors in kind for him, and acted as a defense against the hazing or physical punishment of his Rat by other upperclassmen, unless he deemed the Rat deserving.

Another British public school tradition that was mirrored in a VMI class privilege belonging only to Firsts was "fagging." In the British public school system, an "old boy" could "fag" a "new boy," sending him on an errand. Thus, a First could stop any Rat and direct him to run an errand. Doing so was easy; all Rats were required to walk in the "Rat line" inside barracks. Defined as a straight line along the railings, squaring all corners, while in a "brace" with chin pulled in, Rats walking the Rat line were easy targets.

It should be made clear that everything related here about VMI is as it was in the 1960s. I'm certain that, with women in the Corps today, the custom of physical punishment, as well as a number of other traditions in force while I was a cadet, have been at last abolished.

Delivery of punishment, fagging, and a number of other aspects of life and behavior among the cadets were strictly against the Institute's regulations. If seen by an officer, or the cadet officer of the day, who was honor bound, or "certified," during his period of duty to report any infraction he personally witnessed, any upperclassmen caught doing so would be awarded demerits.

The Institute's regulations were set out in a hardcover blue binder about five by six inches, stowed in a slot built into the bookcase of every cadet room. Referred to as the "blue book," it addressed the official "yin" of life at VMI; the unofficial but rigidly cadet-enforced "yang" of much of what is related above existed separately. Their duality was interesting, and at times highly challenging.

In the cadet glossary of that time, the term "dyke" had many meanings as verbs and nouns. The relationship between a First and his Rat, described above, was a verb: "to dyke." The First's Rat was a noun: his "dyke." A Rat "dyked" his First Classman. The white cross-belts worn on parade were referred to as "cross-dykes." To get dressed for parade was to "dyke out." Various states of uniform dress were referred to as "dyke," as in "class dyke," "gym dyke," "parade dyke," etc. The address system, known as the Turnout, constantly delivered critical information—for example: "Attention in barracks. Uniform for DRC (the noon meal formation) will be class dyke. That is all."

When I was a Rat, my First Class "dyke," an aspiring Marine officer, was cold, demanding, and impersonal. I never spoke to him or saw him again after VMI. When I was a First, my "dyke," Turner, who had grown up in a Navy family from a line of naval officers dating to the Revolution, was a terrific guy; we remain lifelong friends.

PAH-RAAADE, REST!

Every Friday afternoon the entire Corps stood a full open-ranks regimental inspection, followed by a parade. It was a great spectacle if you were an observer on the sidelines, but it was more than a bit of a bore if you were a cadet in the ranks.

In spring and fall, parade dyke was the short-waisted, gray, brass-buttoned tailcoat known as a "coatee." It was worn atop highly starched, white duck trousers. White cross-belts over the coatee were held in front by a highly shined breastplate. A black leather cartridge box anchored the cross-belts in the small of the back.

Rifle-bearing cadets carried a bayonet sheathed on the right hip. A black, oval "shako" with fuzzy black pom-pom and brass VMI faceplate topped the ensemble. All wore white cotton gloves.

Winter parade dyke was a high-black-collared gray blouse over wool trousers with a black side stripe, under a long gray overcoat. The overcoat half cape was turned back and buttoned, revealing a blood-red inner lining. White cross-belts were worn over the cape, with cartridge box, breastplate, and bayonet. The gray, black-brimmed "garrison cap" replaced the shako. All wore black gloves.

Cadet officers and NCOs carried a "saber," actually a straight-bladed infantry sword, sheathed in a metal scabbard on the right hip. During my time at VMI, the engraving on the saber's blade was revised and updated. A cadet committee was formed to review designs. My design was accepted; it's been on all cadet sabers since 1967. All non-saber-bearing cadets carried the M1 rifle.

Parades began with the regimental band sounding "Adjutant's Call" before marching onto the broad, grass-covered parade ground. The regimental staff and Color Guard carrying the American flag and the flags of Virginia and the VMI Corps of Cadets, were accompanied by the two cadet battalions of three companies each. VMI followed the same height-selection process used at West Point, which sorted cadets into companies by height.

Once on the parade ground (known as the Hill), the Corps formed in a long line of companies and was commanded by the cadet regimental commander to stand at "Parade rest!" It was then called to "Attention" and performed a series of precise movements with rifles and sabers, followed by passing in review and marching off the Hill. It was impressive seen from the sidelines, as over a thousand cadets executed the movements in unison with precision.

Parades lasted about forty-five minutes. In late summer or fall, a few cadets might pass out from high heat and humidity, keeling straight over in the ranks, like Grenadier Guardsmen on parade in London.

If the weather was "inclement," a term which included anything from heavy rain to driving snow, parades could be canceled. As part of a hopeful tradition, Rats were taught this ditty, to the tune of "The Arkansas Traveler":

Every time I pray for rain
The darned old Sun comes out again
Sun shines bright while I get dressed
Then it rains like *hell* at "Pah-raaade rest"!

CLASS RINGS

In the fall of its third year, each class at VMI receives its class ring. Ours was fourteen-karat gold, twenty-four pennyweight, inscribed inside with the wearer's name. One side of the ring, the "Institute side," remained the same each year, with the arms of the Institute, surmounted by the statue of *Virginia Mourning Her Dead*, against crossed Confederate and American flags.

Each class designs a unique motif for the other side of the ring, its "class side," and selects a class stone, identical on all rings of that class year. Our class's stone selection was a deep blue zircon. There was a competition to select the design for the "class side" motif. Again my design was selected.

DEATH OF A LEGEND

It was 2 a.m. on a freezing November night in the Valley. I was fast asleep. "You have an emergency call." The corporal of the Guard moved his flashlight away from my face, handed me a phone message slip, and disappeared.

I threw on a bathrobe and went four flights down to the subterranean concourse under Jackson Arch. A row of phone booths yawned blackly along one side. My aunt's number on the slip—not a good omen. The not-unexpected news still hit hard. Dad, who had been declining, had died of pneumonia. Mom was at my grandparents', near the hospital in New York City. Could I come home? Yes, of course.

Up to the Guard Room. Permission to see the officer in charge? Granted. I knocked on the door at the office in Washington Arch where the duty OC slept. That night it was Captain Bob Alsheimer, Airborne and Ranger, so trim and well turned out. His West Point cadet nickname was "Spoony," their slang for "shiny."

He stood in trousers and T-shirt, listening. "Yes, emergency leave, of course. Do you have money?" He reached in his trousers pocket and pulled out twenty dollars. "Take this." Unneeded, I said. He was adamant: "You don't know; just in case. Give our best to your mother. I'm very sorry." A terrific officer.

Flying to La Guardia on a four-engine Eastern DC-7, I watched oil leak from the engine nearest my window, a thin film sheening the cowling in the rising morning light. And many memories of a unique man now gone.

Days later, a dreary, rainy morning on Long Island. The iron-gated, gray-stone-walled National Cemetery, long avenues through huge lawns, serried ranks of white headstones. The honor guard fired three volleys; the officer gave Mom the flag on the casket, folded to a tight triangle.

Father, family man, paratrooper, OSS operator. Forty-six years old. *Finis.*

NEW MARKET

Units of the US Army that have participated in combat attach "battle streamers" to their colors, with the name and date of the actions. VMI is the only military college in the United States that has committed its student body as a combat unit in battle. The regimental colors at VMI carry a blue and gray battle streamer: "NEW MARKET—1864."

In the spring of that long-ago year, the Union Army was advancing up the Shenandoah Valley, a critical source of food and forage for the soldiers, horses, and draft animals of Robert E. Lee's Confederate Army of Northern Virginia.

General Breckinridge, former vice president of the United States and then commander of Confederate forces in the Valley, sent word to Colonel Scott Shipp, VMI's superintendent, to march the cadets north from Lexington to join him. He wasn't certain what it might take to blunt the Union advance. He needed all the forces he could muster. His intent was to hold the cadets in reserve.

Most in their teens, the cadets covered the eighty-six miles on the dirt Valley Pike in four days, with meager rations. Arriving on the outskirts of New Market on the evening of May 14, they slept on a hillside in a light rain. Thunder muttered far off.

The battle was joined next morning, an artillery and infantry duel, with cavalry forays on the flanks. By early afternoon the fight began to turn in the Union's favor; Breckinridge had to commit the cadets. He gave Shipp the order to advance.

The cadet battalion attacked. Across a muddy field, over a number of farm fences, they split into two groups, passing around a farmhouse. There they paused, reassembled, and, under fire, realigned as if on parade, continuing the attack. The rain had so soaked the ground the mud literally sucked the shoes from the feet of many cadets, who ran on with the Corps, toward a battery of four twelve-pound Union cannon.

The Union cannon fired canister: metal cans filled with hundreds of lethal lead balls, scything the cadets' ranks. Yet the boys overran the guns, capturing cannons and bayoneting artillerymen slow to retreat. Their attack broke the Union line, forcing the Union commander to withdraw his forces.

Of the 247 cadets in the VMI battalion's attack, ten were killed outright or died of wounds later, and forty-seven were wounded—about 23 percent casualties of the total force committed. No infantry unit without replacements can sustain that level for long.

In the aftermath of the battle, General Breckinridge rode up to commend the cadets. "Boys," he called out, "you have fought bravely; you will be famous!" To which an unnamed, doubtless hungry cadet replied, "Fame is fine, General, but where are your commissary wagons?"

Captain Henry DuPont (USMA, 1861) was a Union artillery officer on the field at New Market; he narrowly avoided being captured by the cadets. Fifty years later as a United States senator from Delaware, he introduced a bill to appropriate funds to compensate VMI for the destruction of its academic buildings by the Union Army in 1864. The funds were appropriated, used to reconstruct several of the Institute's key buildings.

In addition to its "NEW MARKET" battle streamer on the regimental colors, VMI commemorates the battle in other ways. The cadets' gray overcoats have a horseman's half cape, its inside lined with blood-red fabric. On winter parades, the capes are reversed and buttoned back, displaying their red linings, commemorating the cadets killed and wounded at New Market. On each May 15 anniversary of the battle, the Corps parades with a vacant space in each of the cadet companies in which cadets fell. As the regimental commander intones the names of the twelve dead boys, selected cadets in the ranks respond, "Died on the field of honor, Sir!"

"STONEWALL" JACKSON

Though he was not a VMI graduate, Thomas Jonathan Jackson is one of the many famous names associated with the Institute.

Entering West Point from the part of Virginia that later became West Virginia, he graduated in 1846, distinguishing himself for coolness under fire as an artillery officer in the Mexican War of 1846–48.

From 1851 to 1861 he served at VMI as professor of natural and experimental philosophy (today known as physics) and instructor of artillery. He was didactic, reserved, inflexible, and taciturn. Widely ridiculed by the cadets, who called him "Old Jack" and "Tom Fool," he was eccentric, a hypochondriac, and religious to the verge of fanaticism.

On the eve of the Civil War, in the spring of 1861, Jackson addressed the cadets. In a voice and with a fervor they had not before known. "The time for war has not yet come," he said, "but it *will* come, and that soon. And when it does come, my advice is to draw the sword and throw away the scabbard." The cadets went wild.

In the war that followed, Jackson was transformed into one of the greatest strategists and tacticians of his era. His ferocity as a combat leader is legend. His 1862 campaign in the Shenandoah Valley is studied today at the world's major military colleges. His death from pneumonia, after being mistakenly shot by his own troops at Chancellorsville, was a major blow to the Confederacy.

When I was a cadet, Jackson's statue, gazing out across the vast parade ground toward the profile of House Mountain in the distance, was directly opposite the huge sally port named for him in the Old Barracks. Each time we as Rats passed through Jackson Arch, above our heads was his exhortatory phrase, "You may be whatever you resolve to be." Emerging, we saluted his statue. I thought it appropriate that he kept his back to us; we ignorant fledglings had much yet to prove.

He was a complex, God-fearing man, yet he came from a slave-owning family and owned slaves himself. He was devoted to "Miss Fanny," the slave who raised him. When Jackson lived in Lexington in the 1850s. It wasn't legal to teach slaves to read or write, yet he established a Sunday school for slaves, risking arrest for doing so. During the war he occasionally sent money back from his campaigns to support the school.

In 1906 a memorial stained-glass window to Jackson was established in a Presbyterian church in Roanoke, founded by the son of slaves who had been students in Jackson's Sunday school. He is the only Confederate general to be so memorialized in an African American church.

Jackson is buried in Lexington, surrounded by the graves of many others who fought for the Confederacy. A statue of him stands on a pedestal at his grave site, surrounded by a tall, wrought-iron fence. When on campaign in the Civil War, he had enjoyed lemons when they could be had. To this day, fresh lemons, when in season, are seen on the lawn of his grave site, tossed over the fence by anonymous admirers.

CONTRIBUTIONS

When I was a cadet, the Corps at VMI was about 1,200, smaller than most high schools. Yet the Institute has contributed over 290 general officers and admirals in all the US armed services, and those of several other countries. It has produced a United States secretary of state, a secretary of defense, and secretaries of the Army. Its graduates include General George Marshall, the only soldier to receive the Nobel Prize for Peace; seven recipients of the Congressional Medal of Honor; and thirteen Rhodes Scholars. Graduates have served in every branch of the armed forces, in every war and conflict since the Civil War, amassing legions of awards and decorations for gallantry and heroism in action.

VMI alumni have received the Pulitzer Prize, an Academy Award, an Emmy Award, and a Golden Globe. Alumni include a civil rights martyr recognized by the Episcopal Church, US and state senators and representatives, governors, lieutenant governors, a Supreme Court justice, college and university presidents, and legions of attorneys, physicians, engineers, writers, authors, and corporate presidents and CEOs.

Not too bad for a little military institute in the Shenandoah Valley.

ENOUGH "BADASS" FOR CHESTY

I've mentioned that VMI's culture may be more Marine than Army. That's a fact. I've heard Marine officers refer to the place as "Parris Island in the Shenandoah"; they ought to know.

VMI's association with the Marine Corps goes way back. Beginning with William Upshur in 1902, twenty-five VMI graduates became general officers in the Marine Corps, including Lemuel Shepherd and Randolph Pate, both of whom served as commandants of the Corps.

General John Archer Lejeune, a Naval Academy graduate, served as Marine Corps commandant, and later as superintendent of VMI. Lejeune is famed for commanding the US Army's 2nd Infantry Division in France during World War I. His official portraits show him in his high-collared Marine Corps tunic with "Sam Browne" belt. On his shoulder is the big 2nd Infantry Division insignia with a profile of an American Indian chief in full eagle-feathered war bonnet. Quite a guy.

Without question the most colorful Marine general ever to come from VMI is Lewis "Chesty" Puller. From West Point, Virginia, a town on the James River known for a noxious paper mill, he wanted to join the Army to fight in the Punitive Expedition against Pancho Villa in 1916. But he was underage; his mother wouldn't give her consent.

In 1917 he attended VMI and made it through his Rat year, but left in 1918 to join the Marines to fight in France. He became a Marine second lieutenant but didn't make it to France before the war ended. The Corps contracted; Puller was put on the inactive Reserve list with the rank of corporal.

In the 1920s and early 1930s, the United States engaged in "police actions," intervention and occupation, in countries in Central America and the Caribbean. The objective was to secure American regional influence, safeguard the Panama Canal, and protect the interests of US corporations. Itching for action, Puller served as a lieutenant with the Gendarmerie d'Haiti, a proxy force formed by the United States after its occupation of Haiti.

In 1924, he was recommissioned in the Marine Corps. In the interwar years he served in Nicaragua, China, and twice aboard the USS *Augusta*, then the flagship of the US Asiatic Fleet.

In World War II he commanded a Marine infantry battalion on Guadalcanal and a regiment on Peleliu, two of the critical actions in the Pacific. In the Korean War he commanded a regiment in the landings at Inchon, the advance to the Yalu River, and the battle and subsequent legendary "march-out" to the sea from the Chosin Reservoir in December 1950. During that epic battle, he made the immortal statement, "We've been looking for the enemy for some time now. We've finally found him. We're surrounded. That simplifies things."

"Chesty" retired as a lieutenant general. There may never be another like him. Holder of five Navy Crosses and the Army's Distinguished Service Cross, he is the most decorated Marine in the Corps' long and illustrious history.

At the time of this writing, there is an ongoing discussion among VMI alumni regarding a possible statue of Chesty, to be commissioned for the Institute's campus. While no one can say if such a statue may ever be seen at VMI, one of my classmates' contribution is noteworthy. "If they do decide on a statue to Chesty," he writes, "they'd better make sure they can find enough 'badass' to shovel into the mix."

LIFE TESTS

At VMI we had to complete several "life tests," as they were informally known. Boxing, swimming, dancing, and qualifying on the known-distance, or KD, firing range with the M1 rifle.

Possibly the most psychologically daunting test was the underwater swim. After deep breathing to oxygenate, we stepped off the edge of the Olympic-sized pool in the gym and, without kicking off the wall, swam underwater the full length of the pool, touched the far wall, reversed without surfacing or kicking off, and swam the full length back. VMI's swim coach, nicknamed "Superfish," assured us it was all in our minds. Right.

Boxing. I was sparring with an opponent. We must not have been doing acceptable damage to each other. The boxing coach said, "Are you two roommates or something? I want to see some blood, Misters, or I'll get in and take care of both of you myself." We qualified.

GREAT EXAMPLES

From the caliber of officers assigned to VMI in the mid-1960s, it was evident the Army had a high opinion of the Institute.

In addition to Captain Bob Alsheimer, also assigned as tactical officers were Captains Bob Drudik (West Point, 1957) and Ken Dickinson (VMI, 1957); all were great examples.

Already a minor Army legend when he arrived at VMI, "Ranger Bob" Drudik had led a spirited "Beat Navy!" pregame football rally at West Point, then attacked the escort of the Navy's goat mascot in the stadium on game day in Philadelphia. He is reported to have demonstrated good form with an M1 rifle, with bayonet attached. The midshipman commanding the Navy goat herders whacked him with his ornamental sword. While not qualifying as a combat wound, it nevertheless boosted "Ranger Bob" to an Army legend.

Ken Dickinson was a no-nonsense customer. Like Alsheimer and Drudik, he was Regular Army, Infantry, Airborne, and Ranger. All three had great humor that shone through their facades; I was privileged to count them as friends in my later Army career.

AN AIR FORCE CHRISTMAS PRESENT

My classmate Steve's father was an Air Force general. At Christmas of our Second Class year, he sent his executive aircraft, a twin-engine C-47 transport, to pick up a number of us who lived along the northeastern seaboard. It would drop us off at various air bases on the way to its home base in Upstate New York.

We landed first at Andrews Air Force Base in Maryland, then McGuire in New Jersey, and headed for Stewart, near my mom's home just above West Point, where I would get off.

On the approach into Stewart, the flight crew let me sit in the flight engineer's seat behind the pilot and copilot, with a wide view of the frozen Hudson River countryside, snowbound under gray skies. My headphones were on the pilot's radio traffic. As we neared Stewart, he told the tower the plane had an

O-7 (brigadier general) priority, but no general officer was aboard. He would do an engines-running drop-off of one passenger and immediately depart. The tower cleared him to land.

A blue Air Force station wagon was waiting as the plane taxied up to the ramp in front of Base Operations. The wind and cold as I went down the ladder were ferocious. An Air Force colonel got out of the car, shook my hand, and motioned me to get into the back as the prop blast from the C-47 picked up and the aircraft turned onto the taxiway.

It was warm as toast in that car. The colonel was Stewart Air Force Base's commanding officer; I was floored. He looked over his shoulder at me sitting in the back and asked if I had transport home. I told him I'd planned to call a cab. He said, "Nonsense. You're a guest of the United States Air Force. We'll take you home." They did; it was a great Christmas present.

INDIANTOWN GAP

In the summer of 1966, about 2,500 Army ROTC cadets from colleges east of the Mississippi gathered at Indiantown Gap Military Reservation for six weeks of training. A sprawling post in southeastern Pennsylvania, during World War II, Indiantown (known as IGMR or "the Gap") was a training base for major Army units destined for combat overseas.

In 1966 IGMR was practically unchanged from its World War II appearance, with rows of wooden one-story administration buildings, mess halls, and two-story troop barracks. Built as "temporaries" in record time, over seventy years later many of those same troop barracks can still be found on Army posts.

They were familiar; we had lived in one at Fort Dix in 1948, and hundreds more were at Forts Eustis and Rucker as I was growing up. Long and rectangular, each had a gabled roof, horizontal wood siding, and a projecting, surrounding overhang at the top of the first story. They were almost always painted white, with black, red, or green composition shingle roofs and overhangs. They looked like rows and rows of Chiclets. If you don't know Chiclets, they look like white chewing-gum versions of Army barracks.

An open "platoon bay" on each barracks floor housed rows of double bunks on both sides of a central aisle. Floors were dark green waxed linoleum, which required daily servicing with an electric floor buffer. Each barracks had a latrine and showers at the rear of the ground floor.

I was in "Foxtrot" Company. We were immediately nicknamed "F Troop," after a TV comedy series at that time about a do-nothing-right troop of US cavalry on the Western frontiers. We even had Mosely, our company bugler, an African American cadet who wore a cavalry campaign hat and carried his bugle in every formation.

If Foxtrot was moving from one place to another in a "column of twos" and crossed a street or intersection, two men would double-time forward as road guards to stop traffic as we passed. Mosely would be right with them to play a fanfare as Foxtrot Company made the crossing. Very cool.

Each ROTC cadet company at Indiantown had a staff of Army tactical officers assigned, all of whom were instructors at various ROTC colleges during the academic year. Our company senior tactical officer was a major, with three captains as the platoon "tacs". A seasoned sergeant major was the sole NCO on each company tactical staff. Our sergeant major had a dry wit and a big, foghorn delivery.

My platoon's tactical officer, Captain Alan Shost, was a 1960 West Point graduate, an Artillery officer, and a terrific role model. He was very sharp on detail and looked more than a bit like the actor Robert Vaughn. He called me "Slick." I've never quite understood why, but there it was.

Captain Shost was forever in despair of our ability to march without one or two of us bobbing along out of step. "My grandmother can march better than you clowns, with a brick in her back pocket!" he laughed, and dubbed us the "Granny platoon." We loved it.

While we were out on training, the barracks and latrines were inspected daily. Based on an intense competition in each cadet battalion, movable "Best Latrine" and "Best Urinal" plaques were awarded weekly.

An inspection "buck slip" was filled out daily by the inspecting officer, a copy posted on the bulletin board inside the main door of each barracks, with notations like "dust on window ledge," "improperly displayed footlocker contents," and the like. Our latrine was a perennial problem; it never looked spiffy enough to inspectors. The big, wide, white enamel urinal was a focal point.

After three years at VMI, barracks and room inspections weren't the end of the world. But for some of the guys in ROTC from civilian schools, it was evidently an alien experience. Occasionally we would get a more direct assessment. One evening when we were in formation, the sergeant major boomed out, "Mister Adamson, your bunk this morning looked like a pair of pigs have been fucking in it for four days!"

Out of the corner of my eye, I saw our major and all three captains hustle around the corner of the barracks where they broke up laughing.

We kept struggling to get the damn urinal up to the point it would pass inspection. It was a heavy, white, enameled trough about six feet wide, mounted on the wall at a convenient height. A set of pipes branched from a central fitting in the wall, leading to three flush outlets. After almost a quarter century of intermittent use and neglect, it was a fairly sorry-looking item.

We wanted those plaques. We put our heads together. A couple of the guys bought cans of Bartender's Friend metal cleaner on a weekend in nearby Hershey. Others bought Comet cleanser and Clorox bleach. We all had Brasso for polishing metal.

We attacked the latrine with the zeal of fanatics. We nearly disassembled it, toilets, sinks, and all. We scrubbed every crevice with toothbrushes dipped in Comet, then swabbed with Clorox. We sandpapered the rust off the piping and hit everything else that couldn't get away with Bartender's Friend and elbow grease. We shined the inside of the urinal with a light coat of floor wax. The place didn't look that good when it was new in 1941. We won both plaques, and we kept winning them until we retired them in the sixth and last week.

SHOOTING FOR RECORD

Training that summer at "the Gap" included map and compass work, day and night tactical exercises, classes on a host of other military subjects, and shooting for record with the .30 caliber M1 rifle on the known-distance (K-D) ranges.

The K-D ranges were another aspect of the Army of the Cold War; marksmanship was strongly emphasized. I already knew the basics; my dad had signed me up in the NRA junior marksmanship program at Camp Darby in the mid-1950s, where I shot in competition with bolt-action Remington .22 rifles.

Designed in the 1930s, the Army's .30 caliber M1 rifle was a major departure from the single-shot, bolt-action rifles used by most other armies in World War II. Loaded with a steel clip holding eight rounds, the M1 reloaded automatically after each shot until all eight rounds were expended. When the last round was fired, the empty clip ejected from the rifle with a distinctive PING! locking the breech open for insertion of a new clip.

The semiautomatic function meant the American soldier didn't have to work the rifle's bolt after each shot, affording him a much higher rate of fire than many of his battlefield opponents. General George Patton pronounced the M1 rifle "the greatest battle implement ever devised."

The M1 weighed just under ten pounds. With its walnut stock and "Parkerized" steel barrel, receiver, and sights, it looked, and was, rugged and deadly. Though most combat action was within 250 to 300 yards, in the hands of a well-trained soldier, it could reach out to 500 yards.

On "range days" at the Gap we marched out in the mornings, swinging along with our rifles slung on our shoulders in the early, rising sunlight, with the smell of sage and the promise of heat later in the day.

At the range, the firing points flanked the control tower, with its red "firing in progress" warning flag. The medics were there, their dark green, box-bodied ambulance with a red cross against a big white disk on each side. Green canvas Lister bags hung under shade shelters, bulging with cold, chlorinated water and sweating condensation.

Lying prone at the firing points on canvas mats, heft of the clip inserted, bolt released, slamming the first long brass cartridge with its sharp copper nose home. From the tower loudspeaker: "At two hundred yards, eight rounds. Ready on the right; ready on the left. Ready on the firing line. Targets up! Commence firing."

Target frames rising from behind the berms downrange. Bring the bull's-eye just onto the post and frame of the sights, let out half a breath, hold it steadyyy . . . smooth pressure on the trigger, and CRACK! the recoil punches your shoulder. A whiff of cordite: fireworks with a hint of ammonia. Do it again. And again. With twenty firing points, the racket is intense. Concentrate.

Two days of practice. On day three, we shot for record: the complete "table" of fifty rounds, targets at two hundred, three hundred, and five hundred yards. Prone, standing, sitting, and kneeling. Ten points for each shot in the ten ring of the target. I shot "expert." After that summer, I never fired an M1 in the Army again.

THE END IS NEAR

We knew Captain Shost was due for promotion to major. About the end of the fourth week, our platoon chipped in and ordered a field-grade officer's garrison cap, with the gold oak leaves on the brim, from Luxenberg in New York City. They had been military hatters to Eisenhower, Marshall, and many others of the Army's great generals. We kept it a secret and hoped the hat would get to us before the end of the sixth week.

Along toward the end of the fourth week, Captain Shost told me I was doing very well and had a shot at being selected as one of the top cadets of that summer. By the beginning of the last week, I was in a handful called up for interviews by a board of officers at headquarters.

It was a stifling night; I sweated through a fresh set of khakis, sitting in a hard-backed wooden chair in front of a table of majors and colonels. Two big floor fans made so much racket it was difficult to hear the questions. A few of them wouldn't be in the politically correct Army syllabus today, but whatever I answered must have been acceptable. I was selected as the number-one cadet that summer, receiving a silver bowl from the governor of Pennsylvania at the final cadet brigade review. Over the years Mom kept roses in it, when they were in season. Very nice.

After the parade, on the afternoon of the brigade review, we hung the "Best Urinal" and "Best Latrine" plaques above the urinal and disinfected it with Clorox. We filled it with crushed ice and several cases of bottled beer and threw Captain Shost a party. Our major and all three captains were there.

Shost was surprised and pleased when he opened the hatbox. He went on to a great Army career, retiring as a colonel. He is remembered.

"RATMAN AND WOMBAT"

In my junior and senior years at VMI I created a cartoon strip for the *VMI Cadet*, the Institute's weekly newspaper. Its hero was "Ratman," a pudgy, caped rodent who lived in the "Rat Cave," deep below the VMI parade ground. Assisted by his trusty sidekick "Wombat," Ratman sallied forth to do battle with tactical officers and other real-life targets at VMI.

Each week, cartoon caricatures of actual officers at VMI like Majors "Owlscreamer" and "Underlocker" and Captain "Dickenlittle" were foiled by the clever antics of the dynamic duo. Their targets' names were fictitious, but close enough to the names of the actual officers, along with their unmistakable characteristics.

The cadets weren't Ratman's only fans; I eventually learned that each edition was avidly anticipated by the Institute's officers and faculty, to see who was in Ratman's crosshairs that week. Bets were laid.

At graduation, I crossed the stage to receive my diploma from VMI's superintendent, General George R. E. Shell, a Marine and veteran of Guadalcanal, Tarawa, and Saipan. He shook my hand, then pulled me in close. "Good luck. We're really going to miss Ratman," he said with a big smile.

How about that?

8

FIRST DAY
IN THE ARMY

June 1967

"Do we report with the AIRBORNE tab sewn on," I asked Mike, "or without? We don't want to screw this up; if we do, we'll never hear the end of it."

My VMI classmate Mike thought about it as we looked out the window of the Waffle House at the scene along Bragg Boulevard. It was Thursday, June 15, 1967. The heat outside rose off the pavement in waves. A never-ending stream of traffic moved along the blacktop leading from Fayetteville to the huge army post at Fort Bragg, North Carolina, home of the 82nd Airborne Division, XVIII Airborne Corps, the Special Warfare Center, and the US Army's Special Forces.

Fort Bragg was a huge military city. The businesses on Bragg Boulevard were happy to support it. Wall-to-wall gas stations, bars, fast food and other eateries, dry cleaners, tailor shops, pawnshops, barbers, and a few dives with no windows. Even on Thursday afternoon the parking lots in front of the dives were full. Fayetteville and the Army had a perfect symbiotic relationship.

Mike and I were starting our Army careers. After graduation and commissioning at VMI the preceding Sunday, we had driven to Fayetteville from Lexington, Virginia. We were to report to the 82nd Airborne Division at 0700 the next morning.

"I'm not sure," said Mike. "We never asked at school. If it was critical, you'd imagine someone would have told us, right?" He poked his milkshake with a straw.

It was a ridiculous quandary. We were Distinguished Military Graduates at VMI and were now Regular Army officers. We had both grown up in Army families. Yet we were clueless on this point. We weren't certain if we were supposed to sew on the curved blue shoulder tab with AIRBORNE on it in white letters. The tab capped a red square with a solid blue disk, holding a big white "AA" in its center. Together, they were the shoulder insignia of the 82nd Airborne Division.

Sure, we knew the 82nd was formed in 1971 and was the first of the Army's divisions to be manned with soldiers from all across the country, rather than regionally, like the National Guard outfits. The "AA" stood for "All American."

We knew the division fought in France in World War I, and a sergeant, Alvin York, a crack shot from Tennessee, was awarded the Medal of Honor for single-handedly killing and capturing over a hundred Germans. We knew the 82nd became a parachute division early in World War II and had dropped into battle in North Africa, Sicily, Normandy, and Holland.

So, right, we knew all that. What we didn't know was, should we report in with or without the blue AIRBORNE tab? If we showed up with them and weren't wearing parachute wings, we could get a blast from some officer, any of whom were senior to us, and sent ignominiously packing to slice them off.

On the other hand, if we showed up without them and the protocol was that the tab went with the rest of the insignia, airborne qualified or not, we could just as easily get our tails chewed.

"It's a fifty-fifty chance we'll be OK," I said, "so let's toss a coin. Heads we sew 'em on; tails we don't."

"Works for me," said Mike. The toss came up tails.

No one paid us any attention the next morning as we walked under a short, curved green canopy and up the steps of 82nd Airborne Division headquarters. The gleaming floor of the entry hallway smelled strongly of buffing wax. On either side, glass cases held trophies, plaques, and paratrooper figurines.

One entire wall had a mural depicting a French nightscape, lit by German searchlights, bursting flak, multicolored tracers, and burning aircraft arcing toward the ground. Hundreds of paratroopers leaped from twin-engine C-47 transports, their parachutes trailing away behind the planes like long, descending streams of flocked cotton.

The opposite wall held an enormous set of silver parachute wings, topped with a star within a wreath. Across the center of the parachute were four gold stars. Each signified one of the combat jumps the division had made in World War II.

Beside the entry doors stood the division's "colors," the division's flag with its unique battle streamers; the colors of the United States Army, bearing battle and campaign streamers all the way back to 1775; and the flag of the United States. We were definitely in the major leagues now.

Our orders said to report to the division's administration and personnel office, known as G-1. The directory inside the entrance told us G-1 was down the hall, across from G-4: Logistics. Upstairs were G-3, Operations, and G-2, Intelligence, as were the offices of the commanding general and the division's command sergeant major.

THE COMMAND SERGEANT MAJOR

Several officers passed us without a glance. As we started down the hall, a voice behind us said, "Can I help you, gentlemen?" We turned to see a tall man with a crew cut, in faded, heavily starched fatigues and immaculately polished parachute boots. On both sleeves of his fatigue shirt were three gold vertical chevrons, with three curved gold chevrons beneath. A gold star framed by a wreath occupied the space in the center. He seemed to be about seven feet tall.

He was the command sergeant major, the division's highest-ranking noncommissioned officer. He reported directly to the division commander, a major general.

"Good morning, Sergeant Major!" Mike and I chorused like a pair of Junior Woodchucks. "We're reporting for duty," I added inanely, as though second lieutenants were so rare we needed to describe ourselves to this distinguished career soldier.

"Good morning, gentlemen. Welcome to the 82nd. May I see your orders?" We handed them over. "Hmm." He smiled. "You're in the right place. However," he said, handing them back to us, "may I suggest before you report to G-1, you might want to go back off-post to one of the quick-turnaround tailors on Bragg Boulevard and get those AIRBORNE tabs sewn on. If you show up the way you are now, the G-1 will eat you alive. Count on it."

Mike and I probably set the record for getting it done. We stood awkwardly in our T-shirts while the tailor sewed the tabs on with a big grin. "Every summer it's the same thing," he said. "Every June or July, a few of you lieutenants don't get the word and come in here to get that tab sewn on," he chuckled.

Mike and I looked at each other.

Two hours later, having taken the command sergeant major's advice, we were cordially welcomed by the Division G-1, a lieutenant colonel, and assigned onward to different units.

THE 82ND AIRBORNE DIVISION

In 1967, the 82nd was about sixteen thousand soldiers strong, organized as three brigades of Infantry, plus additional supporting units. Every soldier was a parachutist, having volunteered for the three-week parachute course at Fort Benning and completed its mix of five qualifying day and night jumps.

In order to get to where it needed to go to fulfill its global mission, the 82nd Airborne relied on military airlift units of the US Air Force. Located next to Fort Bragg was Pope Air Force Base, a huge airfield with the C-130 and C-141 transport aircraft needed to lift the division and its supporting units.

"Brutal Utilitarian" would be a charitable description of the architectural style of the huge complex of barracks, headquarters, mess halls, gymnasiums, medical facilities, and other structures that housed the 82nd's soldiers and various units.

"Atrocious" would likely be the first word to come to an artistically sensitive mind. It was a discordant arrangement of off-white or off-tan cement and cinderblock cubes and rectilinear boxes, set in a sea of pavement and worn crabgrass, speckled with a forest of telephone poles, power lines, and antennas. Here and there were gasping trees and arrangements of tired shrubbery. Frank Lloyd Wright it was not.

A HUNG JUMPER

As I walked down Ardennes Street toward the headquarters of my new battalion, I was aware of groups of soldiers standing on the sidewalks, looking at the sky. Droning overhead in a very wide, circular orbit, a dark green, four-engine C-130 Hercules transport towed a soldier behind it at the end of a line.

I couldn't see details. That the soldier was in trouble, though, was evident. Something had to have gone badly wrong when he exited the plane. The nylon static line connecting his parachute to the anchor cable in the aircraft, which was supposed to break free once his parachute was fully out of his backpack tray, had somehow jerked him up taught. Now he was being towed in the slipstream behind four thundering turboprop engines, battered by wind and prop blast, as the plane continued its wide, circular orbit.

It was a very dangerous, potentially fatal situation. Unless they could retrieve the soldier by pulling him into the plane, they couldn't land without turning him into a smear along the runway. If he was conscious, they could cut his static line, allowing him to fall free. He could then activate the smaller reserve parachute all troopers carried on the front of their harness. To execute this last option, the "hung jumper" had to signal to those watching in the plane that he was conscious by putting one or both hands on his helmet. I watched for a few moments. The transport continued its wide, circular orbit.

GLIDER SOLDIERS

My new battalion's headquarters was a one-story affair. An inverted, white, wooden L-shaped frame stood in front, resembling the kind Realtors stake out in front of homes for sale. It supported a hanging square panel with the unit's regimental crest and the names of the lieutenant colonel commanding and the battalion's sergeant major.

Unlike the martial crests of other Infantry regiments of the division, which variously portrayed red devils, winged panthers, or flaming swords, my new battalion's seemed pretty tame. It was a white shield, with a columned, domed temple-like structure in the top half and a dark blue French Cross of Lorraine below. Beneath the shield, a scroll held the regimental motto: "Let's go!"

The battalion headquarters was a smaller version of the division's. The same gleaming, heavily buffed floor; the strong aroma of buffing wax. A smaller collection of framed photos and trophies; the regimental colors, dark blue, with the regimental crest and motto; and a surprising number of battle streamers, for a unit I thought had been created brand new for World War II.

I knew the battalion differed from those in the parachute infantry regiments of the division during World War II. While they jumped into battle wearing parachutes, my new battalion's infantrymen had ridden in gliders, towed by twin-engine aircraft. The battalion was converted to parachute infantry in the 1950s.

I have to confess I was a bit disappointed, in those first hours in the division, in not being assigned to one of the other originally parachute regiments, possibly because I had seen the popular 1962 film *The Longest Day*.

In the film, one of those parachute battalions was first to liberate Sainte Mere Eglise, a French town astride a critical Normandy crossroads, and hold it against German counterattack. John Wayne had played the role of Ben Vandervoort, the legendary commander of the battalion that had done so. Vandervoort broke an ankle in the jump, then ordered a pair of griping paratroopers to tow him toward Sainte Mere Eglise, seated in a two-wheeled ammunition cart. Like many other young males raised in the postwar mythos of American heroism, I thought that was superbly cool.

In World War II my new battalion had flown its "glider men" into Normandy and Holland, taking heavy casualties in the landings and combat operations that followed. The gliders were so tricky to land that in combat situations they were considered write-offs. It also fought as a ground unit in the Battle of the Bulge in December 1944.

The soldiers who rode those gliders into battle were not volunteers, did not receive hazardous duty pay as the paratroopers did, and were at first looked down on by paratroops. They were also not authorized a badge denoting their "winged Infantry" status until late in the war. So it was in that mind-set that I reported in.

I was welcomed by a captain, the battalion's S-1, the admin and personnel officer. He introduced me to the battalion's executive officer, or XO, a red-headed major who sat me down. A soldier brought us coffee while the XO told me the battalion commander was at a conference; I would meet him soon. He asked a few questions about my background, knew a lot about VMI, and told me I would be assigned to the battalion's Bravo Company, commanded by Captain Juan.

Bravo Company, he said, consistently set battalion records in tactics and in their performance in other areas, largely because of Captain Juan's dynamic command style and how he expected his soldiers to be among the very best. I would learn much from Juan, he said; Juan would expect much from me.

I nodded. These men lived in a world where the standards and values of the society outside the military were superseded by a very different set of rules. Every soldier and officer in the battalion, as in the rest of the Army, had given the United States a blank check on their lives, at a time when American soldiers were being regularly killed and wounded in Vietnam.

The XO checked his watch. "Have you been to the Division Museum"?

I didn't know there was one. "No, Sir."

"It's two blocks from here. Why don't you go look around? Pick up some information on our battalion's and the division's history. It's now 1300; report to Bravo Company by 1530. I'll phone them and tell them to expect you." He stood up and shook my hand. "Welcome to the 325th."

The C-130 and its hapless hung jumper were gone when I walked to the Division Museum. I hoped that situation had turned out happily.

SOME REGIMENTAL HISTORY

The first thing I saw at the museum was a CG-4A glider, suspended from the ceiling. Known as a "Waco" for the Ohio-based airplane manufacturer that had built the first ones, it had a tubular steel frame covered in aircraft-grade, doped canvas. The floor was plywood. Wacos were flown by a pilot and copilot. They could carry thirteen soldiers and their equipment, a quarter-ton jeep and four men, or a 75mm "pack" howitzer and a crew of three. Their bluntly rounded, transparent Plexiglas-covered noses were hinged to swing upward, locking in place for loading and unloading.

At the museum I learned that my battalion, and the 325th Infantry, its parent regiment, were the only Infantry unit in the current 82nd Airborne Division that had been part of the original 82nd Division in World War I. There, it had taken part in the reduction of the Saint-Mihiel salient, and in the Meuse Argonne Offensive, two of the pivotal battles of the war. That accounted for the unit's more classic, less flamboyant crest and the many battle streamers I had seen on the regiment's colors.

CAPTAIN JUAN

After the museum, my respect for the battalion had grown when I reported to Bravo Company. The CO's office and company orderly room were on the ground floor of a long, cinder-block, two-story building which also housed the company day room, a troop platoon bay with a double row of bunks on the first floor, the armorer and weapons room in the basement, and two troop platoon bays and latrine and showers on the second floor.

I could hear someone on the phone inside an office to my left as I entered. "CO" was painted on the closed door. No one was in the orderly room. It held two gray steel desks, a file cabinet, and a small table with a ten-cup aluminum coffee percolator, the kind with the glass outside tube and a tilt spigot. Beside the percolator were a few nesting tan melamine mugs and a can of condensed milk with several holes punched in the top. An unsheathed bayonet lay beside the milk can.

On a wooden staff in a floor stand behind one of the empty desks was Bravo Company's guidon, a dark blue, swallow-tailed flag with crossed rifles, and "325" in white.

Mounted on one wall was a large acetate-covered chart with the company's current and future training and parachuting dates, neatly blocked in with colored grease pencils.

On the other was a five-by-eight-foot sheet of plywood painted flat black. Centered in stark white was a huge, beautifully painted pair of curved wings framing a human skull where the parachute would have been. Beneath this arrangement was the legend "DEATH FROM ABOVE" in white capital block letters. Symbology was evidently big mojo in the 82nd.

No one was in the orderly room. I waited until I heard the voice in the CO's office stop and the phone hang up and knocked on the door.

"Enter."

Captain Juan was a powerfully built man with olive complexion, very dark brown eyes, and a short, dark crew cut. I would learn later that as an officer in Brigade 2506, he was captured during the failed 1960 invasion at the Bay of Pigs. Imprisoned and regularly beaten by his communist captors, he and the other prisoners were eventually ransomed from Castro's regime by the Kennedy administration for millions of dollars of medical supplies.

Juan had joined the US Army as a private and sailed through Officer Candidate School at Fort Benning. His fatigues were heavily starched, faded to that shade known by the Marines as "salty." A master parachutist's badge, known as "master blaster wings," embroidered in white was sewn over his left shirt pocket. A curved, black-and-gold RANGER tab crowned the blue-and-white AIRBORNE tab atop the 82nd Airborne Division shoulder patch.

Seated behind his desk, Juan barely looked up from the papers he was signing. He did not invite me to sit down. He did not call for someone to fetch coffee. He did not tell me to "stand at ease."

He did return my salute. "Lootenan'," he began, in a Cuban accent and speech pattern I would later become very used to, and the troops would delight in mimicking, if and when they thought they could get away with it. "The S-1 phoned you were coming." He paused. "So, what am I supposed to do with you?"

"Sir?" I was more than a bit apprehensive. This wasn't exactly a first meeting with promise. I remained at attention.

"Stand at ease. Stand at ease." I relaxed marginally. He continued, "You are reporting to me as a platoon leader, yes? Yet you are not parachute qualified." His eyes locked on mine. "You see my problem?"

"I think so, Sir," I replied. I was ever more thankful I was at least wearing the correct division insignia on my left shoulder.

"Lootenan'," he continued, "until you are parachute qualified, I cannot use you. More, the men will not respect you. Every man here is a jumper. You are a 'leg.'"

He wasn't referring to my abilities; he was pointing out my lack of qualification. In the tight-knit society of these men who jumped out of airplanes, the world was divided into two categories: paratroopers and "legs."

"Leg" came from the fact that paratroopers are trained to land with their legs slightly bent, continuing in a practiced, rolling fall that takes up the impact of hitting the ground at a descent rate of about twenty-six feet a second. Non–airborne qualified soldiers were all "straight-legs," shortened to "leg," and pronounced in a manner that leaves no doubt it refers to some form of lower life.

"First Sergeant!" Juan called over my shoulder. In a few moments the company first sergeant appeared in the doorway. His fatigues were the same faded shade as Juan's, starched stiff as a board. He wore the "master blaster" badge over his shirt pocket, just like Juan's. His black jump boots were shined to mirror status.

"Sir!"

"Call S-1; ask them to put the lootenan' here on TDY orders to Benning for the next available jump class."

The first sergeant looked at me momentarily, then back at Juan. "Yes, Sir!" He disappeared.

Juan said, "Lootenan', you're going to be Airborne qualified when you report back here. Is that understood?"

"Yes, Sir."

"Good. That will be all." I came to attention and saluted. He returned it. That was that.

As the first sergeant handed me back my orders on my way out the door, his expression as much as said, "So long, Lieutenant. Wherever you wind up next, it very likely won't be here."

We'd see about that.

Standing on the steps of the Bravo Company orderly room, I reflected on the very short meeting. Captain Juan hadn't pulled any punches. In my present non-airborne status, I was, as he had put it, useless to him.

He was right; the troops wouldn't respect a new lieutenant until he was jump qualified. His parting words as I went out the door were, "And don' come back without a Ranger tab too."

With my father at Yokohama, 1949. He was my hero.

Visiting the great statue of Buddha at Kamakura on Sunday, 22 June 1950. Returning to Negishi Heights, we learned North Korea had invaded the South.

Many in the American community turned out to see Pan American's new "Strato-cruiser" at Haneda, then Tokyo's only airport, 1951. I'm sitting on the baggage tug.

Negishi Heights, 1951. While my father and a friend talked about a war, somewhere called "grease," I drew airplanes on the sidewalk.

My mother and father, at our quarters at Negishi Heights, Yokohama, 1952.

The Military Sea Transport Service's "General E. D. Patrick" enters San Francisco Bay, 1952. She and her sister MSTS ships made regular runs across the Pacific from San Francisco and Seattle to the Orient.

The Hudson River side-wheeler *Alexander Hamilton*, 1953. A piece of Americana, straight out of a nineteenth-century Currier and Ives lithograph. When she sounded her whistle at the Bear Mountain Bridge, she could be heard as far north as West Point.

A "Bobcat" Cub Scout in Pack 23, West Point, New York, 1954. My mother was our "den mom." First steps, on the trail to Eagle Scout.

My first library card, from the Old Cadet Library at West Point, 1954. With stern portraits of whiskered "Old Army" officers, creaky floorboards, and a musty odor, it was supposedly modeled after the "castle" insignia of the Army's Corps of Engineers.

The American Export Line's beautiful SS *Constitution*. She and her sister ship *Independence* ran between New York, Algeciras, Genoa, and Naples. We sailed for Italy aboard her in 1956, on the voyage immediately after she had taken Grace Kelly to Monaco to marry Prince Rainier.

Our Tuscan home beneath umbrella pines, just off the Via Aurelia in Tirrenia, a beach town south of Pisa and the Arno River.

Bunkers under the umbrella pines, seen from the road between Tirrenia and Camp Darby. Passing them twice daily in school buses, we didn't pay much attention. Years later I learned what might have been stored there, in addition to ordinary military equipment.

A Fiat G.91 jet "strike fighter" in US Army markings at the Army Aviation Center, Fort Rucker, Alabama, 1961. The Army wanted the G.91 to provide its own close air support. Citing the 1949 Key West Agreement between the Army and the Air Force, the Air Force killed the project.

OFFICE OF STRATEGIC SERVICES

HEADQUARTERS 2677ᵀᴴ REGIMENT

A. P. O. 534 U. S. ARMY

1st. Lt. Joseph F. Gioia

O-1178812   Ops. Sup.

APO 512

AF

Signature *Joseph F. Gioia*

Identification Card No. 330

G. G. PARRY JR.
LT. COMDR. U. S. N. R.
SECURITY OFFICER

My father's fluency in Italian led to his World War II service in the Office of Strategic Services in England and Italy. Over the years I met many of his OSS colleagues, a truly unique collection of soldiers, intellectuals, and adventurers. The OSS was the forerunner of the CIA.

My father at OSS Area H in England 1944, with field artillery insignia on his lapels and British and American parachute wings.

A new Eagle Scout, with my mother and brother Dave at Fort Rucker, 1961. My father took the picture; it was a great day.

Senior counselor at the Scout summer camp at Yorktown, Virginia. The summer before going to VMI.

Just before graduation and commissioning as an Army second lieutenant at VMI, June 1967.

Jumpmaster course, 82nd Airborne Division, Fort Bragg, North Carolina, 1967. Two of the men in this photo were killed in Vietnam, two others, myself included, wounded.

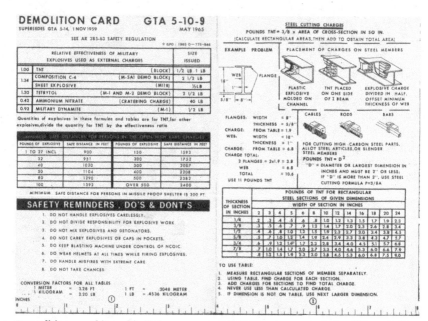

Demolitions card issued in Ranger course, 1967. I've never needed to blow a bridge or derail a train since.

George S, Patton as commanding officer, 11th Armored Cavalry Regiment in Vietnam, 1968. A great soldier and family friend, he retired as a major general. Source: Patton Family Archives.

My infantry platoon in the 82nd Airborne at Fort Bragg, North Carolina, deploying to Vietnam during the Tet Offensive, 1968. Hartnett and Beaver are smoking pipes; Torres, who would discover the mass grave at Hué, stands to the right, with 101st Airborne insignia from a previous combat tour on his right shoulder.

The indomitable Cathy Leroy, the correspondent who talked her way onto the only mass tactical parachute assault of the Vietnam War, in operation Junction City, 1967. Source: Photograph by Bob Cole Courtesy of the Dotation Catherine LeRoy.

Captured at Hué during the Tet Offensive in 1968, French-speaking Cathy Leroy charmed the enemy. Her iconic photo she took of enemy soldiers made the cover of the 16 February 1968 issue of *LIFE* magazine. Source: Courtesy of the Donation Catherine LeRoy.

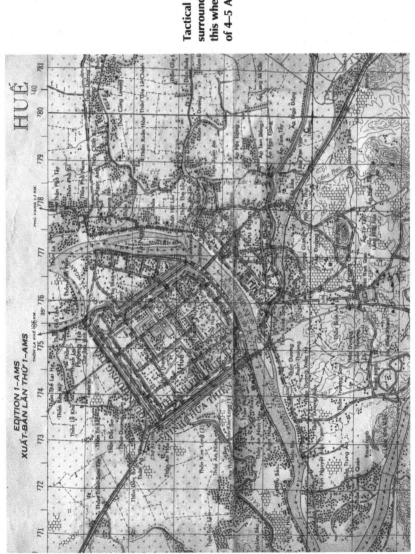

Tactical map sheet of Hué and surrounding area. I was carrying this when wounded on the night of 4–5 April 1968.

Not much cover or concealment in the terrain, as seen behind this group. I am in the center, with Hartnett on my right. Torres stands second from right, beside our sniper, whose M14 bears an early version of the "starlight" passive night-vision scope.

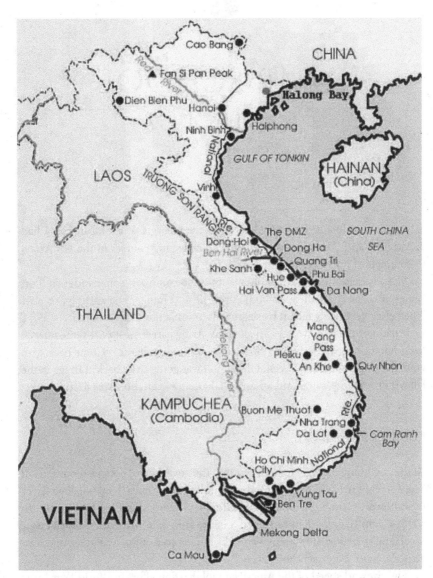

The principal cities of Vietnam are shown on this map. The "DMZ" divides North Vietnam and South Vietnam. Source: Mobile Riverine Force Association.

9

JUMP SCHOOL

June–July 1967

I f North Carolina in June was hot, southern Georgia was a lot hotter. I had Airborne and Ranger, two of the most challenging courses in the US Army, to complete at Fort Benning.

The message from Captain Juan, my first company commander at Fort Bragg, was stark: get through both Airborne and Ranger successfully, or else. The "else" very likely meant reassignment to some non-Airborne unit.

It had not been the way I expected my Army career to start. I remembered the admonition given to young Spartans about to join battle: "Come back with your shields, or on them." Well, I thought, I was going to be back at Bragg in the fall with parachute wings and a Ranger tab; that was all there was to it.

FORT BENNING

At the beginning of the twentieth century, the government bought thousands of acres of marginal land near Columbus, a mill town on the Chattahoochee River in southwest Georgia. Until the United States entered the First World War in 1917, Camp Benning had remained a backwater. After America declared war, several units trained at Benning before becoming part of the AEF, the American Expeditionary Force sent to France.

The size and speed of the American mobilization effort in World War I was astonishing. From a standing Army of just over one hundred thousand in 1917, the United States trained, equipped, and transported over two million men to France by the summer of 1918. Half of them participated in decisive campaigns and battles at Second Marne, Chateau-Thierry, Belleau Wood, Saint-Mihiel, and others before the war ended in November 1918.

After the "Great War," as it was then known, the Army shrank back to a shadow of its wartime strength. A tank school was established at Benning; Dwight Eisenhower and George Patton were both briefly assigned. In 1920 the camp became Fort Benning, a permanent Army post. It has remained the home of American Infantry since.

George Marshall, then a lieutenant colonel and later to become a four-star general and Chief of Staff of the Army, served as assistant commandant of the Infantry School in 1927. He radically revised the Infantry training program, still heavily weighted toward trench warfare tactics, as had been experienced in the recent war.

Under Marshall's leadership, the Infantry School became an incubator for innovative ideas and tactics, many of which became doctrine, to be applied in the crucible of World War II. In the interwar years Marshall carefully watched the officers serving as instructors at the Infantry School. He is said to have kept a list of those with potential to become general officers, in a greatly expanded US Army. Stillwell, Eisenhower, Bradley, Hodges, and others on that list would be jumped several ranks at the beginning of World War II, gaining their stars as the Army grew to nine and a half million men.

AIRBORNE FORCES

The concept of delivering American combat troops to the battlefield by parachute was first contemplated in October–November 1918. At that time, the fortress city of Metz, on the Moselle River in northeastern France, was a heavily defended German strong point. Reducing Metz by conventional artillery bombardment and infantry assault was considered too costly.

A radical plan to take Metz was developed by Brigadier General "Billy" Mitchell and Major Lewis Brereton, two visionary US Army aviators. Soldiers of the 1st Infantry Division would be trained as parachutists. Dropping from converted bombers, they would land behind German lines, near Metz. Their parachute landing, coordinated with a simultaneous ground assault by American infantry, would subject the German defenses to attack from two directions: ground and air. This daring plan presaged the concept of "vertical envelopment," in which troops, either airdropped or air-landed, attack the enemy's position from the rear or flanks, as in the airborne and glider assaults made during the Second World War, more than two decades later.

In the late 1920s, Italy was first to develop airborne infantry units in which all soldiers were trained as parachutists. In 1935, Soviet Russia also conducted large-scale airborne maneuvers, dropping thousands of parachutists, with supporting light vehicles and artillery.

Military attachés from other nations closely watched the Russian maneuvers; among them were officers who would establish Germany's airborne training school in 1936. In its invasions of Norway, Denmark, and Holland in 1940, Germany was first to use parachute infantry and engineer units in combat. German airborne assaults captured key bridges, airfields, and other objectives using several thousand parachutists, and glider-borne troops.

In spite of its 1919 planning for the use of airborne infantry, the US Army was significantly slower than the Europeans in entering the airborne game. A parachute test platoon made the first American military jumps at Fort Benning's Lawson Army Airfield in August 1940. Additional training was conducted in New Jersey on huge 250-foot parachute towers, feature attractions at the 1939 World's Fair. Two of the New Jersey towers were purchased by the Army and reerected at Benning.

In June 1967, I was looking forward to jump school. My father had served in the World War II Office of Strategic Services; he wore both American and British parachute wings on his uniform. Growing up, I knew many of his colleagues who wore the silver American parachutist's badge. I had volunteered for assignment to an airborne unit, and regardless of Captain Juan's peremptory dismissal, I was itching to do it.

GROUND WEEK

After a bumpy flight from Fayetteville down to Columbus on a Southern Airways jet, I signed in at 47th Student Company at Fort Benning. Mike, my VMI classmate with whom I had begun that first memorable day in the Army, signed in a few hours later. While not as brutally straightforward as mine, his 82nd Airborne company commander had sent him to Benning for the next jump class as well. We roomed together in an upstairs portion of the student bachelor officer's quarters. It was a converted World War II troop barracks, divided up almost exactly like the quarters my family lived in at Fort Dix in the late 1940s.

Ground Week of the three-week parachute course started before dawn next morning. Each day's first formations were held on the verge of the huge, flat Airborne Training Area. It was known as the "frying pan" for the incredible heat and humidity generated by the Georgia sun.

Before the sun rose and heat built up, we went through various calisthenics, followed by laps around the perimeter track, in formation. We didn't run individually; we "double-timed" in formation at a fast trot, everyone in step. Running those miles in leather combat boots with little to no arch support probably presaged a lot of foot and ankle problems down the years. The Army didn't seem to care.

I've never understood why so much time in the Army of that time was dedicated to running, in formation, while chanting generally obscene doggerel. It was part of the training ethos of those Cold War years, in which a lot of effort seemed to be expended in ensuring that soldiers were as uncomfortable as possible.

Rather than seeing it as a form of unit bonding, it seemed to be some sort of challenge. You either participated and kept up or were singled out for further attention. Rites of passage? Trial by endurance? I'm sure, but I've never fully understood the utility.

The double-time rhythm enabled chanting while we ran, usually led by whoever was in charge of the formation. He would sing the lead; we responded, as in:

If I die in the combat zone,
Box me up and ship me home.
Tell my gal I done my best,
Bury me in the leaning rest.

More ambitious:

C-130 runnin' down the strip,
Airborne Ranger on a one-way trip.
Mission secret, where unknown,
Don't rightly know if I'm goin' home.
Stand-up, hook-up, shuffle to the door,
Jump right out and count to four.
If my main don't open wide,
I've got another chute by my side.

There were endless variations. Where did we learn them? In the 1960s, as soldiers, officer candidates, or cadets as we moved through basic training, ROTC, or West Point, there was never a formal unit of instruction in "Ridiculous and in Many Cases Outright Obscene Running Chants." It was taught on the side, in the many opportunities while we were "learning the basics" of drill, running, or simply marching as a unit from one place to another.

The instructors in the Airborne Department were all very physically fit noncommissioned officers. In that summer of 1967, they wore faded, starched green fatigue trousers bloused into highly shined Corcoran parachute boots, white T-shirts with their name and rank stenciled across the front, and black baseball hats, on which were pinned their parachute wings and rank insignia. They were verbal, sharp, and quick, awarding twenty or fifty push-ups for the slightest inattention or lack of speed in response to an order.

We were all young, so the physical part of the training was bearable. The heat and humidity, though, were ferocious. We were issued salt tablets and water several times a day. Every so often training paused while we walked under huge frames of overhead pipes with spray nozzles, soaking us with cool water. Minutes later we would be bone dry again. A few became dizzy from the heat; they were told by a "black hat" to go sit in the shade and "pop a salt tablet."

The cinder running track of Eubanks Field circled sets of bleachers, mock-ups of aircraft fuselages, huge sheds covering the swing landing trainers, and platforms from which we practiced parachute landing falls.

The thirty-four-foot towers enabled practicing appropriate exits from jump aircraft. They were big boxes mounted atop four enormous poles, with stair-ways from ground level. On each side of the boxes, a curved doorway opened out into space. Cables ran alongside the doorways, slanting away about seventy-five yards to an earthen berm.

Across the field were three enormous, cross-armed, 250-foot towers, from which we would make our first "free descents" under opened canopies.

Ground Week was focused entirely on how to wear the T-10 military back-pack parachute and the smaller reserve chute, worn in front; the series of orders and movement inside an aircraft leading to exiting in a "good tight body posi-tion"; and how to land, performing a proper parachute landing fall, or PLF, while traveling in any direction.

The Army has an impressive safety record in parachuting. It requires two weeks of training before an airborne student performs his first jumps. I remem-ber the sign on the wall of the parachute packing sheds at Lawson field, where we would draw parachutes for our five qualifying jumps: "The sky, even more than the sea, is unforgiving of the slightest mistake." If ever there was an under-statement, that's one of the best.

COLONEL LAMAR

A memorable moment during Ground Week was the appearance of Colonel Lamar, the commandant of the Airborne Department. It was midafternoon of one of the hottest days in the course. We were variously soaked with sweat or with water from the cooling sprays, but Colonel Lamar, wearing the full Class A uniform of tan shirt and black tie under Army-green blouse, green trousers, and spit-shined parachute boots, looked spotless, dry, and sharp.

He wore the green fore-and-aft cloth flat cap known formally as the overseas cap, less formally as the "piss cutter." On one side of his cap was pinned the silver eagle of a full colonel. On the other was sewn the red-bordered, circular patch designed in World War II, with its embroidered white glider and white parachute against a sky-blue background. His silver Master Parachutist's badge had a single gold star, marking a parachute jump into combat. On his left shoulder looped the green and red, interwoven braided cord of the *fourragère*, awarded to American airborne forces by the Belgian government in World War II. His black Corcoran parachute boots gleamed.

The word was that Colonel Lamar had been commissioned in World War II just in time to be assigned as a second lieutenant to the 82nd Airborne Division, when it badly needed replacement officers following the invasion of Normandy in June 1944. I've been unable to find information on his World War II service, but he was an impressive officer and ran the Airborne Department like an efficient machine. In 1967 there was a great need for qualified parachutists. The Army had two full Airborne divisions of fifteen thousand men each: the 82nd at Fort Bragg and the 101st, then in Vietnam. It had two separate Airborne brigades of about seven thousand men each: the independent 173rd, then in Vietnam, and a brigade of the 1st Air Cavalry Division, also in Vietnam.

In addition, the Army had several Special Forces Groups scattered around the world, all of which were airborne. The Airborne Department trained personnel of other branches of the US armed forces and selected US agencies as parachutists, as well as officers and men from Allied nations.

Colonel Lamar was a highly intelligent man. He had a deep, natural Southern drawl that he could accentuate when he desired. He had come down to see us, he said, to "Pep y'all up a bit." His "pep talk" actually sounded something like this:

> Boys [he pronounced it "Bwahz," drawled with a big smile], ah know y'er hot an' tah'rd. Ah know y'all would rather be behin' a cold beer, or at home with yer girls. Or both! [laughter from our class] But ah know y'er gonna stay the course

and become Yew-nited States Army paratroopers! [cheers, whoops] When y'all graduate, y'er gonna be sharp! Y'er gonna stand out! Y'er gonna be makin' that extra, hazardous duty pay, an' y'er gonna be wearin' those silver wings, an' that glider patch on yer hats, and that foo-rah-jay on yer shoulders [he tapped his *fourragère*], an' those shiny jump boots! Y'er gonna look like a million bucks! Y'er gonna look like heroes, an' the girls'r gonna love yew! An' you know what? You haven't heard a single shot fahr'd yet!

The class was convulsed. We were hooting and hollering. Colonel Lamar knew what he was doing. It made a big difference. Sure, we wanted those wings; to have a soldier of his stature come down and give us that talk, in his "good ol' boy" manner, was absolutely fabulous.

LEARNING THE BASICS

The first week began with learning to tumble, roll, and recover from parachute landing falls. Harnessed and suspended in the landing trainers, we jumped off twenty-foot platforms, swinging back and forth until the black-hatted instructor sergeant released the restraining line without warning, sending us into the sawdust from various heights, forward, backward, and to either side, executing the PLFs.

We lined up inside fuselage mock-ups, endlessly running through the entire series of jumpmaster commands. From "Stand up!" through hooking our static lines to the anchor cable, checking our equipment and the backpack of the man in front, sounding off the count from the last man in the stick forward, to the jumpmaster's command, pointing to the first man, "Stand in the door!"

Jumping from the mock-up doorways and shouting, "One thousand! Two thousand! Three Thousand! Four thousand!" we assumed the tight body position that would prevent spinning in the more than one-hundred-mile-an-hour wind blast, which could twist our parachute canopy and risers as they deployed from the backpack tray.

At the "Four thousand!" count, we reached up with both hands, simulating grasping the two risers extending from our harnesses, looking up to check our canopy. If we didn't see it, or if it was fouled so it wasn't inflating, we would simulate pulling the D handle of our reserve parachutes.

From there it would either be salvation as the reserve opened, or "Katy bar the door" if it didn't, a term I heard often in the Army in those days, denoting a pending catastrophe.

We practiced recovering from being dragged by our parachutes by lying on our backs with the shroud lines and parachute canopy stretched out on the ground behind us. A big, powerful fan inflated the canopy, dragging us until we could twist ourselves to dig in a knee, get to our feet and run around behind the canopy, collapsing it, or release the connector link on one of our harness risers, allowing the canopy to spill its air.

All around in that huge airborne training area were the constant sounds of men running, chanting in the parachute drills, sounding off for the instructors, the droning of aircraft far off, men stamping their boots on the stairs to the thirty-four-foot towers, the roar of the fan inflating chutes for the drag release, the barking of the black hats. And a metallic voice from the 250-foot towers, where the instructor on the ground spoke by bullhorn to men hanging in their harnesses from the towers' arms: "Are you ready on Three? Drop Three!"

Ground Week instilled "muscle knowledge," ensuring that every man performed alike in a situation where a slight error could result in serious injury or a terrible death. I remembered that hung jumper I saw on my first day at Bragg and paid attention.

That first weekend I was tired and stayed pretty much in our quarters to catch up on sleep. I went to the snack bar at the Officers Club on Sunday afternoon. Arrayed around its swimming pool were a number of females on loungers, to whom much attention was paid by a bevy of very fit young officers.

10

TOWER WEEK
July 1967

Compared to Ground Week, Tower Week was actually fun. The thirty-four-foot towers trained us to exit an aircraft properly, leaping out into space. Our harnesses were hooked to a trolley that ran on cables beside the doors on either side of the boxes atop the towers.

As we exited the doors, feet and knees together, both hands on our reserve chutes, heads down, we dropped about six feet and were brought up short, then slid, bouncing and loudly counting to "four thousand!" with our boots and knees together, along the cables, to be stopped and unhooked by other students atop an earthen berm. After we had done it satisfactorily, we were relegated to the berm or to other duties. I was only able to get three rides on the cables before being marked proficient and relegated to the berm detail.

The 250-foot towers were the unsurpassed "E-ticket" rides. They were enormous, of latticed construction, wide enough to straddle a two-story building between their four legs, and tapering to a set of four crossed arms at the very top. Each arm extended seventy feet. Painted in alternating orange and white segments and topped by anticollision air beacons at night, the towers dominated the Benning skyline.

The building at the base of each tower housed the winches for the cables that lifted the jumpers. The cables ran up to pulleys at the top of the tower, out along each arm, through another pulley, and down to the ground. At their ends, each cable connected to a circular ring thirty-five feet in diameter, the size of the deployed canopy of the T-10 parachute. The canopies were rigged, open, to the rings by students, with the black hats supervising.

The rigged canopies in the ring were hoisted a few feet above the student in the harness. Since the canopies were already fully deployed in the ring, there was no need for a reserve, or emergency, parachute. Depending on the wind direction and speed, each tower could hoist and drop two or three students at a time.

The instructor on the ground would give the command to the winch operator in the tower, "Lift Three!" and you had the greatest ride in the school so far, rising above all of Fort Benning and looking way out into Alabama, across the river.

As you reached the top, suspended under the arm, the instructor would call out on the bullhorn, "Are you ready on Three? Drop Three!" The winch pulled you upward a few feet to the release latch, there was a metallic click, your canopy detached from the ring, and you floated down, keeping your feet and knees together, getting ready to execute that perfect PLF.

The cycle of rigging, lifting, and dropping students from the tower was pretty slow. I only managed to jump the tower once, but it was great, a little preview of what was to come in Jump Week. Of note was the fact that when we would make our five jumps, they would be from aircraft flying at twelve hundred feet, five times as high as the towers.

I was in a group rigging a parachute to the ring when a black hat barked out, "Foxtrot Zero Seven! Get over here!" We were out of earshot; I doubt anyone could have heard him with all the yelling and bullhorn noise anyway. He looked at my name tape and said, "You have an emergency call. There's a phone handset in the box on the outside wall of that building." He pointed to the winch house at the base of the tower. "The operator is holding your call. Report back here when you finish."

I ran over, opened the box, and picked up the handset. The operator connected the call. It was my mom; my grandfather had passed away in New York City. In the brief conversation that followed, I asked her if she needed me at home; I could get emergency leave if necessary and restart the jump course in another cycle. Her response was all "Army mom": "No; we'll be OK; you stay at Benning and finish your course. Love from everyone here."

When I reported back, the black hat was another human being for a moment. "Are you OK, Lieutenant?" He looked concerned. I nodded. He stepped back into his instructor role. "Right! Get in there and start rigging!"

DINNER WITH THE GENERAL

The second weekend, I decided to go to the Officers Club for a decent dinner. In those days, on weekends the dining rooms at Officers Clubs on the big Army posts were usually filled with families and groups. I wore a blazer, slacks, and tie and checked in with the host at the door.

"We're all filled up," he said, "but I can ask the gentleman by the window," he indicated a man sitting alone at a table for two, "if he wouldn't mind." He walked over and spoke briefly with an elderly man in a dark blue, almost black coat and black-and-gold striped tie. He nodded, and the host motioned me over.

It was a memorable evening. He was a retired general, a veteran of both world wars. He lived in Columbus. His wife had passed some years before; occasionally he came to the club for dinner. He had steel-gray eyes. He smiled when he heard I was in the airborne course. "They gave Omar Bradley the 82nd, you know, when it was being organized," he said. "He took the parachute course, then they gave the division to Matt Ridgway."

I was fascinated. He had known Patton, Eisenhower, many of the "greats." Of Marshall, he said, "A genius in organization, but couldn't remember names, even of his own secretary. No man is perfect."

At one point I asked him, in the manner of all feckless junior officers, "Sir, if you hadn't been Infantry, what would you have been?"

He smiled. "If I hadn't been Infantry, son, I would have been ashamed."

I've always remembered that evening and chance meeting as a window into another Army and another time. He was a total gentleman at table, but I didn't envy the enemy that had gone up against him on the battlefield.

11

JUMP WEEK

July 1967

Monday dawned bright and hot. Jump Week required five parachute jumps: four in daylight, one at night. Four would be "Hollywood" jumps, without any extra equipment; one would require a Griswold weapons bag, worn on the left side, and a "PAE" bag for personal additional equipment, hung below our reserve chutes. We would do the jumps from two different types of aircraft: the four-engine, turboprop C-130 Hercules and the four-engine jet C-141 Starlifter.

After a last review of the in-aircraft safety procedures and jumpmaster's commands, beginning with the six-minute warning, we were trucked out to Lawson Field. We lined up outside the packing sheds to draw our parachutes from the riggers.

"TRY JUMPING WITHOUT US"

In the original World War II airborne units, the troops packed their own parachutes, but the Army had since evolved to a more efficient solution. Parachute riggers are specialists in parachute packing and preparing various types of equipment loads for aerial delivery by parachute, from personnel to multiple cargo chutes of many sizes and types.

Riggers pack every chute with meticulous detail, supervised at each step. When finished, each signs the little logbook tucked inside a pocket on every parachute. They are intensely proud of their skill and work. Their motto, seen on every rigging shed in the Army, is "Try jumping without us."

At Lawson Field, the packed main and reserve chutes were neatly lined up in long rows on trestle tables, behind which stood the riggers watching us pick them up. Normally, men filed down the table, picking up the last chute in each row. But humans are superstitious. Every so often, for a reason known only to the individual, a soldier would select another.

In such situations, a watching Rigger would take the chute that had been passed by off the table and put it on a table behind him. Nothing was said. I had occasion once to ask a rigger what was done in such a case. He replied, "The rigger will jump that chute, often joining the 'stick' of the man who passed it by, to show we do our jobs right and we stand by our work." Impressive.

THE T-10 PARACHUTE

In the 1960s, the T-10 main parachute we jumped weighed thirty-one pounds. It was on a harness we put on like a backpack, with two straps that hung down in the rear and were brought forward between the legs. The two over-the-shoulder and two crotch straps were snapped into a quick-release buckle on the chest. The buckle had a circular metal disk; rotated ninety degrees and smacked, it released the straps.

The T-10's thirty-five-foot canopy and thirty suspension lines were carefully and tightly folded, secured with rubber bands, then packed tightly with the folded nylon canopy into a deployment bag on the harness's backpack tray.

The apex of the canopy, the small circular hole in the top that lets air flow through, was tied with a "break cord" to a fifteen-foot yellow nylon "static line," gathered and secured across the closed backpack with rubber bands. Enough slack was left in the static line to be passed over the jumper's right shoulder, with its snap hook clipped to the carrying handle of the reserve parachute, worn on the front of the harness. That kept the static line from being fouled until the jumper stood up, at the jumpmaster's command.

After standing up, the jumper connected the snap hook to a steel anchor cable running overhead, down the length of the interior of the aircraft. As he jumped, the static line paid out from the backpack, pulling the canopy from the deployment bag on his backpack tray. When the full length of the canopy and suspension lines were extracted, the "break cord" was snapped by the jumper's weight. The prop blast and speed of the aircraft accelerated the canopy's deployment and inflation.

Developed in the 1950s, the T-10 was packed so that its canopy inflated gradually, slowing the jumper in about four seconds from about 130 miles an hour to a descent under the inflated canopy of about 26 feet per second.

The T-10 was a big improvement over the T-7 parachute of the Second World War. The T-7's canopy snapped open immediately, subjecting the jumper to a severe "opening shock." Even at low speeds of one hundred miles per hour, the T-7's opening shock could rip holsters, canteens, weapons, and cargo packs off the jumper, with the parachute's harness inflicting bruises on shoulders and crotches. In spite of the World War II airborne helmet's unique leather chin cup and double straps, the jumpers' helmets were also occasionally torn off. Bruises inflicted by the harnesses, called "riser marks," were so common on airborne men of that generation that they were considered "symbols of passage."

FIVE JUMPS

All our five qualifying jumps would be by static line. The first two were made on the same day, from turboprop C-130 Hercules transports. Nervous as a plane-load of cats, we focused on every detail. We lined up in two long rows behind the aircraft and were checked front and back by a pair of NCO jumpmasters. Each had passed a rigorous course conducted at Benning or Bragg, covering all aspects of military parachuting. They coordinated with the Air Force flight crew and would control all actions inside the plane, clearing the aircraft's exterior before permitting the first men to stand in the door, and our exits over the drop zone.

As we were each checked and passed, the jumpmasters tapped us on the butt, and we walked up the tail ramp, filling the long webbing seats on either side. It was much hotter than outside; a lot of us were probably sweating from more than the heat, myself included.

The engines started and were run up; the tail ramp whined up and locked. The plane began to move. I was partly scared, mostly excited, hoping I would remember to do everything we had learned in two weeks on the ground, and that the parachutes I was wearing would work. I do remember saying a quick prayer to Saint Michael the Archangel, patron saint of paratroopers.

We took off, climbed out to the peacetime jump altitude of 1,200 feet, beginning a wide "racetrack" circuit. After ten minutes or so, two Air Force crewmen unlocked the troop jump doors on either side, slid them up, and locked them. Immediately the troop compartment filled with cooler air and the roaring of the four turboprop engines.

A few minutes later, one of the jumpmasters stood between the doors in the center of the rows of seats. He held out five fingers extended on one hand, one on the other. "Six minutes!" Every head turned toward him.

"Stand up!" As we stood up and faced him, he lifted both hands above his head, index fingers curled. "Hook up!" We reached up with our right hands and snapped the hooks of our static lines downward onto the anchor cable, giving them a tug downward to ensure they were securely connected.

"Check equipment!" Carefully we each traced the yellow static line of the man in front of us, ensuring it was securely fastened across the man's parachute pack, leading over his right shoulder, not under his arm.

"Sound off for equipment check!"

"OK! OK! OK! OK!" The count was passed up from the rear of each file of jumpers, proceeding to the first man in the stick, who called out, "All OK!"

The jumpmaster, wearing a parachute and hooked to the anchor cable himself, turned to the open starboard, or right-hand, door. Planting his boots on the inside frame, he grasped the door edges. Pushing himself out into the prop blast, looking forward, then aft and down, he ensured there were no aircraft trailing to endanger the jumpers. Pulling himself back in, he repeated the process at the port side door.

I was four or five men back in our stick of jumpers, watching him over the shoulders of the men in front. He pointed to the first man in each file. "Stand in the door!" They shuffled into the door and assumed the jump position, hands grasping the outside of the doors, knees slightly bent. The jumpmaster watched the red light in the panel beside the door. It switched to green. "GO!"

The men ahead of me went out, swept from sight as they cleared the door. I grabbed the door edges and jumped, snapping my hands onto my reserve chute, right hand on the D ring of my reserve, head bent, chin tucked in, feet and knees together.

Films of paratroopers jumping from airplanes don't do justice to the sensation of jumping into the sudden brightness, filled with the roaring engines, windblast, and the incredible feeling of falling away as I counted, "One thousand! Two thousand! Three thousand!" and felt my chute slowing me as it opened at "Four thousand!" I reached up, grabbed the two web risers extending from my shoulders, and looked at that big, beautiful, translucent olive-green canopy overhead.

I was facing back down the track of the plane. A descending series of green parachutes stair-stepped down ahead of me. It was like the 250-foot towers on steroids—far higher, with a whole crowd of people in the air.

We were told to keep a close eye on other jumpers; if one passed beneath you, his canopy would create a dead space, "robbing the air" from yours. If you didn't or couldn't steer away, you were in danger of your chute collapsing. In such cases, jumpers had dropped into the canopy below, entangling both men and, depending on the altitude, plummeting both to severe injury or death.

The T-10 parachute in the 1960s was about as steerable as a boxcar with marshmallows for wheels. You could haul on one riser or the other to try and spill some air from that side of the canopy to make it slowly go in that direction, but as far as steering, good luck.

We were assured there was enough rigidity in the canopy of the jumper below us that we could literally run across it and slide off the edge. What that meant as far as my own canopy staying inflated, I didn't know, and I didn't want to find out.

Fortunately no one was near me; the ride down wasn't more than a minute. Black hats with bullhorns on the drop zone called instructions to jumpers here and there. The last few moments passed rapidly, the ground coming up fast; I hit hard and tumbled in a decent PLF, jumping up and running around to gather my chute.

A punch to my quick release, and the harness fell open. We had stowed our folded gray-green parachute bags behind the quick releases. I laid my bag out on the ground and unzipped it, gathering the parachute harness, canopy and shroud lines in a rolling motion with both arms. Stuffing it all in the bag and zipping it closed, I slung it over my head and carried it on my back as I trotted off the drop zone, keeping a wary eye out for other jumpers coming down around me.

We were trucked back to Lawson Field and did the second jump that afternoon. If there were any jump refusals or injuries, I didn't hear of them. Everyone was tired and pretty happy by the end of the day. We'd had a taste of jumping; we wanted more.

The week passed so fast it was hard to keep track. The third jump was daylight, with equipment: a Griswold weapon bag under the left arm, a PAE cargo bag under the reserve. No weapon; the PAE bag was stuffed with something that just made it fill out. I had seen pictures of the paratroops loading for the D-Day jumps in 1944; both pieces of gear hadn't changed much since.

The third jump was from a C-130, as uneventful as the first two.

The fourth was a night jump, from the C-141 Starlifter. Bigger than the C-130, it was a long, sleek four-engine jet with drooping wings and a high T-tail. We chuted up just after dark, went through the jumpmaster checks, and loaded. The interior was lit only by overhead red lights to preserve our night vision. Under the helmets, our faces and the jumpmasters' were in dark shadow, lending an eerie tone to the scene.

The roar of jets on the flight out to the drop zone was much louder than the C-130's turboprops. The safety checks and jump commands were the same, but our exit was slightly different. The Starlifters had a wind deflector that deployed when the jump doors were opened and locked in the "up" position. Because of them we jumped into surprisingly little turbulence, but once we cleared the deflectors, we shot back and down like leaves on a windy day.

My canopy popped open at the count of three. Floating down through the night, I was surrounded by dark, dangerous blobs; I looked above and behind for jumpers floating in over my canopy, and other jumpers below.

As in previous jumps, the ground came up fast. I wasn't well prepared for it this time. Hitting hard traveling backward, I landed in an uncontrolled "crash and burn" maneuver. Luckily I had no injuries; even better that it was dark and no black hats noticed.

Final jump day was hotter than any in the previous three weeks. I put on fresh fatigues with no rank or shoulder insignia; I was going to report to the Ranger course right after getting those wings; no insignia were allowed in Ranger.

Looking down the runway at the airfield, antennas and structures at the far end seemed to float a few feet off the ground, as in a mirage. Inside the riggers' sheds, huge fans blew the hot, heavy air over us. It was another Hollywood jump; this time when we landed, we would be paratroopers. Neophytes, yes, but you have to start somewhere.

When the canopy popped open and I saw that drop zone between my boots, it was a feeling of relief and accomplishment. The black hats on the ground were booming encouragement upward on their bullhorns: "Lookin' good, jumpers! Lookin' good! Feet and knees together!"

My PLF on that fifth jump was far and away the best of the week. I rolled my chute and hustled over to the marshaling point. Everyone was chattering away; a few of the black hats were shaking hands and slapping troops on the back. We were formed up and called to attention. Colonel Lamar, in starched fatigues and those gleaming jump boots, stood us at ease, congratulated us on becoming paratroopers, then passed down the ranks, handing each of us a set of silver parachute wings.

We were released and stood around pinning the badges on each other and shaking hands. It was a great day. Now I had to get across the post, out to Harmony Church, and report to the Ranger Department. One down, one to go.

12

RANGER

July–September 1967

Colonel Benjamin Church raised a company of the first "rangers" in colonial America in 1676. His men were trained by friendly natives in tribal techniques of scouting, tracking, and fighting. With those skills and the ability to operate far away on the frontiers in areas and terrain not suited to conventional forces, Church's rangers were very different from colonial militiamen or soldiers serving in "regular" British infantry regiments.

The most famous colonial ranger unit, to which contemporary US Army Rangers trace their heritage, was raised by Robert Rogers in 1751 during the French and Indian War. A British officer, Rogers developed his "Rules for Rangers," a set of guidelines for his nine companies of men, covering the basics of their tactics and operations. His "Rogers' Rules" are taught to US Army Rangers today.

At the outset of the American Revolution, Rogers is reported to have offered his services to George Washington, who, suspecting that Rogers might be a British spy, turned him down. Stung by the rebuttal, Rogers proceeded to raise the Queen's Rangers, a unit that conducted patrolling, reconnaissance, and raiding operations, well in advance of British regular forces. As a British officer, Rogers was also responsible for unmasking a young American, a spy, who was returning from a mission in which, in civilian clothes, he had gathered information on the British forces then occupying New York City. On his way back to report on his mission, Nathan Hale met Rogers, also in civilian clothes, in a tavern. Hale mistakenly took Rogers to be another like-minded revolutionary. It was a fatal mistake. Hale was arrested and hanged by the British. He is celebrated as a patriot by the American intelligence community today. At the same time, Rogers is admired by the US Army as the father of its Rangers. History is full of ironies.

EVOLUTION

In World War II, the Army developed independent Ranger battalions, which fought with great effect in Europe and the Pacific as reconnaissance, raiding, and specialized assault forces. Possibly the most famous Ranger operations in each major theater of that war were the assault on a German artillery position atop Pointe du Hoc at Normandy on D-Day in 1944, and the Los Banos prison raid in the Philippines in 1945, freeing 2,417 Allied POWs on the eve of execution by their Japanese guards.

Independent companies of Rangers conducted raiding and reconnaissance missions during the Korean War. After Korea, Ranger companies were disbanded. While no organized Ranger units remained, the Army decided that training in Ranger skills would be beneficial to selected officers and noncommissioned officers. The Ranger Department was established at the Infantry School at Fort Benning, Georgia, in 1951.

THE RANGER COURSE

Developed at Fort Benning, the Ranger course is regarded as the best small-unit leadership course in the Army. Designed to push a student to the extreme limits of his endurance, Ranger demonstrates he can perform at that boundary and beyond. Every man who has graduated from the Ranger course has experienced that lesson.

In the 1960s, the two most intense qualification courses in the Army were Ranger and the longer Special Forces Qualification, or "Q," course. Passing either was an achievement that set graduates distinctly apart from other soldiers.

As a boy, I knew Army officers, friends of my father's, who had graduated from Ranger. Without exception, they were impressive. Like them, I would endure extreme hardship to earn the right to wear that curved black-and-yellow RANGER tab on my left shoulder.

In the 1960s the Ranger course was nine weeks, nonstop, twenty-four hours a day. Divided into three-week phases, the first phase was at Fort Benning, where students were taught the elements of patrolling, land navigation, and a number of other skills.

The Ranger Department used the patrol as a training unit. It defined a patrol as "a unit formed and sent out from a larger unit." Patrols are independent formations, usually operating forward or away from the main body of friendly forces; their makeup and weapons vary according to the mission and type of soldiers available.

Instruction in the three-week "Benning phase" focused on patrols with two different missions. Reconnaissance patrols avoided detection by the enemy while surreptitiously gathering information. Combat or raiding patrols attacked specific targets or objectives, engaging any enemy encountered with maximum violence and/or capturing prisoners for interrogation. Other missions might require a patrol to retrieve a downed "friendly" aviator, contact and lead "friendly" civilian partisans, place mines or other stay-behind munitions, and other nasty chores.

In the Benning phase, intense physical activity, harassment by instructors, and a day-and-night schedule with very little sleep weeded out those judged unlikely to be able to perform in the following six weeks. Ranger classes could easily lose up to 20 percent or more of their students in the Benning phase alone.

In 1967, the heaviest responsibility during patrols was on the student designated as the patrol leader. He had to know his location on the ground at all times and be prepared to maneuver against enemy forces encountered, evade them, or take other actions as necessary. Patrol leaders had to stay on top of the mission at all times (known as maintaining "situational awareness") and think fast in unexpected situations.

Patrols were carried out by day and night at Benning; each required different formations and movements; all required severe restriction of noise, and of lights at night. Those were also the days before GPS; land navigation skills were critical. We'll talk more about that a bit later.

The second three-week phase was conducted at the Mountain Ranger Camp at Dahlonega, Georgia, north of Atlanta. In the mountains of North Georgia, Ranger students learned mountaineering and climbing skills, in addition to conducting more extensive patrolling in the rugged, heavily forested terrain.

The final three weeks were at the Florida Ranger Camp on the huge Eglin Air Force Base reservation, in Florida's northwestern "panhandle." At Eglin, students patrolled in the swamps while learning additional skills in survival and waterborne operations.

At various times during the Vietnam War, the Ranger course also included airborne operations for parachute-qualified students and, in one case at least, experiments in developing instruction in long-range patrolling.

On graduating from the Ranger course at the Florida camp, students were returned to Benning to out-process, then released back to their parent units.

NECESSITIES

As a result of my banishment by Captain Juan, the headquarters of my battalion of the 82nd Airborne had generated orders assigning me to both the Airborne and Ranger classes at Fort Benning. Having completed the parachute training, I was now assigned as a student to Ranger class 2-67. That is, the second Ranger course conducted by the Ranger Department in its 1967 training year. Accompanying my orders was a single mimeographed page advising students to privately purchase an M1950 Korean War–era patrol cap and a good utility knife, as well as various small items such as parachute cord (also known as "shroud line") and extra boot socks.

You might ask why, if the Ranger course was such a big deal, the Army didn't issue a patrol cap and a utility knife, and other goodies like parachute cord and boot socks. The answer was "because." No further logic was offered. During my ten years of active service, I would repeatedly encounter "because" as Army logic, in many different situations.

The unofficial word was the caps, knives, and other items could be bought at Ranger Joe's, an Army-surplus store in downtown Columbus, the former mill town on the Chattahoochee River that abutted Fort Benning. There was a connection between the Army's direction to buy that stuff privately and the convenience of Ranger Joe's, which happened to have it. You never know.

On days before classes reported in to the Ranger Department, young men with military haircuts could be seen at Joe's pawing through a big wooden bin filled with used M1950 patrol caps, all with parallel strips of luminous tape sewn on the rear.

Those luminous "cat's eyes" would be necessary on the long night patrols during the course. In many cases they would be the only way a Ranger could maintain his position with others in his patrol in the total darkness of the forest. The two dim glimmers of light would be critical. Even so, many Rangers, exhausted and on the verge of sleeping standing up during brief patrol halts, dozily stared at spots of luminescent tree bark, remaining standing as their patrol moved silently away.

In addition to the patrol cap, I bought a Ka-Bar combat knife and sheath. Developed as the answer to the Marine Corps' 1942 requirement for a better fighting and utility knife, the Ka-Bar is a full foot long, with a razor-sharp, seven-inch blade. That terrific knife would accompany me through Ranger and two combat deployments in Vietnam. I added an Army demolition knife: a jackknife with four blades and an awl, supposedly of nonconductive steel. Like the Ka-Bar, it was built to last; those knives have never let me down.

HARMONY CHURCH

In 1967, the Ranger Department was in a complex of World War II–era buildings and barracks at Harmony Church, far off in the pines on the eastern side of the huge Fort Benning reservation. Sited roughly between the oddly named towns of Box Springs and Cusseta, in the years before the Army bought the land, Harmony Church was home to a sleepy Baptist congregation. In 1967, the place retained its gentle name, but the curriculum that had replaced the Baptists was downright lethal.

It was close to a hundred degrees on report day for Ranger class 2-67, with humidity in the nineties. If I was lucky, in nine weeks I'd be wearing a Ranger tab. If not, I remembered Captain Juan's parting words. That grim option wasn't worth considering.

After graduating from jump school that morning, I had checked out of the 47th Company and hustled straight out to Harmony Church. Students in our Ranger class signed in at a single-story, flaking, green-roofed wooden building. It was painted in the tan-puke shade of almost all Army buildings of that era, baking in a patch of scrub grass and weeds.

A line of students stretched down the cracked sidewalk in front. Some were pumping out push-ups, counting them in loud voices. Others stood at "parade rest," sweating uneasily as a pair of impressively fit-looking Ranger sergeants in black berets walked up and down, eyeing them like falcons sizing up a collection of pigeons.

Students were admitted to the building one at a time. Stamping our boots—One! Two!—on the porch to bang the dust off and shake our fatigue trousers down over the blousing bands, we swept off our caps, barking out our last name first, initials, and service number.

In 1967, each soldier or officer had a unique Army service number, with a two-letter prefix that identified him as Enlisted Volunteer (RA), Enlisted Reservist (ER), Enlisted Draftee (US), National Guard (NG), or Officer (OF). My serial number was OF112154.

I ran over to the rear of the line, went to "parade rest" with my arms behind me, hands interlocked in the small of my back, feet apart, head up, eyes front, and tried to look invisible. Mentally, I quickly ran through my OF service number; this was no time to screw up.

CAPTAIN MARM

Wearing a black beret pulled down over one eye, a Ranger captain smoking a pipe lounged like a coiled snake against the porch railing, ominously regarding us. A vivid red scar ran down one cheek, disappearing under his chin. He didn't just look mean; he looked deadly.

A bit over a year before, he had been in the first really big battle of the war in Vietnam, in the Ia Drang Valley. As a lieutenant and platoon leader in the 7th Cavalry Regiment of the First Air Cavalry Division, he had single-handedly attacked an enemy machine-gun position, which was killing his men from the cover of a rock-solid termite mound.

He first shot a light antitank rocket at the mound, which withstood the rocket's blast without bothering the gun crew. He then charged the position while under fire, across forty yards of open ground. With his M16 rifle and grenades, he killed the gun crew and a number of other enemy soldiers.

During his attack, he was shot through both cheeks, the bullet narrowly missing taking out his teeth. For his courageous and decisive action he was awarded the Medal of Honor. He was Captain Walt Marm, our class tactical officer, and he would watch each of us as we progressed.

When my turn came, I stepped up onto the porch, did the boot stamp, swept off my patrol cap, and sounded off with my service number. I started to step across the threshold.

His teeth clenched on the pipe stem, Captain Marm growled, "Halt." I froze. He uncoiled from the railing, stepped slowly over to me and tapped a finger against the silver parachute badge pinned above my left shirt pocket. "Why are you wearing these?"

He looked skeptical. The instruction sheet had said to remove all rank and qualification insignia from our uniforms before reporting. He may have thought I had put the wings on for some kind of additional edge.

"Sir, I received them this morning." I had screwed up! I forgot to take them off before reporting.

"You graduated jump school today?" His eyes went to my name tag, then to my face.

"Yes, Sir!"

He removed his pipe. "You're one of those doing Airborne and Ranger back-to-back?"

"Yes, Sir!" I looked straight ahead.

"Hmm. Drive on." I shot through the door.

The rest of that day was a blur of running, push-ups, drawing field gear, more push-ups, pounding up the stairs of an old barracks to rows of bunks, squaring the gear away in the order shown on a mimeographed page on each bunk. Pounding down the stairs, more push-ups, signing for an M14 rifle. Running, running, running. The Ranger sergeants nipped at our heels like terriers, singling now one, now another of us, out for more push-ups.

ALL WE NEEDED TO KNOW

We were issued Ranger handbooks. They were four by five inches and a half-inch thick, held together by a single, very heavy staple at the top center. In 130 two-sided pages, the handbook covered everything we needed to know.

First were formats and checklists: warning orders, complete five-page operational orders, and annexes for subjects such as air movement, resupply, small boat linkups, and detailed debriefings.

Next, summaries of subjects covered in the course, including aerial resupply, fire support, booby traps, demolitions, survival, mountaineering, and a few extras, like prayers: Christian, Protestant, and Jewish. I don't know if the current handbooks include them, but in 1967, prayers were there, and welcome; we were a different country then.

Last, diagrams of training areas and confidence tests so that graduate Rangers could set up Ranger training courses elsewhere. I still have my Ranger handbook, thoroughly beaten up, with evidence of being waterlogged and subsequently dried out, just like its owner.

"TONY" AND "BONY"

Sometime before sunset we stood in formation, in the shade of pines. A pair of sergeants first class stood in front of us. The taller was Sergeant Tony, our Class Tactical NCO. He and his shorter, stockier companion, Sergeant Bony, would assist Captain Marm, bird-dogging us for the next nine weeks.

Tony was Hispanic, lean, and perpetually sarcastic. Bony was all Anglo-Saxon, built like a refrigerator. His favorite adjective was "bony." He used it as other NCO's used "fucking," which we would hear more than enough. His delivery was unique, as in "Straighten your bony backs, you bony Rangers!" as we counted out fifty push-ups, or "Pick up your bony feet!" as we double-timed from one class to another, to the mess hall, to the weapons range, anywhere.

As Ranger students, our fatigue uniforms had no rank, unit, or other insignia. So it was tough to scope where the others came from. Our incoming class was a mix of officers, NCOs, and a few foreign students. There weren't any students in our class who had graduated as new second lieutenants that June from West Point. They were all on graduation leave before reporting for active duty.

SEALS

There was, however, little doubt about four remarkable characters. They made short, barking sounds. They were Navy SEALs. I had never heard of SEALs. Word went around they were the latest version of what we knew as "frogmen" and were some kind of Navy super-ninja special warriors.

They told us they were all assigned to a "SEAL team," another term we'd never heard. One of them said they were doing the Ranger program "just to see what it was like." That was impressive. But none of them were with us in Florida when we graduated. I never knew why.

RANGER BUDDIES

One aspect unique from all other Army instruction at that time was the concept of "Ranger buddies." The training was going to be intense: 24-7 and dangerous. Students had died in Ranger, falling from cliffs in the Mountain phase, drowning in the swamps of Florida, from exothermia in winter, and in a number of other ways. The Army needed us to keep an eye on each other at all times.

We were told to pair off with another student before dawn of the second day. No exceptions. We had two hours to get it sorted out after evening chow, before lights-out. I don't remember how we managed it, but Mike from Indio, California, and I decided to give it a try. He and I would keep each other going in all weather, day and night, for the next eight weeks. We bitched together, shared our C-rations when we had them, and scrounged for food when we didn't. We helped each other on the tactical problems and bucked each other up when we were wet and cold. Mike and I were still together when we graduated in Florida, nine weeks later. I never saw him again after Ranger; I hope he survived Vietnam; I owe him a lot.

Ranger was no time for niceties; it was deadly serious. Everyone was expected to hit it at the same level. No rank, no privileges, no courtesies, no respect for whatever you did in the "outside Army." During the course, our status was, as the sergeants found many occasions to remind us, "lower than whale shit, at the bottom of the ocean." For nine weeks we would remain in that status, addressed as "Ranger" and expected to sound off with "Ranger" and our last names when necessary, which would be often.

While in the Benning phase, we would be in constant motion except for a very few hours of allotted sleep, and no sleep thereafter. The course would run night and day, seven days a week. Instructors would rotate in shifts while we would "drive on."

To say we were apprehensive would be an understatement. The course was "make or break." It was one of the few times in the Army a man proved himself in a version of "trial by fire," not actually in combat. Survive and graduate, receiving the arched, yellow-edged black shoulder tab with RANGER in yellow capital letters, and you had achieved something truly significant. Fail, and you returned to your unit in a state of depression, and in some cases tacit disgrace.

Every student was graded as an individual and on how he performed as a leader and as a team member. Other grades would be assessed for skills he would be expected to master, like mountaineering.

If a man was injured, and many were, depending on the severity they could be "recycled," having to start from the beginning again in a following class. It was also possible to complete the entire nine weeks and still not be awarded the tab. There were rumored to be men who had tried several times, over the full nine-week course, who had never achieved the tab.

A phrase common at that time was that every man "left the course with a tab, or a story."

OFF AND RUNNING

The Benning phase began at 0300 the next morning. Ranger sergeants walked through the barracks banging bars of wood on the covers of the GI trash cans at the end of each barracks floor. "Up! Fall in outside! Move!" In the warm night air, crickets sounding off around us, we formed up, divided into twenty-man increments, and took off on a five-mile run, led by Sergeant Tony and shepherded by other Ranger NCOs.

There was no wind; the temperature was already in the eighties. Sane people elsewhere were asleep in bed; we clocked off the miles. A few men fell out. It would be noted, but they were expected to complete the full five miles. One or two fallouts might be accepted; continued nonperformance would warrant a first counseling session, usually with the student knocking out fifty push-ups as a Ranger sergeant "counseled" in colorful language. If it persisted, that was it; the student would be gone.

AZIMUTH AND PACE

The instruction at Harmony Church during the Benning phase was classroom work and a lot of field application, particularly on land navigation, both day and night. There was no GPS system in 1967; navigation was the old way, by map, compass azimuth, and pace count. My father had taught me and my fellow Boy Scouts in Italy to use the compass and read topographic, or "topo," maps, but the dead-reckoning use of azimuth and pace was new.

There was a pace course marked in several one-hundred-meter lengths laid out at Harmony Church; we each walked it several times to establish how many paces we individually took to travel one hundred meters over various types of terrain.

In the field, we kept a length of parachute cord tied to a buttonhole of our fatigue shirts. Counting our paces, we tied a knot in the cord each one hundred meters traveled. That enabled us to keep the distance along the azimuth. A sharp eye on the compass kept us on course.

The Army's M1950 "lensatic" compass was a critical item. Compact and dark green, it fit in the palm of your hand. It differed from a civilian compass by the sighting wire in a slot in the cover and a sighting tab with a small round magnifying lens. The tab had a notch at its top. A metal thumb loop steadied the compass when you held it up to your eye.

To sight the compass on a distant object, you looked through the slot in the cover, lining up the object with the sighting wire and the notch in the eyepiece. Looking down through the lens, which magnified the compass bezel, marked off in 360 degrees, you saw the azimuth, or direction to the object, on which you needed to travel. The azimuth dial and two little points above and below the sighting wire were luminous. Their soft glow in your palm at night kept you on course.

If you had the azimuth already, say, from a map, you did a little arithmetic to adjust for "magnetic declination," or the difference between magnetic north and true north. Then you turned yourself until the magnetic arrow in the compass rotated around to the adjusted azimuth on the dial and set off.

Keeping track of azimuth and pace count was critical in enabling us to know where we were on the ground at all times. In Vietnam, if you "made contact" with an enemy unit, knowing exactly where you were when you called for artillery or air support could be the difference between life and death.

By the way, are we getting a message here about stuff designed in 1950? M1950 patrol cap? M1950 compass? They made good gear back then; it was still in use decades later. I used that compass on both combat deployments to Vietnam and still have it.

One of the "make or break" tests in the Benning phase was passing the day and night "land navigation" courses. The day course came first. We all started off from the same marker post in the ground.

Each Ranger student was given a small card with the initial azimuth and distance he was to travel to hit the first of five sequential targets in the forest. All the targets were located within a "box" in the forest four thousand meters (four kilometers) on each side—plenty of room to go off course. Targets were green metal disks nailed to trees at shoulder height; each had a unique serial number in yellow paint.

If you were diligent and hit the first target accurately, the azimuth and distance to the next target was painted in smaller numbers in white on the lower half of the disk. Adjusting the compass to the new azimuth, you set off from there toward the second target, and so on.

The distances from target to target varied; some were several hundred meters, and at least one was over a kilometer. So there was plenty of opportunity to wander off course.

I checked to make sure I had set the compass's magnetic declination correctly, then set off on the first azimuth and bearing. I carefully counted the paces, keeping the azimuth bearing under the magnetic needle on the dial. When I had covered the requisite distance, I was standing directly in front of my first target.

Or was I? I looked to my left and right: several other green metal disks were tacked to trees five or ten yards to the left or right of the one I was in front of, all staggered slightly in distance as well. Did I hit the right one, or was one of the other targets the correct one?

I had maintained the azimuth and had diligently counted the distance, so this must be right. I noted the number on the first target on my card, oriented myself and the compass on the distance and azimuth to the second target and set off.

Every target I came to had several other targets tacked to trees around it, each with different numbers, at different distances. If I had made an error in reaching the first target, or any after it, it would have sent me off on the wrong bearing, putting me off course, logging the wrong numbers.

Keeping close attention to each azimuth and bearing, I finished the course in about three hours, arriving at a folding wooden field table set up beside a dirt road on which was a line of trucks. The Ranger sergeant at the table took my card, consulted a sheet on the table, made a mark, and grunted, "Get in the truck."

I had passed the day course. Several others did not; they had arrived at the wrong targets, from which the azimuths and bearing errors compounded themselves. A few students became hopelessly lost and were still out in the woods when night fell.

At 10 p.m., or 2200 hours, the next night we set off on the night course. It was the same drill as in daytime, but we were allowed no lights, relying only on the luminous dials of our compasses.

Arriving at the first target, I found its number was in luminous paint, as were the numbers on the other targets, softly glowing on other trees around me. I could see it would be a lot easier to get snarled up at night than in the daytime. It took longer to walk the night course, too. Those were the days before night-vision equipment. We had to "see" in the dark by ourselves as well as possible; the rest was being very careful.

I took it dead slow, feeling my way with one hand in front to ward off branches and trees, taking care not to fall into ditches or holes, which would have been plainly visible during the day.

I reached the finish about 2 a.m., or 0200. The Ranger sergeant there logged me in. "Not bad," he said. "I see you aced the day course. Where did you learn to read a compass like that?"

"The Boy Scouts, Sergeant."

"The Boy Scouts, huh? That must have been one fucking program. Get in the truck."

So it went.

HOW TO KILL A MAN

The close combat instruction was like nothing I'd experienced at VMI, where boxing was the only physical combat requirement. We gathered around a sunken pit about four feet deep ringed by logs, as a Ranger sergeant, in T-shirt, fatigue trousers, and boots strode out to the center. He wasn't particularly muscled, and he didn't look at all ferocious.

"Who's had experience wrestling?" We looked at each other. A few hands went up. He pointed to the biggest. "You."

The student jumped down into the pit. He looked to have at least a fifty-pound advantage. I don't think I was alone in thinking this was going to be a demonstration of how a small man could destroy a big one, intended to cow the rest of us.

I was wrong. The sergeant said, "You may be in a situation someday when you have to fight for your life. The only rule is, you live; he dies." He beckoned to the Ranger, pointing to a spot directly in front of him. "What we're showing you now is what you need to know to kill a man."

He walked around the student and pointed to points on the body where a blow, with sufficient force, would do just that. Then he said, "Now I'm going to show you that anyone within this distance may think he's got you. He'd be wrong."

In the next ten minutes, the sergeant, without seeming effort, showed how we could turn an attacker's momentum against him, break a number of holds, and disarm an opponent carrying a rifle with fixed bayonet.

Each of the moves was to be finished with a kick to the head or neck, a vicious strike with the edge of the hand, or the use of the attacker's own weapon on one of the deadly body points. None of them was landed on his Ranger student subject with any real force, but it was obvious that all were potentially lethal.

For the rest of the afternoon we paired off, working on the moves demonstrated. As we did so, under the close supervision of the cadre NCOs, we discovered we were able to perform each with increasing confidence and effect. I particularly liked a throw that converted an attacker's charging momentum into his suspension in midair before impacting the ground on his back, enabling either a kick to the head or a chop to the throat.

Next was fighting with the knife. How to attack, how to defend, and where to strike for the fastest and most effective result. The lesson I took away from that segment was to never get into a knife fight.

After a couple of hours, the instructors climbed out of the pit and stood above us. "All right, it's 'last man standing' time! Use what you've learned to see who can stay in the pit the longest. Start now!"

It was a melee that did credit to the instruction. We attacked each other with determination. I saw a few classmates borne to the edge of the pit by several men at once and tossed out. Hardly sporting, I thought, until the same thing happened to me.

In short order there were only a few students left in the pit, circling each other warily until one by one they made a mistake, slipped or fell, and were ejected. Strangely, the last man wasn't in any way a moose, just remarkably elusive and creative.

Would we be able to remember any or all of what we were taught so briefly, in the worst circumstances? Like knife fighting, I've thankfully never had occasion to use it.

The food at Harmony Church was from the standard Army menu; not inspired by Escoffier, but edible and ample. Our caloric burn rate had to be astronomical; the department didn't want us collapsing from starvation during the Benning phase. Word was the food situation would be "different" once we started patrolling in the mountains and in Florida. That turned out to be an understatement.

Before entering the mess at each meal, we had to knock off ten pull-ups on the bars in front, under the eye of one of the sergeants. A few students had trouble getting the required number done and were mercilessly and colorfully harangued while they strained at the bar.

DARBY

After the first week, we moved further out into the oak and slash-pine forests of the huge Benning reservation to Camp Darby, a collection of huts and bleachers named after Colonel William O. Darby, a charismatic Ranger leader in World War II.

We began with nonfiring familiarization with the types of US, allied, and communist weapons we might encounter anywhere in the world. We were all familiar with the then standard M16, so we started with the US M1 Garand and the short M1A carbine. I knew the M1 well, having shot with it on the ranges at Indiantown.

We handled the .45 caliber Thompson submachine gun and the Browning Automatic Rifle, the BAR. Both were very heavy, though they were being supplied, along with the M1, to our physically smaller South Vietnamese allies.

There were a few World War II German weapons, one of which, the MG34 light machine gun, I would later encounter in Vietnam. We handled Soviet and Chinese AK-47s, the SKS automatic rifle, and the Russian PSSh41 submachine gun with its big, round drum magazine.

The pressed-steel French MAT49 9mm submachine gun, icon of their Indochina war, was much like the .45 cal. US M3 "grease gun" of World War II and Korea: both were totally utilitarian in design.

We were shown the new combat shooting stance for the US .45 Colt automatic pistol: facing the target, feet apart with one foot slightly advanced, knees slightly bent, weight slightly forward, elbows slightly bent, pistol hand gripped by the off hand, shooting in line over the sights.

I wasn't surprised when we were told this method was developed by William Fairbairn, a British officer who had trained my father and other OSS agents in World War II. It was much better than the "duelist's" stance that had for long been taught by the Army: feet quartered away from the target, shooting arm outstretched, other hand on the opposite hip.

Fairbairn also designed the famous, needle-shaped "Fairbairn-Sykes" knife issued to the British SOE and American OSS. It was clearly designed for one thing, and that wasn't for opening letters. I still have my father's.

DEMOLITIONS

We moved on to demolitions. The chief instructor, a black Ranger NCO, handed out laminated foldout cards with formulas and diagrams detailing how to calculate, place, and detonate various-sized charges of C-4 and other explosives.

C-4 is a terrific explosive. It is innocent looking, white and moldable, like modeling clay. It came in two-and-a-half-pound oblong blocks wrapped in brown plastic, or in flat half-pound bars also wrapped in brown plastic. Softened by kneading, it can be wrapped around pipes or beams or pressed into cracks or holes.

It takes a severe shock to set off C-4. It can be dropped, walked on, set on fire, or subjected to microwave radiation and it will not explode. But put a blasting cap in it, and the effect is instantly impressive and destructive.

We worked on setting up C-4 "ring-main" charges, designed to detonate in sequence or linearly; "cratering" charges, designed to blow huge holes in roads or airfields; and "cutting charges," detonating inward to cut bridge main suspension cables, rails, or trees. I would supervise setting cutting charges in Vietnam to blow down trees, creating landing zones for helicopters.

We practiced fusing the charges with instant-firing explosive demolition cord, referred to as "detcord," that looked like gray clothesline. Linking C-4 charges with detcord ensured that everything detonated simultaneously. We would also use detcord in Vietnam to link claymore mines and grenades, creating automatic ambushes. More on that later.

We were shown pressure switches and pressure-release devices that could be used to set off booby traps, and blasting caps that could be time-fused, or fired electrically.

The instructor sergeant told us, "If you can see the explosion, it can see you; so keep your fucking heads down." We learned that there was danger from different types of fragmentation and debris, from metal, wood, concrete, or anything else picked up in the blast, which could travel slightly slower than the primary "frag" and was just as deadly.

To knock trains off their tracks, we calculated the charge sizes required, placing wooden blocks simulating C-4 along a stretch of the Columbus and Chattahoochee Railroad's right of way.

As we were busily packing the blocks connected by simulated detcord beside the rails, a freight train came clanging slowly down the line. We all stood back while the demolitions instructor waved to the train crew in the cab. All grins, they waved back. They'd probably watched students packing charges into their tracks for years. You wondered what they were really thinking. I haven't needed to derail a train since.

I still have the demo card, though. You never know.

PATROLLING

Ranger is focused on small-unit leadership, something that can be taught, up to a point. The rest has to come from somewhere in the student's DNA. Some have it; some don't.

Camp Darby was a big, outdoor lab where the instructors would get a good first look at how we acted individually and in groups on the patrol problems we were assigned. We were given a lot of instruction on patrol techniques, conducting more frequent and longer day and night patrols of various types, with varying missions for each.

On those first, short patrols, we carried our M14s, web gear, canteens, and a can or two of C-rations stuffed into cargo pockets on our field trousers. On our webbing patrol harnesses, we hung a colored smoke grenade and our compasses tied to a lanyard of parachute cord. Our canteens and ammunition packs were on our web belts. The twenty-round M14 magazines in the packs were clipped with blank 7.62mm ammunition. I carried my Ka-Bar knife in its sheath on the webbing belt and my demo knife in a pocket.

The terrain around Camp Darby was gently rolling hills covered with scrub oak and slash pine, with a number of creeks and swampy low spots. There was a lot of deadfall timber and dry leaves, so silent movement was a bit of a challenge. It was a good environment to practice the elements of patrolling; much bigger challenges would come in the mountain phase and in Florida.

Keeping a patrol together during daytime was easy; it was also generally easy to have a flank security man or two out on the sides. At night a single-file formation was almost always required, each man maintaining contact with the man ahead, watching the glowing "cat's eyes" tape strips sewn to the back of his patrol cap.

With the starts and stops for map checks and other reasons, unless men were alert, it was easy for a patrol to "break contact" at night because someone wasn't paying attention, had fallen asleep, or was watching luminous tree bark rather than the "cat's eyes" on the man in front.

Periodically the patrol leader would whisper to the man behind him, "Send up the count." The command would ripple back down the line. If the count came back shorter than the number of men the patrol leader knew were behind him, the patrol had to hold up while the errant students were found. This happened all too frequently.

SEEING THINGS

Two training aids in Ranger that aren't formally cited in the course material are exhaustion and hunger. Combining both and observing how we operated under pressure gave the instructors a lot to work with.

We all heard stories of men hallucinating in the Ranger program from sheer fatigue, thinking they were standing in the patrol file at night behind a student who wasn't there, or talking to imaginary people. One man in our class thought he saw a phone booth at midnight in the deep forest. Deciding to call home, he walked smack into a tree and broke his nose. Another man, a student patrol leader, became so exhausted and disoriented that he began to direct the patrol in a wide circular course, doubling back on itself, until the lane instructor relieved him, passing command to another Ranger.

It happened to every one of us in various ways. I saw people who weren't there. I heard things that weren't said. We drove on.

Because many M14 rifles had been lost in previous courses by students who fell asleep or were so exhausted they simply walked away from them, we were required to tie our rifles to ourselves with a length of parachute line known as a "dummy cord," long enough to enable holding the weapon in a firing stance. It was a very good idea.

In addition to the M14, we carried one M60 machine gun on each patrol. The 7.62mm gun was rotated to men designated as gunners. It weighed twenty-six pounds and had a 550-round-per-minute rate of fire. Its feed mechanism was copied from the World War II German MG42, so it rarely jammed. Its barrel could be changed out in seconds with the turn of a locking lever. It was an all-black, wicked-looking weapon, with an authoritative, hammering bark.

During the course, the M60 was "free," with no carrying strap. In Vietnam it could be carried with a general-purpose "GP" webbing strap, slung diagonally to take some of the weight off the gunner's arms. In both cases, it was always carried with a short "ready belt" of about forty rounds in the gun. An assistant gunner carrying a can or two of linked-belt ammunition followed the M60 gunner.

PATROL GRADING

The patrols we ran at Darby were eight to ten students. Each began with a student designated as patrol leader. He would be given the mission for the patrol, with the map coordinates of the objective where the patrol would conduct an attack or other maneuver, or the area in which the patrol would conduct its reconnaissance. The patrol leader was required to organize the patrol, brief it for the given mission, conduct rehearsals if necessary, ensure that every man knew his job, and lead the patrol on that phase of the instruction.

While we were at Darby, as in the mountains and Florida, every student was graded as patrol leader at least twice, some three times. Some students remained patrol leaders over the entire course of a patrol, from briefing to completing the mission. Others would become patrol leaders with little or no warning as patrol leaders were "killed" or swapped out by the lane instructors for any number of reasons, all of which could happen in actual combat situations.

Patrols operated in separate "lanes" in the forest so that they wouldn't run into other student patrols, with the confusion that would ensue. Keeping the patrols in separate lanes enabled the Ranger "lane instructor" assigned to walk with the patrol for that mission to focus, observing and assessing how the patrol leader, and the other members of the patrol, performed.

Lane instructors were Ranger NCOs or officers, many of whom had been to Vietnam one or more times. They knew their stuff and could be fierce. A student patrol leader could be expected to be asked at any time to indicate on the map exactly where the patrol was or how he would react to a hypothetical situation the instructor would describe.

Just as in the real world, there was no end of the sudden situations a lane instructor could pop on a patrol leader. The lane instructor would point with his walking staff: "If you were taken under fire from this direction, what would be your actions?" Or, "You're under a critical time schedule; this man (pointing to another student) has suddenly collapsed from heat or other causes. What are your actions?" Or, "You suspect your 'friendly partisan' guide may actually be leading you into an ambush. What are your actions?"

The decisions made by the student patrol leader could be right or wrong, but the student had to make a decision and not dither in the process. The worst thing a student could do would be to freeze or be indecisive.

We were often told there was no "school solution" to a field problem, no one right answer for all conceivable tactical situations. You had to maintain situational awareness at all times, being creative, making decisions based on the conditions confronted. And quickly. Men could be killed or wounded, or your entire patrol annihilated.

There was a mock grave at Darby with a headstone on which was painted the following:

Here lie the bones of Ranger Jones,
A graduate of this institution.
who died last night in his first firefight
using the "school solution."

OUR AGGRESSOR ENEMY

Without an actual enemy, all the patrol exercises we ran at Darby would have been so much game playing. But there was an enemy out there, the "aggressors," looking to ambush us, or to fight fiercely against us, as we attacked.

Our aggressor enemies were soldiers from a brigade of light Infantry stationed at Fort Benning, supporting all programs of the Infantry Center, including the Ranger Department. The units of the brigade rotated the duty, so one full 750-man battalion was always providing support to Ranger training in all three phases. They were very good, dedicated opponents.

The ammunition used in training was blank, but there was still nothing like being surprised by an aggressor unit—machine guns, automatic weapons, and grenade and artillery simulators exploding with huge concussions. It added more than enough realism to remind us we were training to go up against an enemy halfway around the world who was out to kill us if he could. Patrolling at Darby provided the basics; we would be doing much more in the mountains and in Florida.

SPEED MARCH

On a bright morning at the end of the third week at Darby, we prepared to speed-march back to Harmony Church. We were in light order: patrol harnesses, canteens, and our M14s. The distance was ten miles. Mike and I were one or two back from the head of our column of twos as a skinny little Ranger lane instructor in wire-rimmed glasses with his patrol cap cocked back on his head ambled up and took his place at the front.

Mike looked over at me. "This is gonna be a stroll," he said. "That guy looks like he won't make the distance." Mike was proven wrong in the first hundred yards. The skinny little guy smoked off like a jackrabbit. We were practically running to keep up at a killer pace.

The average Army unit march speed was 120 steps per minute, or about 3.1 miles per hour, which is twice the average human walking speed. The forced-march speed took that up to 4 miles per hour.

We were also on a tank trail: an unimproved dirt road with chunks thrown up by the passage of tracked and wheeled vehicles. So, in addition to the pace, we were constantly contending with the uneven surface.

As we panted along, the sun, temperature, and humidity soared. We were soaked when, at the end of the first hour, the skinny instructor abruptly stopped, turned around, and barked, "Fifteen minutes! Take two salt tabs, conserve water. Check your feet!"

Mike and I collapsed beside the road. I swallowed the tablets with a few strong sips from my canteen. I wanted more but was afraid to drink too much. We pulled our boots and socks off and massaged our red feet as I reviewed how stupid I had to be to volunteer for the Infantry.

The scrawny instructor walked up and down the road, not saying anything but giving us all a good once-over. Other Ranger sergeants moved along, checking feet. I saw a couple of students being helped to a truck that was following the column. They had blistered their feet so badly they couldn't make the rest of the march, and likely the rest of the phase.

I was thankful the truck carrying the lame was well to the rear; all we needed was hauling our tails in a cloud of mogas exhaust.

In the second hour, two men collapsed from heat prostration. The column kept going as a frontline jeep ambulance, designed to carry stretchers, roared ahead to the main post and the hospital. Blisters were one thing; heatstroke was serious business.

Students injured and unable to continue the pace of instruction at any point during the course were "boarded" by the medics and instructors to determine how well they had performed and whether their injury could be healed quickly enough to allow them to join a subsequent class. If so, they would be recycled. Students injured badly enough to fail the board would be returned to their units.

No matter how far into the course a student was injured, if permitted to recycle, when he joined a subsequent class, he had to start over, right from the beginning. Some made minor Ranger history in this process. My classmate Gary was an irrepressibly cheerful guy from New York City. He was injured and allowed to recycle twice before completing the course on his third try and earning the tab. Gary had guts.

Attrition was constant. Men left the course due to failure to perform, accidents, or illness. Some made it all the way to Florida and were found deficient in that phase. A number would finish the course but not be assessed as having performed at the level required to be awarded the tab. They would be credited with having only "completed course requirements."

ASSAULT COURSE

We were at the edge of endurance when our forced-marching column closed in on Harmony Church. Instead of staying on the asphalted road leading into the barracks complex, the little jackrabbit took us off on a dirt road. We knew where that went: the assault course. It was another opportunity to push us up against our limits. Mike and I looked at each other.

We were dispatched on the twenty-five-obstacle course at ten-second intervals. We ran through a maze, crawled through culverts, climbed a cargo net to a platform from which we walked across a beam to another platform, leaped out to grab a rope, and slid down to the ground.

Next was a huge A-frame over a pit full of mud; I grabbed a rope on the edge of the pit and swung out over the mud, but landed short, waist deep in the mud. It was like landing in that honey bucket well in Japan, but far more sanitary.

We did all of it while being yelled at ferociously by the instructors. I didn't take it personally; they were equal-opportunity harassers. We crawled under barbed wire, climbed up and over a wall, negotiated several other obstacles, ran fifty meters to the end, and joined a group of students lying on their backs gasping for air. We were finished.

Or so we thought. A short, stocky Ranger captain was standing over us. "Get on your feet! You think you're tired? What are you going to do in Vietnam when you're tired and you've got men down and dying and they're looking to you? Are you going to lie down like a bunch of pussies? Or are you going to lead? Get up and run it again!" Those were his exact words. We did just that. Then ran it a third time. It was agony. On the third trip through, I was seeing spots. Or were they only gnats?

I look back on that day as one of a very few in the Army where I learned something about myself I would likely never have discovered otherwise: that I could go that extra effort, and it wouldn't kill me. Nothing I would do physically on both deployments in Vietnam came close to the challenge of Ranger.

After the assault course we thought we were done. But there was one last challenge. We fell in and marched a mile to Victory Pond. It would be the final test of the Benning phase. Dog tired but ready, we dropped our harnesses and stacked our M14s. We climbed into a set of bleachers as an instructor described the unique arrangement of poles, cables, and wires behind him.

SLIDE FOR LIFE

The "confidence test" and the "slide for life," he told us, were designed as a check for fear of heights and of water. We would be confronting serious amounts of both in the mountain phase and in Florida.

As I recall, the instructor's description to us on how to negotiate the test was roughly as follows: "Using the foot spikes embedded in its sides, begin by climbing thirty-five feet up the vertical pole on the edge of the pond. From a platform at the top, balance-walk thirty feet out over the water on a plank one foot wide to a set of three steps. Take one step up, one more, and a third to the top. Proceed down two steps to the plank." He paused while our eyes traced the setup over the water in front of us.

"Do another thirty-foot balance-walk along the plank to a platform at a second pole. From there a stout rope is stretched horizontally out over the water to a distant third pole. Crawl out on this rope upside down, with your legs hooked over the rope, to that big, hanging Ranger tab. Slap the tab with one hand. Un-hook your legs from the rope. Hanging by your hands, yell 'Ranger!' like you mean it, and drop into the pond.

"Next, swim to the pond's edge and proceed to another pole. Climb seventy-five feet to the platform at the top. A cable fixed overhead slants away across the pond and down, ending in the water near the shoreline. A Ranger instructor with a red flag will be on the shore, in line with you and the cable.

"Reach up and grab both handles of a trolley on the cable, over your head. At a wave of the flag by the instructor, lift your feet and begin an accelerating slide out and down across the pond. When the instructor waves the flag a second time, let go of the trolley, keeping your feet together, and drop into the water."

We sat in the bleachers, watching our classmates hit that setup. Some fell off the plank, landing in the pond; they swam out and lined up to do it again in a group that stood off to the side. Those who finished the tests climbed, soaking wet, back into the bleachers and kibitzed those still negotiating them. There was a lot of hooting and ribald calling; I'm certain the instructors welcomed it. Anything to put us under more pressure and distraction.

I couldn't wait to get on that setup; a drop into the pond was going to be fabulous after sweating through that forced march and three trips through the assault course. Plus I had mud up to my waist from missing that damn "Tarzan of the Jungle" rope swing over the mud pit. Good thing the department hadn't figured out they could stock the pond with alligators.

When my turn came, I realized the trick was not to look down. Focus out in front, keep your balance, put one foot in front of the other. The step-up thing was the trickiest; you had to shift your weight to maintain balance. The inverted sloth crawl out along the rope to the Ranger tab was unique, but if sloths could do it, so could I.

The drop into the pond was great. I swam out, hustled over to the slide test, and went up that pole like a shot. It was twice as high as the first poles but seemed about five times as much; the Ranger instructor on the far shore looked like an ant. I grabbed the trolley, he waved the flag, and I was off. The acceleration was terrific. As he waved the flag again, I let go and hit the water like a bomb. Fabulous!

We marched to the barracks, cleaned and turned in our M14s at the arms room, and hit the showers to scrub the crud off from Darby. We would leave for the Mountain camp at Dahlonega at 0500 the next morning. We had six hours off, to report back by 2100. It was the only few hours of downtime we were allowed from the program in the nine-week course.

We had survived the Benning phase. There was a lot of banter and grab-ass. One of the students' parents arrived to take their son into Columbus for a fast dinner. They invited Mike and me along; we threw on jeans and T-shirts and joined them.

We had only been away from civilization for three weeks, but it seemed much longer. I can't recall where we ate. It was a bit unreal. We were in an intensive program training for leadership in the war half a world away. Around us ordinary people were chatting and enjoying their dinner. I wondered if they had anyone, or knew anyone, at risk. Very likely, since Columbus was an Army town. If so, you wouldn't know it. Life went on.

13

MOUNTAINS

August 1967

The stars were out as we formed up early the next morning. A line of two-and-a-half-ton trucks with hooped canvas covers stood in the street. We climbed in and ranged ourselves along the bench seats on either side. A few lay down on the steel truck beds and went to sleep. The drivers shoved the tailgates up with clangs and pinned them. Engines revved. With much gear shifting and exhaust blatting, we were off for the Mountain camp, and the Chattahoochee National Forest.

SUNDAY IN ATLANTA

As we rolled north, a few more joined the men on the floor and went to sleep. I moved over to the edge of the bench near the tailgate and watched the country-side roll by as dawn came and the sun rose.

There was an interstate from Columbus to Atlanta; we didn't take it. Our convoy rolled along Georgia state roads, through a succession of sleepy little towns. Weathered, red brick buildings, a store or two, an occasional gas station. Swaybacked old barns bore faded, painted ads for snuff, Dr. Pepper soda, and brands of farm feed.

We passed long fields of crops. Here and there a skeletal, metal Aeromotor windmill, its vane folded, towered over a galvanized water tub at its base for livestock. Horses and mules watched impassively from pastures.

Atlanta was a big town in 1967, but nothing like the world-class big city it would become in the next couple of decades. Our convoy arrived on sunny suburban streets at just the time church services were letting out. In those days people dressed for Sundays. Family groups stood in the sun around church steps, looking curiously at us as our line of big, Army-green trucks ground by. There were a few very attractive young females; one or two in our truck cracked a few crude remarks and were told good-naturedly by others to "shut the fuck up." A typical Ranger Sunday. We drove on.

GOLD COUNTRY

Dahlonega is about seventy miles north of Atlanta, on the edge of a vast national forest and the Tennessee Valley Divide. The 1820 discovery of gold in the mountains nearby catapulted the Cherokee-named town to such prominence that a branch of the US Mint was established during the brief boom period that followed.

Nothing of real note followed until 1952 when the Army, drawing on its experience in mountain operations in Italy in World War II and the then ongoing bitter mountain combat in Korea, established the Mountain Ranger Camp about ten miles northwest of town.

In 1967 the Mountain camp was a collection of green-roofed wooden huts, a mess hall, a few administrative buildings, bleachers, and sand pits. The huts had bare wood floors, a couple of hanging lightbulbs, and folding, bare, wood-framed canvas cots. My memory of the place is a series of planar relationships, everything perched on various levels, disappearing into the surrounding forested hills.

RANGERS ON THE ROCKS

Our trucks ground up the twisting roads on the flank of 3,100-foot Yonah Mountain, dominating the surrounding hills in the national forest and topped by a sheer granite face. We were headed for mountaineering instruction, known as "Rangers and ropes on the rocks." We had to pass all aspects of this segment of the course; our ability to function on patrols in the mountains might require some or all of it.

The mountaineering delivered at Yonah was outstanding. Ranger instructor NCOs began with demonstrations of various climbing techniques, culminating in a master sergeant traversing out under a forty-foot cliff overhang. With nothing below but hundreds of feet of air, he moved along by clipping his line sequentially into snap links connected to steel pitons hammered into the rock overhead.

Thankfully we weren't going to have to execute that hazard, but it showed us how we should be confident in the equipment. I was confident I would never voluntarily try anything like it.

We learned critical knots, among them the square knot, known to sailors as the "reef knot"; bowline; figure eight on a bight; and the prusik, a friction knot with a number of applications. If all this sounds like ancient Greek, each has a specific purpose. We tied them over and over. Then, blindfolded, we tied them again.

While civilians may know the oblong steel ring with a spring-loaded gate as a carabiner, in the Army's glossary it was a snap link. A length of climbing rope tied around our waists and crotch and secured by a square knot served as "Swiss seats," onto which we clipped our snap links, through which the rappelling ropes ran.

We used a single rope to rappel, traversing down a cliff or a mountainside in bounds. We learned to do it from higher and higher points, trusting the ropes, gaining confidence, enabling us to make bigger and bigger bounds, sailing out and down along a cliff face.

It was one of the few times in the course we actually did something that was fun. Once we mastered rappelling, we learned to evacuate casualties down the cliffs, one man on the rappel ropes on either side of the casualty being lowered from above on a belay line.

Mountaineering is "up" as well as "down"; we practiced free-climbing, with pitons and belay lines, secured to our Swiss seats by a second student below us as we climbed. When we climbed while "on belay," there was that huge element of safety.

Belay climbing required preparing the cliff face as you ascended, hammering pitons into the rock, moving your safety snap link to successive pitons above as you climbed—not exactly the stealthiest mode.

It's one thing to do all this in daylight in light climbing gear, and usually in good weather, as most recreational climbers do. Military mountaineering is all-weather, day and night, with rucksacks, weapons, and whatever additional gear is required for the mission. Not for neophytes.

10TH MOUNTAIN DIVISION

Much of what we were learning had been developed for military application by the 10th Mountain Infantry Division in World War II. A new unit with a unique mission, the 10th had trained in Colorado before being deployed to the Italian front.

Because of the many famous climbers and skiers in the division, including Olympic contenders, plus a large number of college graduates, many from the Ivy League, General Eisenhower once referred to the 10th Mountain while it was still training in the States as "a bunch of playboys." But once it was deployed in Italy the division executed audacious mountain combat operations, capturing Riva Ridge and Monte Belvedere, gateways to the Po Valley, which had stalled the Allied offensive for months.

After the war, veterans of the 10th Mountain went on to build the American ski industry, serve in the executive ranks of the Sierra Club, and found Nike, the company that became a world name in recreational and sports footwear.

Little of that was known to us as we climbed like ants against the rock face of Yonah, or bounded down it in ever-increasing leaps. Every now and then there was a moment to appreciate the view, stretching for miles above the forested, surrounding hills. The heat of summer brought the sharp bite of pine to us. The burring of woodpeckers and the calls of other mountain birds were a constant background accompaniment.

The air was heavy with the foretaste of rain as we boarded the trucks for the run back down to the Mountain camp. Masses of darkening thunderheads were stacking far up in the sky to the southeast.

MOUNTAIN PATROLS

After a fast meal in the mess hall, we found a pile of rucksacks and a case of boxed C-rations in our hut. A sheaf of 1:25,000 scale US Geodetic Survey topographic maps lay on a cot. I picked one up. It was shaded almost solid green; we were definitely going to be operating in deep forest. And mountains. Steep ones from the zillions of contour lines, so close together they looked like solid brown shapes under all that green.

The map border was titled "Suches–Noontoola." I found Suches, a crossroad town about ten miles from Dahlonega, near Woody Gap in the national forest. I couldn't find Noontoola. It didn't matter; we weren't going to be visiting either.

The rucksacks were shapeless, weathered, faded green nylon bags on scuffed, nicked, in some cases bent, dark brown aluminum frames. Stained and dirty, many were torn. A few were soaking wet. Turned in by the class preceding ours, they were harbingers of what was ahead. Mike looked at them for a moment, nudged the pile with a boot. "Shit," he said, "what happened to the guys that were wearing these?" We would find out soon enough.

A figure appeared in the doorway. A captain in patrol cap, with twin "cat's eyes" tapes sewn on the back, brim lowered so that his eyes were in shadow. In faded fatigues and web gear, he was about six feet and lean, carrying a hiking staff. All the lane instructors had them; homemade, hickory or ash. They were for balance on the hills, as pointers, and for the occasional whacking of a student dozing or not paying attention.

"You Rangers get yourselves a ruck," he said, slowly looking around at us. "Be out on the bleachers in five minutes with your weapons. One map and one C-ration each. Full canteens. Move." He disappeared.

We looked at each other, then scrambled to unsnarl the pile. Webbing straps, shroud line, and other tangled cords made separating the mess a challenge. The ruck I got looked like it was run over by a truck, bearing the imprint of something suspiciously like a tire tread mark.

Dotted around the hut area were structures with slanted roofs supported by vertical beams, open on all sides. Each sheltered a set of bleachers seating about twenty Rangers. In front of each bleacher were a blackboard and sand table. The sand could be sculpted, with little markers added to depict friendly and enemy units, and a number of other embellishments. The one in front of our bleachers was filled only with sand.

The captain held a small, green, hard-covered notebook. He flipped it open. "Get out your handbooks." He turned to the blackboard. "Here's where we start on what you learned at Darby." He pointed to Jack. "You're the patrol leader. Come down here." He took Jack off a few paces, pointed out a number of things on Jack's map, and spoke to him in a low voice as Jack wrote in his own notebook.

We strained to hear but couldn't make it out. "Any questions?" Jack had a couple. We still couldn't make out the answers. Then, "Use the sand table if you feel it helps. You have fifteen minutes to organize, brief, and be ready to go." The captain pointed past us to a truck on the road behind the bleachers. He stepped over to the side and waited.

Jack went to the sand table and did some fast scooping, shaping, and smoothing. He referred to his notebook and briefed us as follows, in the five-paragraph format used for a field order:

"Situation: We're operating against the aggressor enemy," he began. "They will be patrolling in our designated area, so a high state of alert and noise and light discipline are required during the movement to our objective.

"Mission: Get out your maps. The mission is to conduct a combat patrol to attack and destroy an aggressor position at these coordinates, on or before 0500 tomorrow. That is our objective. Write them down." He gave us the eight-digit map coordinates as we scribbled in our notebooks.

"Execution: We will move over this mountain and down this slope to the objective." He pointed to the mound he had made in the sand table. "As we near the objective, I will conduct a leader's reconnaissance."

"Admin and Command: We will organize the patrol as follows." He named each of us with our tasks: point man, security team leader, pace man, radio operator, assault team leader and assault team, machine gunner and assistant machine gunner, and assistant patrol leader, who would bring up the rear and ensure that the patrol didn't break contact.

"Our actions at the objective will be as follows." Using a stick, he showed how he planned for us to secure the area and attack the objective. "I will designate a rally point short of the objective in this general area." He indicated with the stick. "We will fall back to the rally point on completing the attack." He continued with the signals to initiate the attack and to break contact and withdraw to the rally point.

He gave us the radio frequency for the PRC-25 backpack FM radio and our patrol's radio call sign. "We each have one meal; hold off on those until after we've attacked the objective by 0500 tomorrow. Any questions?"

We had a couple, then we loaded up in the truck. Thunder rumbled in the distance. As we climbed in, it began to rain. The drive out to our patrol launch point took about a half hour, grinding up a twisting, narrow mountain road. The rain drummed on the truck's canvas cover. The foliage was so dense the view back down the road was like a glistening, green tunnel.

We deployed into patrol formation as Jack had briefed and started up the mountain. The forest smelled intense. Rain, earth, and leaves, combined with an undernote of decay. We were soaked in two minutes. It wasn't cold. Yet.

The memory of that first Mountain phase patrol is sharp. The slope was steep; we were moving on the azimuth Jack had briefed. It was still light, so we moved easily. There was a lot of deadfall and leaves on the forest floor, but the rain muffled the sound of our boots on the wet leaves. I was the pace man, just behind the man carrying the radio, who was just behind Jack. The lane instructor moved up and down the file.

We counted the paces; at every hundred we tied a knot in the parachute line pace cord tied to the buttonhole of our fatigue shirts. Our pace count was accurate for moving on flat ground; allowance was made for distance applied to hiking up and down hills. It was guesswork, but between us, as we paused for periodic map checks under the scrutiny of the lane instructor, we stayed on top of our locations.

In addition to the pace, the ability to read the map contour lines and translate them to the actual hills, valleys, and other features was critical. Inability to master this could result in the patrol missing its objective or, worse, becoming lost.

There was a legendary story of the Ranger student who, after studying his map and looking at the surrounding terrain, replied to the lane instructor's question as to his location, "I think we're on that hilltop over there." Fail.

It wasn't all an uphill slog; the mountainside was slashed by ravines and ridges that ran in diagonals off our azimuth. As a result, we were moving down into small valleys and up over the ridges. As we traversed one of the valleys and began the upslope, furious ripping bursts of machine-gun and rifle fire opened up on our left, from the high ground behind us. With the majority of the patrol in the low area below the aggressor ambush, most of us were in the "kill zone" of that gun.

Everyone hit the ground, firing back with their M14s. Our M60 gunner opened up as well, but the aggressors were in a well-concealed position beneath a lot of heavy log deadfall, so how effective our shooting would have been was anyone's guess.

Silent until now, the lane instructor was standing over Jack, shouting down at him, "What do you do now, patrol leader? That position is gonna smoke your people! What do you do now?" He threw a few grenade simulators on the ground just far enough away that their blasts didn't injure anyone but did add to the immediacy of the situation.

Jack was clearly more than a little flustered. He didn't have time to really react before the lane instructor called out, "Cease fire! Cease fire!" The shooting from the aggressors died down and stopped, though there were a few catcalls from up the hill.

"You didn't have any flank security out, patrol leader," the instructor said to Jack. "You're dead." He turned to Bill, who was carrying the radio. "He's dead. You're the new patrol leader. What are your actions now?" Just like that.

MOONSHINE

Little known to us at the time was the coordination by the Ranger Department of our patrol movements with local law enforcement and Park Service rangers.

In the 1960s, there were quite a number of illegal stills producing various alcoholic products, operating in secluded hollows on state and federal lands. They could be shifted rapidly, and the men who ran the stills were frequently armed. The last thing the Army wanted was a patrol of Ranger students carrying fearsome weapons, but with blank ammunition, stumbling across one of those operations.

In that backwoods environment and culture, many of the men on both sides of the illicit alcohol and law enforcement issue had grown up together or knew of each other's movements. Word was that an informal information-sharing arrangement, never attributable but always current, enabled the Army to plan its patrol lanes so that potentially dangerous encounters didn't happen.

It could also be deadly. There were situations in which some states' National Guard "loaned" assets to law enforcement efforts. In later years I knew an Army officer who was originally commissioned into a southern state's National Guard. In the late 1950s, he flew as a backseat observer in a Guard light military aircraft, working with the state police detecting illegal stills in heavily forested mountain areas. The pilot made a few low passes over a suspected still site. The plane's engine was hit by rifle fire from the ground; the pilot was killed in the crash. Though injured, my friend escaped. He remained convinced that if they had caught him, the "moonshiners" would have finished him as well.

CHICKEN DINNER

We began that first Mountain phase patrol with a single C-ration apiece. We ate that after we successfully attacked the initial objective the next morning. We needed food; the temperature had dropped during the night, and the rain hadn't let up. We were soaked and damn hungry. We would stay that way for the next day and a half, without food.

A fresh lane instructor took over; I was designated patrol leader. We were to make contact with friendly partisans at a grid coordinate in the mountains and receive the latest intelligence from them on an aggressor convoy expected in their area early that afternoon. Organizing the patrol on the intelligence we would receive, we were to ambush the convoy, killing or capturing a senior aggressor officer, and retrieve maps and documents he would be carrying.

We reorganized; another student took over as patrol leader. The new mission was to move to a clearing on the side of the mountain to receive an airdrop of rations. Good news. We arrived about a half hour before drop time. The lane instructor called an administrative halt to the exercise and motioned for us to gather around. "Your chow is coming in via U-6 Beaver. The drop will demonstrate how an ordinary poncho can be used for small payloads. A poncho has been fashioned into an expedient parachute."

The lane instructor pulled a rolled-up VS-17 ground-to-air signal panel from his pack and gave us a quick demonstration on how to use it to signal to aircraft overhead. It was simple and clever. About six by two feet, dark green on one side, bright fluorescent orange on the other. It could be laid down flat on the ground with the bright side up and would be unmistakable to an aircraft flying overhead, as long as there was no obstruction to the view. On this mountainside clearing, it was perfect.

If radio contact was not available, it could also be used to signal aircraft with Morse code, by "popping" the panel open and closed in short or long dots or dashes, flashing the bright side upward. We were thinking, "Expedient parachute; signal panel. Great." If food was on that drop, we didn't care if they used a poncho, bedsheet, or a shower curtain.

Drop time came and went. No sign of the U-6. We waited. About twenty minutes later an aircraft buzz was followed by the olive-green, high-winged, single-engine Beaver, zooming over the trees and circling. Either the panel had worked, or more likely the flight crew did this for every Ranger class and knew precisely where we were.

The plane banked away, circled, then came in straight and low. A crate fell from the door; for a moment the poncho fashioned as a parachute snapped taught above it, then one of the lines tied to a corner of the poncho broke. The crate dropped straight in from several hundred feet, the poncho fluttering above it. Preceded by a loud squawk, it smashed into the ground about ten feet from the panel with the sound of splintered wood.

A squawk!? We hustled over to find a smashed wood fruit crate containing three dead chickens and three empty .50 caliber ammunition cans. The lane instructor stood looking philosophically at the dead fowl. They appeared remarkably untouched, except for a corona of feathers surrounding the crate, which had burst out in a circle of splintered wood.

"Well, there're your rations. Doesn't look like you'll have to kill 'em. You move out on the next leg in an hour." He walked to the edge of clearing, sat down on a log, and checked his watch.

We went at it. Our performance was equal measures of innovation and desperation. We had the dead chickens, the smashed crate for fuel, and three ammo cans. Perhaps the cans were for stewing the birds; we had no time for that.

Several started pulling the feathers off the birds; a couple of others unlimbered knives, gutted them, and cut the heads off. We wound up with three crudely sectioned chickens with feathers still sticking out in patches. Not exactly a Julia Childs presentation, but we weren't picky.

We built a very small pyramid of splintered wood. With the clank of a student's lighter, we had fire. Adding more and more kindling, we eventually built it up to appreciable size and kept it fed. We skewered the sectioned chicken on sharpened branches. I don't think we had them turning over the flames more than fifteen minutes before we started tearing into it. No time or place for table manners; we were damned hungry.

THE STORM

The wind began to pick up in late evening. From the base of the trees we could see the forest canopy surging in the gusts. Sheet lightning and thunder far off heralded the coming storm.

It was a hellish night. As the storm built, we climbed up a mountain, pausing to frequently send up the count. Losing a man or breaking contact in this situation would be dangerous. Past 0200 we had crossed the shoulder below the crown of the mountain and were on a downslope so steep it was hard to maintain balance. We were semisliding down the face of the mountain sideways, reaching with one boot down while keeping the other planted upslope. Lightning sheeted across the treetops with immense hammerings of thunder. Bolts hit ridges around us. The wind increased from howling to a deep, constant roar. I remembered that sound; it was the same as in Yokohama when I watched the typhoon tear the roof off the warehouse down the street.

Shouting as loud as we could, it was still nearly impossible to hear each other. Trees were being blown down; we felt the vibration of their impacts on the mountainside through our boots. Rain seemed to come as much up from below, out of the ground, as from above. Everything was glimpsed in freeze-frame, lit by stark white strobing flashes.

The dial of my compass wouldn't settle; it swung over 180 degrees clockwise, then back. I'd never seen a compass act like that. Were we on top of some huge deposit of magnetite or other ore? I held it out to the lane instructor. He watched, pulled his own compass off his harness, saw its swing, and shook his head. As close to my ear as he could, he shouted, "What are your actions?"

It wasn't safe. I made a decision. "Pull everyone in, tie to trees!" I yelled. He nodded. I passed the word. We used our Swiss seat ropes, tying ourselves in sitting, legs pointed downslope. I reached over to the patrol's RTO, the student designated as the radiotelephone operator beside me, got the handset, and put it to my ear. Static, barely heard over the roar of the storm. No need tempting a lightning strike; I bent the blade antenna down, tucking it into the webbing of the RTO's rucksack.

The lane instructor tied in on my other side. Riding out the storm was the objective now. The wind continued howling through the night as the rain lashed at us. We were soaked; I was thankful it wasn't that cold. I pulled my legs up and laid my rifle across my knees. Hard to believe in the midst of that maelstrom, but once we were secured against sliding down the hill, I fell asleep. So did the lane instructor and others in the patrol.

I woke just before dawn; the rain had dwindled to a shower. The wind had died significantly. There was a faint, scratchy voice in the radio handset. We were back in the game. We woke everyone and moved on with the mission. I expected the lane instructor to relieve me or downcheck me; for whatever reason he did not.

Later we learned the storm had caused significant flooding and knocked out power in many North Georgia communities. The Ranger Department kept field training going.

Through the next day and night, the weather gradually improved. The sun returned; one mission followed another. New patrol leaders were switched in. We drove on, with little rest and minimal food. At one point, after conducting an attack on an aggressor outpost, Mike and I sat, exhausted, with our backs against a pair of trees, listening to our stomachs rumbling. Suddenly he stood up, walked over to a fallen tree, and reached underneath. In his hand was a perfect green bell pepper, as shiny as in the supermarket. Not large, but food. Without a word he unsheathed his knife, cut it in two, and handed me half. It was fantastic. Even today, over fifty years later, I can taste it. Incredible. How it grew there is a mystery, but when the mysterious works in your favor, don't question it.

I don't mean to convey the impression I'm complaining about the weather. Were the heat and humidity at Benning significant? Yes; we had heat casualties. Was the storm in the mountains, which hammered Georgia and northwest Florida, a memorable experience? Absolutely. I was surprised to find no mention of a hurricane in the summer of 1967; it certainly qualified as one in my book. But the summer weather we endured in Ranger Class 2 was nothing compared with the challenges we knew confronted those in Class 5, which began in late fall and continued into January 1968. Those poor guys operated in cold, rain, and, not infrequently, hail and snow.

Class 5 is infamously known as "Frostbite Five"; the only class given a break during the course, between the Benning and Florida phases, to take a week off for Christmas and New Year. They've earned it. I know men who went through the program in Class 5 who still have periodic bad dreams about the cold and hunger they endured in the North Georgia mountains.

We made it through the Mountain patrols with the class losing a number to falls, blisters, and, in a couple of cases, deciding they'd had enough.

14

SWAMPS
September 1967

WELCOME TO FLORIDA

We slept most of the way from Benning down to the Florida Ranger camp in the canvas-covered two-and-a-half-tons. Somewhere near Shalimar we cross-loaded into long, open "cattle trailers" pulled by prime movers.

We had heard about the "greeting" Ranger classes sometimes received.

As we rumbled along a raised two-lane blacktop road bordered on both sides by swamp, we scanned the sky. A shout of "There they are!" pulled our attention around directly to the rear. Two dots in the sky rapidly closed on us. The truck drivers hit the brakes; we came to a shuddering stop.

In seconds, a pair of F-4 Phantom fighter-bombers blasted low overhead, pulling up as they roared away in afterburner. Preset explosive charges on both sides of the road blew fountaining geysers in the swamp, simulating the bombs the jets would have dropped on us.

Black-hatted Ranger NCOs suddenly appeared, yelling, "Get your asses OFF those fucking trucks! Get into that SWAMP! They're gonna be BACK! You better light those birds UP!"

In moments we were chest deep in the ooze, holding our weapons over our heads. Sure enough, the F-4s banked in a wide circle and lined up for another pass. We all blazed away with our M14s with blanks, but even with live ammunition it would have taken a lucky shot, a true "golden BB," to bring down one of those monsters.

MAJOR ALVIN

The Air Force flew off for a cold beer. We sucked ourselves out of the water and swamp grass, to be met by Major Alvin, legendary commander of the Florida camp. He stood on the hood of one of the prime movers. Hands on hips, he glowered down at us.

We were drawn to Alvin like mice to the Pied Piper. Even in the hard-assed world of special operators, he was unique. He was Airborne, Ranger, *and* Special Forces, plus a few other specialties that were probably classified. He had served as a US exchange officer assigned to the Special Air Service, the British equivalent of our Special Forces. While playing football in college, he had been drafted by the NFL. He turned them down to join the Army. He was reported to have said, "Nobody dies on a football field; what kind of challenge is *that?*"

Legend had it that Alvin, flying in a Huey on a patrol insertion in Vietnam, had taken a 7.62mm hit to the chest, just before leaping to the ground. The door gunner had laid him out on the floor of the helicopter, packing plastic wrap from a radio battery into the hole in his chest to keep the air seal and prevent his lung from collapsing.

Alvin was alive, but barely. They flew him straight to the field hospital, where a surgeon, assessing the severity of the wound, was evidently slow in his response. Like a striking snake, Alvin's hand shot out, grabbing the doctor by the throat with a grip of steel. He pulled the man's face down, whispering hoarsely. Whatever Alvin said was enough to "encourage" the doctor to operate immediately, saving his life.

Now he stood looking down on us as though we were termites. His eyes ranged over our entire soaking-wet, motley crew. His jaw worked on a wad of chew. "Ah hear you people think y'er shit-hot," he growled. He spat over the side of the truck, narrowly missing a student, who hopped to the side. "Ah hear you think you've got all the answers. Ah hear you hope Florida is gonna be a walk in the sun."

He paused, spit, and looked us over. "So here's the picture. We've had a lot of rain, and the swamps are nice and hah." He grinned and spit again. "So if you think we're gonna back off on patrollin' just 'cause of a little rain, think again. Ah don't much care if you drown out here, but you're goin' to go the full program. Mah people are gonna make sure of it."

He paused and spit a final stream of juice. When he growled, it was at least an octave lower. "Now, git this straight. There's on'y three ways yer gonna leave Florida: dead, washed out, or Rangers. Git on those trucks."

GATORS

The Florida Ranger camp was at Auxiliary Field One, at Eglin Air Force Base. During World War II, "Aux One" had served as an outlying, isolated airfield to the main Eglin Field complex. In 1967 the Ranger camp headquarters was in the old World War II green-roofed, one-story operations building; it still had the square, glassed-in airfield control tower extending from its roof.

Two things distinguished the Florida Ranger camp from the Mountains and Benning. The first was the pond beside the headquarters building. About the size of a very small swimming pool, it was surrounded by a grass verge, enclosed in steel cyclone fencing. Lounging in the murky water was a pair of alligators—big, dark green, motionless. I got the feeling if the fence wasn't there, they could move very fast.

The "story" was that Alvin had had the pond dug and filled, and the grassed area fenced, then engaged a couple of local "good ol' boys" to produce the reptiles. Occasionally the gators made a sound I will never forget. I don't mind admitting it scared the hell out of me the first time; its memory hasn't diminished. A mix of hissing, gurgling, and roaring, it was delivered with the gator raising its head and tail just above the water while vibrating its body.

That gator roar was absolutely primeval. It reminded us that relatives of those killers were alive and well all over northwestern Florida. The fact that no Ranger student was eaten by an alligator didn't matter to us one bit; we were spooked. I'd bet Alvin had exactly that in mind when he added those giant lizards: one more psychological factor.

Nice touch, just like his "welcoming" speech.

THE TOKYO RAIDERS

The second distinguishing feature was a pair of faded but still visible white lines painted on the old runway in front of the headquarters building. Several hundred feet apart, they extended across the width of the concrete. They were a part of American military history, vestiges of a secret operation daring in its audacity, unique in its delivery.

The lines marked the distance necessary for twin-engine, US Army B-25 Mitchell bombers to be able to take off from the deck of a 1942 US Navy aircraft carrier. They were the remnants of secret training conducted by the squadron that would become famous as the "Tokyo Raiders."

In early 1942, America was stinging from the surprise attack inflicted by Japan on the US Pacific Fleet at Pearl Harbor, resulting in the sinking of several battleships and other naval vessels, and over two thousand Americans killed.

Two weeks after Pearl Harbor, President Roosevelt directed that Japan was to be bombed, as soon as possible. Yet at the time, the Japanese home islands were beyond the range of any American land-based aircraft. What to do?

An audacious plan was developed. Could B-25 bombers take off from the limited length of an aircraft carrier deck? If so, they could be transported by a carrier to within striking range of Japan. They could then bomb several Japanese cities, continuing on to land at airfields in China, in areas controlled by Chinese forces that were then allied with the United States.

A squadron of B-25s was chosen for the project. They flew to Eglin, where Lieutenant Colonel James Doolittle, a famous former test pilot and aviation engineer, commanded the operation.

There is a myth that Doolittle's flyers were hand selected before being given the opportunity to volunteer. Not so; the B-25 squadron selected was flying antisubmarine patrols in the Pacific Northwest and was ordered to Eglin, no details given. On arriving, the entire squadron was secretly briefed by Doolittle on the intended mission. He told them that any man desiring to could drop out, no questions asked. Not one did.

At Auxiliary Field One, the B-25 crews practiced taking off within the limits of the lines painted on the runway. They represented the deck of the USS *Hornet*, the aircraft carrier that would take them to within launching range of Japan.

The mission was flown; Japan was bombed. Within three months of Japan's attack on Pearl Harbor, the United States reached out across the Pacific, bombing Tokyo and several other Japanese cities.

The "Tokyo Raiders" became legends. Their painted lines, still on the runway at the Florida camp twenty-five years later, were an inspiration to all of us.

SWAMPS

As in the Mountain phase, the Florida instructors wasted no time. We were issued maps; classes were held in the Barn, a big three-sided shed, before we went to the swamps. The "local reptile" segment of instruction got our complete attention. Various specimens slithered or coiled in wire mesh cages on tables, their forked tongues flicking, as an instructor detailed their color, habits, and generally bad attitudes. Water moccasins were most numerous, reinforced by lots of rattlesnakes, copperheads, and, deadliest of them all, the occasional coral snake.

Eglin Air Force Base is in the Florida "panhandle": that part of the state that sticks out to the west, at its very top. We were told that because of its combination of swamps, bayous, and flat, dry land, the panhandle had the state's highest snake population. But, said the instructor, "if you don't bother them, they won't bother you." As for the alligators, he continued, they were actually quite timid and would do anything to distance themselves from big, bad Ranger patrols.

"Are you kidding?" we thought. "What happens when we're waist deep in the swamp at night and one of those poisonous water moccasins comes swimming along? Or we step on any of those bad-attitude snakes in the dark?" As for alligators, we decided that "timid" stuff was ridiculous. Blank ammo would be useless against them; going *mano a mano* with a giant lizard with our knives didn't sound promising either.

We were cautioned that we would be spending a good deal of time at least waist deep in water at night. That turned out to be an understatement. The storm that passed through the southeastern states during our last week in the Mountain phase raised the Florida swamps to record highs. We were issued rubber bags to go inside our rucksacks. "Goosenecking" them by tightly twisting, bending the twist, and cinching it tightly with parachute cord ensured the contents wouldn't get soaked in the swamps. "Terrific," muttered Mike. "Where the hell were these in the mountains?"

On our first patrols, we gained greater confidence in "dead reckoning" navigation by azimuth and pace, since there were almost no terrain features except for the water obstacles. This skill would frequently pay off for me in Vietnam.

Our missions changed irregularly. We attacked aggressor encampments, liberated a prisoner, rescued a downed pilot, contacted friendly partisans, built rope bridges across streams and passed the men and gear on them, and paddled ten-man rubber boats at night through swamps that had everything but boa constrictors hanging from the trees. We did it around the clock, with almost no food. We continued to see things at night, and patrol leaders were relieved or revolved without predictability.

WILDLIFE

Except for mosquitoes, which hunted us in hordes, no one was bitten or eaten by the snakes or alligators we feared. I wouldn't be at all surprised if they were all part of the Ranger program anyway. When they came off duty, they probably put on their patrol caps and slithered over to the "O" Club for a few shots with the lane instructors.

Were any of these fears or concerns irrational? Possibly. No students came to harm from the wildlife. But let's not kid ourselves; the snakes were poisonous. And the gators? Well, parts of Florida are likely as wild as before the Spanish first arrived. If they aren't, let humans leave for a year or two, and they'll revert. They're out in the savannah and the swamps, in big numbers.

Another factor may be the innate ability of wildlife to understand that starving Ranger students are likely to put any creature they come across on the menu, in short order. So, best to stay well away from them. Perhaps that knowledge is transmitted genetically; if so, it would explain why, during the entirety of the nine-week course, we saw almost no wildlife that could be converted to dinner.

The swamps and creeks at Eglin were high because of the recent storms, and at night, wading through deep water in the creeks and bayous, following the "cat's eyes" tapes on the back of the student ahead, it was easy to step into a sinkhole over your head. Ranger students had drowned in those swamps. We felt our way very carefully.

DUNE MOON

When we had the chance to notice, the night sky was beautiful. The moon and stars together were bright and clear. Moonlight filtering down under the trees was almost silver, bright enough for us to make our way. It was also an additional hazard. The aggressors were out in force; moon and starlight helped them as well.

A few nights into the first patrol I noticed intermittent, very low-level bursts of light in the sky. Just above the level of the background, ambient light, definitely unnatural, it was like extremely weak photoflashes. After seeing it several times at irregular intervals, I thought I was hallucinating; we were all experiencing a bit of that anyway. The next night I noticed it again. I checked with others; they'd been seeing it too, but like me they weren't about to mention it to the lane instructors, who seemed not to notice.

Years later I learned that DUNE MOON, a classified project, was conducted at Eglin in the summer of 1967. It tested dropping electronic sensors from various types of aircraft. The low-level bursts of illumination we saw were part of the project.

DUNE MOON was the result of deep thinking by a group known as the "Jasons": civilian academics brought together occasionally to consider lofty concepts for the Defense Department. They proposed an "electronic fence" that would interdict supplies moving by truck from North Vietnam down the Ho Chi Minh Trail, inside then neutral Cambodia and Laos, and along the border between South Vietnam and Cambodia.

Electronic sensors would be airdropped in huge numbers. They would be camouflaged as tree limbs, rocks, and reportedly as animal droppings. Registering local magnetic disturbances and vibration and transmitting their readings by wireless, they were intended to detect vehicles. If both magnetic and seismic sensors alerted at any point along the road network, it would more than likely be from the passage of vehicles. Aircraft, either on-station patrolling the night sky or launched from bases in Vietnam or Thailand, would use flares or infrared to locate and attack the trucks.

The Jasons, by the way, are still doing their deep thinking. I had occasion to work with them on a project decades later; their imagination is indeed "outside the box."

The 460,000-acre Eglin reservation is home to cypress, oak, and magnolia in the lowlands and swamps, and slash and longleaf pine on the sandy flat regions. Plenty of undergrowth filled in the gaps. It was generally easy to move through, but the aggressor was out in force; security was critical, and more than one student got clocked for leading a patrol into an ambush.

LRP's

We stayed out for four or five days, switching missions and patrol leaders. It rained, we starved; it rained more. We kept starving, sucked it up, and drove on. Shortly after returning from the first series of patrols, one of the lane instructors motioned to me to accompany him. My buddy Mike looked at me with an eyebrow raised. I shrugged; no idea.

At the Barn I found four other students sitting on the lowest level of bleacher seats. The tall, lean officer who had signaled to me was joined by another, shorter and built like a football tackle. He told us they had both served with the 1st Infantry Division in Vietnam and had brought back an idea. "You men," he said, "are here as part of an experiment." We looked at each other. "We are developing a possible future segment of instruction in the Florida phase built around long-range patrol techniques. LRP (he pronounced it "lurp") units in Vietnam are bringing back critical information to their parent organizations. We believe there is a future for these types of units; we will teach you men a bit of what we know. You will then be deployed on two separate missions for the remainder of the Florida phase, to test your ability to function using LRP techniques and tactics. One of these will be a daytime "walk-in"; the other will begin with a night parachute drop and a "walk back."

"In case you're wondering why you've been selected," he continued, "you have been assessed as having completed the requirements for the course. You are all airborne qualified. Your participation in this development of the LRP segment is voluntary. Consider yourselves to have volunteered. The Ranger Department thanks you." He smiled wryly. "But understand this: if you fail to perform in this experiment, we can reevaluate your scores for course completion."

No problem; we got the message loud and clear, and were eager. I had heard of LRP units but knew nothing about them other than that they usually operated far away from their parent units and had to stay damn quiet in order not to be compromised. This was a chance to do something different, and learn in the process.

In the next two days the captains gave us a fast course in LRP techniques and tactics. If ordinary patrolling required cautious movement, LRP required something approaching Zen. Every sense had to be alert. LRP patrols were much smaller than the patrols we were running in the mountains and Florida.

SOG

At the time we didn't know that in Vietnam a highly classified unit known as MACV-SOG was conducting patrols "over the fence" into neutral Cambodia and Laos, running deep reconnaissance against the same road network and enemy truck traffic for which DUNE MOON was developing its future electronic sensors.

Innocuously titled "Studies and Observation Group," a name I don't think fooled anyone, SOG was in-country in Vietnam in 1964, in the very earliest days of US ground force commitment. Its Special Forces reconnaissance men were among the most skilled and courageous in the Army.

Named for American states or poisonous snakes, each SOG recon team had two and sometimes three Americans, augmented by five to six indigenous Montagnard, Vietnamese, or ethnic Chinese. Insertion was by helicopter, generally at very last light, sometimes after the aircraft had made several "false insertions." The team would quickly make its way off the landing site and into deep jungle, there to go to ground and wait, all senses tuned, listening for any sign that it was detected.

SOG teams made quite a dent in the enemy's efforts by calling in air strikes against truck parks and convoys, ammunition, and other storage sites that were camouflaged so well that aerial observation could not ordinarily detect them. They also conducted prisoner snatch missions and in a couple of then highly classified operations "salted" doctored enemy ammunition in full AK-47 magazines along the trails, where they might be found by passing NVA soldiers. Loaded into an actual AK, the results would be fatal to the shooter.

The North Vietnamese enemy knew SOG teams were operating. Unknown until after the war, there was a double agent in the South Vietnamese headquarters with which SOG headquarters was required to coordinate all its missions. The agent fed information to Hanoi; the enemy sent specially trained units after the teams, sometimes using dogs to track them. Entire teams disappeared, failing to come up on the radio for their first communications check after insertion. After the war, the North Vietnamese agent was honored as a hero by his government. Many SOG men are still listed as missing in action.

LRP PATROLS

Our first LRP patrol would be a point reconnaissance. We painted our faces and arms with black and green camouflage sticks, securing all equipment so that nothing rattled or made noise as we jumped up and down for our patrol leader's equipment and sound check.

We loaded in the back of a three-quarter-ton "weapons carrier," our "simulated helicopter," and were driven to the insertion point. Jumping off the truck, we made our way deep into the savannah and went to ground in a star formation, each man's boots in the middle, all with weapons facing out. We remained motionless for an hour, listening. The next leg of the patrol was a slow and cautious movement to the reconnaissance objective: a bend in a creek from which we were to observe the waterway, a road bordering it on the far bank, and an aggressor outpost on the road.

We went to ground in a huge clump of saw grass at the base of a thicket of pines. Over the next twenty-four hours we observed and noted truck, jeep, and foot traffic on the road, and the changing of the four-man aggressor group that manned the outpost, which entailed raising and lowering the aggressor's "Circle Trigon" flag, on which was a green triangle inside a green circle.

The aggressors gave no indication they were aware of our presence in the area; possibly they were given a series of tasks and actions to perform at specific times. We did note the passage of two aggressor patrols, one on each bank of the creek, but we remained undetected. At the end of the observation period, we quietly withdrew to a grid coordinate where we called by radio for extraction and were picked up by the same three-quarter-ton "helicopter."

Our mission debrief generally pleased the two captains; we had gotten most of what we were expected to see, though we had missed a couple of others. The next day was spent briefing and preparing for the "walk back" patrol, which would begin with a night parachute drop. We would conduct a reconnaissance as we made our way back on foot to friendly lines, reporting on anything of military value that we would see.

NIGHT JUMP

At about 9 p.m. we were trucked to Hurlburt Field, another outlying airfield on the huge Eglin reservation. Hurlburt was the base of the Air Commandos, a special operations unit I hadn't previously known of. An assortment of aircraft occupied the ramp: C-130 transports; a couple of twin-engine C-47s of World War II fame, with some kind of weapon pointing out the port-side cargo door; a few high-winged, single-engine aircraft; and some big, single-engine AD-1 Skyraiders, known during the Vietnam War as "Sandys" or "Spads."

At the end of the flight line near a taxiway, our truck pulled up behind a high-winged, twin-engine C-123 transport. It had two piston engines, with small jet engines mounted outboard of each. Painted in green, black, and brown camouflage, it was a smaller version of the big C-130 Hercules.

The C-123 had evolved from a late-1940s design for a huge, all-metal troop-carrying glider. It had gone through a couple of design and power evolutions and had almost been relegated to obscurity. But the Air Force's interest in reviving it was sparked by the Army's introduction into Vietnam of its own twin-engine, prop-driven CV-7 Caribou transport.

Flown by Army aviators, the Caribou was ideal for operations in and out of short-field, unimproved conditions. The Air Force wasn't about to relinquish that role to the Army, so the C-123 was rejuvenated. Deployed to Vietnam, it served in several roles, mostly as a tactical transport, but also as a spray aircraft for Agent Orange and other defoliants, under a project code-named RANCH HAND. The Army, unimpressed, kept flying their Caribous.

I would be carrying the radio on this patrol; the jumpmaster, a Ranger sergeant, helped me rig it under my reserve parachute, with a twenty-foot bungee lowering line on a quick release. Just before landing, I would trip the release at about treetop height, letting the radio fall to the end of the line so that it would hit the ground first.

The PRC-25 radio was a steel box with handset, battery, and antenna. Weighing just over twenty-three pounds, hitting the ground while still hooked to it could cause severe injury. Why was that important? Twenty-three pounds is about as much as a full twenty-four-can case of beer, or soda. You don't want to be wearing something like that across your legs when you're coming down at about twenty-six feet per second.

The jumpmaster checked our parachutes and equipment carefully, front and back. We loaded, taking our places on the nylon-covered, tube-framed bench seats. This would be my sixth parachute jump, the first after airborne school a few weeks earlier. I was looking forward to it. Usually the sixth jump was celebrated back at your "parent" unit. In the raunchy humor of the day, it was considered your "cherry" jump; the hapless "newbie" was often required to wear a special steel helmet, on which would be painted a big red cherry. Better to log this one doing something useful.

For officers, the cherry jump was often followed at the Officers Club after 1800 the same day by several rounds of drinks for other officers of his unit, all on his tab. This celebration is not to be confused with the far more rigorous and alcoholic "Prop Blast" ceremony celebrated for new officers in many airborne units, about which we will learn more later.

What made this jump unusual was that we would be "tailgating" the C-123; the rear ramp would be lowered to horizontal, and we would walk off rather than jump from the doors, as we had done in the airborne course.

The jumpmaster reviewed all the jump commands with us, and the Air Force loadmaster gave us a quick safety briefing. The aircraft commander, a major, told us we would be jumping from well above 800 feet. The jumps at Benning had been from 1,200 feet. I figured the Air Force knew what they were doing; I was concerned about getting rid of the radio before I hit the ground.

The engines started and ran up; we taxied out and took off. The flight to the drop zone was brief. At ten minutes from jump, the tailgate wound down with a whine; the roar of engines and the cool night air rushed into the cargo compartment. Framed in the huge rectangular opening in the rear of the aircraft, the moon was up and about three-quarters full, dusting a thin, flat layer of silver clouds. Far off, the lights of a big city twinkled on the horizon. Below was darkness.

The Ranger jumpmaster did his safety check, then held out both hands. "Six minutes!" Then, "Stand up!" At his command we clipped our static line snap hooks to the anchor cable running just over our heads, checked the back of the man in front of us, and sounded off the count.

"OK! OK! OK! OK!" the first man in our stick pointed at the jumpmaster. "All OK!"

"Stand in the door!" The first man shuffled to the edge of the ramp as we followed close behind. I was second in the stick. The light in the panel beside the jumpmaster winked from red to green. "Go!"

The first man stepped out and dropped out of sight. I went right behind, had a good body position, and really felt the weight of the radio as I counted, "One thousand! Two thousand! Three thousand! Four . . ." I was beginning to reach up for my risers to check my canopy when WHAM! I hit the ground with the radio, unreleased, still under my reserve.

I literally saw stars; I wasn't sure if I had broken anything. I was completely unprepared for it. I lay there with that damned radio slewed to one side, still hooked to my harness. I moved my feet; my ankles seemed OK, but I had really taken a wallop across the shins.

The DZSO, the drop zone safety officer, a Ranger lieutenant, came running over, cursing, "Shit! Are you hurt? Don't move!" He checked me over, then hustled off to check the others. He had a jeep with a radio; he called a halt to the problem while he summoned a medic from a nearby aggressor unit. After about an hour, while we walked around to see if we could function OK, we all agreed we would press on with the problem.

We had definitely been dropped lower than briefed and were variously banged up, but no one had broken anything. Looking back, I think the fact that we weren't tensed up may have helped. It sure would have been better to have gotten rid of that radio and landed as we were trained to do. When we did get word a few days later from the Air Force, it was essentially, "Gee! Sorry 'bout that!" which was one of the throwaway lines of that time.

The rest of our second LRP problem went without a hitch. Dinged as we were, we moved extra slowly and debriefed on everything we saw, which again seemed to satisfy the captains. I don't know if the Ranger Department ever did elect to add LRP techniques to the Florida phase; no one I've met since who's gone through the program has mentioned it.

A day or so later, as the rest of our class completed their long patrols. As at the end of the Benning phase, there was a lot of grab-ass and bantering. It was a unique feeling of having crossed a threshold, of achieving something each of us had earned and of having learned something about himself. There was no way I could know it then, but nothing I would do in combat would equal the physical challenges I had faced and met in Ranger.

TABS

On a bright morning in mid-September, we formed up on the runway in front of the camp headquarters building. Our boots were on the white line painted there for Doolittle's raiders in 1942. The camp adjutant followed Major Alvin down the line, reading off our names as Alvin pinned the black-and-gold RANGER tabs on our left shoulders. I remember a set of steel-gray eyes, a wink, a smile, a strong handshake, and "Well done, Ranger."

The Columbus airport on the morning we left Benning to return to our units was the last time I saw anyone in my Ranger class except for Bland, a VMI classmate who was recycled due to severely blistered feet. He graduated with the tab in a following class. As a combat leader he would perform superbly in Vietnam, earning the Silver Star for gallantry in action. We will see him again a bit later in this story.

I've wondered, down the years, whatever happened to those four cocky SEALs. Were they, literally, fish out of water? The 1960s were before SEALs evolved into extended operations on land as much as at sea; perhaps they weren't ready for it yet? Or were they pulled out for some operation elsewhere? I guess we'll never know.

I would meet Sergeant Bony years later, when the 82nd Airborne was re-organizing in the 1980s and the 505th Parachute Infantry Regiment was being reactivated as a full regiment. I was invited to return to Fort Bragg to hang the "TET COUNTER-OFFENSIVE 1968" battle streamer on the regimental colors.

It was a great honor. I was a civilian then; I wore a suit and tie. Bony stood with a group of other NCOs. I went over to them. "Sergeant Bony, you were one of our class Tac NCOs in Ranger in 1967." I put out my hand. "What you taught us saved my tail in Vietnam. Thank you." We both smiled; it was a great moment.

OPSEC

Growing up, I had seen Ranger class photos on the walls of various friends of my father's. They all looked uniformly cool; groups of wolf-lean, grinning men, each with a new RANGER tab pinned to his left shoulder. Years later I looked in my files for ours; there didn't seem to be one. I couldn't remember a class photo being taken. I might have been elsewhere in the Florida camp area, could have missed it altogether. Odd, but possible.

I called the Ranger Training Department. It was a full command by then, too, no longer a mere training department. The Army had a combat regiment of Rangers as well, with tough, assault-type missions.

I spoke with the command sergeant major. He had another NCO pull my class's file. We chatted a bit, then, "Sir, there is no photo of your class in the file. There is no notation as to why, but I would guess it was due to OPSEC, operational security."

That was interesting. "Was that a common practice at that time, sergeant major?"

"No, Sir, not common, but there were a few, in those years during Vietnam." There was a pause. Then, "My guess is someone was in your class who someone else didn't want their picture taken."

That made sense. There could have been men in the course from any number of other government agencies, or foreign armies, who might be doing clandestine work afterward. Because none of us wore insignia, you didn't know if the man next to you was enlisted or officer, what organization he was from, or even if he was American.

BACK TO BRAGG

But that was in the future. On that fall morning in 1967 at the Columbus airport, traveling on orders in our short-sleeved, tropical-weight tan uniforms, we wore that new RANGER tab on our left shoulders with more than a little pride. Four or five of us were booked on a Southern Air flight to Fayetteville, returning to the 82nd Airborne.

As we boarded the 727, we all smiled at the two very attractive stewardesses, one blonde, the other brunette. They were both definitely appreciated. We settled in our seats as the blonde looked down the long aisle and grinned, holding the microphone for the usual preflight safety talk.

She had a great Southern drawl. "We want to give a special welcome to some of our passengers today, who we see have graduated from the Ranger course." She paused as we looked at each other. A couple of the guys leaned out into the aisle for a better look. "And we want to make sure you boys know that if there's anything we can do to make this flight more enjoyable for y'all . . ."

Wow! We grinned at each other. We were practically bouncing in our seats.

She paused; the suspense was perfect. "Y'all can just ferget it!" The plane erupted in laughter. They were terrific.

"HOW DO YOU LIKE YOURS, SIR?"

The next day I shined my jump boots and "broke starch" on a fresh set of fatigues, with the RANGER tab and parachute wings sewn on. I drove in to the battalion area. On my way up the walk to the Bravo Company CP, a sergeant called a work detail to attention with, "All the way, SIR!" a big grin and sharp salute. One of the men on the way out the entrance stepped back and held the door with a smile and the same greeting. Something had definitely changed.

When I reported in to Captain Juan, his reception couldn't have been more different than four months before, when he'd banished me like some pestilential outcast. He came around his desk and shook my hand, pulling up a chair with the other. "Welcome back, Lieutenant! Siddown, siddown!" He was all questions as the first sergeant, smiling, came in with two cups of coffee in those ever-present, tan melamine mugs.

"How do you like yours, Sir?" He asked.

I was home.

JOHN WAYNE TOOK OUR FUN AWAY

Ironically, I had to turn around after a few weeks at Bragg and go back to Fort Benning, this time for the Infantry Officer Basic Course. It was one of the rungs on the Army's "professional schooling" ladder. In IOBC, Infantry second lieutenants were taught the duties and responsibilities of a rifle platoon leader, and the tactics we were expected to use in various field situations. Classroom work was combined with plenty of field application.

The final field exercise of the course was "Rifle Platoon in the Night Attack." The night exercise was intended to give us an opportunity to experience all aspects of the attack. Normally it was conducted with profuse blank ammunition, flares, and artillery and grenade simulators—a lot of light and noise, which was what the real thing would be like.

Our class's night attack exercise was entirely different. A movie was being filmed at Benning that fall. Starring John Wayne and a number of other Hollywood notables, *The Green Berets*, based on a best-selling book of the same title by Robin Moore, would become one of the iconic films of the Vietnam War.

The Green Berets cast haunted a number of the watering holes around Benning. Some were regulars at the "Bunker Bar" at the Officers Club, where they ran up truly Hollywood-sized tabs.

The Army's Special Forces was an almost mystical organization then; publicity from Moore's book and a best-selling song, "The Ballad of the Green Berets" by Barry Sadler, a Green Beret staff sergeant himself, added to the mystique.

Our IOBC class's night attack problem coincided with the night the movie's production crew filmed an "attack by Vietcong guerrillas" on the film's "Special Forces camp" in "Vietnam." Faithfully constructed to look like an actual Special Forces camp in Vietnam, the filming was taking place on a different part of the reservation.

To support that night's filming, helicopters, artillery, a huge amount of pyrotechnics, and other support by the Army at Fort Benning was dedicated to the production. Any sound made or lights shown by our class in our night attack, though it would be made miles away, might affect the sound or lighting effects for the filming. As a result, we attacked the hilltop position designated as our "final objective" with no pyrotechnics, no support, and no blank ammunition.

Imagine a full class of Infantry lieutenants, all of whom were eventually going to the real war in Vietnam, walking up that hill, going, "Bang-bang-bang!" in total darkness, like kids playing war games, while the Hollywood crowd filmed their epic.

Once we seized the objective atop our hill, we could see all the way across the Benning reservation to where all the fantasy fighting was going on. With flares hanging in the sky and lots of explosions, it looked very authentic.

15

"PROP BLASTED"

October 1967

A week or so after I reported back to the battalion from the Infantry Officer Basic Course at Benning, Captain Juan stopped me in the hall outside the arms room. "1700 Friday at the 82nd Annex. You're gonna get prop blasted." He grinned. "You'll have company; I think we have seven in this year's intake. Fresh meat." He rubbed his hands together. Not a good sign.

By "fresh meat" he meant the other new lieutenants who joined the battalion during the summer, directly out of jump school, or, like me and a couple of others, after finishing Ranger. Yes, we were all jump qualified. But there was one more hurdle to being accepted as members of the Airborne, that unusual fraternity that trusts their lives to an armful of nylon and gravity.

I had mixed feelings about the prop blast. I'd heard about the rite for years. It began in 1940, when the Army was experimenting with the parachuting of infantry at Fort Benning. A number of young officers were making their first jumps. Bill Yarborough, then a captain, and Bill Ryder, a lieutenant and leader of the parachute test platoon, decided some sort of ceremony would be in order. An accompanying, unique mixture of liquor would also be appropriate.

At that first prop blast, the "punch" was a mix of champagne for "altitude," vodka for "blast," and sugar and lemon juice, for happiness and sorrow. The deadly punch was chugged from a "prop-blast mug": a 75mm shell casing, to which were attached two ripcord handles from a T-3 chest-pack parachute. "Geronimo" was engraved on one side of the mug, the names of the officers who participated on the other.

"Geronimo!" was the yell given by officers and men as they jumped during the first parachute tests, to prove to the others that they had their full wits about them. A Western film by that name had shown at the post theater the week before; the chief's name was chosen because it was unmistakable. "Geronimo!" later became the motto of the 509th Parachute Infantry Regiment.

The list of twelve officers engraved on the 1940 mug is a "who's who" of future Airborne leaders and commanders. Yarborough went on to design and patent the US Army's silver parachute wings, the first sets of which were handmade by the firm of Bailey Banks & Biddle in Philadelphia, and became a lieutenant general. General officer's stars similarly fell on several of the others.

The 1940 prop blast couldn't have been too outrageous; wives attended as guests and observers. Reportedly, participants yelled "Geronimo!" as each man jumped off a chair and performed a parachute landing fall. He then drank from the mug as all assembled chanted, "One thousand! Two thousand! Three thousand! Four thousand!"

As a rite of passage, I was ready for the blast and looked forward to it. But there was another, darker aspect. Over the years, it had evolved from a convivial off-duty gathering of airborne men having a few good belts to something more like a fraternity hazing session. Participants were directed by those already prop-blasted in earlier ceremonies to consume bigger and bigger amounts of prop-blast punch, which had become increasingly powerful.

In two recent instances, young lieutenant participants had consumed so much punch that they were rendered unconscious. Hauled to their beds and left, unattended, to "sleep it off," sometime during the ensuing hours, they vomited, aspirated their own vomit, and died.

On the Friday evening of the ceremony, I turned the Austin-Healey off Longstreet Road, bumped over the railroad tracks, and parked at the 82nd Airborne Annex. It was a beautiful day; the sun was just about to set; the air carried the smell of pine and heather. North Carolina in autumn.

The Annex was a separate, smaller club than the big, much older and more formal Officers Club on Main Post. It served not only officers of the 82nd but of many of Bragg's other airborne units as well. It was a rambling one-story brick building surrounded by pines, with a bar, a stage, a big dining room that could be sectioned off, and an adjoining barber shop and shoe-shine concession.

The Annex entry was a step up from the parking lot onto a stone doorstep. On entering, every man stamped his Corcoran jump boots: One! Two! shaking his fatigue trousers down over the blousing bands at his boot tops. It was habitual, reflexive.

The Annex was informal. Not rowdy, except in the bar on certain evenings, but not at all buttoned-down. "Fatigues and boots" were acceptable at any time. The informality was heightened by an aspect I look back on from over half a century, as at a very different Army. Every weekday, the lunch crowd packed the Annex. A long buffet and steam table ran along one wall; at its end was a big tub of bottled beer in crushed ice; it was constantly replenished. Drinks could be ordered at table. The bar did a booming business.

I frequently saw officers put away more than a few, then return to their units for the remainder of the duty day. I wasn't much of a drinker at that time: a few occasional beers as a cadet was about it; hard drinks and wine were still out there in the future. It was clear the Army of 1967 ran as much on alcohol as it did on caffeine. It ran on enormous amounts of caffeine.

Was midday drinking a function of the war going on halfway around the world, or a result of it? The war's shadowy specter was present in the Annex every day. Everyone was coming or going, likely at the risk of death or wounding. Those who had been there knew what the war could do. Those not yet gone, myself included, heard many stories.

The war was hard on some families, brutal on others. That turbulence manifested itself at the Annex as well. Repetitive year-long combat "tours" (an odd term, as though our experiences in Vietnam were arranged by the travel firm of Thomas Cooke), with a nine-month interval between, placed huge burdens on the wives. When a man came up for reassignment to Vietnam, his family had to clear their on-post quarters by the date of his departure. The Army didn't care where they went. Many wives remained close to Bragg, living off-post. The commissary and PX were affordable resources, especially for those with children. Womack Army Hospital was also there for dependent medical care.

Sadly, there were some women who stayed close to Bragg while their husbands were in Vietnam, who frequented the Annex enough to be noticeable. It was a severely unhappy time. The war slowly eroded the Army in Vietnam, and marriages and families at home.

When I arrived on the evening of our battalion's prop blast, a portion of the dining area was partitioned off. A bar was set up in a corner; several of the battalion's officers with master wings appeared to have already been there for some time. Trays with hors d'ouvres stood on a table against one wall. A full dinner off the club menu for all attending would follow our blasting.

On a side table covered with white linen was a silver punch bowl and ladle, both with German "alloy purity" and the Nazi eagle and swastika stamped on them, captured in France in 1944. Around the bowl were eight double-handled silver mugs, commissioned after the war from Bailey Banks & Biddle. Each was engraved with the regiment's airborne campaigns: North Africa, Sicily, Normandy, Holland, the Ardennes, and the Rhine.

They are also the division's war campaigns; the names ring the upper walls of the division football stadium at Fort Bragg, where the year before Bob Hope had brought his troupe for a gala Christmas show. Hope squinted up at the names, against the glare of the spotlights, and quipped into the mike, "It looks like you boys play a hell of an 'away schedule'!" The troops went wild.

Foursome tables were pulled back, providing space for a mock-up of the inside of an aircraft. Rather, a simulation of a portion of the aircraft. A platform raised about two feet off the floor supported a railing down one side, leading to a strongly supported jump door. The apparatus could be conveniently knocked down and reassembled for other prop blasts. Very neat.

Hoots greeted me and the other newbies as we arrived. "Fresh meat!" "Greenhorns!" "You'll be sorry!" I wasn't sorry about getting metaphorically blasted, just that the cost of our seniors' prodigious bar tabs, the food, and the rental of the jump rig, room, and staff would be divvied up and on our Officers Club bills at the end of the month.

The blast commenced about 1800, or 6 p.m. Unlike the 1940 event, ours was a stag affair. The humor and comments would have pegged the needle in the red on a profanity meter.

We were lined up and subjected to garrulous quizzing on airborne procedures and technical terms, sizes of canopies, numbers of shroud lines, aperture diameters, descent speeds, and on and on. A favorite was the Airborne Department's definition of the ordinary zipper: a "quick-fit cargo tie-down slide fastener." Try saying that several times, quickly.

Any mistake made in this inquisition required successive hits of punch from the prop-blast mugs. After the quiz session, it was into the fuselage mock-up to go through the entire pre-jump sequence, jumpmastered by Chuck, the Alpha Company CO. We had to precisely execute the motions of "stand up," "check equipment," "sound off for equipment check," "hook up," "check static lines," "count off," "send up the count," and "stand in the door," followed by vigorous exits with a good tight body position and PLF's onto the club floor.

None of our landing falls was judged acceptable, requiring more punch and back through the sequence again. Juan and Norm, the Charlie Company commander, were most vocal. Norm pulled out a chair. "Goddammit! My daughter can do a better PLF than you amateurs! I'll show you a PLF!" He jumped off and hit the floor like a sack of potatoes, lying there laughing. Juan, roaring, poured his drink on him, then hustled to the bar for a refill.

"Holy shit," one of the lieutenants muttered, "we may have to go into action with these guys someday."

"Silence!" roared Norm. "Mutiny! More punch!"

After three or four tries and a lot more punch, we were "passed accepted." We each scrawled our signature in the battalion Prop Blast Book and were welcomed into the fraternity.

The lesson of the drunken, dead lieutenants must have been on the minds of our seniors; none of us were exactly blotto, but we definitely didn't need any accompanying booze for the dinner that followed. The seniors were more in danger, if anyone. It was quite an evening.

Decades later I had occasion to return to Bragg. The Annex was completely gone, replaced by a field of young pines. Only the doorstep remained, half hidden in brush, its surface worn smooth by thousands of parachute boots.

16

HUNTING GENERALS

November 1967

A beautiful North Carolina autumn; great splashes of red and gold mixed with green pine of the forest. Six battalions of the 82nd Airborne Division parachuted into the western reaches of the Fort Bragg reservation. It was the start of a massive field-training exercise, an FTX, named PINELAND VI.

The six battalions were the "friendlies." Our battalion would play the guerrilla force; the "enemy." We had parachuted into the maneuver area a week earlier, going to work creating "hides" and safe areas; caching weapons, food, and gear; and preparing to make nuisances of ourselves.

With the maneuver underway, the friendly battalions were loosed to chase us. At six-to-one odds, "Jumpin' John," our battalion commander, was in high anxiety. But to Captain Juan, our slightly mad Cuban-born company commander, the odds were in our favor. Unconventional warfare? He was in his element.

Among the Army's characters, Captain Juan was a standout. The rumor was that his parents, big landowners, got him out of Cuba to Miami when Castro took over in 1959. Powerfully built, he was one of hundreds recruited by the CIA for a planned clandestine invasion of Cuba. As a swimmer, he went ashore the night before the invasion in April 1961 to survey the beach at Playa Girón, afterward infamous as the "Bay of Pigs." Captured by Castro's forces when the invasion failed, he and others were sent to prison, where they were starved and regularly beaten.

The Kennedy administration eventually ransomed the prisoners for $53 million worth of food and medical supplies. Processed through Homestead Air Force Base, Juan was one of those offered enlistment in the US Army. He starred in Officer Candidate School at Fort Benning and was commissioned in Infantry. A fierce anticommunist, he sought assignments verging on the impossible.

The FTX "scenario" designated the maneuver as taking place in the mythical nation of "Pineland." The maneuver area included several actual North Carolina towns. Our battalion, known as the "Pineland Liberation Army" (PLA), played the part of an insurgent force attempting to subvert and overthrow the government of Pineland. We relied on the support of sympathetic citizens of Pineland. Each year, selected residents of the area looked forward to playing various roles.

Pineland was a US ally nation; its "capitol" was in the actual town of Ansonville, North Carolina. Responding to a request from the premiere of Pineland (the mayor of Ansonville), the US president authorized the 82nd Airborne to provide assistance.

As the PLA guerrilla force, most of us were in jeans, sweatshirts, windbreakers, and a combination of military uniform and equipment. We had a mixed bag of vehicles: jeeps, a few civilian cars, and a pickup truck or two. No one shaved. We had the bravado of hyped-up, badassed guerrillas. We cultivated sneering demeanors, peppering our speech with *hombre, amigo, viva!*, and *huelga!*

Juan kicked even that up a notch. He had the appearance of a revolutionary on hot sauce. He wore a bandana, a big non-US revolver on his hip, jeans, and a multicolored serape. The troops loved it.

We had all the usual army weaponry: M16 rifles, M60 machine guns, M79 grenade launchers, and even the 90mm recoilless rifle. One thing we were not carrying was the Colt .45 pistol. They were issued to officers, some noncoms, and men on crew-served weapons, but too many pistols were being "lost" on parachute jumps. The opening shock of a parachute could flip a pistol out of the standard leather holster, which had a single snap in its flap. North Carolina must have been dotted with rusting .45s. I never understood why we didn't design a more severe holster or adopt the British method: a simple lanyard to the butt of the weapon, the other end fastened to the holster.

Because of the lost pistol problem, Major General John Deane, the 82nd's division commander, issued a directive that no .45 pistols were to be taken to the field. Officers would wear empty holsters. Most officers stuffed a pair or two of boot socks, or a number of candy bars, in them.

My thought was if my soldiers had to carry their assigned weapons, I wasn't about to lead them with a holster stuffed with boot socks. On a weekend leave in New York City in October, I went to FAO Schwarz, the famous toy store. For $1.98, I bought a plastic Colt .45 toy pistol, detailed very closely to the issue US

Army .45. It was so authentic to the real thing in design and color, you couldn't tell the difference, except for the weight. The magazine even had wooden bullets that ejected as you worked the slide. Equipped with my *ersatz* pistol, I jumped with the battalion on the FTX.

During the maneuver, we rested by day in camouflaged forest hideouts, striking by night at various friendly forces targets. We ambushed convoys, liaison vehicles, and wiring parties and probed various units' night defense perimeters.

In addition to making nuisances of ourselves, we were given a few specific missions: covert agent extraction, propaganda operations, exfiltration of a downed PLA pilot, and "assassination" of a Pineland politician.

Meanwhile, the six friendly US battalions would be hunting us day and night. They had their own combat and reconnaissance patrols out with vengeance, and light aircraft and scout helicopters prowled above the forest's canopy.

On the second or third afternoon of our guerilla idyll, Juan called me to the company command post. Moving carefully, with an eye and ear cocked for the friendly force's aircraft buzzing over the forest, I stayed in the shadows, keeping a camouflaged poncho liner over me.

Juan's CP was in a little ravine under thick pines. His radio operators had spread his bedroll and gear and were busy cooking C-rations with smokeless heat tabs. Juan had his back to a tree, chewing reflectively on a leaf. He had a dangerous look in his eye.

"Have a seat." He swept his hand over the pine needles next to him. I assumed a cross-legged posture and waited. He lowered his voice. "I have a mission for you. A very dangerous mission." He paused for effect. "You are going to penetrate the friendly forces command post and kill or capture General Deane."

Holy shit! In his better moments, Juan could be creative, but this was off the charts. Attack a battalion command post, a communications center, the airfield itself, maybe even the ammunition dump. Possible. But the "friendly forces" command post was the actual division command post. It would be guarded by at least a full company of combat Military Police, plus maybe a special "palace guard" of infantry, a reinforced platoon, even a whole company. It would probably be ringed with double razor wire, and likely there would be only one way in and out.

I thought about it. Assuming we got in, we'd have to get out again. It was an FTX, so we wouldn't kill anybody or shoot the place up, which was what we'd do in a real situation. On the other hand, what a juicy target! If General Deane was in when we came calling, he might have the assistant division commanders with him, both of whom were one-star brigadiers, plus a whole basketful of light colonels, majors, and captains.

It might turn out to be a suicide run, but that was the benefit of an FTX; you could try out all kinds of things. If you were careful, no one got hurt, except for their pride.

"Sounds dangerous, Sir," I said. "Count me in."

"Very good!" he said, smiling. "Run your reconnaissance tomorrow, and make a plan. Let me have it by tomorrow night. If everything goes well, you make your move within twenty-four hours after that. Any questions?"

"No, Sir."

"Good. Get moving."

Back at my platoon CP, Rip, my platoon sergeant, shook his head admiringly. "Sir, I gotta hand it to the Old Man. He's gonna get us all killed with this one."

"Maybe," I said, "but tomorrow morning we're going to be at the division CP to have a look at the setup."

It took us three predawn hours to work our way very quietly into a spot where we could view the command post. Rip and I were using sniper's veils and good camouflage, so we looked like just another couple of clusters of leaves and vegetation on the forest floor. I would have liked full "ghillie suits"; they were totally effective for camouflage, but they were issued only to snipers.

The CP, a small military town of tents and inflatable structures, arranged in orderly formation, was in a huge open field. One large, long wall tent in the middle was likely the briefing tent. We could see sentries at the entrances to a few other tents, which I assumed to be S-3 operations, S-2 intelligence, and division signals. Several radio and other masts stood in the middle of the complex, braced with guy wires.

Off to the side was a landing zone; arriving and departing helicopters provided useful cover noise and activity. The droning of a couple of big diesel generators provided additional, constant background "gray noise."

Surprisingly there was very little effective patrolling around the outside of the double-concertina wire perimeter. Every few hours a three-man security team would walk the perimeter outside the wire. They never ventured out more than fifty meters or so. Military Police manned a security checkpoint at the entrance. There might be roving security inside, but no one seemed to be seriously hunting outside for anyone looking in.

We watched what came and went through the main entrance: mostly jeeps and a few three-quarter-ton weapons carriers. Every vehicle stopped at the entry barrier, a wooden frame woven with barbed wire. The barrier was covered by an M60 machine gun in a sandbagged position, sited to sweep the entry. Passes were checked, and the barrier moved aside.

At mealtimes, a two-and-a-half-ton mess truck, escorted by an MP jeep, came down the road through the forest from the division's "trains" area, carrying hot food in marmite cans. The trains area was about two miles away near the airfield; it held the division's supply, maintenance, and transportation units.

The mess truck pulled up in the vehicle park inside the perimeter. A work detail offloaded the insulated marmite cans to a dining area under a big, green canvas overhead awning.

The headquarters soldiers rotated to the mess point, going through the serving line with their mess kits. Mess helpers ladled out food. Some took their food back to their workplaces; others ate at benches beneath the awning. Everyone washed their mess kits afterward in galvanized cans full of hot, soapy water. The immersion heaters sent clouds of steam into the chill air. When the wind shifted, we caught the aroma of roast beef, with an overtone of kerosene from the heaters.

Rip and I stayed very still while little forest bugs crawled up and down our arms. The sentries at the front gate and inside were relieved every three hours. The mess truck and jeep came down the road from the division trains again—same process as before.

We watched until sunset, then very slowly crawled backward, pausing every few minutes, until we'd gone far enough to rise to a crouch and leave without detection.

Back at our company CP, the best plan seemed risky; I gave it a low chance. Juan thought it was great. But he wasn't going on the raid.

At 1100 the next day, twenty of us were lying back in the forest at a curve in the access road. Cleanly shaved, I was outfitted in regulation "friendly forces" uniform; the rest of the men stayed in guerrilla attire. We had a spotter with a radio well up the road toward the division trains area. At 1145 he sent us a prearranged single code word that the mess convoy was on time and on the way. Quickly, Smitty drove my jeep just off the road. Several of the men helped him very, very carefully to turn it on its side against a tree. Smitty was also shaved and fully outfitted in "friendly forces" uniform and web gear. He lay down beside the jeep. Rip smeared ketchup on his forehead and cheek, pooled a little under his head and out onto the road, then hauled for the wood line to join us.

A few minutes later, we heard the growl of military engines. The jeep and truck swept around the bend at a good rate. I had a momentary fear they'd sail right past Smitty, but the lead jeep driver jammed on his brakes hard. The truck banged into its rear, not hard enough to hurt anyone but hard enough to distract the men in the vehicles.

An MP lieutenant jumped from the jeep; the driver of the truck did the same. They ran over to Smitty. The rest of the troops in the jeep and truck were frozen in that moment, confronted with what they thought was a real emergency.

I was impressed they reacted so quickly, but this was our moment. Mac and his people got the drop on the rescuers. A group of stunned faces were staring down the muzzles of rifles and machine guns. My .45 was aimed in the air to one side of the MP lieutenant. It's not nice to point guns at people if you don't intend to shoot them.

"OK," I said very quietly to him, "have your people put their hands on top of their heads, please."

He looked disgusted. The oldest trick in the book and he fell for it. Worse, we'd taken advantage of Boy Scout instincts.

"Ah, shit," he sighed.

"No one can fault you," I said. "You thought it was a real accident, a trooper injured. You did the right thing."

The truck driver, standing beside him, smiled and put his hands on his head. Slowly, the MP lieutenant did the same. His expression remained grim.

Rip didn't waste a moment. He had the cooks, servers, and MPs out of the vehicles and bundled off into the woods under guard. Smitty wiped the ketchup off and hopped into the MP jeep. The raiders got into the bed of the truck under the hooped canvas cover and below the line of vision of the tailgate. I jumped into the jeep after relieving the lieutenant of his black arm brassard with the big white "MP" on it. We were off.

The next few minutes were like fast-forward video with moments of freeze-frame. We rolled up to the CP perimeter at moderate speed. Instead of slowing, we sped up and barreled straight through, knocking the barrier flying, sending the sergeant of the guard jumping aside. A tossed smoke grenade landed in the machine-gun position, theoretically "destroying" it. We braked to a halt at the entrance to the big briefing tent, where Rip got the drop with his M16 on the single MP at the door, barking, "Freeze!"

I saw a maneuver umpire, identified by white tape around his helmet and a white armband, swinging his clipboard and wristwatch up together as he noted the time and began writing.

Our troops leaped out of the mess truck in various directions, some to the G-3 tent, others to the signals center. A stuttering of small-arms fire began. Ours or theirs, I didn't know; no time to care. Into the briefing tent with my .45 held muzzle up. In the second or so it took to get my bearings, I saw we'd hit the jackpot.

There were a lot more people than we'd expected. All the seats were filled. A staff major froze in mid-briefing, a pointer in one hand, its tip resting on a map on a big easel.

The jackpot was sitting in front of the major. Lieutenant General Throckmorton, the XVIII Corps commanding general. Beside him was Major General Deane, the 82nd Airborne Division's commander. Both generals craned around looking at us as we appeared behind them and to both sides. The rest of the space was filled with colonels, lieutenant colonels, and majors.

"Sir," I said to General Deane, "you're my prisoner, or a casualty."

He rose to his feet, face darkening. "Now just a minute, here!" he began.

He was cut off by General Throckmorton. "I'm afraid he's got us, John." Throckmorton was grinning, enjoying the moment. I saw another umpire scribbling away and figured we'd done our job. It was time to get out of there before things got ugly.

I holstered my pistol, came to attention, and saluted the generals. Throckmorton returned it, but Deane was looking at me intently. I turned to go and heard his voice ring out. "Just a moment, Lieutenant. There is an order prohibiting pistols carried in the field. What are you doing with a sidearm?"

"Sir, this isn't a real pistol," I replied. "It's a toy." It must have sounded as stupid as I felt saying it, but there it was.

"A . . . a *toy*!?" He was incredulous. "Let me see that!" He had his hand out. I unshipped the .45 and passed it to him, muzzle in the air. While he squinted at it, I told him I'd bought it at Schwartz—thought it would add realism to training, without risk of losing a real weapon.

The generals acted as though they didn't hear a word. They passed the gun back and forth, working the slide, ejecting the clip, thumbing the wooden bullets in and out. They were really into it. They muttered, "Very clever!" And, "Lighter than the real thing, but very close."

Deane mused, "Could we get enough for everyone? We could order a few thousand just for use on exercises. Could go Army-wide; solve the loss problem in training." Meanwhile, the staff officers were sitting like deer in headlights. Then Deane said, resignedly, "No; wouldn't work. Imagine what the press would do with a story about the 82nd going to the field with toy pistols."

Throckmorton grunted affirmatively, a little ruefully. Deane handed me the pistol, like a boy reluctant to give up a really neat thing. He was smiling very, very slightly. "Made by Mattel, too, I see. All right, Lieutenant, as the Corps commander has said, 'you got me.' Good work. Now get yourself out of here."

"Yes, Sir! All the way, Sir!" I saluted again, and picking up Rip at the entrance, we made as graceful an exit as possible. I've always remembered how the 82nd Airborne came *that* close to making history in the toy pistol business.

17

"LIGHT AT THE END OF THE TUNNEL"

Autumn 1967

During the fall of 1967, the American war in Vietnam ground on. At home, polls showed that the rising numbers of US troops killed and wounded had begun to raise the question whether we should be in Vietnam at all. In addition to growing protests against the war, an attitude on the part of the general public to "finish it or get out" began to emerge. Seeking assurance of his strategy, Lyndon Johnson reached out to the CIA and the Defense Department for affirmation. The response was unsettling. The CIA's estimate of the size of effective North Vietnamese and Vietcong guerrilla forces in the South came in considerably higher than that of the military's. If the CIA's numbers were correct, the United States had not yet reached the "crossover point" claimed by General William Westmoreland, commander of all US forces in Vietnam. He maintained that attrition of communist fighters on the battlefield in South Vietnam had surpassed the North's ability to effectively replenish its fighting manpower.

If it had not, the war could grind on indefinitely. Sensitive to the mood of the American public in that second full year of US combat action, Johnson called General Westmoreland back to Washington in November for "consultations" and presentation to the media. During that visit, in a briefing at the National Press Club, Westmoreland reaffirmed the military's strategy and progress in Vietnam, stating that the war had reached the point "where the end begins to come into view." Another statement made by him, one that would haunt him for the rest of his life, was that we had begun to see "light at the end of the tunnel."

Westmoreland's optimistic assessment of progress was based on various metrics. After each combat action in Vietnam, the numbers of enemy killed were reported up the chain of command. These "body count" reports were closely scrutinized for their estimated effect on the ability of the enemy to maintain his fighting efficiency. But the enemy was very good at removing his dead; often blood trails were all that were left, causing many US units to "guesstimate" the number of enemy killed. In time, and under rising pressure from higher command levels, these guesses became highly unrealistic. Civilians killed in combat situations were also often included as "padding" in body-count reports by units seeking to assuage the constant demand for "better operational results." "Kill ratios"—the relationships of X number of enemy dead to Y number of US dead—were also cited. The reliability of these arid, lethal numbers was questionable, fueling potentially inaccurate assessments of real progress. Based on these numbers and other intelligence assessments, by the end of November 1967 the US military command in Vietnam was optimistic.

The North Vietnamese enemy, however, were not at all of the same mind. As early as April 1967, their high command had begun planning for a coordinated, massive, all-out surprise offensive in the South. It would strike simultaneously at every major South Vietnamese city and town, and at almost every US and South Vietnamese military base or installation of significance. A special assault team was dedicated to attack and occupy the US embassy in Saigon.

The surprise assault would be launched in January 1968, during the period of "Tet," the Vietnamese Lunar New Year. Tet is the biggest celebration of the Vietnamese year, a time for cleaning house, gathering for family reunions, making pilgrimages, and settling debts. The Vietnamese people travel long distances to be with family during Tet. In the weeks before, it could seem as though half the population was on the roads. In the last week of January, the enemy would capitalize on that turbulence to mask the movement of his guerrilla units, supplies, and special attack teams into place.

In the autumn of 1967, I was informed I could expect alert orders to Vietnam, likely departing sometime in mid- to late summer 1968. There was no way as a new lieutenant I could request assignment to a particular unit in-country. I could as easily be assigned as an adviser to a South Vietnamese Army unit. I would have to wait and see what the "needs of the Army" would be.

As it developed, I would not have to wait long.

18

"HOLD YOUR
UNIT IN READINESS"

December 1967

Captain Juan closed the door to his office. "Have a seat." He folded his hands together on the desktop. "What I'm going to tell you is classified. We've been tasked to provide one platoon, to be held in readiness, for a special mission. I've chosen you and your men." He looked at the ceiling for a moment, then said, "You are to move your platoon to Pope Field at 1800 this evening. An escort officer from XVIII Airborne Corps headquarters will accompany you. At present this mission is classified TOP SECRET. Do you understand?"

"Yes, Sir. May I ask the nature of the mission?"

"I can't tell you anything more at this time. If we get any phone calls, your men's families will be told that your platoon is on an extended no-notice field exercise. I know I can count on you. Good luck."

"Yes, Sir." I stood up, saluted, and left. Outside, Rip, my platoon sergeant, waited on the company steps. I told him the news. He said there was no "scuttlebutt," no rumblings of anything out of the ordinary. We were both in the dark.

Rip went up to the platoon bay to alert the men, stress the security blackout on the mission, have them square their TA-50 equipment away, and draw weapons from the arms room. At 1800 he fell the troops out on the grass in front of the company barracks. I looked them over. They were good soldiers; everything was as required.

A Military Intelligence major from XVIII Airborne Corps appeared with a stiff tan folder with a red border and a red diagonal stripe across it. He riffled through several pages; extracting one, he held it out to me. On a single sheet were TDY, temporary duty orders, assigning my platoon to Headquarters, XVIII Corps, for an indefinite period. Authorization for the orders was

"VOCO," verbal orders of the commanding general, 82nd Airborne Division. This was big stuff.

I nodded. "Understood, Sir."

"OK, Lieutenant, let's get your men over to Pope. Once you're settled in, you and your men will be in isolation until further notice. No one leaves the site; there will be no communication with the outside. Do you understand?"

"Yes, Sir."

We mounted up in two trucks. The major preceded us in a staff car. Half an hour later we were in a huge hangar at the airfield. Air Police secured the entrance; Rip and I showed our IDs and signed in. I signed for the men.

Rows of cots made up with bedding were aligned at one end. A briefing board with a locked cover was mounted on an easel in front of rows of folding chairs in a second area. In a third, a pair of mess attendants were opening insulated marmite containers of hot food, providing a mess line next to rows of tables and more chairs. Spartan as they were, all conveniences were afforded. It was evident we were going nowhere for the time being.

The Army major and an Air Force counterpart took me aside while Rip got the men sorted out and their gear stowed beneath their cots. The weapons were secured in an armorer's cage at the back of the hangar.

The Army officer spoke first. "Lieutenant, your platoon is being held in readiness as a possible reaction force in support of a mission currently being flown in space." I must have registered surprise; he smiled briefly. "There is a possibility that the mission may have to come out of orbit early. If so, you and your men will be dropped as close to the touchdown point of the payload as possible. Once on the ground, you are to locate the payload and secure it until relieved by either a land force or additional airborne forces. You are to secure it against any attempted intrusion by third parties and hold until relieved. Do you understand?"

"Yes, Sir. May I ask where we might be going?"

The Air Force officer replied, "At present we believe it may land along a band of territory crossing equatorial Africa. We're planning to airlift you and your men by C-141 to a site in the region. You will be held in readiness there. Once the location of the touchdown site is known, you will be flown to the area by C-130 and dropped as nearly as possible to that location. You will receive further instructions tomorrow. We anticipate your departure from here within forty-eight hours."

It was mysterious. But we weren't in their business; our job was to do what we were briefed to do. No one mentioned humans; they referred to a "payload." I wondered why those running the mission being flown wouldn't know a lot sooner whether their "payload" was going to come down early. I also didn't know who the "third parties" might be, but I assumed we'd find out the next day.

After the evening meal, which, prepared by the Air Force, was better than we had back at the battalion, a medical team showed up. We all got gamma globulin inoculations to boost our general immunity to disease. They stung, forming a lump under the skin for a few hours until the fluid was absorbed. In those days, anyone in the military changing continents usually got hammered with gamma globulin; it felt like a lump of peanut butter, warm and happy under your skin. Still, if we were facing malaria, dengue fever, and a host of other potential parasitical and waterborne diseases, it wasn't a bad idea.

Rip and I sat together after our shots, each with one of those ubiquitous, tan-colored melamine mugs of coffee. I rubbed my arm. "I don't understand," I said. "A separate paratroop platoon, detached from an airborne company? To jump onto a missile or whatever, somewhere in Africa? A single platoon? Doesn't the Army have outfits that are specialized in this kind of thing, like Special Forces?"

Rip stirred his coffee. "Good question, Sir. But Captain Juan would have asked the same question, wouldn't he? And here we are."

"You're right," I said. I was anything but certain. I wasn't aware of what the Army did or didn't have available. The war in Vietnam seemed to be pulling into itself almost everything in the Army that wasn't nailed down. But General Westmoreland had briefed the Chiefs and Congress a couple of weeks before. He said we were starting to see "light at the end of the tunnel."

Next morning we got the full "word" on the mission. The two majors reappeared, accompanied by a tanned civilian in a short-sleeved, wash-and-wear white shirt, clip-on black tie, black slacks, and black loafers. He wore sunglasses, which he did not take off indoors, and a gold watch big enough to serve as a weapon in a bar fight. If it wasn't a Rolex, it was close.

He introduced himself as "Mr. Smith." Unlocking and flipping the cover off the briefing board, he gave Rip and me a detailed briefing on where we might be going and what we might encounter. He indicated countries we might be parachuted into, a procession of names from the headlines of the day: the Republic of Congo, Gabon, Rwanda, Burundi, and Tanzania.

Mr. Smith knew, or seemed to know, the histories of the countries and the leaders of each in detail, as well as side notes on various guerrilla efforts and bandit gangs. There were characters in his briefing that were straight out of *Terry and the Pirates*. An action comic strip of the day, it starred a handsome American Air Force officer who was always chasing or being chased by exotic bandits. He was always accompanied by gorgeous, exotic women. There were no exotic women in Mr. Smith's briefing. I was wishing I had paid more attention to current events.

Rip and I busied ourselves passing on to the troops what they needed to know in terms of our mission, a number of scenarios we might be confronted with, a few possible actions on marshaling after the jump, and the order and movement from there. I was surprised by how little curiosity the men seemed to have. Fly to Africa. Wait there. Fly to some spot in the middle of the continent. Drop onto . . . what? Sand? Swamp? Jungle? Find the payload. Secure it. Hold it until relieved. Against anyone. "Fine, Sir. No problem."

Few of the men had any further comment, although one or two looked more than a little skeptical. They weren't alone. In the back of my mind I kept wondering why this task fell on us instead of the CIA's paramilitary people or our own Special Forces.

One possible answer was the size of the force required. A Special Forces A-team was twelve officers and NCOs. They were highly trained to lead a much larger force of "indigenous" troops, recruited from the local area, almost always in guerrilla operations. They were force multipliers, not commandos.

And this wasn't a training mission. The task we were briefed for was search, secure, and hold; a defensive operation. I didn't know anything about the CIA's capabilities, but I assumed they had people who could handle something like this.

There had been a number of rebellions, riots, massacres, and other disturbances in Africa in the 1950s and 1960s that resulted in military action, mostly by British, French, and Belgian forces. I guessed we would know more as time went on. We settled down to wait for the flight to Africa.

It never came. On the evening of the second day, the Army lieutenant colonel appeared and handed me another single-sheet order. It released us from "special duties" and returned us to the 82nd Airborne Division. No explanation given.

On our arrival back at the company, Juan was all smiles. "Great job," he said. "Outstanding." But I had a nagging feeling there was something more to it. Years later I found out there were no manned space missions during the period in which we were held in readiness to go to Africa. Project Gemini sent no manned missions into space after 1966; Project Apollo's first manned mission was December 1968. There is no mention of any other space mission of any kind. Was it a clandestine military mission? Was there any mission at all? I guess we will never know.

The only proof it happened is a single line in my officer efficiency report, written and signed by Juan and endorsed by our battalion commander in

February 1969, covering the preceding six months. "This officer organized and prepared his platoon for a recent highly classified mission, keeping his men in readiness and well informed at all times."

As for my thinking there might be something more to Juan's simple "Good job," I wouldn't be surprised if the mission order, which came from XVIII Airborne Corps to the 82nd Airborne Division, didn't have a "back channel" chit attached to it, the kind of personal note generals write to each other. They are informal, usually detached and destroyed after being read by the recipient. If such a message was passed from General Throckmorton at XVIII Airborne Corps to General Deane at the 82nd Airborne Division, it could have said something like, "John—this looks like just the thing for that lieutenant and his men who got the drop on us during PINELAND VI."

Our infantry company stopped briefly at a Marine CAT (civic action team) compound just outside Hué. A few days later, we discovered the mass grave of men, women, and children murdered by the enemy. I wasn't smiling much after that.

Home on convalescent leave in 1968, with my Austin-Healey 3000 Mk III. The last year they made that great car.

Back in the 82nd Airborne in summer 1968, wearing my father's World War II OSS "smock" for a jump from a De Havilland U-6 Beaver.

With the regimental colors of the 508th Parachute Infantry Regiment. Attached are embroidered "battle streamers," each bearing the name of a campaign or battle in which the unit participated. A French *fourragère* is also attached, denoting the 508th's parachute jump into Normandy on the night of 5–6 June 1944.

Commanding B Company, 2nd Battalion, 508th Airborne, as a first lieutenant during a 1968 division-sized FTX (field exercise) in North Carolina.

Prepared to escort visiting General Aurelio de Lira Tavares, chief of staff of the Brazilian Army as he inspects my company, Fort Bragg, North Carolina, November 1968.

Briefing General Aurelio de Lira Tavares, chief of staff of the Brazilian Army, Fort Bragg, North Carolina, November 1968.

We took this company picture when I turned over command of B Company, 2nd Battalion, 508th Parachute Infantry. "Death from Above" was our informal motto. I left for Vietnam again several days later.

When I joined the 1st Air Cavalry in Vietnam in April 1969, I went back to leading a platoon until the company command slot opened up. These were some of my great soldiers.

As company commander of A Company, 1st Battalion, 5th Cavalry. Though we had a cavalry designation, we were a light infantry, "rucksack" outfit.

Rod carries a 7.62mm M60 medium machine gun, weighing just under twenty-four pounds. An assistant gunner trailed Rod and each of the other machine gunners with two two-hundred-round cans of linked-belt ammunition.

Just shy of a dozen Alpha company troopers on a motorized "mule" on a two-day stand-down from the field. Looming in the distance is the "Black Virgin" mountain, Nui Ba Den.

Waiting for a serial of inbound Hueys in 1969, to be flown into a combat assault, somewhere along the Cambodian border. We mounted so many of these "charlie-alphas" the division awarded Air Medals to its combat infantrymen.

UH1-D "Hueys" of the second lift have just deposited my troopers on the ground in 1969 in a very large LZ near the Cambodian border.

My jungle boots, worn on both Vietnam tours, all the dye washed out, replaced by the reddish, iron-rich laterite dirt of III Corps. Note the dog tag laced into the right boot. I donated the boots in 2011 to the Army Center for Military History; they are a permanent part of the Army's history.

The promotion ceremony took me by surprise. With two generals visiting his headquarters, Lieutenant Colonel "Pete" beams as I shake hands with Major General Elvy Roberts, commanding 1st Air Cavalry Division. Not shown is Brigadier General "Uncle Art" Hurow, who flew from Saigon for the occasion.

Brigadier General Arthur Hurow, one of our family's closest friends. Born in Poland, he served as a combat infantry officer in Italy in World War II.

Marilyn Genz was a TWA stewardess who toured our LZ during her weeklong visit in 1969 to the 1st Air Cavalry Division. Her vest, now in the Division Museum, is decorated with many pins and badges. After her visit, she was known as the "Sweetheart of the Cav."

Though tongue-in-cheek, this cartoon was close to reality. It didn't take long for new replacements to the infantry units in the 1st Air Cavalry Division to turn into seasoned field soldiers.

Nui Ba Den, an extinct volcano known as the "Black Virgin Mountain," rises over three thousand feet near the Cambodian border. A Special Forces unit occupied its summit while the NVA held many caves honeycombing its interior.

I'm on the radio, likely to battalion, whose call sign was GENERAL MOTORS. The density of the rainforest we operated in can be seen behind me.

Butch and Don sling a huge wild boar, killed the night before after wandering into one of our ambushes. We airlifted it back to battalion, where "Mess Daddy," our senior mess sergeant from Louisiana, had it cleaned, cooked, and sent back out to the field units as gumbo.

A terrific battalion commander,
Lieutenant Colonel Ras' was focused on
the mission, intuitive, tactically astute,
and concerned for his soldiers' well-
being.

Christmas

Season's Greetings from the
First Air Cavalry Division
in the Field in Vietnam - 1969

An unusually peaceful scene on the division's Christmas card, 1969. Home and
Christmas were very far away that year.

Not a formal ceremony but full of meaning. Lieutenant Colonel Ras' presents the Silver Star.

In War Zone C, one of the hottest areas in III Corps Tactical Zone. I'm carrying the CAR15 and a belt full of extra magazines as we bring in a resupply "log bird."

Foxhole Delivery Service
Provided by
B Co. 229 Avn. Bn.
Rice Paddy Deliveries
On Call
Foggy Peaks
Appointment Only

BRAVO COMPANY

229TH AVN BN (AH)

"The Stacked Deck Bn"

Has had the privilege of supporting you.
Killer Spade provides fastest, safest delivery.
We are listed in your SOI.

A little humor in the midst of war. KILLER SPADE's "business card," handed to me by the resupply (log bird) pilots from the 229th Assault Helicopter Battalion.

Clean fatigues make the man. But I'm still wearing those washed-out jungle boots.

Our brigade's base area, under the rubber trees of the old French Terre Rouge (Red Earth) plantation at Quan Loi. Sandbags are stacked against the walls, affording some cover against mortar and rockets fragments. There was no such protection for the roofs.

"Loach" pilot with his scout helicopter. These men were fearless, admired by every infantryman in the division. One such pilot flew me to the hospital when I came down with severe malaria.

⑲

"THIS IS NO EXERCISE"

Early February 1968

It was below freezing in Florida. In the coldest winter in decades, agricultural fortunes in the Sunshine State were being devastated.

Our brigade of the 82nd Airborne Division, about five thousand men, was on LONG THRUST, an extended field exercise. The maneuvers began in the last week of January, with day and night parachute drops into the savannah, scrub, and pine forests around Camp Blanding, near Jacksonville.

Very cold days brought weak sunshine. In the freezing nights, we ambushed and patrolled by the watery light of an evasive moon, dodging behind scudding clouds.

We had flown out of Pope Air Force Base on the heels of breaking news that all hell had broken loose in Vietnam. On the last night of January, Vietcong units had attacked across the country, striking at major US and South Vietnamese military bases and key cities: Saigon, Da Nang, Qui Nhon, Pleiku, and the ancient Imperial City of Hué.

Word was the US embassy in Saigon had been attacked by a "sapper" assault team. They killed the American Military Police on guard, blew a hole in the perimeter wall, and penetrated the embassy, where they were hunted down and killed the next day. I later learned that one of my school classmates in Italy was among the American MPs killed.

While the news was surprising, it didn't immediately concern us. We were in a big Army. As chaotic as the reports described, that real war was half a world away. Our attention was focused on the near-term missions in our maneuver scenario in Florida. Vietnam would be there for all of us, as individual replacements, somewhere down the road.

At 0230 my platoon's PRC-25 radio on the company command net hissed to life. Marion, my laconic radio operator, whispered a few words in reply and held the handset out to me.

Captain Juan was on the other end. Mission change. Move to an assault airstrip about four kilometers, or "clicks," away. I checked the map with a red penlight. "Are we still tactical, over?"

"Negative," said Juan. "Put your people on the road. The FTX is canceled."

I pulled in our ambushes; that took half an hour. We headed out on a tank trail, with big chunks of dirt torn up by the tracks. We made good time on the margins, the troops swinging along in a fast night march. No talking. Not from discipline; to save breath. Airborne Infantry is lightest of the light; we prided ourselves on getting from one place to another faster than the movement tables projected.

Long before we reached the airfield, bonfires reflected off the windy clouds glowed and jumped; stars gleamed in the breaks. We came out of a wall of pine to a clearing fifty or so yards across, thousands of yards long. An airstrip had been built there in World War II; it would take our turboprop C-130 Hercules transports. An air liaison control team with jeeps, radios, and lights was positioned on one side.

Ranged along the near side of the strip, groups of soldiers gathered around big fires. Some stood hip-sprung, talking. A few were lying feet to the fire or propped on an elbow.

With a wolfish grin, Juan climbed on the hood of a jeep, making "gather-round-me" motions with his arms. "We're going back to Bragg in the morning." Scattered cheers. "Check your gear; get some sleep. We'll be flown out at first light."

A two-and-a-half-ton truck pulled up with marmite cans of hot food and coffee. Cook's helpers began unloading, doling out the food to a quickly forming line.

After ensuring that my troops were fed and sorted out, I wrapped up in my sleeping bag, looked at the moon, dreamed of hot sun, white sand, babes in bikinis, palm trees, and oranges. So much for Florida.

Late next morning, after a bumpy flight up the East Coast, we landed at Pope. Trucks took us to the battalion area. The rest of the day was cleaning gear and turning in weapons and equipment at the arms room. Rip and the squad leaders made sure the troops showered down, changed to clean fatigues, and headed for chow and their bunks.

Well after dark, I pointed my Austin-Healey out the Yadkin Road gate toward the house in Ponderosa Pines. Two VMI classmates and I rented it from a

Special Forces sergeant major who was then in Vietnam. It was fully furnished down to silverware and crystal. A huge oil painting overlooked the dining table: Saint Michael the Archangel, with flaming sword and Corcoran jump boots, his wings spread, sword in hand, among paratroopers floating down from a fleet of twin-engine C-119 Flying Boxcar transports from the 1950s.

We never ate in the dining room.

I looked forward to a hot shower and some sleep. Bill, a VMI classmate in a different battalion, was the only one at the house, puttering around the kitchen.

"How'd it go?" He stirred a pot.

"Not bad."

"Anything new?"

"Nope; froze our asses off. It'll take me a year to thaw out. Any more of that 'Florida sunshine' stuff and we'd all have died of exposure."

In the shower I stood a long time under very hot water. That stuff about oranges, beaches, and palm trees? For the travel posters. I toweled off, pulled on a clean T-shirt, and fell into bed.

Bill was shaking my shoulder. My company's CQ, the charge-of-quarters soldier on duty after hours to mind the phone, was on the line. I padded into the kitchen.

That night it was Ramirez, a sharp young Puerto Rican SP4. "Sir, we're alerted again. Everyone's being recalled."

"OK, I'll be right in, Ramirez. Thank you."

I looked at the kitchen clock: an hour and forty-five minutes since I walked into the house. I pulled on fresh fatigues and boots; muttered to Bill about someone waiting until we got sorted out and in bed, just to pull another alert; and left.

The night sky was clear and cold, with a little northwest wind. As I pulled up to the stop at Yadkin Road, the Fayetteville AM station was playing "Lucy in the Sky with Diamonds."

But something was odd. At that hour, traffic going onto Fort Bragg should be minimal. Tonight it was bumper to bumper, all going onto the post.

I thought, "This is no exercise."

I drove back to the house. Bill had his feet up, watching TV. "Hey, something's going on. Do you have any spare boot socks?" Bill rummaged around in his room and pulled out four pairs.

The battalion area along Ardennes Street was bustling. MPs shook out concertina barbed wire across both ends of the block, white engineer tape woven through to make the barrier visible. I showed my ID card and was checked off the battalion roster.

A string of two-and-a-half-tons parked nose-to-tail down the center of the street was being loaded. Heavy, wire-bound wooden crates of 5.56mm ammunition. Boxes of fat, green M-21 fragmentation grenades, each nested in its thick, black cardboard cylinder. Jerry cans of water.

A line of M-151 field ambulances stood off to the side. The battalion surgeon and medics updated inoculation records, men getting on-the-spot shots.

I trotted up the steps to the company barracks. Juan, the first sergeant, and two of the other lieutenants were in his office. The division was alerted, he said. Third Brigade was being ordered to Vietnam. The rest of the division was to stand to in case the order expanded to the other brigades.

Our battalion was in 2nd Brigade. Juan said each of the companies in our brigade was detailed to provide one full platoon, to augment a company in 3rd Brigade.

He dismissed the other lieutenants. The first sergeant remained. Juan lowered his voice. "There is a by-name order for you on this movement. I would have sent you anyway. Your platoon is the best I've got," he said. "Good luck; keep your head down. We'll see each other again someday." He held out his hand.

Mystified, I went upstairs to the platoon bay to give Rip and the men the word. I didn't say anything about the "by-name" business to Rip or the troops. We didn't need resentment because I'd been tagged for this movement; the sudden orders meant a number of my soldiers would be returning to Vietnam well within the normal nine-month reassignment interval from their last combat tours.

At about midnight, we marched over to the 3rd Brigade area. Our new company's commander was a first lieutenant. He had no combat experience. Same for the other lieutenants. Most of the men did; I wondered what they might be thinking.

We were assigned a platoon bay. Rip made sure everyone had a bunk. The mess hall, open all night, would feed the men hot soup and sandwiches. Most of the troops put their gear under the bunks and, fully clothed, tried to get some sleep.

We were alerted two hours later. Trucks were arriving in the street below. Boots pounded down the stairs; the air was streaked with mogas exhaust. Tailgates banged down. Sergeants called off names. Troops swung their A-bags up and clambered in, stuffing themselves along the bench seats.

I had one boot on the step to the cab when I heard my name over the chaos. I stepped down. Bland, my VMI roommate and classmate, was grinning from ear to ear. He was the 3rd Brigade's historian. "I knew you wouldn't want to miss this!" He punched me on the shoulder. "This is history! See you in-country!" Before I could reply, he hustled off.

I was speechless. I was going to Vietnam because my VMI buddy figured I wouldn't want to "miss this"? What the hell? I stood there for a moment. Well, I would be going eventually; now was as good a time as ever. I'd be going with my platoon, too; we knew each other, had trained and operated together. That was a very good thing.

We lurched off in a discord of double-clutching and blatting of exhausts. Down the familiar streets, past the barracks areas of the 1st and 2nd Brigades on our left, their low, concrete-block battalion headquarters fronting Ardennes Street. The bigger brigade headquarters buildings slid past on our right. Pale faces of the night-duty CQs stared out at us from the dimmed windows.

We rolled down Ardennes Street past Bastogne, Eindhoven, Carentan, Biazza Ridge—all named for battles fought long ago. Turning onto Longstreet Road, we ground off toward Pope Field.

Generator-driven light racks flooded the flight line. Rows of huge, four-engine C-141 Starlifter jet transports were aligned, T-tails standing high above. Nylon-webbing-shrouded pallets were forklifted into the transports' cargo holds. Troops in helmets, field jackets, fatigues, and boots stood in long lines boarding other planes by the forward doors.

We were grouped by "chalks" of 120 men, checked off by an Army admin sergeant. I was the only officer in my chalk. Our Air Force loadmaster wore a gray flight suit, with headphones, a boom mike, and a long cable connecting him to the plane. He was talking to the pilot up front. It was his airplane; we would be his responsibility until we arrived on the other side of the world.

Our C-141 had rear-facing passenger seats on each side of the central aisle—a bit like airline seats, but not as comfortable. There were no windows. The troop jump doors on either side at the rear of the hold held small round view ports. The interior space was huge, a long tube lit by overhead lights, filled along the floor by the rows of seats. Cables and ducts ran along the overhead. A slanting pressure bulkhead at the tail end of the tube locked the compartment. Behind that bulkhead were huge clamshell doors that could be opened to receive freight, or to drop cargo.

A voice on the overhead speakers told us we would be flying from Pope to Elmendorf Air Force Base in Alaska. We would refuel there. From Alaska, the second leg would be to Kadena Air Force Base on Okinawa. The third leg would be down across the South China Sea to Vietnam. Total flying time was estimated at eighteen hours, not including ground time at the refueling stops.

We took off at 0400. As the wheels slammed into the uplocks, the men were silent, wrapped in their own thoughts. Mine were full of questions.

The interior lights were dimmed shortly after takeoff. Some of the men dozed. Many were stressed at leaving their families and loved ones on short notice; more than half had returned from a full year's combat tour less than nine months before.

Hours out of Pope, I made my way aft, to the view port in one of the troop jump doors. Below, bright sunlight gleamed on snowcapped mountains. I asked the loadmaster where we were. "Beats me, Sir." He shrugged and grinned. "Canada someplace? The South Pole?" He returned to the magazine he was reading.

Elmendorf was freezing, crystal clear, boring. We refueled, careful not to let the troops wander too far from the airplane. They were trained in some survival skills; evasion and escape all the way back to North Carolina might look better than another Vietnam tour.

We climbed again, heading westward over the North Pacific. At Kadena we were told there was a hold on all southbound flights. We deplaned, cautioned to stay ready for short-notice departure.

Rumors circulated: we were being recalled, Ho Chi Minh died, LBJ and McNamara changed their minds, and so on. The troops were bused to the mess hall, officers to the Officers Club, open early. There were as many Airborne lieutenants and captains as at a brigade "officers' call" at Bragg.

We all crowded into the bar and the dining room for steaks and fries. It might be the last decent meal for a while. The Air Force's club didn't disappoint; the steaks were great.

The flight down to Vietnam was uneventful until the very end. Night fell again as we tracked down across the South China Sea. The interior lights were dimmed. I'd given up trying to sleep. There was a tap on my shoulder. The loadmaster leaned over: "Aircraft commander wants to see you, Lieutenant."

I climbed the several steps to the flight deck. A major was flying in the left seat. He and the officer in the right seat both wore odd, white plastic headgear that looked like bicycle helmets.

"Good morning, Lieutenant," he said. "I want to let you know what our options might be on arrival at Chu Lai. Right now the field is closed; the base is reporting incoming rocket and mortar fire. So I'll make a decision in the next few minutes as to whether to go in or just orbit around out here for a while until things calm down."

"Yes, Sir," I replied.

"Now, if I do decide to go in, I'm going to do a very steep descent, roll out and land, and do what's called an engines-running offload. Do you know what that means?"

I'd never heard the term. "No, Sir."

"Once we touch down, we'll slow down very quickly. I'll open the aft cargo doors and lower the tail ramp to just below the horizontal. I'll taxi slowly down the runway, and you and your men will deplane from the ramp. You have to get off the aircraft and off the runway quickly. When I get to the far end of the runway, I'm going to button everything up and turn right around. Then I'm going to come straight back up that runway at full takeoff power. Do you understand?"

"Yes, Sir."

"Good. Brief your people to head immediately left or right after they hit the runway, take cover in the ditches on either side, and stay down until we're fully clear."

"Yes, Sir."

"Good. Now, this last part is very important. Make absolutely sure you have all your men off my runway, and very sure you take every bit of your gear with you. Sucking a pack or a rifle into one of my engines is going to just ruin my day." He smiled. "Do you have that?"

Over the major's shoulder I saw the most beautiful moon, floating in a cloudless sky sparkled with stars. Surreal.

"Yes, Sir."

He smiled again. "This isn't a normal procedure, but that's the way we'll play it. OK. Good luck to you and your men. I'll keep you posted on what I decide to do."

"Yes, Sir." I went back down to the troop bay and got a cup of coffee from the big thermos strapped to the bulkhead. About forty minutes passed. The loadmaster tapped my shoulder; the major was going for the straight-in approach.

I walked back to the aft end of the compartment. The loadmaster handed me a mike on a long cord. As I began speaking, he switched the interior illumination from dim white light to red. I waited until everyone was awake and I had their full attention.

"All right, let's listen up, men," I said. "We're going to be landing in a few minutes at Chu Lai, on the coast of Vietnam. We'll be saying good-bye to our Air Force friends. They've done their job in getting us here. Now we start ours. Here's the way we're going to handle landing and unloading."

I described the situation as the major had explained it. "It's not the way we've trained to exit these airplanes (scattered nervous laughter from a few of the troops), but we *will* get off as specified, and fast. After you get off the tail ramp, go left or right, head for the ditches on both sides, and stay there until you get word otherwise. Make absolutely sure you take *everything* with you. Do *not* leave anything on the runway. Let's all do this right."

The descent was very steep, almost a dive, probably to cut down on exposure to possible ground fire. True to his word, the major hit the brakes hard when we touched down, then gave us a slow, smooth roll to offload.

I was first off the ramp; the heat and humidity, mixed with the kerosene smell of JP-4 fuel, hit me like a wet rag. Before I got to the ditch on the side of the very wide runway, I was in a complete sweat, and would pretty much stay that way until I left Vietnam.

The ditch was half full of water; we all went in up to our waists, keeping our weapons and gear up on the dry side of the bank. Out along what I guessed to be the far perimeter of the base, there were parachute flares, floating down from the high overcast sky, trailing sputtering smoke, casting a yellowish, shifting light. I didn't hear any incoming mortar or rocket rounds, or any outgoing artillery. In fact, it was pretty quiet for an airbase that was recently under attack.

In less time than I expected, the major taxied the C-141 down to the end of the strip, turned around, locked the brakes, and ran up the engines. We could hear the whine increasing to a full roar. Then he came smoking back up the runway, going flat out. The wings flashed over us as he passed. I had never been that close to a big jet; it was impressive. As the plane rotated for takeoff and began its climb-out, the "all clear" began to wail from sirens across the base.

Slowly we climbed out of the water. Not the most decorous entry to a combat zone. Our small portion of the 82nd Airborne had arrived in Vietnam.

20

THE TET OFFENSIVE

February–April 1968

A MASS GRAVE

February. After a couple of days of in-country orientation at Chu Lai, we flew north, through an enormous storm, landing at the Marine combat base at Phu Bai, just below Hué.

Pronounced "h'way," the ancient Imperial City and seat of Vietnamese emperors had been attacked and occupied overnight by local Vietcong guerilla fighters. They were reinforced by North Vietnamese units that had marched at night for days to join in the assault. Some American and South Vietnamese units based in the city were surrounded and fighting for their lives. The Marines had moved combat units into Hué; ferocious fighting was ongoing, house-to-house and street-to-street. The enormous citadel, a fortress with stone walls feet thick dominating the Perfume River, was taken and held by the enemy. A huge, red, yellow-starred flag flew atop the citadel's tall central flagstaff, easily visible to all.

The Marine base at Phu Bai was chaos: serials of air transports landed incessantly, bringing in troops and supplies. Helicopters of all kinds clattered overhead. We had arrived on the edge of a battle that would become as famous for the war in Vietnam as Gettysburg was in the American Civil War.

It rained incessantly. The temperature fell to the lower forties at night; we were issued "sleeping shirts." With them under our jungle fatigues and wrapped in a poncho liner, we were only marginally warm. I almost empathized with the enemy; Hanoi was several hundred miles north—they were probably freezing up there. If I were them I'd likely want to invade the South myself, just to get warm.

During the fighting, Hué stank of burned wood, rotting corpses, and shit. Bodies in the river, canals, and on the streets. A bridge over the moat led to a classic, peak-roofed gate in the citadel wall. Today it's a photo site for tourists. In 1968, across the moat from the gate, a burned-out Citroën held four carbonized bodies; they aren't in the tourist photos.

The sound track at Hué was small arms, artillery, helicopters, and prop aircraft. The clouds were too low for jets. Every now and then, beefy, propeller-driven A-1 "Spads" dropped under the overcast for gun and rocket runs along the river.

The rains stopped in early March, the low, gray clouds replaced by glaring sun, shimmering heat waves rising from the white, sandy soil.

There is a photo of our outfit, pausing at a Marine civil action team's CAT compound on the outskirts of Hué. My radio operator and I sit among rucksacks, weapons stacked against a flagpole in the compound center, sandbagged bunkers in the background. Several of my troopers stand talking; one of them has removed his shirt to get a bit of sun.

I'm smiling, but Marion, my RTO, looks apprehensive. He went home to South Carolina untouched; I was the one who got creased.

After what came next, I didn't smile for a long time.

A day or so later we were on the western edge of the old Imperial City, out on the flats along the north bank of the Perfume River, upstream from the Imperial tombs. During their withdrawal from the fierce battle that shot Hué to pieces, the North Vietnamese and Vietcong discarded or buried weapons and explosives. Our mission that day was to find anything the NVA and VC had left in our company's operating sector.

Captain Zeke, our company commander, had his three infantry platoons spread out to cover as much ground as possible. My soldiers moved slowly forward, spread about ten feet apart.

Late morning. Another platoon's soldiers walked past a ten-pound, canvas-wrapped satchel charge lying in the open in low brush. Zeke erupted, prodding Fleener, who was carrying the radio on the company net. "Dammit! Pass the word! Keep people's eyes open!"

Fleener keyed the black plastic handset. Around a wad of spearmint gum, he droned a flat twang, "Niner-Niner from Six: now keep yer people's eyes open. Six India out."

We moved on. Torrés, one of my sergeants, saw a pale root poking up from the ground. With a whiff of death, the root snapped into focus. He dropped down on one knee. It was a human elbow, the crook of it. Some shreds of skin and white bone. He'd seen skin and bone like that; the stench took him back to New Mexico, where it was hot as hell in the saguaro cactus. Looked like the shank of a calf, maybe, that wandered from its mother. Hit by something—coyotes, mountain lion.

The sun pounded down. Zeke came over. "OK, dig it out." He was eager; enemy dead might be intelligence bonanzas. Buddhism holds that the souls of the unburied wander forever. The enemy buried their dead when they couldn't carry them. They weren't tight on field security; buried NVA or VC might have maps, diaries, or other information.

Several troopers opened their folding shovels. The first spade of dirt brought a wave of rotting stench. Men retched. Zeke backed away. The troops broke out wolf-snouted M-24 gas masks. With more digging, bloated bodies appeared. Civilians; mostly men, some women, a few children. Almost all Vietnamese. Four Caucasians; two men, two women.

All had their hands tied behind them with rope or wire; most were shot in the nape of the neck or back of the head, a few in the face. Rope and wire cut into the skin of some who may have struggled.

The enemy had come to Hué with lists. During the weeks of occupation, roundups and trials were held; betrayals and denouncements followed. People were led away; others simply disappeared. While the enemy held the city, the local VC came out into the open; they were seen, identified. Many who recognized them were killed, to eliminate them as witnesses.

We later learned that documents found on the bodies were those of ordinary civilians; teachers, students, merchants. The Caucasians were a West German medical team, missing from the beginning of the offensive.

The stink burrowed into our gear, took days to leave us. In the States, academics like Noam Chomsky claimed the mass murders at Hué were a "CIA trick." Chomsky didn't stand in that reeking trench.

ONTOS

Combined operations can produce surprises. Related by an Army lieutenant in another battalion at Hué, this example is particularly interesting.

Noon, in the western suburbs. The lieutenant moved his platoon down a street along the north side of the Perfume River, near the old municipal hospital.

On the far side of an intersection ahead, a badly shot up ARVN jeep had crashed against a concrete utility pole. Several bodies were sprawled in and around it in pools of blood.

The lieutenant took a very quick look from down at pavement level at the corner, around the edge of the wall to his right. The enemy had a heavy machine gun across the intersection ahead. It was on the second-story balcony of the second house to the right from the intersection, diagonally across the street. Several NVA or VC were up there, with strips of red-and-blue cloth pinned to the shoulders of their khaki shirts.

That heavy gun commanded the intersection; he couldn't advance across. The houses up and down the street on his side had high-walled gardens; he couldn't flank the gun. What to do?

He described the situation by radio to his company commander. "Wait one," came back. In a few minutes his CO was back on the line. "Stand fast; we're sending support." No details.

He waited. The low clouds were full of rain; the throaty drone of prop-driven A-1 Spads came from east along the river. Far off, a battery of artillery banged away. Automatic weapons chattered somewhere ahead. There was no movement in the immediate area. Nearby, the sound of a baby wailing, quickly suppressed.

From down the street behind came the sound of an engine. His sergeant tapped his shoulder; "What the hell is *that*?" The tone made him turn quickly. An angular, pyramidal vehicle on rubber tracks, it made remarkably little noise. Three long, parallel tubes were clamped along each side. The vehicle stopped, idling, a few yards to the rear of his command group. A Marine in a tanker helmet popped out of the hatch on top.

The lieutenant recognized the long tubes as 106mm recoilless rifles, three on each side. The Marine looked to be about nineteen years old. "Understand you got a problem, Sir. What can we do to help?"

"Yeah. There's a heavy gun across the street ahead, diagonally right, in the second story of a house. Second from the corner, on the far side of the street." With his finger he traced a diagram of the intersection on the sidewalk, and the house across where the gun was sited. "They're up there on a balcony; I don't think they know we're here."

The kid in the helmet thought a bit, then leaned forward and talked with the driver below and in front of him, whose hatch was open. The lieutenant couldn't make out what they were saying. After a moment, the driver nodded, dropped down, and closed his hatch.

The kid said, "OK, Sir, here's what we can do. When I give you the go sign," he waved his hand, "like this, have your guys throw all the smoke they can out there, and then a couple of frags behind them. Throw the frags *really* far out, as far across as they can. After that, leave it to us."

For a moment the lieutenant thought the Marine was joking. The armor, if that was what it was, on that toy with the recoilless guns didn't look like it would stop anything bigger than a light machine-gun bullet. A heavy MG might make Swiss cheese out of it. But, he figured, the kid had to know what he was doing. "OK, if you're for it," he said. "Are those things loaded?"

"Yes, Sir. All six," said the Marine, with a grin.

The sergeant passed the word; several of the men unclipped smoke grenades and held them. Two more were ready with fat, olive-green M26 frags. "OK," said the lieutenant, "when you're ready."

The Marine nodded and dropped down into the vehicle. A moment later, his hand above the edge of his hatch waved twice.

"Smoke!" said the lieutenant. It happened in seconds. The grenades arced far out into the street, spewing yellow and purple clouds. The heavy gun in the balcony opened up, green tracer tearing chunks out of the surface of the street. "Frags!" The men threw them as far across the street as they could. Everyone hit the ground. The flashes and twin CRUMPCRUMP! of the frags flashed in the clouds of multicolored smoke.

Racing partway out into the intersection, the little vehicle pivoted half right, facing the house. The enemy gun hammered harshly again, but it was shooting blind. With an almighty roar, a huge sheet of flame shot out behind the vehicle. The back blast from all six recoilless rifles knocked down a section of the wall behind it.

From around the corner came the huge explosion of all six 106mm rounds detonating. The lieutenant dropped down and took another look around the base of the wall. Flame and smoke shot up from a huge gap where the villa with the gun had been.

The vehicle reversed, stopping beside the group of slack-jawed soldiers. The kid stuck his head out. "Anything else you need, Sir?"

The lieutenant was momentarily speechless. Then, "Damn! I guess not! What do you call that thing?"

"Ontos, Sir."

"Whatever! Thanks a lot! You made our day!"

"Any time, Sir. Semper Fi!" With that, the lethal little vehicle pivoted on its tracks and whined back down the street.

There was a moment of silence in the command group, broken by the sergeant. "Why the hell," he growled, "don't *we* have something like that?"

INTO THE PADDIES

Canals and dykes sectioned the flat paddies. Shimmering heat haze drew our eyes to mirages on the far tree lines, where huts and palms seemed suspended, floating in air.

An ARVN unit crossed our front, riding atop dark-green armored personnel carriers. The South Vietnamese soldiers clustered atop laughed at us, waving, as we plodded along. We watched the APCs ford a canal, the lead vehicle nosing in, pushing a bow wave of muddy water. At the far bank, its tracks sliced into the soft mud, unable to get traction. Tracks whirling, engine whining, it dug itself deeper into the bank. Two more carriers crossed the canal. All became mired. We turned off the bank. Lighter on the land, we moved cross-country. Enraged roaring followed us for a long time.

CATHY MEETS THE ENEMY

At about that time I heard a rumor about a French woman combat reporter who had bicycled into Hué at the height of the fighting and got herself captured by the NVA. Incredibly, she had talked her captors into permitting her to photograph NVA soldiers. As the story went, she was afterward released by the enemy unharmed. Her name was Catherine LeRoy.

Odd things happen in war, but this sounded particularly fanciful. We had found the four West Germans in that trench; why would the enemy let a French-woman go? But a week or so later, in one of the inbound mailbags, there was the latest issue of *LIFE* magazine. On its cover was LeRoy's photo of a pair of NVA soldiers in Hué during the occupation. Inside was her feature article, detailing the story as I had heard it.

In a war full of unique characters, Cathy LeRoy stood out. With no training as a journalist, she had flown to Vietnam on her own, got a camera, and set off as a war correspondent. She had talked her way into parachuting on operation JUNCTION CITY with the 173rd Airborne Brigade, the only correspondent allowed to do so. She had covered the savage fighting by the Marines to take Hill 881. She had gone to Khe Sanh during the siege there. She could curse like a trooper. She was one of a kind.

"STREET WITHOUT JOY"

Detached from our old company, my platoon had started out as an "orphan." In time we got to know our new unit. The lieutenants were all good officers; two were West Point graduates. All were Ranger qualified. Platoon sergeants and other NCOs were competent professionals.

Some of the soldiers had been in-country before. They knew the basics from experience: dispersion, awareness, digging in, stringing trip flares, patrolling, ambushing, noise discipline. The rest tried to learn fast.

The French named Highway 1, the main coastal road, "the street without joy," for the dead and wounded they had lost up and down its length. On a night ambush patrol in the hills west of that road, we went into position at a trail junction in solid darkness. Everything was done by feel and slow motion, low whispers. I lay beside Ross, our Irish M60 machine gunner. The draft had plucked him off a construction site in New York City. He was pissed when they told him he either served or it was back to Ireland. He found he liked the Army; he went to jump school and did a year in Vietnam with the Airborne brigade of the 1st Cavalry Division. Now he was back again.

Ross was the shortest man in my platoon besides Torrés. His bush hat brim worn low over the eyes, he could have been farming in Ireland. I asked him once about his plans after the Army. "Ah well, I'm thinking there'll always be demand for a man with me skills." He grinned. I don't think he was referring to construction.

There is a photo of our patrol's return next morning. Seven men, most smiling. It is a clear day, the hills behind covered only by ankle-high brush. Bob, the sniper at far right, cradles the wood-stocked M14 with a PVS-1 "starlight" scope, the first night observation device. When switched on, it whined like sexed-up mosquitoes; the scope picture, green and aqueous, was crude but effective.

Next, Torrés, who nosed out the mass grave at Hué. Munras stands beside him carrying the radio, his arm on Torrés's shoulder. I'm next, arm over Munras's back, M16 in right hand, muzzle down, and yes, I had fixed my bayonet to the weapon.

Then Ross, the heavy black M60 balanced on his right shoulder, holding an extended leg of the bipod, two linked belts of ammunition for the gun slung crosswise. Beside him, two troopers whose names escape me. Both tall, one with a hat as big as a sombrero. Torrés, Munras, and me in M1950 patrol caps, Ross in his Irish farmer's bush hat.

MORTARS AND MINES

Next day began with a bright morning, mist low in the valleys, clear on the hilltops, blue skies. From our vantage I looked across at soldiers on a far ridge, lined up for breakfast at a field mess. I don't recall if the ridge was an extension of our unit's or another's.

They were all out in the open, grouped together, nicely bunched up. I ran over to Zeke. "Sir, can you get them on the horn over there?" He swiveled to see where I was pointing, grunted "Shit!" and reached for the radio handset as we saw puffs of the enemy's mortar rounds impacting. The bursts, just a few, hit one after the other. Seconds later, the CRUMPCRUMPCRUMP! of the explosions reached us. Several men killed or wounded.

The same morning, a sudden, dull detonation. A jeep suspended in midair, two soldiers hovering momentarily above it. During the night, the road to the firebase from the valley floor had been mined. We had mine detectors; they weren't used. Lessons were learned the hard way.

PK's

We moved out into the plains. Close to a hundred degrees, no wind, no shade; humidity around ninety. During the French Indochina War from 1946 to 1954, outposts had been built every few kilometers along major roads. Lonely, bleak cement pillboxes, with a watchtower and open water cistern. Designated "PKs," for *postes kilometres*, they were manned by Vietnamese, Lao, or Cambodian troops of the French Union forces.

They were also referred to by the French Army as *appât de buse*, or "buzzard bait"; lonely targets for night raids by the Vietminh. In such cases, dawn usually found the defenders dead, their weapons and meager supplies removed by the enemy.

On this numbingly hot afternoon we paused at one of those stark, long-abandoned posts. Men broke out their canteens; Zeke talked to battalion on the radio. A couple of my troops sat on the rim of the cistern, filled with scummy green water. Without warning, a young sergeant E5 stiffened, fell backward, and disappeared. He wore a helmet, load-bearing gear, and boots.

One of the men shucked off his boots and gear and dove in, but he was gone. The cistern was deep. After an hour and repeated dives, his body was recovered. Otherwise a good soldier, he had been chewing on a wad of C-4 plastic explosive as if it were gum. Claimed he liked the taste. Several men warned him it was likely dangerous. His death was a ridiculous loss. It wouldn't be the last of that kind I would see.

SITTING DUCKS

Another searingly hot midday, we were strung out along a canal dyke bordered by a line of trees providing welcome shade. Zeke and the company CP were back down the canal about a hundred meters. Half the men were breaking into C-rations; the others kept watch. Across from the other bank, green rice paddies stretched away to a far-off, thin green line of trees. The haze made them seem to float in the air.

A nonsmoker, I was trading the cigarettes in my ration pack for the foil-covered chocolate discs in my RTO's B-2 unit. With no warning, M16 fire cracked out farther down the dyke. More shots snapped off; men eating snatched their weapons. There was no sound of return fire.

I hustled down to my lead squad. Two troopers were sitting in the shade, laughing as they took potshots at a group of ducks in the water about fifty meters further down. They snapped off a couple of rounds; the ducks squawked and paddled around, outraged, as small geysers of water shot up where the shots were hitting.

"Knock it off!" I came up behind them. They looked at me, surprised. "Someone owns those ducks. If you want to turn some farmer into a VC, if he isn't already one, just shoot his ducks. Understand?"

"Yes, Sir!"

Grumbling, I went back up the dyke, leaving Rip, my platoon sergeant, descending on them with their squad leader. Zeke was at the CP on the radio. I stood by while he finished. "What was that about?" I explained; he shook his head. "All right, keep an eye on them."

"Yes, Sir. But, something else."

"What?"

"Clear day, no wind, no enemy, over open sights. And those two couldn't hit a bunch of sitting ducks? We may have bigger problems."

He grinned. "You may be right. Be sure you're behind them in the next fight."

Zeke decided to leverage our coverage of the company's area of operations. Dividing it into rough thirds, he assigned one of his three rifle platoons to each. We were on our own.

THE BOY ON THE DYKE

Leading or commanding men in combat is a huge responsibility; a wrong decision or bad move can get people seriously hurt or killed. It was the first time I had independent control of my little unit.

We were operating well within the range fan of the artillery battery supporting our battalion. If need be I could call for fire or for air support. I had the platoon medic in my little CP group. Most of my men were experienced combat veterans. Still, I was apprehensive. It was like learning to drive; daunting at first, easier as you went along.

Overlaid was the experience of finding that mass grave. It really impacted me. I was concerned; that was a good thing. But, more importantly, I was very focused on the mission of killing communists.

It turned out to be a walk in the sun; the enemy moved further west and south, into the hills. We trekked across paddies and dykes, searched a few huts, explored tree lines. I sent out a few small patrols under experienced NCOs; no result. We found a rice cache camouflaged at the base of a saw palm thicket and scattered it.

Uneventful. Except for the afternoon of the first day. On a dyke bordering paddies in the middle of nowhere, we came upon an old man and a little boy. There was no village nearby. The man was bent over the boy, shielding him from the glare of the sun with his big conical straw hat. He was crying.

The boy was on his back, having some kind of breathing attack, gasping for air. My first reaction was that it might be a ruse. We carefully checked the old man and the boy for anything concealed. Nothing. My medic quickly examined the boy. "Severe asthma or something else. He'll probably die out here eventually. Nothing I can do." The old man kept crying and babbling in Vietnamese, which none of us spoke. I looked at Rip. He shrugged. My medic stood up.

I turned to Marion for the radio handset and called Zeke, requesting medevac, specifying that the casualty was a noncombat civilian with a breathing problem. It was damned audacious to call for air evac for a civilian, a noncombat casualty at that.

The memory of what we'd found at the massacre made me want to help. The boy was likely to die; we had the means to do something. The request would probably be denied, but it was worth a try.

Surprisingly, Zeke didn't object. A few minutes later, the medevac pilot came up on my radio. We threw out a smoke grenade. The Huey descended steeply, flared, and touched down. Two of my men lifted the boy and carried him to the helicopter.

One door gunner jumped off and ran a quick frisk of the old man and the boy, then helped the old man in. The boy lay on the floor. The old man sat on the webbing seat running crosswise. As the pilot pulled pitch and the ship lifted, the old man looked out at us. Palms together, he bowed his head repeatedly.

We continued searching. At dusk we linked up with the company. Zeke took me aside. He had listened to my description of the situation and passed the request up the chain. Afterward he received a scorching rebuke for calling a medevac for a civilian; air evac assets were for American casualties. But, he said, it was approved and the mission was flown. We might have done some good.

I've always remembered and admired Zeke for that. I like to think our medical people did what was necessary for the boy: he survived the war, made it to America, went to college on a scholarship. Right?

Not likely.

"DANGEROUS DAN"

When our brigade deployed to Vietnam, Major Jake was commanding. He was well respected by the officers and NCOs. But Infantry battalions rate lieutenant colonels as commanders. Our battalion couldn't be left to a major. Jake was pulled up to brigade staff. We got a new lieutenant colonel.

Shortly after he took over, the new battalion CO visited his companies. The day before the visit, word came down from battalion: everyone, no exception, was to write the letters "DDD-O" on both sides of all canvas helmet covers. Block capital letters, ink, two inches high, four wide. No explanation.

The directive resulted in muttering and shaking of heads at various levels, but it was the word. We complied, using ballpoint pens that came with the "sundry packs" of toilet articles, magazines, playing cards, and writing paper.

Our company was atop a ridge overlooking Highway 1, just south of Hué. The new CO's command helicopter landed in a blast of rotor wash, blowing the few poncho liners the troops had rigged for shade off the hill.

Our new commander arrived in starched jungle fatigues and shined jungle boots. His clean helmet cover displayed the DDD-O lettering, crisply applied on each side. Closely trailing him was the battalion sergeant major, his helmet also neatly lettered. The sergeant major carried a sawed-off black pool cue, which he used as a pointer, jabbing at various equipment and troopers.

Zeke escorted the CO around the company's perimeter. Eventually they arrived at my platoon's sector, covering two routes up into our position from steep draws that ran down the back side of the ridge. I walked the CO along our portion of the defense, showing him the siting-in and fields of fire of our machine guns. I indicated on the map and pointed out on the ground the mortar and artillery concentrations that covered the dead spaces, and the interlocking fields of fire between my platoon's and the adjoining platoons' positions.

He nodded, then asked, "How are you fixed for smokes?"

We had plenty of colored smoke grenades, I said, and fragmentation and white phosphorus as well. He looked at me as if he'd just noticed I could speak. "That wasn't my question, Lieutenant. I want to know if your men are getting their cigarettes." The sergeant major stood impassively behind the CO, tapping his trouser leg with the pool cue.

Either the colonel knew of some cigarette problem, or he was unaware they came with every C-ration unit. The troops were in no danger of running out of "smokes." I replied, "Yes, Sir, they are."

After the CO's ship lifted off and the men were retrieving their poncho liners, Zeke gathered the platoon leaders. Overall, he told us, the colonel was satisfied with our position. But he wasn't at all pleased with the sloppiness of a few of the troops' job of putting the directed lettering on their helmets.

The CO had told Zeke his nickname was "Dangerous Dan"; "DDD-O" stood for "Dangerous Dan's Demons, Bar None." He wanted everyone to know that, and the number of helmets he had identified as unsatisfactory were to be relettered, ASAP. The botched covers being unsatisfactory, we would need new helmet covers, also ASAP.

Patton had his pistols; MacArthur had his corncob pipe. Dangerous Dan was going to have "DDD-O" all over every man in the battalion. He rated the availability of cigarettes at a high level of concern.

Shortly after that visit, word came down the CO had been wounded while visiting another unit; no details given. The CO replacing Dangerous Dan said to get rid of the lettering. We all got new helmet covers. We kept patrolling.

The day Johnson stated he wouldn't stand for reelection, we were back on that ridge. Johnson's speech was delivered in the evening in the States; it was high noon in Vietnam. A group of us listened on a transistor radio tuned to AFVN, broadcasting the speech live. So Tet brought down a sitting president. Nobody on our hilltop seemed to care much. We were on the other side of the world, neck deep in the war.

The log bird that day brought water, rations, and mail. I leafed through the Asian edition of *Time*, printed on flimsy paper. The business section had a picture of the Golden Gate Bridge, seen through a window, between two men seated facing each other in jackets and ties. Coffee cups were on the table. One man read a newspaper; the other was looking out at the bridge. The caption said they were riding a ferry across the bay to work in San Francisco, from some town with an unusual name. The article explained that regular ferry service had begun between Marin County and San Francisco. I showed the picture to Marion. "Look at this. Is that cool or what? Ride to work on a boat, and get a great view doing it?"

"If you say so, Sir." Marion opened a B-2 ration can. He was right to be disinterested; like Johnson's speech, nothing in the *Time* article had any effect on us. Years later, in a different life, I would take that same ferry to work in San Francisco from Sausalito, the oddly named town in the article.

WOUNDED

A week or so later we shifted to another area of operations, a bit further inland. The company's night defense perimeter was on an elongated, irregular hilltop. We moved up onto the hill very late; it was dark by the time we had our positions in place. My platoon sector covered a portion of the flank that looked north.

From my position we could see almost all the way west to the foothills of the A Shau Valley, north across the river to Hué, east almost to the sprawling base at Phu Bai, hidden by more hills, where we had landed in February.

There were a few high clouds that night, stars shining between; cool but not cold. Unusual to have such a panoramic view. Marion and I shared a position with the platoon medic, behind my first squad. Rip was off to my right, on the other side of a draw that led up the hill.

I sat with my back against my rucksack, looking up at the stars. Beautiful night. Suddenly a sheaf of rockets burst from the hills off to our left, arcing in fiery orange streaks across the sky, to impact in the Phu Bai base behind the hills to our right.

Almost immediately artillery and mortars began firing illumination from various points across our field of view. The flares popped into life high above, swaying down, leaving smoking trails above the parachutes. Their light was orange-white, casting constantly shifting shadows. You kept your vision down; looking directly at the flares left dark streaks in your night-adapted eyes.

I told Marion to get some sleep; I'd wake him about midnight. The medic would take the third radio watch in the hours before dawn. Nothing happened for the next couple of hours; a few aircraft high above, helicopters, intermittent "harassment and interdiction" fire by our artillery, toward the mountains in the west.

At midnight I woke Marion. When I was sure he was awake, I picked up my M16 and headed over to Rip's position. We would check the rest of the sector. I moved across the draw, looking down the hill. Flares were coming down; the bushes cast swaying shadows.

Down and to the left in the draw, a wavering bush snapped into backlighted silhouette: the head and shoulders of a man. Another was just behind him, a bit further down. For a moment I thought they were my soldiers, from first squad, then realized the draw was wider than I thought and they were coming uphill. Fatal mistake; they were enemy, and close!

I pulled my M16 up and shot pretty much from the hip. It was on semiautomatic; as I pulled the trigger again, it felt like I'd been hit in the arm with a ball bat. I dropped down and shouted for Rip. There was no pain; my arm was numb.

It happened in seconds. I stayed in a crouch, expecting them to come right up that draw. Nothing happened. The whole hillside was awake; there was no further shooting. I hustled back to the platoon CP and called Zeke on the radio. The medic wrapped a quick pressure dressing around my wrist and hand. I couldn't feel anything from the elbow down.

Zeke called for more illumination; it was in the air very quickly. After that fast exchange, there was nothing more to our front. No movement. To this day, I have no idea what that was. A recon? A probe? Were they lost? Did they even know we were on that hill? Combat is full of unknowns; I would see many more.

MEDEVAC

The jet engines wound down. The huge clamshells at the rear of the plane whined open; the tail ramp lowered. From inside the big C-141 transport, the view was an early evening sky, perfectly clear, the sun setting behind a range of hills. The air was clean and fresh. After a long flight from Japan, we were at Travis Air Force Base, north of San Francisco.

I was unsettled at the dialogue I'd experienced with a couple of the medical people in Japan. I didn't think I was that badly hurt and had said so at our battalion aid station in Vietnam. That was met with smiles and assurances that I'd be returning to the unit after a few days.

I was passed through the medical chain in-country, the injury examined and assessed at each step. At the evacuation hospital on the coast, I was told that possible nerve injury required surgery in Japan. Vietnam was "a septic environment." That made no sense; if the Army could do surgery on serious cases in-country, what was so different about a light wound?

At the hospital in Japan, the surgeon tapped the lighted X-ray. "You're lucky; if that had come in a fraction of an inch lower, it would have likely shattered your forearm and taken out your elbow." But, he said, surgery likely wasn't needed; with therapy to regain full motion, it would heal.

Shortly after, I was told I'd be sent to CONUS, the continental United States, for convalescence. I'd stated I wanted to return to my unit. I was being shunted back to the States?

I must have been emphatic; I was referred to a pleasant major, who turned out to be a psychiatrist. He counseled me about "survivor's guilt." "Perfectly normal," he said. "We see it all the time. Don't worry, Lieutenant; the war will still be there on your next tour. Have a nice day."

Further protest brought the admonition that if I kept "complaining" I could be referred to the hospital's commandant for disciplinary action. At that point I resigned myself. The major was right; the war would still be there.

FITZSIMONS

At the Air Force hospital at Travis, I was asked which medical facility I preferred to be sent to. I put down Valley Forge in Pennsylvania or Walter Reed in Washington, DC; they seemed closest to my home in New York. But due to the Tet Offensive, both those hospitals were full. The next day my name came up for transfer to Fitzsimons General Hospital in Denver.

A blue Air Force van drove several of us, in blue pajamas and bathrobes, out to the flight line. We passed a line of C-141s and several C-130s and stopped beside a boarding stairway that led up to the door of a true museum piece. A silver, four-engine prop transport on tricycle gear. A C-54 Douglas Skymaster, it was straight out of the 1950s. I half expected to see Harry Truman standing at the top of the stairs grinning and waving his hat.

The C-54 was the executive transport for the commander of the Colorado Air National Guard. A glass cabinet on the bulkhead facing the door had those push-in white plastic letters on black felt background that you used to see at restaurants or movie theaters: "Welcome Aboard 'Old Blue.'"

The flight out to Colorado was memorable. There were headphones at each seat; the cabin crew switched them to Glenn Miller big band music, all the way to Denver.

From Buckley Air Force Base we were bused to Fitzsimons, an enormous hospital in Aurora, east of Denver. When built out there in 1918, Fitzsimons sat in the middle of open prairie. By 1968, suburban Denver had grown out and around it.

The main building, of enormous 1930s architecture, towered above everything around it. Fitzsimons was full; beds were taken up with serious wounded. Walking cases slept on folding beds in the hallways. The fighting during Tet was taking a severe bite out of our soldiers in Vietnam.

I knew I wasn't going to be there long. After leaving the brigade in Vietnam, I belonged to the Army medical system. If I had to be in the States, I wanted to be reassigned to the 82nd Airborne at Bragg. I was pretty sure if I didn't do anything about it, the Army could assign me any number of places.

The day after arriving, I found the office of the hospital administrator. A Medical Service Corps captain behind a gray steel desk listened to my request. As I explained my request, he took several swigs of coffee from a mug. He put the mug down and half smiled patiently; people probably came in with this kind of request all the time.

"I hear you, Lieutenant." He moved a piece of paper from one side of the desk to the other. "We'd like to accommodate. But the system works in its own way. We'll transfer you to 'casual status' when you're able to be released on convalescent leave. You'll have to report back here for reassignment when your leave is over. By then the system will have determined where you'll go next. Is that clear?"

Very clear, and not at all encouraging.

THE FIRST PURPLE HEARTS

In early June, I was on convalescent leave in New Windsor, New York, just over Storm King Mountain from West Point. A pleasant little town with its feet in the eighteenth century, New Windsor is home to two noteworthy events in American military history.

First was a little-known potential mutiny of the officers of the Continental Army, and the threat of military action by the Army against Congress.

In 1782–83, eight thousand soldiers of the Continental Army were in camp at New Windsor. The British surrender at Yorktown, Virginia, in 1781 had ended active combat, but the peace treaty was still being negotiated in France. Meanwhile, the British army and navy still occupied New York City and other eastern ports.

George Washington, commander of the Continental Army, maintained his headquarters near New Windsor. He feared that if the treaty negotiations in France failed, the British might attempt a restart of the war. In readiness for a possible spring 1783 military campaign, he kept the Army at New Windsor.

At the same time, Washington was faced with a potential mutiny of the Army's officers. They had served diligently in the war; many had lost homes, property, and family members. They were owed back pay, land grants, and pensions. Now, Congress was slow in approving the awards, ignoring the officers' appeals for redress.

Washington learned that a conspiracy was brewing, to march on Congress and demand payment, at the threat of arms. He asked a subordinate to call all the officers to a meeting.

They assembled, grumbling, expecting to hear from the subordinate. Instead, Washington himself entered. In his opening remarks, he counseled patience, decrying the threat of use of armed force against Congress. Then he paused, fumbling for a pair of reading glasses. His officers had never before seen him require them. "Gentlemen," he began, "you will permit me to put on spectacles, for I have not only grown gray, but almost blind, in the service of my country."

Several who were present wrote later that, seeing their beloved commander so worn by his duties, hardened combat officers openly wept. Washington's remarks defused the anger; the nascent revolt stood down. Since that day, the US Army has adhered to the principal tenet of subordination to civilian authority.

New Windsor is also noted as the site of the first award, in 1782, of what today is known as the Purple Heart. Three soldiers who had distinguished themselves during the war were awarded the Badge of Military Merit, presented by Washington himself.

Only one survives. Awarded to Sergeant Elijah Churchill of the 2nd Light Dragoons, it is a cream-colored armband, on which is embroidered a large purple heart. The word "Merit" in white appears on the heart, surrounded by embroidered vines. It can be seen at the National Purple Heart Hall of Honor at New Windsor.

The modern Purple Heart medal is directly descended from those first awards. It is heart-shaped, bearing Washington's profile, on a purple ribbon edged in white. On the reverse in raised letters is the inscription "For Military Merit."

1968

It was a year of severe unrest at home and abroad. In just the few months before I arrived home on leave in late May, North Korea captured the USS *Pueblo*, an electronic intelligence ship; the Tet Offensive in Vietnam caught American forces almost completely off guard. American troops massacred five hundred Vietnamese civilians at My Lai; Martin Luther King Jr. was assassinated; and Lyndon Johnson announced that he would not seek reelection as president.

Still to come in 1968 were the riots at the Democratic National Convention in Chicago, the murder of Bobby Kennedy, Arlo Guthrie's introduction of his twenty-minute song "Alice's Restaurant" at the Newport Folk Festival, and the Soviet Army's invasion and occupation of Czechoslovakia.

In late May I was in a quandary. I was on "casual status," not assigned to any Army unit. I technically belonged to Fitzsimons General Hospital in Denver. I had no idea what my next assignment would be.

I had a couple of physical therapy appointments at the hospital at West Point to follow up on getting my arm and hand back in shape. I could almost fully rotate the arm, but it was still pretty stiff.

21

82ND AIRBORNE

May 1968–April 1969

BUMPER NUMBERS

On the way to one of my medical appointments, I was stopped at an intersection at West Point, behind an Army two-and-a-half-ton truck. I idly looked at the truck's bumper numbers to see what outfit it belonged to.

At that moment, however, I was more interested in the engine temperature of my '67 Austin-Healey 3000 Mk III. A hot sports car and the last year it was produced, the radiator fan ran off a belt drive to the engine. When the engine was idling, the fan hardly moved. So, after checking the temperature, I looked up at the truck, and zowie!

I'm smiling as I write this. Deciphering Army bumper numbers was like reading a code. Military aficionados make a hobby of it, much like train-spotting is a hobby in the UK.

In 1968 the numbers and letters on the front and back of a military vehicle told the unit it belonged to, and the bigger unit that unit belonged to. The numbers on the back of that truck were:

82 AB - HQ 2/508

Translated, the truck belonged to the headquarters of the 2nd Battalion, 508th Infantry, a unit of the 82nd Airborne Division.

There was only one likely reason that truck from the 82nd Airborne at Fort Bragg, North Carolina, could be at West Point in late May. Each summer, cadets who have finished their Plebe (freshman) year go through six weeks of military training at Camp Buckner, on the big West Point reservation. Each summer an Army unit goes to West Point, on temporary duty, to support the cadets' summer training. In the summer of 1968, a battalion of the 82nd Airborne was very likely at West Point for that duty.

From my three years as a boy at West Point in the 1950s, I knew the summer support units were based at Camp Natural Bridge on the West Point reservation. After my hospital appointment, I drove the Healey out Route 293, past my old Cub Scout and summer camp site at Round Pond, to the turnoff to Camp Natural Bridge. I was wearing tennis shorts, Top-Sider moccasins, tennis shorts, and a short-sleeved Madras shirt. Hardly military.

"CASUAL" NO LONGER

The buildings at Natural Bridge were one-story, green wooden affairs looking more like a Scout camp than a military post. A blue metal swallow-tailed guidon with white crossed rifles, with HHC 2-508 ABN lettered on it in white, hung in front of the headquarters.

As I opened the screen door and stepped in, a Spec-4 clerk typing at a desk looked up, curious. "Can I help you?" He likely thought I was lost; I certainly didn't look "regulation."

"Yes, I hope so. Is the S-1 in?"

He narrowed his eyes a bit. If I was asking for the S-1, I must know something about the Army. "Wait here, please."

Shortly, a captain followed him back in from an office behind the Spec-4's desk. "What can I do for you?"

I explained that I had been in the division's 3rd Brigade in Vietnam and was now on casual status, still assigned to the hospital. I'd been trying to be reassigned to the 82nd.

"May I see your ID card?" he said. I handed it to him. "Hmm." He looked me up and down. "Do you normally drop into a headquarters dressed like that?" He was smiling. "Wait here."

Presently he was back. "Come with me, Lieutenant." We went through another door, further back in the building. The battalion commander, a lieutenant colonel, looked up from signing papers. I stood at attention; saluting in civilian clothes wasn't in order. "The adjutant tells me you're looking for a job. Is that right?"

"Yes, Sir. I've been asking to be reassigned to the 82nd, and am due to return to Fitzsimons in a week."

The colonel asked how 3rd Brigade was doing in Vietnam, what my duties were in-country, how I was wounded, and whom I had talked to about reassignment. After a few minutes, he said, "OK, go have some coffee out front if you like. Don't leave the building."

The S-1 stayed with the colonel. I went out to the entry. The Spec-4 pointed to the percolator, with its condensed milk can and, yes, accompanying bayonet.

About ten minutes later the S-1 came out. "The colonel has spoken with Division G-1 at Fort Bragg. You're assigned to this battalion, and further down to Bravo Company. Be here 0700 Monday. If you don't have fatigues, get them. Your temporary orders authorization is VOCO: verbal orders of the commanding officer. Permanent orders will follow." He held out his hand. "Welcome to the 508th." We shook.

I smiled all the way back over Storm King to Mom's house.

SUMMER SUPPORT

My new job was executive officer to Captain Rick, commanding Bravo Company. He was a "mustang," from Seaside, California, next to Fort Ord. The term referred to officers who served as enlisted men before they were commissioned. It's from the days of the "Army of the West." Wild horses that roamed the plains, mustangs could be caught and trained, but they retained a streak of the wild. Rick was a professional, a charismatic natural leader; he also had a great sense of humor.

Among other training missions during that summer, Bravo Company ran the M60 machine-gun instruction and conducted a live-fire demonstration during a segment on Infantry Platoon in the Defense.

M60 RANGE

The machine-gun range almost got me in very hot water with the New York State Police. One morning after all the NCOs and soldiers had dispersed out to the various training sites, Sergeant Jerry called from the M60 range. He was a cheerful African American and a crack shot; his normal duties were on the division pistol team. Two of the M60 machine guns on the range had problems, he said, and cadets were waiting to shoot. Could we get a couple of replacement guns down to him ASAP?

All Bravo Company's vehicles had departed for the morning's training sites. But the armorer had two M60s ready to go. The range was about five miles away; training was waiting. I could get there in no time in the Healey. The armorer put the two guns in the back of the car, which had its top down. They were just long enough so they wouldn't lie flat on the rear bucket seats; their matte-black snouts stuck up at a slant, just above the folded-down car top. The armorer stuffed several cans of 7.62mm linked-belt ammunition under the guns and in the foot wells in front of the bucket seats. "Can't never have too much linked belt, Sir," he grinned.

About a mile from the range, I looked in the Healey's mirror. Wall-to-wall red lights. A state police car was right on my bumper. I pulled over. The trooper was on his radio for a few minutes, likely calling in my license plate number. He unhooked the flap of his pistol holster as he walked up to my driver's side door. I kept my hands on the steering wheel.

He looked me and the guns over. Good thing I was in uniform. "May I see your identification and license?" I carefully extracted both. He studied them. "Why are you carrying these?" He pointed to the guns.

I explained I was taking them to the range for training the cadets. He thought that over, tapping the cards on the palm of his hand. He put them in his ticket book. "All right. Here's what we will do. I will follow you to the range. You will drive at the posted speed. If you think your little roller skate can outrun my cruiser, think again. Is that clear?"

Very clear. When I pulled up at the range, followed closely by the police cruiser, Sergeant Jerry was grinning from ear to ear. He and a helper hustled the guns out to the firing points. The sound was almost deafening; we had ten M60s working, and the cadets were having a ball shooting at targets in their fire lanes.

The state trooper was talking on his radio. I walked over and waited until he had finished. "Thanks for being understanding. I realize it wasn't the brightest thing to do."

"Don't mention it, Lieutenant. Next time, try to use a truck, or a jeep or something."

"I will. I wonder, if you have a couple of minutes, if you'd like to put a few rounds downrange. If it's allowable."

It was his turn to grin from ear to ear. He left that range a happy man.

HOW WOULD DAD DO IT?

Rick detailed me to narrate the live-fire demonstration for Infantry Platoon in Defense. It was a stock feature of every summer's course of instruction. Held at a range with bleachers facing targets placed against a berm across a shallow valley, about three hundred meters to the front, it showed off all the weapons of a full infantry platoon and demonstrated their impressive firepower.

Each paratrooper in a forty-seven-man platoon was equipped with either the M16 rifle, capable of semi- or fully automatic fire; the 40mm grenade launcher; the M60 machine gun; or the 90mm recoilless rifle, capable of defeating tanks or blowing open bunkers.

Every year the "Platoon in Defense" class was held in the same way. The cadets would arrive by truck and climb into the bleachers. Arrayed across their front, a platoon of soldiers stood next to the various weapons on mats, set up to fire. The narrator identified each weapon. As he did so, the soldiers fired the weapons singly, then in a "mad minute," all the platoon's weapons firing together. Riflemen shot at individual targets; machine gunners swept their sectors with red tracers; grenadiers lobbed their high-explosive 40mm grenades onto targets in their sectors; the 90mm recoilless rifles, located on each flank, fired with their characteristic backblasts and the big detonations of their high-explosive rounds.

It was impressive; a platoon could throw a lot of weight. But to me, something was missing.

A day later my driver and I were headed out to one of the training sites. "OK, stop here." We pulled over. I got out and walked to the bank of one of the lakes. It had changed some; a lot of vegetation since fourteen years before. But it was the same spot.

My father had arranged for me and a couple of the neighbor kids to be there one afternoon in the summer of 1954. The class was on "field expedient" solutions. That day the cadets watched a driver race a jeep into the lake; it promptly sank to the level of the seats. The driver sloshed back to the bank; the jeep was towed back out.

Another jeep was driven onto a canvas tarp at the water's edge. Folded up over the front, back, and sides and lashed together, the tarp gave the jeep buoyancy. Lifted by four men on a side and slid into the water, the jeep was easily floated. It was another of Dad's out-of-the-box solutions.

Uncle Art once told me that when he and Dad were lieutenants in the 9th Infantry Division at Fort Dix in the postwar years, their unit was given the task of moving several "Quonset huts" to a new site several blocks away in a very short time span.

The Quonsets were half-cylindrical, twenty by forty-eight feet, made of curved metal shell sections bolted together. To unbolt and completely disassemble each hut, transport the sections, and reassemble them would take a long time. Dad suggested they simply unbolt each Quonset from its foundation, and then, with forty men on each side, they would pick up the buildings and walk them down the road to the new location. A man with a T-shaped pushbroom atop each end of the roof lifted telephone wires as they passed. They finished the assignment in record time. Afterward, Art and Dad threw a barbecue and bought beer for the men.

I thought, how would my father do the platoon demonstration? A day later, I went to Rick with a suggestion. He listened and smiled. "That will definitely be different. Before we go live with it, you'll have to do a dry run for the colonel and Major Mike and get their sign-off."

Major Mike was a Marine Corps officer assigned to the Academy as an instructor. The platoon firepower demonstration was in his summer instruction area.

I got the platoon leader and men of our demonstration platoon together and described what we were going to do. You could see the smiles start as the troops looked at each other. We walked over the ground of the demonstration area, selected the positions, and got to work.

A few days later, we did the full-dress dry run for the colonel, Rick, and Major Mike. No shooting; just showing how the demonstration would progress from the moment the cadets arrived to the moment the shooting began.

The colonel was intrigued; he said he would bring the battalion XO and invite a couple of other officers he knew on the Academy staff. Major Mike said it was something he would expect a Marine to think of. Major Mike later became a Marine general, so I'll take that as a compliment.

On the day, the cadets arrived on time and climbed into the bleachers, chattering away. In front was the valley. Across the valley were the targets. In front of the bleachers was the usual terrain: bushes, grass, a tree here and there. In the center was a lectern and microphone arrangement. A pair of loudspeakers flanked the bleachers. No narrator was evident; there wasn't a soldier in sight.

The cadets chattered among themselves. Then a voice boomed from the loudspeakers: "Gentlemen, may we have your attention, please?" The talking died down. "Good afternoon. Welcome to 'Infantry Platoon in the Defense.'"

The cadets looked around. The lectern was empty. The voice continued. "This afternoon you will see the capabilities of an infantry platoon in defensive position. Our soldiers today are from 2nd Battalion, 508th Parachute Infantry. A complete infantry platoon is now dug in across your front in defensive positions, prepared to deliver tremendous firepower to the targets downrange. Can you see them?"

There was a lot of chatter, exclamations of disbelief, and so on. The voice continued, "The reason you may not see anything to your front is we've decided to combine today's defense demonstration with a lesson in camouflage. If you can't see my soldiers, gentlemen, neither can the enemy. Remember this day when you become platoon leaders yourselves. Now, let's see what we have for you."

At that point, camouflaged as a bush, directly in front of the bleachers, I stood up and took off my helmet, which had the background shrubbery woven into its camouflage band. I walked to the lectern. Before the cadets arrived, my troops were in well-camouflaged defensive positions. One by one, going from the cadets' left and across their front, I introduced my soldiers, with each type of weapon. As they were identified, they stood up, waved, then disappeared back into the camouflage.

It definitely got the cadets' attention. The firepower demonstration went off without a hitch. Combining camouflage with the platoon in defense and firepower demonstration was very likely the kind of approach my father would have taken.

LIBERTY JUMP

In late June, word came down from headquarters. On Thursday, July 4, the battalion would conduct a mass parachute jump at Liberty, New York, about thirty miles northwest of West Point. Liberty had officially invited the entire battalion to a barbecue, sponsored by a number of local organizations, to be held after the jump.

Liberty is a small town in Sullivan County, New York; beautiful, rolling dairy country. During the Revolution, when it was much smaller, it contributed over three hundred men as militia and soldiers in the Continental Army. In 1968, though controversy over the war in Vietnam was growing, Liberty remained patriotic. Their July 4 was a much-looked-forward-to, big event.

Liberty was also in the heart of an area known for its popularity as a summer vacation spot for Jewish families, largely from New York City and its suburban environments. So much so that the region was colloquially known as the "Jewish Alps," and the many resorts that catered to Jewish families as the "Borscht Belt." Grossinger's, a huge 1,200-acre resort just outside Liberty, was preeminent of the hostelries.

On the morning of the 4th, a truck convoy took the battalion, minus a small, griping stay-behind element who would miss the post-jump party, to Stewart Air Force Base, ten miles north of West Point. During World War II, Stewart had trained West Point cadets to fly. Many wound up in fighters and bombers; many never returned.

As our truck convoy rolled past Base Operations and out to the C-130s on the flight line, I remembered the Air Force's gracious treatment of a sole VMI cadet, home on Christmas leave. Could that really have been only two years before? It seemed like a hundred years.

Liberty was a "Hollywood" jump. No equipment. We drew our parachutes, ran the jumpmaster checks, and loaded into the C-130s. The flight out to the DZ was about twenty minutes.

The loadmasters locked the doors in the up positions; soon we were streaming out into a perfect summer's day. Blue skies; high, white clouds; and an enormous green field below. As I descended under my canopy, keeping a wary eye out for other jumpers, I was amazed at the number of people who had come out to see the drop. They seemed to be ranged along one side of the DZ about five or six deep. It was going to be a big party.

I did a reasonably good PLF, gathered my chute, and trotted over to the trucks. We were driven to the outskirts of town, de-trucked, and formed up by companies. We marched through Liberty in fatigues, boots, and helmets; no band, no flags, but the steady tread of seven hundred pairs of boots was nonetheless impressive. Spectators lined the streets on both sides, waving American flags and cheering.

The barbecue was first class. The people were friendly; the speeches were bearable. If anyone misbehaved, I didn't see it. We returned to Natural Bridge with memories of a great day, and the knowledge that there were many Americans who were proud of their soldiers. Sadly, that feeling would be diminishing; the war was eating it away like waves washing sand from a beach.

FIRST COMMAND

Shortly after we returned to Fort Bragg, Rick, on orders to Vietnam himself, took me aside. "I recommended you take the company," he said. "The colonel agreed."

Wow. I was stunned. I was in grade as a first lieutenant only a few months at the time; there were captains itching to command an Airborne infantry company.

Rick put it in cold perspective. "The colonel thinks you've got what it takes. So don't fuck up; if you do, you'll be relieved."

I determined neither of those events would occur.

TWO GREAT LIEUTENANTS

I was fortunate to have very good officers. Two were particularly outstanding.

Mac came to us in September 1968. Graduating *magna cum laude* in history from Harvard in June 1967, he immediately enlisted in the Army as a private. Passing out as honor graduate of his class at Infantry Officer Candidate School (OCS) at Fort Benning, he went through jump school, then reported to our battalion.

Mac's Harvard degree and his communication talents were recognized; he was held on battalion staff as Assistant S-1 (Administration). Itching to serve with soldiers, he regularly requested transfer to one of the battalion's rifle companies. The colonel wasn't about to let a man with Mac's talents out of the "head shed," so Mac eventually forced the issue. Telephoning the Department of the Army, he requested assignment to Vietnam. When that unorthodox message traffic crossed the colonel's desk for approval, the colonel relented; Mac was assigned down to us in Bravo Company.

Mac and I shortly established that our fathers had both served in the OSS in World War II. Mac's dad was legendary; he fought in one of the International Brigades during the Spanish Civil War, taking part in the bitter fighting in University City in Madrid. As an American officer in the OSS in 1944, he led one of the famed "Jedburgh" teams, parachuting into France immediately following D-Day, to lead French resistance fighters against the occupying Germans. The Jeds' mission was to delay German units from reaching the Normandy area. They were so successful that some German units didn't reach the Normandy area for over a week. After the war, Mac's father earned a PhD in classics and eventually chaired the Harvard Institute for Hellenic Studies in Washington, DC.

I asked Mac why he had enlisted as a private to go to Officer Candidate School rather than seek a commission via ROTC while at university. We both were aware that if he hadn't made the grade at OCS, he would have been on a plane to Vietnam as a replacement rifleman in short order. Mac's answer was straightforward. His intent was to lead American soldiers in combat, he said; he wasn't about to stand in front of them as an officer from some "pussy" ROTC program at Harvard. His words exactly.

Mac went on to the 173rd Airborne Brigade in Vietnam, was wounded and decorated for combat leadership, then left the Army. He did his masters and PhD in history at Yale, became a prominent military historian and author, and eventually chaired the Department of History at the London School of Economics.

Mac was thoughtful, concise, and dutiful, one of the best officers I had the privilege to serve with in the Army. Not surprisingly, years afterward, he was inducted into the OCS Hall of Fame at Fort Benning. We have remained close friends ever since those early days together in Bravo Company.

Paul was equally professional. From a Massachusetts family with a historically Navy background, his grandfather encouraged him to join the Army. Good man, that grandfather; the Army got a great soldier.

Like Mac, Paul enlisted as a private, went through Infantry OCS in 1968 at Fort Benning, then jump school, and straight to the 82nd. He was my company executive officer. Quiet, decisive, and thorough, he was always impeccably turned out. Years later, I learned he would dash across post at midday for a change into another set of freshly starched fatigues.

Paul ran bed check of the troops every night, then set up a cot in my office to catch a few hours' sleep. The company CQ would wake him in time to clean up, get dressed, and stow the cot. He was working at his desk in the company office before I came in every morning.

Paul served as one of the jumpmasters on almost all of our parachute jumps. In the field, he was as attentive to detail and thorough in execution as in garrison. He was an asset to the company and the Army.

He went on to get his Ranger tab, then serve with the 23rd Infantry (Americal) Division in Vietnam, several times taking over his infantry company when it lost its commander. His battalion commander was Norman Schwarzkopf, then a lieutenant colonel, who would become a four-star general, commanding DESERT STORM. Paul's brigade commander in the Americal Division was Joe Clemons, famed for his heroic counterattack in Korea in the battle for Pork Chop Hill.

After Vietnam, Paul commanded an A-team in the 7th Special Forces Group at Fort Bragg, and an infantry company in the 82nd Airborne. Initially commissioned as a Reserve officer, like my father he was later commissioned in the Regular Army. He retired as a full colonel. Like Mac, he was inducted into the OCS Hall of Fame at Fort Benning.

I mention Mac and Paul as representative of the caliber of officers I was fortunate to work with. Both products of Officer Candidate School, as my father had been, they were among the very best of our generation.

"ARE YOU STILL HERE?"

A landing against organized and highly trained opposition is probably the most difficult undertaking which military forces are called upon to undertake.

—George C. Marshall, General of the Army, 1943

An airborne operation involves the air movement into an objective area of combat forces and their logistic support, for execution of a tactical, operational, or strategic mission.

—FM 3-90, *Tactics*, appendix C

It was January 1969; our company was to execute a night jump with full combat gear onto a DZ on the western Fort Bragg reservation. From there we would move cross-country to attack and hold an objective airstrip by dawn, for follow-on landings of troops and equipment.

Except for the fact that we would be in-flight only about a half hour or so before the jump, it was a condensed version of the kind of assignment we were prepared to carry out, anywhere in the world.

The troops were up for it. We briefed at the company and moved out to Pope Field in trucks. The base and the flight line were dark, except for light stanchions beside a C-141 jet transport, far down at the end.

It was a freezing cold night. Clear, light winds, a little moon, bright stars. The riggers had two lines of main and reserve parachutes laid out. Our breath steaming in the night air, we chuted up and did the jumpmaster checks. We boarded everyone by the port-side forward door, just behind and below the flight deck.

There were no crew in the plane as we climbed in and took seats on the nylon benches. The aircraft was dark, as freezing cold inside as out. Eventually a van pulled up; the crew climbed aboard without saying a word. The lights came on; the engines started. The loadmaster slid the door shut and locked it. Heated air began circulating. Looking down the interior of the aircraft, I saw a few of the troops doze off; others chatted among themselves. I settled back and waited for us to get moving.

After about ten minutes, the engines wound down and stopped. The load-master unlocked the door and opened it. The van returned; the flight crew came down the few steps, filing out the door. None of them seemed to notice us. The last crew member stopped, stuck his head back in, and said, "Are you still here? The airplane's broken; we won't be flying tonight." He went down the steps and into the van, which drove off.

I won't repeat any of the remarks from the troops. I unbuckled my seat and shucked off my main and reserve chutes. It was a long, cold walk to Base Ops. I called the duty officer at battalion. They sent trucks; we went home.

I later learned that the report on that fiasco went all the way to the division's commanding general. I can only imagine the rocket that went from him to the Air Force.

ON THE RECEIVING END

Shortly after that episode, I was Drop Zone Safety Officer for another battalion's mass tactical night jump, onto SICILY drop zone.

The DZSO is the man in control on the ground in peacetime; he maintains contact with the troop carrier aircraft by radio. He monitors conditions on the DZ and can call off the drop if the wind speed rises above a certain level, or if other factors might endanger troops in the air or on the ground.

On that night, my driver and I took my jeep out to SICILY DZ, followed by a pair of field ambulances and a few trucks to recover the troops' parachutes. We arrived at midnight, parking along one side of the drop zone.

Easily half a mile wide and about two miles long, SICILY DZ had been scraped down to bare earth by the engineers many years ago. In 1968 it was the biggest drop zone on Fort Bragg. Other DZs at Bragg were HOLLAND, NORMANDY, SAINTE MERE EGLISE, and SALERNO. All were named for combat drops or actions by the 82nd Airborne Division during World War II.

It was another clear, starry night; just a sliver of moon, almost no wind. I stood beside the jeep, chatting with the medics. Eventually the lead C-141 Starlifter came up on the DZSO frequency on the jeep's radio. Winds were light; no other air traffic, no obstacles. I cleared the aircraft to drop.

The long line of C-141s flew a wide arc out over the countryside, then turned inbound toward the DZ. They would fly parallel to the drop zone, turn to cross along its base, turn again aligned with the DZ's center axis, and start dropping troops.

"There they are," said a medic. The transports had their navigation lights on. We heard the rumble of their jet engines as the twinkling lights paraded past, a couple of miles out, along the far side of the DZ.

Then an interesting thing happened. I had never been on the ground before at the receiving end of a night drop. Sure, the planes were obvious with their nav lights on as we watched them go by, down the far side of the DZ. But as they turned and lined up coming toward us, they were dead silent. All that jet noise was trailing behind them. We could see their lights, but in combat those would be turned off.

Seven hundred battle-ready troops were headed straight at us. If this had been an actual tactical drop, there would be little to no warning.

"Execute, execute," squawked the radio. Twelve hundred feet above us, troops were streaming out the jump doors, but we couldn't see anything except the transports' wingtip lights. As the jets passed overhead, the engines' roar returned, fading as they flew away.

For a few moments, silence. I looked up. It was deathly still. Then the stars began to be blotted out by big, black mushrooms. Suddenly, amid the eerie whoosh of air displaced by many canopies, jumpers were thumping down out in the dark in front of us. Soon, hundreds of men were arriving in the darkness.

That's what it would be like on the receiving end; a force like that, in the middle of the night, dropping on the enemy without notice.

IRF DEMONSTRATION

The 82nd Airborne Division's mission was global: be ready to go anywhere in the world and fight on arrival. Word could be received at any time to send troops; the division maintained a Division Ready Force, rotated among its three brigades. The DRF Brigade assigned one of its battalions as the ready battalion; one of the battalion's companies was designated the Initial Ready Force.

The IRF company was the standing by 24-7 spearhead of the division. Sequestered in barracks, its vehicles and equipment were packed for airdrop and prepositioned for rapid load-out at Pope Field.

It happened that Bravo Company's turn as our battalion's IRF company was coming up in the very near future. I was summoned to battalion headquarters; Colonel Johns sat me down in his office. "Division is receiving a visitor while your company is standing IRF. Brigade says it's important he gets an up-close look at our rapid deployment capability. Nothing official, but apparently there are aspects of diplomatic importance to his visit. That is sensitive; keep it to yourself." He looked at me to make sure I got it. I nodded. "Division wants him to see the IRF company," he continued. "Can you handle it?"

"We can do it, Sir. May I ask who the visitor is?"

The colonel read from a paper on his desk. "General Aurelio Tavares. He is minister of the Brazilian Army. That's equivalent to our Army chief of staff in DC. Word is he is strongly pro-US. He commanded Brazil's Expeditionary Force in World War II. A note here says he's also written over thirty books on history." The colonel looked up and smiled. "Just the ticket for another history major, don't you think?"

How the colonel knew I majored in history at VMI was surprising. But I learned early never to underestimate him. "We'll make sure he and his people get the right impression, Sir."

"Very good. Go to it."

I headed back to the company and huddled with First Sergeant Bernard. He was a "by-the-book man" with a fixed habit of addressing me in the third person, "Old Army" style. "Does the lieutenant think this is a good idea?" Or, "Does the lieutenant desire that I take this action?" It was a bit unsettling.

Bernard was a combat veteran of Korea and a master paratrooper, with only a year left until retirement at twenty years. Rumor had it he had been a senior captain in the 101st Airborne, the Army's other parachute division. He was a Reserve officer, not a Regular; along with several thousand other unfortunates in a recent reduction in force, as a commissioned officer he had been considered "excess to the requirements of the Army in a RIF."

He was given a choice: he could leave the Army without a pension, or he could accept demotion to NCO rank, transfer to another division, serve the remaining few years to twenty, and retire on his officer's pension. He chose the latter.

It must have been difficult, as a former officer of higher rank and greater combat experience, to serve under a lieutenant. He was doing it day by day, with no deviation. Hence the distance and the formality.

Bernard was an impressive soldier: serious, dedicated, brooking no nonsense. I respected him greatly and knew he would get any job done right. He was a definite asset.

We talked over coffee in my office. As always, Bernard sat ramrod straight in the chair. His fatigues were starched with creases that could have carved roast beef. His jump boots were mirrors. The first sergeant's three chevrons up and three rockers down, with the centered diamond, stood out on his sleeves.

I recapped the colonel's briefing, how he desired that we make a strong impression on the visitor. "Top," I continued, using the informal term for first sergeant, "How would you suggest we handle this?"

Bernard had a square jaw, pale blue eyes, and a silver brush cut. "If the lieutenant might consider, it may be impressive to the visitors to see something besides a static display."

"What do you have in mind?"

"I've seen these demonstrations before. The troops are all drawn up in formation; the visitors arrive and walk around looking at the men and the equipment. Dull, if I may say."

"I agree. So?"

"Suppose they arrive in the company area, and there's just the lieutenant, the company's guidon bearer, and myself. All the equipment is laid out for inspection: the jeeps, the recoilless rifles, the mortars, the radios, the prepacked drop loads of ammunition and rations. The machine guns. We can have the gear that's actually inside one of the prepacked loads laid out on a tarp in front of one of them, all squared away."

"Where are the troops?"

"They're lined up in the hallways in the barracks. At the lieutenant's word, I blow the whistle to have them fall out. They come bounding out both doors, forming up by platoons. Then the lieutenant presents the company and escorts the visiting general through the ranks."

That's how we did it. As additional flair, every man's face and hands were daubed with green-and-brown camouflage greasepaint. We all carried our assigned weapons; I had a real .45 ACP in my holster for this one.

General Tavares turned out to be a surprisingly affable man; he shook my hand after I saluted him. He thanked me in excellent English for taking the time to provide the demonstration and said he was very much looking forward to it. If he was wondering where the rest of the soldiers in my company were, he didn't show it.

Behind the general were his two Brazilian Army aides, our colonel, and Major General Seitz, the 82nd Airborne Division's commander. General Seitz seemed a little puzzled as to why there were no troops present, but said nothing. There were also a couple of civilians in dark suits and sunglasses. I assumed they were from the State Department.

At my command, Bernard blew the whistle; the barracks doors popped open. The troops pounded down the steps and formed up. Their face and hand camouflage was a bit incongruous with their starched, fresh fatigues and shined boots, but they looked very sharp. A full company of infantry, about 170 men, with all their vehicles, weapons, and gear, is an impressive sight.

I escorted General Tavares along the lines; he stopped every now and then and shook a soldier's hand, smiling. It was a nice touch; you didn't see much of that in the US Army.

Everyone was pleased; Colonel Johns was beaming, and General Seitz smiled as General Tavares complimented him on his fine soldiers.

That was about it. A year later, General Tavares was in a *junta* of Brazilian generals that seized control of the government. General Tavares himself became president of Brazil.

Years later, out of the Army, I had occasion to speak with General Seitz, himself by then retired. I reminded him of the readiness demonstration for General Tavares. A big smile crossed his face. "I believe he got the message the United States was a strong friend of Brazil. Good job."

I remembered the suits, the ones in sunglasses. I guess they weren't from State after all.

NOT THE BEST OPERATION

First Sergeant Bernard retired. A handshake and a salute. "First Sergeant," I said, and meant it, "I owe you more than you know. I greatly appreciate your assistance and advice."

He squared up; his gray eyes looked straight into mine. "You'll do fine, Lieutenant. Good luck." It was the only time he dropped the third person. Then he was gone.

Our new first sergeant was Tuttle; short, solidly built, with four rows of ribbons and two gold combat stars on his wings. He had jumped into Normandy as a private with the regiment on D-Day, and into Holland in the fall of the same year in operation MARKET GARDEN.

He was nearing the end of thirty years of service. A field-weathered man of few words, he growled rather than spoke and rarely raised his voice. He didn't have to; the troops held him in awe.

Tuttle wasn't as distant as Bernard, but he was just as professional. He probably thought it was odd that a first lieutenant was commanding a company; there was no shortage of captains rotating in and out of the division. Whatever his thoughts on that, he kept them to himself.

Returning from one of our field exercises, the troops squared their weapons and gear away by midday. We had set a brigade record for movement to contact and seizure of our objective, under an unusual set of operational circumstances.

Tuttle stopped inside the door to my office. I was signing over 150 individual meal cards; the Army never tired of sending that stuff through. "Sir, if you're not busy later today, a couple of the other NCOs and I will buy you a beer at the NCO Club."

I looked up, surprised. That kind of offer didn't come often. "Absolutely, Top. Happy to. Thanks. What time should I show up?"

"1800, Sir. There's some good music laid on, and the beer isn't bad." Understatement. It turned out the club had booked Merle Haggard for that evening. He sang his great trademark song, "Okie from Muskogee." It brought the house down. Sergeants were standing on the tables, hollering and hooting. Haggard ate it up. I was honored to be there.

He was right about the beer, too. None of that cat piss from a keg; we both had a couple of San Miguels. The time seemed right to ask a question I'd been waiting for. "Top, what was it like, at Normandy?"

He waited a few seconds, drank some more beer. I wasn't sure he'd heard me; the band wasn't that loud. He looked straight at me. "Well, Sir, there has never been such a fucked up operation."

I must have seemed surprised. He went on. "No, I don't mean they shouldn't have dropped us where they did. I mean what happened." He drank some more beer. "My stick of troopers landed off target, but we gathered up some strays. And during the night, little groups of us got together here and there, and wherever we could, well, Sir, we really fucked the Krauts."

"But the next morning, see, the sun didn't come up so much as it was a heavy overcast. As it got light, we saw troopers drowned out in the fields; the Krauts had flooded them. Even more, our guys were hanging dead in the trees." He paused and took another swig.

"What about Holland?" I asked.

"Worse. That was a daylight jump. It's one thing to go in at night and the Krauts shooting flak blind at the planes, but this time we came out right over them; they could hardly miss."

"What happened?"

"They shot down a number of our C-47s. Our plane was hit, too, but my stick got out OK, right over a battery of 88's. The gunners were kids, teenagers. No local security. We landed all around them. Evened the score for Normandy.

22

1ST AIR CAVALRY DIVISION

April 1969–April 1970

In April I returned to Vietnam for a second combat assignment. I remembered that reeking ditch full of bodies at Hué and being shunted out of the country. I had a score to settle.

At that time, reassignment to Vietnam was nine months after returning to the continental United States (CONUS). There was an informal policy that if you had been evacuated to CONUS as a result of a combat wound, you could request assignment to a particular unit in-country on the next tour. No guarantees; the needs of the Army came first.

Even so, junior officers on assignment to specific units could have their orders changed anyway when they stepped off the plane in Vietnam. Some combat units like the 101st Airborne Division, 173rd Airborne Brigade, and 1st Air Cavalry Division, were frequently shifted to where the heaviest fighting was. They needed a lot of junior officer replacements.

Emmett, a close friend, graduated from West Point in June 1967, went to the 2nd Infantry Division in Korea, then through Airborne, Ranger, and the Special Forces Qualification, or Q course, in the States. Arriving in Vietnam as a first lieutenant, he had orders assigning him to the 5th Special Forces Group. At Tan Son Nhut airport outside Saigon, he was told he could choose between three non–Special Forces combat units instead, all of which required immediate officer replacements. It wasn't unusual. He chose the 173rd Airborne Brigade and commanded an infantry company.

As a result of the informal reassignment policy, a few months before my rotation date back to Vietnam I requested assignment to the 1st Air Cavalry Division. It was a great division with a strong combat record. In a few weeks my orders came back from the Department of the Army; I was confirmed for assignment to the "1st Cav."

On a rainy morning in April, I said good-bye to my mom and brother. It was going to be a hard year for Mom. My father had passed away a few years before. I was returning to the war. My brother, Dave, who with my mom had endured Dad's illness, decline, and death while I was away at VMI, was just entering college in Boston. He would be in all the cross-currents and arguments surrounding the war.

The TWA flight to California was uneventful, as was the United Airlines MAC-PAC flight to Vietnam. I gave one of the stewardesses Mom's telephone number, asked her to call. Weeks later, when the mail caught up, Mom wrote that she received the call.

The flight to Vietnam was very different from the year before. Instead of jumping into a water-filled runway ditch from the ramp of a C-141 at 2 a.m., I arrived on a charter flight at Tan Son Nhut airport at noon. The hammering heat and humidity, though, were the same as before.

THE "1ST CAV"

The first of the Army's "airmobile" divisions, the 1st Air Cavalry Division, was about fifteen thousand strong. With more than four hundred helicopters of various types, it could move its nine light infantry battalions like chess pieces, supplying them and supporting them with artillery and "down-in-the-weeds" air support from armed helicopter gunships.

The 1st Cav fought some very big battles in Vietnam, most famously in November 1965 in the Ia Drang Valley, near the Cambodian border. In that fight, a battalion of the 7th Cavalry went "belt buckle to belt buckle" with a full regiment-plus of North Vietnamese infantry, at landing zone (LZ) X-RAY. The lessons learned at the Ia Drang, and other fights like it, were part of the tactical doctrine we used in the field in 1969.

The 1st Cav's insignia was a large yellow shield bearing a horse's head in black profile, with a diagonal black stripe across the shield, representing the old mounted cavalry trooper's blanket roll.

In Vietnam, the division's nine maneuver battalions were "airmobile infantry," airlifted into action by helicopter. While they carried the unit designations of cavalry regiments of the "Army in the West," they were light infantry: "rucksack" outfits, operating for weeks at a time in the jungle.

After confirmation of my orders at Tan Son Nhut and a quick briefing for new arrivals, I flew north by C-130 to the division's base area at An Khe, in the Central Highlands. There, I was in-processed and assigned onward to 1st Battalion, 5th Cavalry, in III Corps Tactical Zone, north of Tay Ninh.

On the evening of my arrival at my new battalion's rear area at Tay Ninh, I learned I would be flying out to the battalion's forward firebase in the morning. Meanwhile, I could pick a cot in one of the "transient hooches" across the dirt street.

Hooches were plywood rear-area buildings, fifty feet long by twenty-five wide, metal roofed with a wide overhang, screened all around from waist high to ceiling. Sandbags were stacked to waist high along the outside walls against fragments or small-arms fire. There was no protection for the roofs.

I looked into the dim interior of one of the hooches. Folding canvas cots lined both sides of a wide aisle. Some had mosquito netting; most didn't. From the gear on or under the cots, a number of others would be sleeping there, but it was still early evening. A single figure was asleep on the cot farthest from the door. I picked one nearest the exit. If I needed to get out, I might be in a hurry.

I walked toward the mess hall, a larger building. Suddenly WHIZ! and a huge explosion four or five buildings away. Pieces of something buzzed past like enraged hornets. A chunk of burning plywood flew by and skipped off the ground. Moments later a siren began wailing, not far away.

A hooch and a truck beside it had taken a direct hit from either a rocket or heavy mortar. Likely a rocket; mortars didn't "whiz"; they "shuffled," like the rustling of a curtain. It was a single explosion, too; mortars usually arrived in groups. The enemy loaded the tubes up to get several rounds in the air at once, then hauled ass to get away from possible artillery counterbattery.

Pieces of the truck were scattered over the roadway. Just before the rocket hit, the driver had left the truck to go to the mess hall. Two men in the hooch weren't so lucky; they were spread all over the impact area.

That heavy 140 mm rocket must have been shipped south all the way from North Vietnam; the enemy had lugged it across the border and through the jungle to set it in position to launch against the Tay Ninh base. Net effect: one truck and hooch destroyed, two men killed; no change to the war.

I decided to pass on dinner, crossing to the Officers Club for a beer. There I met another lieutenant, just in from one of the infantry companies in the field to attend a court-martial as a witness.

His jungle fatigues were faded, as were his jungle boots. They were covered with what appeared to be ingrained reddish dirt. Nicks and scratches covered his hands and wrists. His company was out on the border. "Getting through the bamboo is fierce," he said. "It can take a day to do a couple of clicks. The rubber is easier going, but much more dangerous. Trees are in straight rows, like a checkerboard. No underbrush. Clear shots from about five directions." He took a swig of San Miguel. Morale in his unit, he said, "could be better. We lost our CO in a fight last week. He was good, but unlucky."

The night wasn't quiet. Not far away, diesel-driven generators droned. A mortar chugged hoarsely; parachute flares popped high overhead. Lurid orange-white, they swayed gently down, leaving smoky trails in the sky.

On the other side of the airstrip, an artillery battery shot a fire mission, banging away through a number of outgoing rounds. Was it "harassment and interdiction," or for a unit in contact? "H & I" fire was aimed at map coordinates where the enemy was thought likely to be moving at night; completely blind shooting. I wondered if H & I actually hit anything, and if it did whether it landed on the enemy, civilians, or wildlife.

I went back to the hooch and stretched out, thinking. It had been a long day. Being in-country again was a bit strange, but these people seemed to generally have their act together. From my vantage near the door, I saw straight out through a sizable hole in the tin roof I hadn't noticed in the daytime, framing a patch of night sky, a dusting of stars. Lightning and far-off thunder, seconds behind. I drifted off to an edgy, unsettled sleep.

LZ DOLLY

Next day brought more heat, higher humidity. A UH1-D "Huey" supply helicopter was headed out to the battalion five base and loading zone, or LZ. I signed out and caught a ride to the pad. In a few minutes I was on a Huey, with mailbags, equipment, and two replacement first lieutenants.

The battalion's forward firebase and landing zone was on LZ DOLLY on top of Nui Ong, a long hill mass overlooking one of the enormous rubber plantations.

The Huey climbed out of Tay Ninh headed north. The two first lieutenants evidently knew each other. As we clattered out toward DOLLY, I tried talking with them, but they weren't interested. From their rings, I assumed they were classmates from the same school. Likely this was their first Vietnam tour; they were probably as nervous as I was a year before. Hell, I was still nervous, but not nearly as much as I had been then.

Leaning back on the nylon seat, I looked the helicopter over. It was a flying pickup truck, really; practically everything was a bit nicked, scratched, and faded. A sturdy bird, though; hundreds like it were hauling troops, mail, ammunition, water, and supplies in the combat zone.

The aviator up front in the right seat was the pilot, a warrant officer. Probably twenty or twenty-one, back home he was likely good at high school math and science, worked on cars. Same for the other warrant, on the left, across the radio console. Both wore Nomex flight suits and gloves. The Nomex looked itchy; fire protection was worth a lot of itchiness.

Neither commissioned officers nor NCOs, warrant officers were specialists. Their job was to fly the aircraft, and do it well. Vietnam brought a need for thousands of helicopter pilots. Commissioning that many new lieutenants would clog the promotion system, so the Army hugely expanded the ranks of aviation warrants.

Both wore dark olive-green aircrew helmets with light-green plastic visors. Both wore .45 Colt pistols in shoulder holsters. A short-barreled CAR15 submachine gun and a claymore bag full of magazines for it was slung across the back of the pilot's seat. If the bird went down, that CAR15 and the bag of mags would be very useful. I'd bet he was on his second tour.

There were no autopilots in helicopters; they had to be hand-flown all the time. The pilot was flying this one, his gloved hands on the collective and stick. The bird gently rose and fell, yawing a little from side to side.

Lips pursed against his boom mike, the other warrant talked on the radio. Jotting notes in grease pencil on a plastic-covered map, he held it up to the pilot and pointed the pencil to a spot. The pilot nodded. The warrant on the left reached down, dialed in a new radio frequency, and began talking.

We moved into a gentle bank to the right, holding it, flying a big, wide circle. The sun chased shadows around the troop compartment. The door gunners in the side pockets leaned over their pedestal-mounted M6D's looking down. Below was a huge rubber plantation, stretching miles in every direction.

The other two lieutenants weren't paying much attention. I leaned over and tapped the door gunner on my side. He looked around, his eyes concealed behind his visor. "What's up?" I shouted.

"A unit's in contact off the LZ. Artillery's shooting support. We're holding out here, get cleared when they turn it off." I nodded.

We held the circle for about five minutes, then suddenly banked hard and flew straight ahead, in constant descent. Over their shoulders and between the flyers' helmets up front I saw only sky. Suddenly there was a green hill line directly ahead, topped with tall trees. We were flying right at it.

The only place to land was a saddle on the ridge, with steep drop-offs on either side. A military shanty town was strung out left and right with barbed wire, bunkers, sandbags, metal culvert, and radio antennas, all scattered about the base.

Five sandbagged circles held a battery of 105mm howitzers. A group of smaller sandbagged circles held heavy, 4.2-inch mortars. Other structures seemed to be made of curved steel culvert and mountains of green sandbags.

We flared in to land, touching down in a blast of dirt and pebbles. I jumped off with the other lieutenants as two soldiers leaped on, stripped to the waist and covered in red dust. They grabbed a pair of red nylon bags of mail and leaped off. Two others, helmeted, tired, in dirty, torn fatigues, with weapons, rucksacks, and huge smiles, jumped aboard. They were very likely going home.

We turned away as the helicopter lifted off, rotor blast spraying us with more dirt and pebbles. The whole turnaround had taken about fifteen seconds. In a few moments the howitzers were banging away again. I was aware of other sounds: the whistle and roar of jet aircraft and the clatter of helicopter gunships. The sounds of action out in the rubber carried up to the ridgetop.

Men in various stages of uniform or stripped to the waist were standing on bunkers, some with field glasses, some shading their eyes, looking out across the tops of the rubber trees. Like everything else, they were covered with red dust.

The artillery shut off again. F-100 jet fighter-bombers camouflaged dirty green, brown, and black rolled into fast, low passes over the forest canopy. Silver napalm cans glittered from their wings, followed by orange-black billows of smoke filtering up through the treetops.

There was an easy-but-tough look to the men I saw watching the show; professionals watching the work of other professionals. Many were from the infantry company that was on the LZ for base defense. They were doing a couple of weeks' relatively easy "palace guard" duty while the other companies continued in the field, before taking their own turns.

The two new lieutenants looked as if they'd somehow taken a wrong turn, unexpectedly arriving in an unfamiliar, threatening neighborhood.

A captain with a clipboard appeared at the edge of the helipad. He motioned us over. We gathered in front of him and saluted, a little raggedly. He returned it, looked us over. "Gentlemen, welcome to the battalion. I'm the S-1 (the battalion's personnel and administrative officer). In a few minutes you'll be meeting the battalion commander. At the moment," he smiled, without humor, "he is a bit occupied. Follow me. I'll show you where you can wait without posing a risk to yourselves, and the rest of us."

The lieutenants laughed nervously; the S-1 acted like he didn't hear it. We walked up the ridge to the TOC, the battalion's tactical operations center, heart and nerve center of the LZ. Built partly above ground, mostly below, the TOC's upper walls were composed of dirt-filled howitzer ammunition crates, surrounded on the outside by multiple layers of green, woven-nylon sandbags.

Its below-ground portion was covered by huge steel culvert halves, with several layers of sandbags on top of them. Cyclone-wire "standoff" fencing was suspended on poles over the entire arrangement. The standoff would detonate incoming mortars and rockets before they penetrated to the interior of the TOC. From the tallest of the jumble of radio antennas and masts above the TOC, an American flag drooped in the windless heat.

The S-1 led us onto a raised platform at the side of the TOC. A couple of battered sling chairs sat on it beside an empty Styrofoam blood plasma shipping container. There was no railing; one wrong step and it was a steep fall of about thirty feet to a ledge. Past that, the cliff dropped over a hundred feet straight down into the tree canopies of the rubber plantation below.

"Stay here. Don't bother anyone; they're busy. The CO will be with you shortly." It wasn't a suggestion. The niceties over, the S-1 disappeared inside.

From our perch, we had an even better view of the events below. The firing died down; the Air Force went home. A pair of Cobra gunships were finishing gun runs. The forward air controller continued to orbit above the scene of the action. His little Cessna L-19 Bird Dog made lazy figure eights, like a student flying a Saturday afternoon pattern.

Yellow smoke rose above the trees. A Huey dropped down into the canopy. The men watching on the bunkers climbed down.

COLONEL PETE

Though commanded by lieutenant colonels, the battalion commanders were addressed as "colonel." One moment, there were just the three of us. The next, Colonel Pete was standing with the S-1 at his shoulder. He was compact, wiry. He wore very faded jungle fatigues, sleeves rolled up on muscled arms. He had a blond brush cut, pale blue eyes, and wire-rimmed glasses. His nose was broken, maybe more than once. Much later, I learned he had boxed as a cadet at West Point in the amateur "Golden Gloves" category.

The colonel looked us over, then wordlessly reached out his hand. In a practiced motion, the S-1 put the clipboard in it, like a nurse slaps a scalpel into the hand of a surgeon.

The colonel held the clipboard but didn't look at it. He regarded us without expression. Suddenly he smiled. Genuine, with warmth. "It's been a very busy day. I trust you'll forgive the lack of ceremony. One of the companies ran into a pretty good-sized force out there. They were likely intending to move up this ridge at some point and bother us." His smile disappeared. "They won't be bothering anyone."

He looked at the clipboard. "It's always a pleasure to welcome new young infantry officers. Plenty of work for everyone, so let's start with you, Lieutenant." He gestured to the officer standing on the far side of our little group. "What job would you like in the battalion?"

The lieutenant's answer was unique. I've remembered it word for word. He cleared his throat and straightened up. "Sir," he said, "I believe I can serve the battalion best as the assistant S-3 for Air Operations."

That was as much as saying, "Sir, I acknowledge we're in the middle of a war, and my proper place as an infantry lieutenant is in the field. However, my belief is that I will be much more valuable to you here on this hilltop, in the TOC, studying maps and working radios, acting as a traffic cop for your air support."

Colonel Pete listened without expression. He lifted his head just a fraction, as though sniffing the air. He breathed out a single word. "Really." The S-1 was expressionless.

He turned to the other lieutenant. "And you, Lieutenant? What would you like as your assignment?"

The second officer's answer was even better articulated. "Sir," he said, "I believe my talents can best be expressed as liaison officer to brigade, or to division."

Wow! In the lexicon of twenty-something-year-old junior officers, that was rarified! No one but full colonels and above spoke like that. Delivered, under the circumstances, with aplomb as well. He was a junior officer like me, but his vision had to be on a plane far above mine. Liaison to brigade! To division!

It was as much as saying, "Sir, you and I are men of the world. I'm sure you can appreciate I'm not interested in being on this hilltop, covered in dust. Designate me as your liaison to command levels where there is intellectual challenge, as well as air-conditioning, hot showers, good chow, and regular mail."

The colonel's eyes narrowed further. "Do tell." The S-1 assumed the same look. His jaw line tightened.

The colonel turned to me. He looked at the clipboard again. "And you, Lieutenant? How about you? I see you're second time in-country, from the 82nd. Wounded the first time."

"Yes, Sir."

"Where was that? Up north?"

"Yes, Sir, near Hué, April of last year."

"What was your assignment?"

"Platoon leader, Sir."

"Good, good." The colonel paused for a moment. "Well, how about it? What's your dream assignment?"

"Sir, with all respect, I'd like command of a company."

He looked at the clipboard again. "Says here you've got nine months of company command behind you already. In the 82nd, at Bragg?"

"Yes, Sir."

The two lieutenants craned around to see better; the colonel ignored them. He nodded. "Command. Admirable ambition. Admirable. I think the best thing for you at present, though, is to go in as XO of a line company. Alpha Company could use you right now. Their XO, Lieutenant Holtzman, is due to come out of the field soon. How about we send you out to relieve Holtzman and understudy Captain Cecil, the Alpha Company CO, until you make captain?"

Although pitched as a question, it was a command, not an invitation. "Sir, I'd be happy to."

"Excellent. You go with Sergeant Smithers here." Another figure materialized behind the S-1, although the colonel made no sign of recognizing his arrival. "He'll get you sorted out."

He turned to the two lieutenants. His voice dropped an octave, his tone changed. "As for you, I have a few things to say."

Sergeant Smithers, a lanky figure in jungle fatigues, cleared his throat as a signal that it was time for us to move. I moved. From the little I caught of the one-sided conversation between the colonel and the lieutenants as we moved off, it wasn't the best start to their assignments. Colonel Pete must have been very disappointed. He could have made them simply disappear; no one who served in the battalion at that time remembers them.

ALPHA COMPANY

"What do you have by way of gear, Sir?" Sergeant Smithers led me across the LZ to a bunker overlooking the rubber plantations stretching far away.

"Not much, except for what's in this kit bag."

"No problem. This is Alpha Company's rear area; they'll fit you out. Zack!" He leaned into the bunker. "New officer here." He turned to me. "Good luck, Sir. Welcome to the battalion." He saluted and headed back up to the TOC.

Sergeant Zack, Alpha Company's rear NCO on the LZ, sported a web belt and holstered .45. Covered head to foot in red dust, his eyes and teeth gleamed whitely. In a few minutes I was sorting through a collection of gear: rucksack, patrol harness, poncho, seven days' C-rations, two filled canteens, frags, smoke grenades, M16 rifle, and ammunition. Augmented by my Ka-Bar and a few goodies I'd brought, Abercrombie & Fitch couldn't do better.

Ten minutes later I was on another Huey, hauling the last run of water, ammunition, rations, spare radio batteries, and a few sacks of mail out to Alpha Company.

The flight was short. The pilot lifted the helicopter off the pad and swooped down the ridgeline like a crazed barn swallow. Just before we smashed into the tops of the rubber trees below, he pulled up on the cyclic. We soared out across the top of the canopy, going like a bat out of hell. That kind of flying always scared the hell out of me. Watching the treetops flick by just below, it appeared we were moments away from hooking a skid and cartwheeling in a burning ball of wreckage to the jungle floor. But at that height, just above the trees, we were actually safer than flying higher. We were gone before the enemy could get a bead on us.

We slowed, banked left, and dropped into the same hole in the trees I'd seen the other helicopters dip into earlier. As we hovered slowly down below layers of canopy, we entered a strange realm of unearthly and permanent twilight, though the sun was shining above.

I was impressed by the height of the rubber trees, standing arrow straight and close to a hundred feet tall. Planted as the lieutenant the night before at Tay Ninh had said: in a grid, so stepping out between two trees exposed you to view and fire from four or five directions. The floor of the plantation was flat, littered with layers of dead leaves. The effect, in the watery light that managed to penetrate the canopy, was of being in an aquarium.

As the Huey touched down, around the clearing men were either standing or sitting, talking on radios, consulting maps, eating, cleaning weapons. Unseen, farther off, the majority of the company was alert, on guard, facing outward in platoon sectors.

Everyone had helmets on; one or two men had shirts off. As I jumped off the ship, two men leaped aboard, throwing out a mailbag, water jugs, ammunition, and batteries. An officer with several days' beard, looking like he needed a good night's sleep, passed me without a word or glance, threw his rucksack in, and climbed aboard.

The pilot spooled up the engine, pulled pitch, and climbed. Several men on the edge of the clearing waved at the departing officer; a few flashed the "V" peace sign. I kept my head down against the rotor blast until the ship rose, then looked around.

A lot of eyes were on me, as though I had literally dropped from outer space. No one made a move. I stood looking at them. They looked at me. Their faces, beneath their helmets, carried little expression. After a moment I saw a figure making an "over here" motion with his hand. Standing in a small group of radio operators and people with maps, he was Captain Cecil, the commanding officer. I had arrived at Alpha Company, my new home.

Several weeks later we returned to LZ DOLLY for our turn at base defense. The day after we landed, Cecil shook my hand and passed command of Alpha Company to me. He smiled. "Now don't fuck up," he said.

I'd heard that before.

Thirty years later, Steve Holtzman, the lieutenant who passed me without a word to board the Huey on that long-ago afternoon, sat in my California living room. From Steve, I got the other side of the story of my arrival in the company that day.

I told him how no one had at first said a word when I landed among them; they regarded me like an odd creature from a zoo. He laughed. "Because they didn't know what to expect. Just before you showed up, Cecil called me over and said, 'Holtzman, this is your lucky day. Your replacement is coming in on that bird. Grab your gear, you're going out. This new guy must have a pair of balls like John Wayne. The S-1 says a couple of other lieutenants committed career suicide in front of Colonel Pete, and the third guy, the one they're sending us as your replacement, says he wants to take over a rifle company.'"

THE BIG PICTURE

During the war, South Vietnam was divided into four military "Corps Tactical Zones." "Corps" rhymes with "core." The Corps' zones were designated I through IV, from north to south. I and II Corps (referred to as "Eye" and "Two" Corps), generally mountainous and bordered partially by Laos, extended southward from the 17th parallel which divided North and South Vietnam. III ("Three") Corps included Saigon; generally flat country with rolling hills, its rainforests and rubber plantations extending north and west to the Cambodian border. Southernmost IV ("Four") Corps was marsh, rice paddies, and the tropical savannah of the Mekong Delta.

Seven air bases in Thailand supported the war, their fighters and bombers flying against targets in North and South Vietnam. Heavy B-52 bombers based on Guam made twelve-hour round trips to unload tons of bombs in Vietnam along the borders and in Cambodia and Laos.

From offshore in the Tonkin Gulf, the Navy's carrier task groups launched constant air strikes against the North. Cruisers, destroyers, and an occasional World War II–era battleship bombarded shore installations, shot up coastal traffic, and laid mines along the coast. "Swift" patrol boats prowled the coast and up the rivers in the South. It was a big war.

RUBBER PLANTATIONS

In the early twentieth century, French companies cleared vast tracts of rainforest for the cultivation of rubber trees; the work was all by hand. In searing heat and high humidity, Cochin-Chinese natives labored under primitive conditions, cutting and clearing away enormous trees and underbrush, vines, and bamboo. Ninety percent of the workers contracted malaria, the disease estimated by historians to have killed half of all humans that ever lived.

Rubber trees were planted in geometrically ordered rows and columns. Mature enough in seven years for sap to be harvested, workers scored each tree diagonally downward. Latex sap flowed into cups positioned at the scorings' bottoms. The largest plantation in the III Corps zone was said to be operated by Michelin, the French company producing automobile tires. Half a world away from France, the manager of the Terre Rouge (Red Earth) plantation at our Brigade base at Quan Loi lived in a white villa set in green lawns surrounded by shade trees, with a tennis court and swimming pool.

The US government paid indemnity to the French plantation companies for every rubber tree damaged by military operations. It was rumored the French companies paid the NVA and Vietcong enemy not to destroy the trees. War is full of ironies.

In the plantations, the light was aqueous-blue tinted, the ground matted with dead leaves. Huge colonies of earth-boring termites built mounds several feet high and just as wide, hard as portland cement. Trees planted in grids, ten feet apart, allowed lateral and diagonal visibility up to fifty meters. If we could see that far, so could the enemy. Access roads cut through the plantations; the enemy used them as high-speed marching routes.

One of our company's memorable firefights began with the point team coming up to one such road. A column of North Vietnamese infantry was crossing much farther down, accompanied by a number of ducks. Quickly brought forward, an M60 machine-gun team lay on the edge of the road, sighting on the crossing men. Our point man stepped out into the road. Doffing his helmet, he waved it above his head, a hell of an audacious act. Thinking he was another of them, the enemy waved back. Our M60 opened up, accompanied by a hail of 40mm M79 grenades. In the ensuing fight, the fate of the ducks was unknown.

RAINFORESTS

The trees were eighty to ninety feet tall, with triple canopies. Everything fought for the spare daylight filtering through, in a diverse and competitive ecosystem. At twenty or thirty feet, the trees sent out a network of branches, their interleaved vegetation forming the first canopy. It was another thirty feet to the second meshed canopy, and the treetops formed the third. Thick underbrush to about six feet covered the forest floor, with tangled vines, bushes, and thickets of bamboo so dense we often hacked through with machetes in intense, trapped heat.

Animals and birds were in constant motion and relationship with the forest. Moving in steamy twilight in the dry season and watery twilight in the monsoon, we heard wildlife above but seldom saw it. At ground level were sun bears, wild boars, knee-high barking deer, dirty-brown game hens scratching and shuffling, and tough little grunting peccaries, capable of impressive bursts of speed.

A big boar once wandered into the kill zone of one of our night ambushes. Setting off a trip flare, it was shot by the M-60 gun team. There is a picture of the beast next morning, slung from a pole hoisted by two soldiers. Airlifted back to the LZ, it was sectioned and the slugs removed. After inspection of the meat by the battalion surgeon, our senior mess warrant sent freshly barbecued pork out by air to the infantry companies.

On another night a sun bear ambled down a forest track, straight into one of our ambushes. We didn't eat the bear.

NUI BA DEN

For most of my command time, we operated in War Zone "C," north of Tay Ninh along the Cambodian border, and in adjoining Binh Long Province. To say those were "hot" areas was an understatement. North Vietnamese Army units were there in force.

Along that border, the terrain was low, thickly forested rolling hills, dominated by Nui Ba Den, the "Black Virgin" mountain, visible for miles. The huge cone of an extinct volcano, it rose over three thousand feet. Accessible only by air, a US Special Forces outpost occupied the summit. The enemy was on the mountain, too. He dug tunnels and enlarged caves, using them for shelter from artillery and air strikes and to launch periodic attacks on the Americans at the summit.

Looming above the surrounding landscape, against a sky filled with huge clouds laced with shafts of sun, Nui Ba Den was a memorable sight. The clouds climbed above the forest canopies to tops at twenty thousand feet, casting slow-moving shadows across the mountain's flanks. Seen from a helicopter, the effect of dark shadows against the green of the mountainside forests was like the mottled coloring on a frog's back.

Westward across the Cambodian border, the enemy rested in base areas within easy marching distance of our operational areas inside Vietnam. His units could shelter and be augmented there, as they arrived from their long march south on the trail, or withdraw and be refitted there from combat losses across the border. We could not pursue him with ground forces; until the "Cambodian incursion" in 1970, his Cambodian sanctuary remained a major advantage.

Though the North's soldiers made the long journey to the South on foot along the trail, the majority of supplies for the enemy's units and base areas in southernmost III and IV Corps did not come, as American media often erroneously reported, down the trail as well. Rather, they were landed by communist-flagged and other shipping at the Cambodian port of Sihanoukville. There was no need for the enemy to man-pack them from Sihanoukville to his base areas just inside the border; he used hired civilian trucks to move them, on a Cambodian highway built with American USAID money.

OUR ENEMY SOLDIER

In the rainforests and rubber plantations north of Tay Ninh and close to the Cambodian border, the enemy soldier in our battalion's area of operations or AO was from the 272nd and 273rd regiments of the North Vietnamese Army, the NVA.

He wasn't Vietcong; they were South Vietnamese guerrillas, local fighers, usually operating from or in the vicinity of towns and villages. There were almost no towns or villages in our operational area. Our enemy soldier was North Vietnamese. Though there was a hard core of "regular," experienced soldiers in the North Vietnamese Army, some of whom had fought the French, most of the enemy's soldiers were drafted.

The North's leadership was intent on continuing to send our enemy soldier, and thousands like him, down the long series of roads and trails to fight in the South. The trip could take months. Along the way, he was subject to malaria, dysentery, fierce storms with lightning strikes, floods, and occasional attack by wild animals, in addition to airstrikes and bombings by American fighter-bombers and B-52s.

There was no one-year combat tour in the South for our enemy soldier; like his fellows, he was "in for the duration." There was no home leave for him, either; he had no regular mail or other means of communicating with his family in the North.

What, then, was our enemy soldier like in 1969? What did he carry? What support could he call on? First, he was dedicated. His communist forebears had been fighting since 1946, first against the French, then against the South Vietnamese, lastly against us. Though there were likely times when he was lonely and frightened, like almost all soldiers are in war, he was generally courageous.

A comparison of assets available to both sides supports this. We had air superiority. On-call air support delivered bombs, rockets, napalm, and other ordnance. Our aircraft moved troops and supplies all over the country. The NVA soldier had none of these in the South. We had tanks and armored personnel carriers, armed with cannon and machine guns. Except for an attack by Russian-built PT-76 light tanks on the Special Forces camp at far northern Lang Vei near the Laotian border in 1968, his army had no armored vehicles in the South.

In spite of our advantages, at places and times of his choosing he would attack, almost invariably armed with no more than AK47s, B40 rockets, light machine guns, and mortars.

We had one of the most sophisticated medical systems in the world, with on-call medevac helicopters able to retrieve our wounded on the battlefield. There was no evacuation chain for NVA wounded; he was lucky if his comrades could drag him off the battlefield. His army was also chronically short of medicines and medical supplies.

His units suffered high rates of malaria, so much so that the North appealed to its Chinese allies for any way to alleviate the disease. The result was a secret kept for decades. In response to the North's request, the Chinese put a special medical team to work on "Project 523," headed by a young woman doctor. Searching centuries of ancient Chinese medical texts, the 523 team discovered a fourth-century AD manuscript noting a cold fusion of the herb artemisinin, "sweet wormwood," as effective against malaria.

China and the North kept the find a state secret, only releasing it to the world in 1985. As a result, the doctor who headed Project 523 became the first Chinese woman to receive the Nobel Prize for Medicine.

Our enemy soldier was generally tough and capable of carrying heavy loads, but was almost never seen with the kind of rucksacks that we carried like pack animals. He traveled light, with a canteen, a bag filled with balls of cooked rice and fish, a small glass bottle filled with oil and a wick for night illumination, an AK47 or B40, ammunition, and a grenade or two. He might also carry a rolled-up, rubberized plastic hammock. Strung between two trees, it let him sleep suspended above the hard, cold (and often wet) ground.

His uniform was a green or khaki short-sleeved shirt and long or short trousers. He wore floppy bush hats or lightweight pith helmets. Somewhere on his person, usually on his hat, was a red, enameled star. If he was an officer, his aluminum belt buckle had a star engraved on it. A pair of rubber sandals completed his field attire.

He was resourceful. Though he didn't have the ordnance and munitions we did, his ability to improvise was impressive. In certain areas he excavated, reinforced, and lived in vast systems of underground tunnels and shelters, perfectly camouflaged, and impervious to almost anything we could put on them except heavy bombing strikes. Kitchens in these underground complexes had cleverly vented channels to disperse smoke from the cooking fires.

He salvaged unexploded US and South Vietnamese artillery rounds, turning them into improvised explosive devices. He extracted the explosive filling from salvaged artillery rounds to pack into "Chinese claymores": round, metal, dishpan-sized blast devices used as booby traps, attached to trip wires along trails. Filled with glass, nails, scrap metal, and rocks, they were lethal. He retrieved discarded, empty American C-ration cans, filled them with explosive, a detonator, and rocks, glass, and scrap metal. He set them beside trails, connected to trip wires.

As demonstrated all over the South, particularly by the massacre of thousands of civilians at Hué in 1968, our enemy soldier and his Vietcong allies weren't bound by Western rules of war. He committed widespread atrocities without hesitation, often eliminating South Vietnamese officials and their families at the village level as an example to others. Americans captured in South Vietnam also endured starvation and privation similar to that suffered by prisoners in Japanese prison camps in World War II.

His tactics weren't sophisticated. They didn't need to be. If he collided with us when he was on the move in forests or plantations, he knew we had enormous on-call combat support. In those sudden, unexpected "meeting engagements," his choices were to fight or flee. After the first vicious interchange of fire, he would usually attempt to break contact and withdraw.

If he chose to fight, he would need to get as close as possible to us so that we would be reluctant to call artillery or air for fear of hitting our own troops. The occasions when he would come in and "grab us by the belt buckle" were rare, but other units that encountered such situations paid a heavy price in casualties. Situations like this required the term "danger close" when calling for artillery or air support. More on that later.

While I always respected our NVA soldier as an enemy, I nonetheless intended to kill him. I fully understood that he intended to do the same to me.

TACTICS

Tactics are how you control the movement and maneuver of the forces you have in battle in order to achieve an objective or mission. They can be proactive or reactive. If you're attacking an enemy or maneuvering against him to overpower and destroy him, your tactics are proactive. If you're surprised by the enemy or defending, your tactics are reactive. Either way, it's about control and maneuver; using what you have in the best way you can to accomplish the mission.

What were my tactics as a company commander? Let's start with what I had to work with, then look at our mission and a couple of other factors.

FOGGY DAY

Alpha Company (radio call sign FOGGY DAY) was light infantry and airmobile. We were frequently airlifted into the field by helicopter, but once on the ground, we lived and fought with what we carried.

The Army's Table of Organization and Equipment (TO&E) specifies the exact number of soldiers allocated to each type of unit, with their job specifications and equipment. The 1969 TO&E for a light infantry company specified 6 officers and 165 men.

We were also generally understrength. On 1 June 1969, our company's morning report tabulated 127 enlisted and NCOs and 5 officers, for a total of 132 present for duty.

Each company had several men who took care of administration, supply, and maintenance. They were the company's executive officer (XO), supply sergeant, company clerk, armorer, and field radio mechanic. Except for the XO, they did not go into the field with us; they were instead split between the brigade's rear base and our battalion's forward firebase, or LZ.

The company clerk was critical; he compiled and submitted the morning report, a by-line and by-name itemization of every man's status, turned in daily to battalion by a certain hour. The morning report was used to determine rations, supply of other items, leave, medical issues, and time served for promotion. The company clerk also handled a number of other administrative issues.

Subtracting the men noted above from our morning report strength, our actual effective "field strength" was 127 officers and men.

In the field, our company command group was myself, as company commander, and my two radiotelephone operators (RTOs), each of whom carried a PRC-77 FM backpack radio. One radio was on the company's command frequency, the other on the battalion's command frequency. "Biggy," my pace man, walked directly behind me, keeping his own pace to compare with mine. "Doc", our company senior medic, completed the command group.

I carried the CAR15, a short-barreled version of the M16 with a telescoping stock, using the same 5.56mm ammunition. I almost always had a map or compass in my left hand, so I carried the CAR15 in my right or rested it on the ammunition pack on the webbing on that side. It had a canvas general-purpose (GP) strap that let me sling it on my right shoulder, muzzle down, so I was able to quickly swing it up. That could free my right hand for a radio handset if I had the map in my left.

I also carried a .45 ACP pistol in a holster on my right. I cleaned and lightly oiled it and my CAR15 every day. Almost every man had a shaving brush; we used them to periodically brush the dust off the receiver groups and bolts of our weapons.

The M16s and CAR15s had a hinged metal dust cover that snapped closed over the breech. I made sure mine was closed every time I charged the weapon.

Our company had three infantry platoons. Each was led by a second lieutenant, with his RTO and PRC-77 radio on the company command net; a platoon sergeant; and a platoon medic.

Each platoon had three rifle squads of between eight and ten men each, and a weapons squad of eight men. Rifle squad weapons were M16 rifles and M79 40mm grenade launchers. We attached the weapons squad soldiers to the rifle squads. They carried the 90mm recoilless rifle, two in each platoon, and the M60 machine guns, also two in each platoon. The 90mm and M60 gunners each had an assistant gunner-ammunition bearer, who carried one or two cans of linked-belt ammunition for the machine gun or rounds for the 90mm. Weapons squad men also carried the .45 pistol.

An artillery forward observer, a lieutenant, and his radio operator accompanied my company headquarters element. They were from the five-gun 105mm howitzer battery on the battalion firebase. That battery provided direct support to the battalion's companies in the field.

Our artillery forward observer, or FO, was Lieutenant Paul, with his RTO's PRC-77 on the artillery radio net. Paul's call sign was GUIDON FOUR TWO. The artillery battery of 105s was TRAIL SPIKE.

Remember those old cannon on two wheels with a single heavy thing sticking down in the rear that rested on the ground? That heavy thing was the gun's "trail." The "trail spike" was a sturdy pole the crew stuck in a hole in the very end of the trail. They would use it to lever the trail up to shift the gun left and right.

Our field medics were assigned from the battalion's medical element, headed by Doc G., a slightly crazy but highly talented guy from New York. Our battalion's radio call sign was GENERAL MOTORS. Our company call sign on the battalion radio net was FOGGY DAY. Our battalion's other infantry companies' call signs were FENCE POST, DOUBLE TIME, and BLACK GOLD.

MISSION

Our mission was to find the enemy, "fix" him, and kill or capture him. Once we found him, "fixing" him meant engaging and holding him in place in order to finish him with the weapons we carried, plus the combat support we could call on.

There were no "front lines" in Vietnam; the enemy could be anywhere. In heavily forested terrain, it was like playing a lethal game of blindman's bluff. We knew he was out there. While we had generally good intelligence, except on rare occasions we didn't know precisely where he was, but by moving, patrolling, and ambushing, we would find him.

So, where to look? Each major infantry unit in Vietnam had its own area of operations, or AO. The 1st Air Cavalry Division divided its huge AO among its three infantry brigades; each brigade divided its AO among its three infantry battalions.

Within each battalion, the commander, a lieutenant colonel, reviewed and assessed the information provided by his Operations and Intelligence and staff, determining how to best allocate the battalion's AO among his three infantry companies.

Based on the battalion commander's decisions, the companies were assigned their own AOs. Irregular outlines on the map, each came with a bit of intelligence, periodically updated, as to what battalion headquarters believed might be in our AO.

Our AOs were remote, far away from any major town or village. They were designated "free-fire zones": anything that moved in the AO could be considered enemy and engaged without further clearance. There was a dichotomy in that directive, however. We knew there had always been itinerant woodcutters and charcoal burners operating in that region. They weren't "legitimate," but they weren't enemy either.

To give you an idea how remote and unique our AOs were, the entire massive region the 1st Air Cavalry Division operated in along the Cambodian border in 1969–70 is today a UN World Heritage Zone, containing some of the world's most valuable animal habitats and ecosystems.

COMBAT SUPPORT

In the field, we could call for supporting fire from the battalion's five direct-support 105mm howitzers at TRAIL SPIKE, and on heavier, longer-range artillery if we needed it.

We could call on scout helicopters and Cobra attack helicopters. We could call for close air support from Air Force fighter-bombers by talking to the forward air controllers, or FACs. They could be in single-engine L-19 Bird Dog observation aircraft, or twin-engine OV-10 Broncos. The FACs could direct jets (known as "fast movers"), usually F-100 Super Sabers or F-4 Phantoms, carrying bombs, rockets, napalm, or all three. This is where the term "danger close" was used.

Finally, there was medevac: emergency medical evacuation helicopters, call sign DUSTOFF. Their pilots were experienced and fearless.

The radio call signs and frequencies for all the support units, and the other infantry companies in our battalion, were on a plastic-covered card I carried in my shirt pocket, tied to a length of parachute cord, fastened to a buttonhole. The card was our unit's signal operating index, or SOI, an abbreviated radio "phone book."

I've been asked which of the weapons in my infantry company I thought were most powerful. My answer invariably surprises. It was the PRC-77 radio. With it, I could call for all the support mentioned above, with firepower far greater than the weapons we carried ourselves.

OUR SOLDIERS

FOGGY DAY was a rucksack outfit. We were frequently airlifted by helicopter on "combat assaults," then submerging in the jungle like a submarine at sea.

Quietly patrolling and ambushing, we stayed in the field for weeks at a time. About every fifth or sixth day we were resupplied by helicopter.

Seven in ten of our company's men had been leading ordinary lives when their draft notices came. Many had been raised on stories of their father's or uncles' World War II service and John Wayne movies. They didn't ask to come to the war, but when they were called, they left everything they'd known and reported.

Molding them into soldiers, the Army trained them to kill, then flew them halfway around the world to fight in a war growing ever more unpopular at home. Each soldier was assigned a military occupational specialty, or MOS code, designating his specific job. With few exceptions, our men were MOS 11B: "Eleven Bravos." Infantrymen, the backbone of the Army. Not professionals by any means on arrival in-country, within a month or two in the field they could almost claim that status.

They were Tom, Onzie, Woody, Fuzzy, Mario, Jay, Jack, Dink, Benny, and over a hundred others. Most knew little about the history of the war or its geopolitical aspects. Most carried no real *animus* against the enemy they would confront. All were liable to death or mutilation, any minute of every day.

With slight variation, they looked much like soldiers and Marines in the Pacific in World War II. They wore jungle fatigues, jungle boots, and canvas-covered steel helmets. On their harnesses they carried fragmentation and colored smoke grenades, two canteens of water, possibly a Ka-Bar or sheath knife, and canvas ammunition packs filled with twenty-round magazines for their M16 rifles.

They carried the M16, the M79 40mm grenade launcher, the M60 machine gun, or the heavy, short-barreled 90mm recoilless.

They were like pack animals, carrying upwards of sixty pounds of gear, water, and ammunition; more if they were radio operators or machine gunners. I was impressed by how they endured it all, especially the draftees.

They carried radio sets, the very first "starlight" night-vision scopes, and spare batteries. Medics carried bulging medical aid bags.

On or in their rucksacks, they carried spare boot socks, more ammunition, more water, claymore mines, more linked-belt ammunition, small antipersonnel mines, extra ammunition for the recoilless rifles, empty sandbags, and folding shovels.

They carried iodine tablets to kill bugs in the water. They carried powdered Kool-Aid sent from home to cut the awful taste of the iodine. Against malaria, they carried orange dapsone tabs and white chloroquine pills. We took the white pill every day. If we could remember which day was Monday, we took the big orange tab then as well.

All field units had serious malaria problems. If exhausted and the troops' resistance was down, as it usually was, antimalaria tablets were about as useless as the issued insect repellent.

They didn't carry anything preventing amoebic dysentery or the immersion foot that hit so many in the monsoon, when feet swelled up and skin could peel off in strips.

They carried canned C-rations, or dehydrated long-range patrol rations. They carried chunks of C-4 plastic explosive to heat the rations.

They wore a pair of metal dog tags embossed with their name, service number, blood type, and religion, if any. In my company, one was worn on a chain around the neck, the other laced into a boot, doubling the chances one tag would be recovered.

They carried Bibles, missals, hymnals, prayer books, good luck charms, and talismans, or nothing at all. I never heard anyone belittle another for what he believed in. I did hear pleas and promises to God under fire.

They carried all these things, in the rain and heat and fighting, for the full year. They bitched, like all soldiers bitch. But it was a strangely proud bitching. If you asked them what they were fighting for, they weren't hesitant. They weren't fighting for South Vietnam. They weren't fighting for Mom, the flag, or apple pie. They were fighting to survive the war so that they could go home. What they were really fighting for, they wouldn't realize until years later, was each other.

One day, near the actual end of that endless year in the field, they would board a helicopter on the back haul to the rear area and turn in their weapons and gear. They would shower, put on a clean uniform, and begin the long trip home.

They would consider themselves anything but "heroic." Resigned, committed, wary; all of those applied. Yet a number of them did things in the chaos of engagements that were astonishingly heroic. To most of them, their service in Vietnam would turn out to be the most astonishing feat of their lives.

ROUTINE

When I took command in May 1969, I had a lot to learn about the company: what the men and NCOs were like, how they operated, the hundred little things that knitted them together as a combat unit.

It was evident they knew what they were doing, and did it with a minimum of fuss. They were weathered, as men who live in the field and sleep on the ground are weathered. Their helmet covers, jungle fatigues, equipment, and boots were faded. The NCOs, especially the E5s, were incredibly young.

Days in the field began with a stand-to just before dawn; everyone up, weapons at the ready. We retrieved the trip flares and claymore antipersonnel mines set out the evening before. Night ambushes came in. Half the men had C-rations or long-range patrol rations; the others stood watch.

We broke down the defense perimeter, emptied sandbags filled with dirt from their fighting positions, and rolled and strapped them to the rucksacks. Each man carried four or five sandbags and a wood-handled folding shovel, one of the best pieces of equipment in the Army.

Each soldier wore an over-the-shoulder web harness connected to a webbing belt. Hung on the harness were smoke and fragmentation grenades. On the webbing belt were his ammunition packs, one on each side, with four magazines in each, filled with eighteen or twenty rounds of 5.56mm ammunition for his M16. One or two one-quart plastic canteens in a steel canteen cup, in a canvas carrier. An aid pack with a pressure bandage. Some men had a sheath knife on the web belt as well.

The webbing harness with its gear was his load-bearing equipment (LBE). Everything he needed to fight was on his LBE. Things he didn't need to fight went into the rucksack. The left shoulder strap of the rucksack had a quick-release; a pull on the tab dropped the ruck and freed the soldier for action.

Every morning I determined the direction the company would take leaving the forward operating base, or FOB. The lead platoon would head out on the designated azimuth, then the command group, then the other platoons joining in trail.

As we moved, I kept an eye on the map and counted my paces. I looked in all directions, considering what my options would be if we made contact. I assessed the terrain, the weather, everything around us. Periodically I would coordinate my pace count with my pace man, who walked behind me.

In very thick forest it was difficult to keep flank security in contact with the main body; we moved in an extended column of twos, sometimes in file, with platoons in trail. There were many times when the entire outfit was halted while the point team broke brush. Very hard going.

To cover as much territory as possible, every several hundred meters I stopped the company. We sent a small five- or six-man patrol out on either side, with instructions to the patrol leaders to move out several hundred meters or so, "buttonhook" right, proceed fifty meters, and return to the company.

We remained prepared to move immediately to support if the patrols made contact. Even with this technique, we were only covering a strip of ground at best a few hundred meters wide.

Our day was filled with movement and patrolling. Occasionally we dropped a "stay-behind" ambush. A designated group would go quietly to ground, facing back down the direction we had come from, while the company moved over them and continued on the original azimuth. Usually there was no result. In a couple of instances, after ten or twenty minutes there was a savage burst of firing as the stay-behind killed an enemy "watcher" trailing us.

Toward the end of my command time, we emplaced automatic ambushes—a "necklace" of fragmentation grenades connected with detcord, camouflaged, and laid down on one side of a trail. The firing cap for the necklace connected to a trip wire at ankle height across the trail. The detcord connecting the grenades extended to the firing cap of a claymore antipersonnel mine in a tree, its blast zone directed back down the line of the trail. Very effective.

Toward 4 or 5 in the afternoon, I chose a position on which to emplace a night defense perimeter, which we referred to as the forward operating base, or FOB (rhymes with "fob"). If we crossed trails during the day, or our patrols had crossed them, I might, depending on signs of foot traffic, have one or more ambushed during the night.

The company, minus men detailed for ambushes that night, dug fighting holes big enough for two to three men to fight from without getting in each other's way. The empty sandbags were filled with dirt from the holes. If possible, we cut branches to lay over bags two high around the holes, then covered them with more bags, providing overhead cover.

The night ambush patrols ate, rested a bit, then headed out to be near their ambush sites before dark. I ensured the patrol leaders coordinated with me on the locations I wanted them to go to on the map.

Ambushes were usually between five hundred and one thousand meters from the FOB. The patrol leaders knew to conduct a careful recon before they moved into their sites. At the patrol leader's discretion, he could wait until dark, then move his ambush into the intended location.

We plotted artillery around the ambush locations in case they needed support during the night. We maintained radio watch all night. In the CP group, we rotated radio watch among ourselves. Periodic sitreps (situation reports) with the ambushes was by "breaking squelch": keying the radio handset made a distinctive sound, breaking the carrier wave of the signal. Two clicks in response from the ambush was "all OK." If we didn't get that response back, the man on the radio at their end had dozed off (it happened), or something else was in progress, we would find out one way or the other.

We slept on the ground. Every man had a sheet of "mortar plastic," transparent plastic sheeting that came in the boxes in which mortar ammunition was packed. Laid out on the ground, it insulated the soldier from the damp earth. Some troops carried the issued olive-drab air mattress; blown up just enough to keep the soldier off the ground, they afforded a modicum of comfort.

In all cases, staying as low as possible during the night meant a chance of survival in case of sudden enemy attack. A year or so before I joined the company, the company commander slept in a captured NVA hammock. One day he made the cardinal error of setting up the company's night defensive perimeter around one of the old French PKs. Bad decision; the PK was very likely registered on the maps the NVA used during the night to lob four fast 82mm mortar rounds into the company's perimeter.

Everyone sleeping flat on the ground survived, scrambling into their fighting holes. Not so the company commander; he was killed instantly, suspended high enough in his hammock to catch a lethal sheet of steel fragments from the mortar bursts.

Nights in the rainforest or jungle were full of incessant sounds. The calls of the "fuck you" geckos, the chattering and singing of nocturnal birds, and the rustlings of animals foraging. And, always, the constant whine of mosquitoes.

Just before dawn, everyone was awake for stand-to, weapons at the ready. So began another day in the field.

NOISE AND LIGHT

When the company was moving in daytime, there was no talking at a normal conversational level; we kept our voices down. Also, there was absolutely no smoking on the move; it was astonishing how far that scent traveled. In several instances we picked up the enemy early because his people were smoking. On another occasion, we heard him early due to noise he was making.

At night there was severe light discipline; no lights whatever, at any time. This was tough on the smokers; they had to "light up" at night down in their fighting holes or under a poncho. When smoking, they had to shield the cigarette's glow. If I had to do a map check, I did it with a flashlight with a red filter over its lens, under a poncho.

We almost always traveled cross-country, staying off trails. Danger areas to us in daytime, we ambushed the enemy on them at night.

Point duty rotated among the three platoons, each sending out a point man and slack man behind him as their lead element. We had a machine-gun team well forward in the lead platoon.

Often the point man would have to "break trail," moving through virgin brush, with his M16 at the ready. I had great respect for the soldiers who performed this dangerous job day after day. On 5 June 1969, the day they were killed, Jack and Dink were walking point and slack respectively.

If we had to cross an open space, we shook the company out so that the lead platoon would have the other two platoons echeloned back on either side. The formation would close up again as we reentered forest or plantation.

I always positioned myself just behind the lead platoon leader. Moments counted in a firefight. I needed to have as good a grip on what was happening as possible, and fast. At the same time, I didn't want to impede the lead platoon leader's ability to get his men forward as quickly as possible.

My maneuver decisions on making contact were to determine the size and direction of the enemy fire; bring as much of my firepower forward while protecting my flanks. My forward observer would handle the artillery. I would also handle close air support if it was needed or available. If we could bring overwhelming combat power from our supporting arms on the enemy, risking my soldiers for no reason made little sense.

There was a lag in every contact between Lieutenant Paul's call to the artillery, in which he verified and passed our coordinates, and the response of the first rounds. In that interval, we quickly established a base and volume of fire. If the enemy broke contact, Paul would have the artillery range shots out from our contact to hit him as he withdrew. In many cases after a contact, multiple blood trails verified Artillery's reputation as the biggest killer on the battlefield.

In the time I commanded, we didn't capture enemy alive. Enemy soldiers remaining on the field after our contacts were dead. If anyone on the other side intended to surrender, we didn't see it. The NVA weren't as fanatical as the Japanese in World War II; they did surrender. They were also captured wounded. It just worked out that in our contacts, neither of those occurred.

LEADERSHIP

Situations requiring leadership were many and varied; no two were the same. Here are only a few.

Leadership Is Inspiration

When I took command a few weeks after I arrived, I decided a few things needed to be said. I remembered how the men bunched up on that ridgeline on my first tour the year before were killed and wounded by getting mortared, and other mistakes resulting in casualties from inattention or complacency.

At the first opportunity when we were back on LZ DOLLY for a turn at perimeter defense, I found an appropriate, secure place and sat the three platoons down separately for a very brief talk.

"We're all in this fight together. I've watched you in the field and believe our company is an effective fighting unit. But I want to make a few things clear. The shortest way home alive at the end of your year here is through the enemy. If he determines you're weak or lack determination, he'll attack you. Keep him off balance, on his back foot, and he'll have his own skin to worry about.

"We need to keep always in mind that our mission out here is to find him, and kill him if we can. When we're in contact, we'll fix him in place and call artillery and air to destroy him. But we need to be much more aggressive in our ambushing and patrolling. If you look to your officers and NCOs, keep alert, and watch out for each other. We'll all do fine."

Leadership Is Innovation

When I joined the company, I noticed there was a distinct distancing between men who were in the field for months and new arrivals. I began a system in which platoon leaders paired new replacements with field-experienced men. As a result, the experienced men started a competition to see how fast they could bring their new men up the curve on things it usually took weeks or months to learn. Company morale went up a notch, along with combat efficiency.

Leadership Is Encouragement

On another day, we had a very violent, fast contact. We all hit the ground at the first bursts of firing. There were the usual first moments of establishing the size and weight of the fight and the enemy's position and capabilities. I called in the contact while the men hit hard with small arms and grenades from the M79s. Paul brought in the artillery; we hammered them for a few minutes. We took no casualties. The enemy broke contact, and we moved up in pursuit. We could hear attack helicopters in the distance, hitting his people with rocket and grenade fire.

A few minutes into that movement, my RTO handed me the company command net handset. One of the lieutenants behind me was on the line. His platoon was missing a soldier.

It was a new man. I went with a patrol from his platoon back over the ground, found him face down in tall grass, shaking but unhurt. I got down on one knee and talked to him a bit until he regained some stability. He was OK but scared to death. He turned out to be a great field soldier.

Leadership Is Firmness

On another morning after we stood to and retrieved our night ambushes, one of the platoon leaders came to the CP with a new replacement who asked to speak with me. My policy was any soldier had access, as long as he went to his platoon leader or platoon sergeant first.

What I learned shocked and angered me. The trooper was a good kid, about nineteen, assigned to one of the rifle squads.

"Sir, we were on ambush last night."

"I know. What about it?"

"Well, Sir, we didn't go where we were supposed to be. Me and (he named another soldier) knew it, but we didn't say anything. But Sir, I was scared. If we weren't where we were supposed to be, what if we got hit?"

He was right about being scared; he had every reason to be. Ambushes were to be placed where I showed their patrol leaders I wanted them to be on the map. Expecting them to be there, Paul and I plotted artillery concentrations around them to be called on if the ambushes made contact during the night.

I called in the ambush patrol leader and the other experienced soldier. It was true; they had elected to shelter in a hollow they found on the way to the designated ambush site. Remaining there, they sent in periodic "nothing to report" sitreps by radio.

It was disturbing on two levels. First, their mission was to go to a specific spot because I thought a trail junction they would set up on was a likely route of enemy movement. If an enemy unit headed down that trail in our direction during the night, the ambush would hit it with everything they had, giving us warning.

Second, they hid out only a hundred meters or so in front of our night position. If the enemy passed them and hit us, we would have opened up with everything we had and would likely have fired artillery out there, not knowing they weren't where they were supposed to be.

I wasn't about to put them on a charge and send them to the rear for disciplinary action. They were experienced soldiers. Understrength as we were, we needed every man.

The next night, I had them both move five hundred meters out from the company, to a map location I specified and coordinated with them. There they spent the night, alone in the forest. They got the message, and so did every man in the company. We never had that problem again.

Leadership Is Compassion

Gerry, one of my platoon sergeants, had been wounded four times; twice on his first tour, twice with the company. He was a good man; stolid, not terribly imaginative. He took his soldiering seriously. Like "Pigpen," the character in the *Peanuts* cartoons who was a magnet to dust and dirt, Gerry attracted enemy frag.

One afternoon in deep rainforest, Gerry took a "buttonhook" patrol out from the main body. About half an hour later my RTO handed me the handset. Gerry had found a cache of rice in bags, he reported, on dunnage keeping it off the ground, covered with plastic and camouflaged with brush. There were some wires under the dunnage. He was going to check them out.

I was halfway through saying, "Don't do that!" when whump! from far off. Gerry's RTO was on the phone, breathlessly reporting that Gerry was hit and down. I took a compass bearing and headed the company in that direction, ready for anything.

Gerry had several frag wounds. He was conscious but in a bit of shock. I called a medevac. As we were loading him, I leaned over and said, loud enough for him to hear over the rotors, but not for anyone else, "Gerry, you're going to live through this war! You're not coming back to the field!" I squeezed his hand. He smiled weakly; they flew him out. I sent word back to battalion to reassign him to a rear-area job. After the war, he followed a successful career as a detective in the Los Angeles Police Department.

Leadership Is Eternal Responsibility

Once I was counseled by a senior officer "not to be too worried about your men." Incredible. My mission and my men were uppermost in my mind at all times. We were very good at our mission, and though my company lost very few men, I remember each of their deaths vividly. They were good men, in a war few understood.

BATTALION OFFICERS

I was fortunate to land in a truly great battalion. Colonel Pete and Colonel Ras' were both terrific battalion commanders.

Like Colonel Pete, Colonel Ras' was a commander and leader who inspired confidence. He called his soldiers his "pennies." "I hoard every one," he said, "and don't intend to spend one of them without very good reason."

In early 1970, the battalion's LZ was just below the Cambodian border, and under almost daily attack. A CBS news team flew in and interviewed Colonel Ras' as the base took sudden incoming fire. The reporter and cameraman both hit the ground. In the ensuing film, the picture swings wildly as the cameraman ducks; the picture, after a few moments of blurred motion, again centers on Ras', who hadn't flinched. He was standing upright, looking down at the cameraman with a half smile that as much as said, "You can't get good footage from down there, son."

The battalion staff and company commanders were all dedicated professionals. Mike, our battalion S-2 Intelligence, spoke fluent Russian; he eventually wound up commanding the Army's Russian Area Studies Institute in Germany. Gene, our S-3 Operations, was Special Forces on his previous tour, calm, avuncular. Earl, our battalion Signal officer, was terrific; we never had problems in communications. Phil, S-4 Supply, pulled rabbits out of hats, producing impossible-to-find cases of steaks, gallons of freshly made ice cream, and other goodies. All were flown out to the companies in the field.

George took over Alpha Company when I came down with malaria. A West Point graduate, he was initially accepted at VMI but elected to put in two years at Georgia Tech before going to West Point. That was VMI's loss. He was a terrific field soldier, racking up an impressive kill rate with some unique modifications of the state of tactics at the time.

Jay commanded Bravo Company. A former NCO and OCS graduate, he was a hard driver with a terrific sense of tactics, and care for his men. Severely wounded in-country a year or so before while leading a mechanized infantry company, word came back after that fight that he had died on the medevac helicopter. His unit wrote him off.

Long after the war, someone from Jay's prior outfit discovered he had survived. A congressman directed the Army to research the records. Eventually, several of us who commanded companies when Jay had Bravo Company went down to Fort Benning, to see him awarded the Distinguished Service Cross.

LIEUTENANTS

The Army went through second lieutenants in Vietnam at a respectable rate. Not as drastic as the World War II classic line, "the life expectancy of a second lieutenant is fifteen minutes," but many were killed or wounded. Because they were leading, at the front or near it, in many cases identifiable to the enemy. Because they were new and hadn't yet gained experience or "field knowledge." Because of happenstance; combat is relentlessly arbitrary. I should know; my encounter with the enemy on that hillside in 1967 was the result of precisely such random circumstance, and my error in not siting the positions covering that draw closer together. I was damn lucky, and learned from it.

In general, my lieutenants were good. My executive officer was a mustang, an NCO before commissioning. The platoon leaders were OCS or ROTC, with one West Point graduate. Another, with us briefly before being hit, was from the bayous of Louisiana, with an accent strong enough to require an interpreter. They all tried hard and were generally liked and respected. Three were wounded; none were killed.

RON

We were a couple of days into taking our turn at perimeter defense on LZ DOLLY. As a field radio mechanic, Ron was one of our stay-behind element, remaining on the battalion firebase. One morning he showed up at the bunker I was using as the company CP. "Sir, can I make a request?"

He was a squared-away soldier, knew his radio stuff. We had no complaints in the communications department. "Sure. Have you run it by the first sergeant and exec?"

"Yes, Sir. They said to see you."

"OK, what's up?"

"Well, Sir, I'd like to go to the field."

As the radio mech, Ron's job wasn't out in the woods with us. Any number of our riflemen would gladly trade places with him if they could; life on the LZ was a lot more pleasant than humping a rucksack in the field.

I was a little puzzled; didn't get it right away. "We don't need you out there in the field, Ron. Your radios work fine. If we have to get anything fixed, we swap it out; you take care of that from back here."

He shuffled his feet a little. "Sir, I mean I'd like to switch MOSs. I want to go to the field as an Eleven Bravo.

Wow! That was new. As a field radio mechanic, Ron's MOS was 31E, referred to as a "Thirty-One Echo." He wanted to change to 11B, or "Eleven Bravo," the MOS for an infantryman.

Ron was a man the Army had trained to repair radios; he did a very good job of it and was at a lot less risk than anyone out in the boonies. He wanted to become a combat infantryman? No wonder the first sergeant and exec had said go talk to the CO. Afterward, they likely looked at each other, raised their eyebrows, and made little rotating motions beside their heads with their index fingers.

This was serious stuff. I sat him down. He was determined about wanting to transfer to one of the platoons and soldier as an infantryman. He said he understood the risks, had thought about it for some time, and was waiting for us to be back on the firebase before bringing it up.

"Hmm," I said, "I can't give you an answer until I talk to the S-1 and the Signal officer. No promises."

"OK, Sir. I'll stand by."

Surprisingly there was no problem with the S-1 as far as personnel, though he shared the attitude of my exec and first sergeant; he thought Ron was nuts. But he would put in a request for a replacement radio mech if it was OK with Earl, the battalion's Signal officer.

"I had a suspicion that's what he wanted," said Earl. We were sitting outside the TOC. Earl spent a lot of time in there, making sure communications ran faultlessly. His area was a critical part of the adage, "A unit needs to be able to move, shoot, and communicate." Because of his diligence, we never had a communications problem, and the colonel made certain we company commanders appreciated it. We did.

Earl was also an Airborne soldier; he had served with the 82nd. We had that in common. "He mentioned something about it a month or so ago," he continued, "but I thought it was just casual. Tell you what; let me see if we can get a replacement out here for him. If I can do that, he's yours, the crazy bastard. Have to admire him for it, though."

That's how it worked out. I assigned Ron to one of the platoons; his lieutenant paired him with an experienced field man. He turned out to be a great combat soldier. The added benefit was that if anything went wrong with one of our radios, well, we had an expert on them, lugging an M16 and a ruck right along with us.

Ron went on after Vietnam to OCS and eventually retired as a full colonel. How about that?

FIREFIGHTS

Our tracers were bright red, the enemy's neon green. Was there some agreement about that, between us and the Russians and Chinese, like the NFL deciding offside rules?

Contacts at night were red and green strobes, shouts, and rocket-propelled grenades exploding in trees. Artillery arrived with shattering sounds, like huge loads of flat wooden boards dropped from a great height onto a concrete floor.

The first moments of contact were always like being on an express train, before adrenalin surged and everything seemed to slow down.

There were oddities: an NVA canteen sailing by during a fight while I was talking on the radio. Just the canteen in midair. We retrieved it later. I still have it.

Bits of leaves, clipped by enemy fire, fluttering down to land on my arm as I talked on the radio.

One of my troopers' shots hit an NVA soldier's chest harness carrying RPG rockets. The resulting massive blast and shockwave silenced both sides for a few moments. Then the fight resumed.

One of my men's rucksack was shot to bits on his back as he lay prone, by his platoon's M60 gunner, a few feet behind him in dense brush. The gunner apologized profusely afterward.

Our missions could change in a moment. I was once briefing my XO on a last-minute mission change. "Wow," he said, "we're really gonna get dropped in the shit on this one."

I thought for a moment as I folded my map, remembering that honey bucket well in Japan. "Nah," I said. "I've been there. It's survivable."

Years later, an officer who came into the Army decades after Vietnam asked me if there was any "order" to those fights. The Army's term for them then was "meeting engagements." Very formal. The reality was, as one of my soldiers wrote years later, "like a knife fight between blindfolded men in a dirt-floor Texas bar."

During my command time, we lost four men killed and a few wounded. In June 1969, we lost Jack and Dink, two good men. Jack was one of the best men I had in both tours. On that morning, he was up on point, Dink behind him. We were in dense forest with thick ground cover. The enemy let them walk into a fire field, thinned just at knee height; they hit Jack and Dink in the first burst. Bennie, forwardmost on an M60 gun, stood upright shooting it out; a slug shattered his arm.

It was close-in. At first contact, everyone hit the ground and effectively vanished. It was hard to see where my soldiers were. I needed to move to find people, to organize and direct the action. Most reacted quickly; a couple had frozen. I grabbed men, talked to them, had them repeat back; then, "OK, go!"

The company command net was jammed; Jack had a radio, his hand clenched on "transmit." With no radio, my being right behind the lead platoon leader and close to the action helped. It was over in minutes; the enemy broke contact.

"LEAD DICK"

Pat commanded Charlie Company. One day in midsummer 1969, we were in thick forest on the Cambodian border. We had just paused for a map check. The day was quiet; the usual background sounds of birds in the canopy, nothing else.

I was reaching for the battalion radio net handset to call in a sitrep when there was a sudden, far-off burst of AK47 fire. A hell of a firefight developed as we listened: M16s and M60 machine guns, the enemy's AKs, and heavier explosions of their shoulder-fired B40 rockets.

B40s, Russian-made RPGs, rocket-propelled grenades, were designed as antitank weapons. The NVA used them as antipersonnel weapons. They weren't grenades; they were finned rocket projectiles with a nasty shaped-explosive charge in the nose that could burn through steel armor. If an RPG hit anywhere near you, there was a good chance you would be killed or severely wounded. When they hit a tree, they blew out huge shards of wood and splinters. Yes, there were casualties from wood fragments.

When the firing erupted, Pat was carrying his M16 rifle with the receiver group resting on the ammunition pack, on the right side of his load-bearing harness. The firefight opened with a hail of enemy automatic weapons fire and several RPGs. Pat later said he saw a burst of orange light as an RPG detonated right on the flash hider, the slotted fixture at the very end of the barrel, of his M16. No sound, just the flash.

The concussion from the blast knocked him backward and stunned him. By some freak chance, all the shrapnel from the RPG, except for a few tiny bits that wounded him in the groin and legs, missing any critical equipment, blew past on either side of him. After that fight, he was referred to in the battalion as "Lead Dick."

THE HAUNTED PATROL

We had one exceptional night ambush that puzzles me to this day.

The five-man patrol was led by an experienced soldier. They departed just before sunset, moving to a grid location I identified on the map as the fork in a trail. The enemy was using the trails at night in this sector; chances were they might hit a group up the trail from the fork. They would, as always, conduct a careful recon before going into position.

Fine. But just past midnight, my RTO handed me the handset; on the other end was the ambush patrol leader. Even allowing for the distortion of sound over radio and his low voice, it was evident he was shaken. He asked to withdraw the patrol.

There had been no enemy activity. He could not describe the problem other than that something he could not explain had happened. Lights, voices, wind, but no humans. What!?

I thought for a moment. If they were spooked about something, they were no longer calm, deadly ambushers. OK, I told him, come on in; we're alerted. The company went to stand-to, with every man awake, armed, alert. I told the patrol leader to stop fifty meters out and give me the word by radio they were on their way in. He did so; the sector they were entering disarmed their trip flares.

At the CP, the young soldier was breathing hard and apologetic. Doc checked his pulse. A little erratic, he said, and accelerated. I sat the patrol leader down and had him drink some water.

His tale was remarkable. They had passed an old, overgrown shrine on the way to the trail junction. Not on the trail, deep in the woods. It was clear there had been no activity there for a very long time. They moved on another fifty or so meters, found the trail, checked it, then set up a linear ambush along one side.

Darkness came, sudden and total in the deep forest at that latitude, like turning off a switch. They waited. For the first few hours, he said, there were the normal sounds: insects, geckos calling far off in the trees.

At around 2300, or 11 p.m., all the night noises stopped. Not so much stopped, he said, as the activity and volume faded to an almost leaden silence. It was as if, he continued, the silence drifted down from the canopy overhead, like something tangible.

Then a very gentle breeze, a slight change in the air, but growing. *That* was unusual; there was no breeze under that rainforest canopy, ever, except during the monsoon. This was the middle of the dry season, when the air was hot, still, and humid.

The breeze grew to a light wind. They could sense leaves stirring in the canopy, but there was no sound. It grew until it was moving tree limbs overhead.

Then they heard voices: weird, distorted, as though wailing. Colored lights floated in the wind, with the odor of incense. Each man felt something else they couldn't describe well: an ominous, malevolent presence.

To put it mildly, they were shit scared. Yes, they were soldiers, trained and ready. But this was something far outside what they expected from a potential enemy.

The wind grew to a cold gale; the canopy overhead was swaying. Lights hovered in the blast; the voices grew in volume. Then suddenly, almost instantly, it was over. The canopy settled; the wind, voices, and lights were gone. The heavy, humid, still night slid back. The insects and geckos resumed.

I debriefed the men individually; their experience was the same. Though the ambush site was no more than several hundred meters away, we had experienced no change in conditions at our night perimeter.

My medic said if they weren't each in a mild state of shock, it was close. There was no further activity the remainder of that night.

VERY CLOSE CALL

We were on a firebase very close to the Cambodian border. Airlifted to the base that afternoon, we waited for pickup by another serial of helicopters, to be combat assaulted into a new AO. By evening the lift aircraft scheduled to pick us up hadn't appeared.

Just at twilight, I sat on the sandbagged ring around one of the LZ's five 105mm howitzers. Both my radio operators were on my left. Biggie, my pace man, was on my right. We were looking at my map. Behind us the howitzer's crew prepared a fire mission. The gun captain called out the azimuth and deflection, the crew responding.

There was a sudden, soundless white flicker, like a fluorescent light when first switched on. The blast slammed me against the sandbagged side of the bunker we were facing, knocking me a little dizzy. Other explosions hammered the LZ.

"I'm hit!" Biggie yelled. He was on the ground writhing, trying to reach his lower back, covered in blood. I grabbed him and, with one of the radio operators, dragged him into the bunker. The floor was covered with men; no one else seemed hurt. Outside, more explosions, yelling.

I reached for Biggie's back; a hot shard of steel, solidly stuck, burned my fingers. He was in incredible pain. We couldn't do anything except hold him as he thrashed on the floor.

The attack was over in moments. The fragment was lodged in Biggie's kidney. Doc and the medics shot him full of morphine. We sent him out on a medevac that came in just before dark and went out immediately. Several men had been killed, including the crew on the gun we were sitting beside; a number were wounded. From the concentration of the impacts, it was most likely heavy mortars.

I must have hit something or something hit me on the way to getting pasted against that bunker. I could barely walk. My ankle was swollen to about half again normal size. We taped it up tight. Years later that damn injury wore out my left hip. Eventually I had to have a full ankle replacement as well.

We waited the next day for an airlift out, but air assets were tied up elsewhere. In late afternoon, I coordinated with the S-3 on a new AO, closer in. We would hike to it. We went through the wire an hour after dark and moved off in a file through the rubber. Several thousand meters later we halted, going to a defensive perimeter, without digging in, the men prone with their weapons facing out. We went to watch-on, watch-off alert. Those who were able slept where they were.

TERMITES

Atop enormous subterranean colonies, termites created earthen mounds from two to five feet tall and several feet across, hard as concrete. In a fight, they could be used as cover from enemy fire.

An hour or so after we set up our hasty night perimeter, we experienced nature up close. Unaware, we halted atop one of the colonies. In daylight we likely would have seen one or more of the mounds; in total darkness we hadn't a clue. Attracted by our vibration and body heat, they came burrowing up through the ground, angry, hungry, or both. Just under an inch long with strong mandibles, they were all over our fatigues and equipment.

I radioed battalion that we were changing location "due to attack by enemy termites." That message made the rounds all the way up to division as one of the more unique.

A SURPRISE VISITOR

The rains began in late May. The first storms were tentative, like an orchestra tuning up. An hour's rain, a pause to rearrange the sheet music, then again, this time with *gusto*. In a day or so, it was coming down nonstop.

We lived in an aqueous world, moved through sodden jungle, stayed wet, ate wet, slept wet. Men came down with immersion foot. I evacuated John, one of my radio operators, his feet swelled up white, bloated. Pushing a finger against them left an indention that took time to fill out, like the Pillsbury "doughboy." Others developed debilitating ringworm—not a worm at all; a fungal infection.

We passed into an upland area with huge trees with thick canopies, admitting little light; a kind of gloomy twilight, though my watch said it was high noon.

We paused for a map check. The ground was soaked; we sat on our rucksacks. I had my back against the trunk of a towering tree. Paul, my artillery FO, sat facing me. I spread my acetate-covered map on my knee; we both bent over it, our radio operators around us.

Except for the rain, there was no sound. The jungle life that would be making a racket was trying to stay dry. Suddenly from above came the sound of branches breaking, leaves shoved aside cascading down through the canopy overhead, growing in volume. We froze. Something big grazed my left shoulder, hitting the ground with a heavy, wet SPLAT! No one moved, it happened that fast. We stared at a humped brown mound of fur.

Paul spoke first. "Damn! It's a sloth!"

My company RTO craned over to look. "Is it dead?" I nudged it with my boot. It wasn't one of those cute little sloths you see in zoos; this guy was *big*.

"I don't know," I said. "I thought these things are supposed to stay up in the trees."

It wasn't dead. As we watched, it moved, slowly. But then, everything sloths *do* is slow. Its eyes opened; it looked at us with a strange sort of grin, but that was its face coloring. Very slowly, it stretched out an arm with long, sharp claws; then the other, *very slowly* climbing back up the trunk. Its big brown eyes didn't leave us. Until it disappeared in the canopy overhead, we watched it, watching us.

Somewhere in Vietnam there may be an old, gray sloth, boring all the little kiddy sloths with stories about the day he dropped in on very strange animals, way down there on the ground floor.

FIELD RATIONS

We carried several olive-drab-metal-canned C-ration meals in our rucksacks. Enough for five or six days added a lot of weight to water, ammunition, weapons, and gear.

Each meal weighed just under three pounds, providing 1,200 calories. The main-course cans were one of twelve choices, such as beef steak, spaghetti and meatballs, ham and lima beans, and turkey loaf. I'll spare you the outrageous names the troops dubbed a few of them.

Each had a dessert unit: pound cake, cinnamon roll, fruit salad, or peaches in syrup. An accessory pack had instant coffee, sugar, salt, creamer, toilet paper, and four cigarettes. It was very much a "smoke 'em if you got 'em" Army.

A hard white plastic spoon came with every meal, and one of the most ingenious pieces of equipment ever devised: the P-38 can opener. A small folding blade on a simple metal tab for a handle, it could zip open a ration can in seconds. Troops carried them on their dog tag chains.

Improvising on C-ration menus became a game. One of my RTOs was a wizard at *caffé mocha*. Mixing several coffee, sugar, and cream packets in hot water, he shaved two discs of foil-wrapped milk chocolate into the brew. *Voila!*

The Tabasco company in Louisiana sent thousands of small red bottles of their hot sauce to Vietnam. Each came with a *Charlie Ration Cookbook*. A stroke of marketing genius, it was illustrated in the style of the famous *Beetle Bailey* World War II comic strip. Different C-rations could be combined with a dash of Tabasco sauce to create "foxhole dinner for two," "cease-fire casserole," or "patrol chicken soup." We tried a few. We survived.

The Army issued solid-fuel tablets for heating C-rations. But it didn't provide a simple, folding metal stove for supporting the cans while heating. By the late 1960s, just such a stove, developed by the German Army in World War II, was in use by several armies. It's sold worldwide today under the "Esbit" trademark. We heated our Cs on "expedient stoves" made from empty ration cans, punched several times around the bottom with a "church key" for air flow. A can of food or coffee could be balanced on top.

We ignored the issued heating tabs; too weak. Our preferred fuel was a small chunk of C-4 plastic explosive torn from the brown-plastic-wrapped bars of it we carried. With ventilation, C-4 was stable, burning with a blue-white flame of very high intensity.

In midsummer 1969, we received long-range patrol rations, or "lurps." Lightweight, freeze-dried, vacuum-packed in plastic bags; we added water, hot or cold. They were tasty and came in eight flavors, including chicken with rice, chili con carne, and beef stew. A cereal or fruitcake bar, and two foil-wrapped milk chocolate discs. Much tastier than Cs, lurps were bigger in volume, providing 1,500 calories. You can buy the same "lurp" units today in backpacking stores, under the "Mountain House" brand.

Decades later I learned the Army had considered providing a stove like the World War II German design. But the test troops got their fingers pinched, so it was deemed "dangerous." As combat infantrymen, we were each draped with enough hardware to practically take out a small town. Not providing a stove because we might get our fingers pinched shows the gap between the people in the rear and the troops out at "the sharp edge."

LOG BIRDS

Every fourth or fifth day we were resupplied by helicopter, referred to as being "logged," for logistics. Always a Huey, the log bird brought rations, ammunition, new fatigues, boots as needed, mail, radio batteries, and big, wobbly plastic "blivets" of clean drinking water. Every so often it brought replacement soldiers, and hot food in insulated marmite cans.

The log bird would take out men going to the rear for various reasons, and the lucky ones nearing their "dates of expected return from overseas service," known to all of us as DEROS, pronounced "DEE-roce." I tried to send DEROS men out a week or so before their last in-country date. They could decompress a bit and begin the out-processing that would put them on a "freedom bird," the chartered jets that took us home to the States.

Getting ready to bring in a log bird meant finding a landing zone big enough for the rotor disk of the Huey, with a bit of margin. On this day we were in triple-canopy rainforest. As we moved during the morning, I kept thinking we might have to blow down a few trees with C-4 to create enough space to land the bird. But just before midday, we skirted an opening that looked like it could take a single ship, though it would be a tight squeeze.

We stopped. Two patrols went out to scout enemy that might threaten the operation. Finding none, I put security out around the clearing; radioed battalion that we had a one-ship LZ, though a tight one; and sent the encrypted map coordinates. We waited.

You could hear Hueys long before they were near you. Their rotor sound had a characteristic *popopop!* as the rotor tips actually broke the sound barrier.

My RTO handed me the handset. The helo pilot spoke in that choppy fashion you can replicate by talking while you repeatedly hit your Adam's apple, if you ever get the urge. "Ahh . . . FOGGY DAY SIX . . . KILLER SPADE SIX THREE, inbound your location. Pop smoke, over."

I gestured to one of my CP group. He pulled the pin on a smoke grenade and threw it out into the clearing. Bright yellow smoke surged out, slowly rising up through the rain, above the trees.

"KILLER SPADE SIX THREE, FOGGY DAY SIX . . . smoke is out, over."

There was a pause while the helo sound got louder, then, "Ahh . . . FOGGY DAY SIX . . . I have Loopy Lemon, over."

We used the names of popular powdered drink mix flavors back home to identify smoke colors. Occasionally the enemy would throw a captured smoke grenade out as well, hoping to lure the helicopter into small-arms range and shoot it down. If the helicopter pilot called out a color other than the one we threw, we warned him off and called artillery onto the location of the spurious smoke.

"DAY SIX . . . roger on Loopy Lemon, over." The rotor sound got louder. The Huey slid over the edge of the hole, hovering directly above. The pilot descended straight down, both door gunners hanging out on the skids on each side, watching the tail boom. There were no rear or side mirrors on those birds for the pilot; the door gunners gave him feedback on that tail rotor, which had no more than a five-foot swing clearance either way.

It was superb flying, but I watched it with concern. We really needed the supplies. We *didn't* need a crashed aircraft and casualties.

KILLER SPADE was the call sign for Bravo Company of the 229th Assault Helicopter Battalion. They were old friends and had flown us into many combat assaults. Each of the 229th's helicopter companies had a different playing card suit symbol on the left- and right-side pilot doors. Bravo Company's was a black spade inside a blue square. The other companies had diamonds, clubs, or hearts. The battalion's radio call sign was STACKED DECK.

Down it came, rotors clearing the trees by no more than four feet or so. It settled gently on the floor of the clearing. A couple of my men jumped aboard and tossed out the supplies. I ran over, ducking my head. "Good to see you! Many thanks!" I yelled in the left-side window.

Their helmet visors down, the two guys in the front seats nodded. The warrant on the left grinned and handed me a business card through his window. I was floored. A *business card*!? They both laughed soundlessly, nodding their heads. I waved and scurried back to the CP group.

The blade pitch changed; the ship picked up to a low hover, paused, then slowly and smoothly went straight back up until it was just above treetop height. It did a pedal turn and departed. As the rotor sounds faded in the distance, I looked at the card. One side had the division's horsehead-and-chevron insignia and:

BRAVO COMPANY
"The Stacked Deck Battalion"
Has had the privilege of supporting you.
KILLER SPADE provides fastest, safest delivery.
We are listed in your SOI.

The reverse read:

Foxhole Delivery Service
Provided by KILLER SPADE
Rice Paddy Deliveries on Call
Foggy Peaks by Appointment Only

I have that card today, still ingrained with the red laterite dirt that covered everything in our part of Vietnam. Every time I've seen it, I smile.

MEN ON THE MOON

High noon, deep in the rainforest on the Cambodian border. Midnight in the States. We had stopped to send out patrols. My RTO handed me the handset on the battalion frequency radio. On the other end was Major Gene, our battalion S-3: "Be advised we have just landed on the moon. That is all."

I stared at the handset, then at the faces of the young, tired, sweating soldiers in my command group. "Roger, thank you," I replied and handed the handset back. "We just landed men on the moon," I said. "Pass the good word."

Their expressions were a unique blend of "No shit?" and "So what?" Surreal. We moved on.

MG34

"Have a look at this, Six." One of my squad leaders dropped an unusual-looking light machine gun in front of us. Long and slender, with a pistol grip, buttstock, and bipod. I recognized it as an MG34, the belt-fed German infantry weapon I'd seen in the Ranger course. Carved in this one's wooden buttstock was an inscription in Vietnamese and an exclamation mark.

I sent for Truong, our "Kit Carson scout." A former VC who had surrendered to the South Vietnamese, he'd volunteered to work with American units as an interpreter and adviser on enemy capabilities.

The paper that came with him from S-2 said he was kidnapped from his village by the Vietcong and forced to carry ammunition and equipment. He had escaped and surrendered to a South Vietnamese unit when he found the opportunity.

Nothing new to that situation; during their Indochina war, the French had done the same, using natives and even enemy soldiers as bearers for equipment, or laborers. The French labeled them PIMs: "temporary military prisoners."

How had that MG34 gotten into the hands of the NVA enemy halfway around the world in 1969? The likely answer was that it was captured by the French during the Second World War, or seized thereafter. When French forces went to Indochina in the late 1940s, Foreign Legion units went with them. The Legion had a big postwar enlistment of former German Wehrmacht soldiers, even a few who had been in the SS.

The French weren't terribly choosy; they had a colonial war to fight. The Germans were willing to do it and were battle-hardened soldiers. When Legion units went to Indochina, some were equipped with captured German weapons. The MG34 was efficient and deadly. The gun may well also have been captured by the Vietminh during the French Indochina War, or it may have been part of the weapons stocks left by the French when they withdrew in 1954. Assigned to an NVA unit, it wound up in our hands.

I imagined the inscription on our captured gun to be an exhortation like, "Kill the Imperialists!" Truong went down on one knee, turning the stock so he could better read the inscription. We waited. He looked up and smiled. "It say, 'Oil gun, or not work.'"

TRUONG

Truong was a slight, gentle guy. I never did determine what happened to his family, whether the VC killed them or whether he still had a village to return to. He never talked about it; I didn't ask. He kept pretty much to himself, tagging along at the rear of the command group.

In contacts, he stayed well down; he wasn't a fighter. He was, though, a very good discerner of enemy activity. He knew their movement styles, how they built their temporary and more permanent fighting positions, what they carried, how they were motivated. His English was *very* basic, but with hand movements and drawing on the ground with a stick, we managed to communicate.

He wore US jungle fatigues, size extra small, and rubber-soled sandals rather than American boots. When he showed up, coming off a log bird with the rations, water, ammunition, and mail like another inventory item, he had a nametape over his pocket, on which was stenciled CONG.

Vietnamese names are three or four syllables—the first is the family name. His full name was Truong Van Cong. So his name tape should have read TRU-ONG. Some dolt in the rear, who should have known better, sent him to us with a nametape sure to generate comments from the men: "They have to *label* these guys as Vietcong now, or what?"

UNCLE ART

Art Hurow and my father were lieutenants together in the late 1940s at Fort Dix. We were practically next-door neighbors in Japan. Art and his wife, Ruth, were so close to our family I called them Uncle Art and Aunt Ruth.

A Polish immigrant, Art arrived in New York in the late 1930s. Enlisting shortly after Pearl Harbor, he became an infantry officer, seeing extensive combat action in Italy. Like my father, Art stayed in the Army, and like Dad, he'd "had enough of loud noises," transferring to the Transportation Corps. He was a terrific officer, and a great general.

One day in June 1969, I was with my infantry company in the field. I had taken command a few weeks before when Cecil had rotated to battalion staff. We were out on an operation about eight days by then. To me, the morning was like any other. I was focused on our mission and all things related to it. We could look to another week or so in the field before being rotated back to LZ DOLLY for our turn at base defense. At about 0900, I was surprised to get a radio call from battalion to move the company to a pickup position. I was to be flown, individually, back to DOLLY "for a meeting." That was all the message stated.

It was odd; I reviewed our movement, our current mission, trying to reason why a company in the field would have its commander extracted. If we put the company in a good defensive posture, I was confident my XO could hold down the unit while I was away.

We found a clearing big enough to take a single Huey. I thoroughly briefed my lieutenant, made sure he had a good grip on the situation, and flew out as the sole passenger.

The S-1, our battalion adjutant, met the helicopter. "The colonel wants to see you at the TOC at noon. Get cleaned up and a change of fatigues." No details. I didn't ask; I assumed other company commanders had also been extracted from the field for the meeting. I'd find out soon enough.

When I reported to the tactical operations center, I was astonished to see Uncle Art. He stood next to our division commander, Major General Roberts. Colonel Pete, our battalion commander, was grinning from ear to ear.

Art shook my hand, closed his other hand over it, and held it. "Don't tell me you forgot the date?" Suddenly it clicked. It was the 10th of June, the day I was to be promoted to captain. I hadn't kept track of dates; in the field, all days were pretty much alike.

A brief ceremony followed. Art had a set of captain's twin silver bars, the old kind, heavy, with the pin-and-catch back, rather than the lighter, modern version with two posts-and-keepers. "These are an old pair of mine," he said. "I thought you'd like to have them."

It was another moment when the Army became family. Art kept track of the days; he flew from Saigon all the way out to our battalion LZ. Colonel Pete was delighted to have two generals on his turf. I could imagine the coordination that went into getting those generals together.

A cup of coffee, more handshakes, then I flew back out to my company. The troops enjoyed hearing about it. We picked up where we had left off, hunting for the enemy.

Years after the war, out of the Army and attending a conference as a guest at the War College in Carlisle, Pennsylvania, I met another civilian attendee at an evening reception. We got to talking about Vietnam; he had served as an Army officer there as well. After a few minutes, I learned he was Art's aide. When I told him about Art flying from Saigon out to LZ DOLLY just for that promotion, he exclaimed, "That was *you?*"

As he related, his life as Art's aide was pretty stable and comfortable in Saigon; it wasn't exactly a danger zone. The night before, Art told him, "We're going out to 'Indian territory' in the morning to see a young tiger get promoted; he's the son of my best friend. You'd better arm up!"

He said Art's command helicopter flew north and kept flying north. Art told him that if they went down in the rainforest or the rubber, they would be eaten alive by the NVA. They kept flying north, all the way to the Cambodian border. And there was LZ DOLLY. He said he had never been so far from Saigon; that flight "gave him the willies."

Hilarious. To me, being on the battalion firebase was almost as safe as being back in the States. It's all relative, right?

MAJOR MINOR

He was our battalion XO, second in command to the colonel, ensuring that the colonel's orders and desires were carried out. A West Point graduate, he was a professional and highly competent officer. He divided his time between the battalion's forward firebase and its rear area under the rubber trees at the brigade base at Quan Loi, where he had his own "hooch."

Major Minor seemed highly concerned that there was going to be a revolution or racial war at home. I assumed his belief was based on his perception of the "black power" culture prevalent at that time in the States, and very much so in the Army in Vietnam. Many black soldiers went around in the rear areas with much larger than "regulation" hair styles, some with "afro" combs stuck in them. When meeting each other, they executed intricate "daps": a series of fist bumps and hand clasps signifying cultural unity. Some found it off-putting; I thought it was interesting, and noticed that most of that was practically nonexistent in units actually out in the field.

Major Minor carried a holstered .45 ACP pistol at all times. I was told the battalion armorers had cautioned him it wasn't safe to have a round in the chamber unless he was preparing to shoot. But he carried it holstered, with a round chambered for instant use.

One evening after flying back from the battalion firebase, he was in his hooch, shifting the pistol in its holster from his field harness to the web belt he wore in the rear, always with the holstered pistol. The pistol fired, the bullet hitting him squarely in the chest. He died before a medic could get there.

DEATHS BY ACCIDENT

People find it hard to believe if I tell them I saw more American soldiers die in Vietnam from accidents than in combat.

In war, things happen without warning, very fast. Sometimes men are on the wrong side of circumstance. And there's always the "Darwin" component: those who die as a result of unsafe behavior or bad judgment, like the sergeant who chewed C-4 and the Major Minor. There were many more.

Two soldiers I passed one stifling afternoon at Quan Loi, for example. Playing catch with a fragmentation grenade. I couldn't believe it.

"OK, you men know better. Someone's liable to get hurt."

They looked affronted. "Yes, Sir."

I walked on, thinking they had to be rear-area people; field soldiers were unlikely to mess with something that lethal just for kicks. I was well on my way along under the rubber trees when the WHUMP! of a grenade detonating came from far behind.

CRIMSON TIDE 106

On a sweltering afternoon at the Quan Loi airstrip, I was waiting for a flight out to the firebase. Our rear-area supply people were loading out some of our battalion's equipment on a twin-rotor CH-47 Chinook; I would go along as a passenger.

The Chinooks were big helicopters that carried troops or cargo inside and external cargo on a hook or in slings. The division had two heavy-lift battalions of Chinooks; their radio call signs were CRIMSON TIDE and LONG HORN.

There was a lot of activity on the other side of the airstrip. Prepackaged material for a new firebase being built out in the rainforest was picked up and flown out by a series of Chinooks and a powerful CH-54 Skycrane. Loads of steel culvert, steel planking, balk timber, coils of wire, pallets of thousands of empty sandbags, and other matériel were laid out on cargo nets that would become sling loads carried beneath the helicopters.

A D-6 Caterpillar bulldozer was also being airlifted. Broken down into three pieces, it would be landed at the new firebase site and assembled there by men from the division's combat engineer battalion.

Because of their weight, the components were flown out in three lifts by the Skycrane. With its drooping pilot/crane operator cabin; its single, massive five-bladed rotor; and its slender fuselage, it resembled an enormous dragonfly. It had just departed with the Cat's dozer blade and its hydraulic pistons hanging beneath it.

The amount of lift an aircraft generates is directly related to air temperature and altitude. On a very hot day, lift is significantly decreased. This was a *very* hot day. There was a lot of racket: helicopters, four-engine C-130 transports, and high-powered, twin-engine OV-10 Bronco turboprops, flown by the forward air controllers.

Over it all, we became suddenly aware of a different sound: engines straining to the "redline" limit. Across the airstrip, a CRIMSON TIDE Chinook was dragging its hanging sling load across the ground. Its rotors, normally horizontal, seemed to be bent slightly upward, indicating it was straining to lift its load in the high-heat condition.

Pieces of steel planking began shedding from the nylon webbing cargo net. There was a rapid snapping or popping sound. The Chinook then literally sat down on the sling load in an extreme nose-down attitude, its rotors almost striking the runway. We were transfixed; they were definitely in trouble. Why they didn't shut down the engines is a mystery.

What happened next was fast. The Chinook popped back up to about one hundred feet, with the load swinging wildly beneath it. The effect made the big helicopter fishtail and jerk around. The sling load either separated or was punched off by the crew.

Suddenly relieved of the sling weight, the Chinook shot higher while rolling to the left, finally going completely inverted. There was an explosion as the rear pylon and rotor broke off. The forward section plummeted down, slamming into the ground with tremendous force. The wreckage didn't burn. Five men died.

MAIL AND MARS

We had two options to communicate with home. Mail took about a week to get to the States, another week for a reply. You wrote "Free" on the upper right of the envelope; no stamp needed. If you were on an LZ or firebase, or further to the rear, you dropped letters in red nylon mailbags hanging at various places. Outbound mail was collected every couple of days, winding up on chartered aircraft to the States.

If you were in the field, on log days word was passed to get outgoing mail up to the company CP. It went out on the log bird. If you didn't have paper, you could write a message on the side of a piece of cardboard torn from a C-ration box, write "Free" in the corner, and it would get to the address in the States.

The other option was voice. It was possible to speak with someone in the States using a quirky, unpredictable combination of radio and telephone known as MARS: the Military Amateur Radio System. At some bases in Vietnam, radio communication units had a MARS phone box mounted on the outside wall or on a nearby post. Inside the box was a telephone handset on a hook, without the rotary dial. The handset was connected to a radio operator's station inside.

At certain hours, usually at night when atmospheric conditions were amenable, the military radio operator would attempt to make contact with a volunteer civilian amateur radio operator (known as a "ham" operator) in the States. As long as the radio link held between them, the ham operator could "patch" the radio call from Vietnam into the civilian telephone lines.

To use the MARS system to call home, you went to the communications facility sometime during the night when the system was "live." You joined a line of others at the MARS box. Calls were handled by an operator inside on a first come, first served basis. When it was your turn, you gave the MARS radio operator the number you wanted to call in the States.

The MARS operator passed the number to the stateside ham operator. The ham operator dialed the number in the Bell Telephone civilian phone system. If someone answered, the ham operator told them there was an incoming call from Vietnam. Also, they had to say "over" each time they finished speaking so that the call could be switched back to you. You also had to say "over" so that the ham operator could switch it back.

The ham operator finally stated that if anything of a military nature was heard being discussed, the MARS operator at the Vietnam end, who was also listening, would cut the call off. Your entire call would be limited to five minutes. With two strangers monitoring and with having to say "over," conversations could be a little strained, but it was better than nothing.

If your call did go through, the connection could be spotty; sometimes you could hardly make out what the other person was saying. Sometimes the phone at the stateside end would simply go unanswered; those days were long before answering machines. Sometimes you would hear a "busy" signal. In both of the latter cases, it was "Sorry, Charlie, try again some other day."

Just before Christmas 1969, I was at Quan Loi, just below the Cambodian border. It was a good-sized base with a big airstrip and a MARS terminal. I joined a long line of other soldiers waiting to make calls. It was 7 p.m.; with the time difference, it was 8 a.m. at home. It was also about ninety degrees at Quan Loi, with very heavy humidity. Moisture in the air formed halos around lights enveloped by swarms of bugs.

While we were waiting in the MARS line, Quan Loi was hit with a mortar attack. The first incoming round exploded far down the runway. The next hit a helicopter or aircraft parked in a revetment; it blew up in a spectacular fireball. Other explosions walked toward us.

The rational action was to try to find cover. All around us, men ran for the shelter of bunkers. But we all hit the ground where we were and stayed there, getting as flat as possible. Not one man moved from his place in line. When it was over, we stood up and dusted ourselves off. I don't remember a word being spoken.

My call went through; Mom was surprised and happy to hear from me. After we had spoken for a few minutes, she asked how things were *really* going. "Pretty quiet, Mom," I replied. "Just another day here, over."

AFVN

In the States, Vietnam was very much a television war. In-country, unless you were somewhere in the rear areas, there wasn't much TV. Radio, though, was everywhere. The Armed Forces Vietnam network (AFVN) did its best to replicate stateside radio formats, salted with "public service messages" on reenlistment, R & R sites to visit, and reminders to take the antimalaria pills. There was a popular "spoof" Vietcong reenlistment spiel the men parodied for weeks.

Almost everywhere in-country on an LZ, firebase, or in the rear, we could pick up AFVN's *Dawnbusters* program at 0600, with its wake-up call of "Gooood Morning, Vietnam!" and its mix of rock, "Top 40," some mildly off-color jokes and commentary, and a nod to the "unit of the day."

News on the Hour and the *Stateside Survey* summarized events back home. Without question, the most popular song aired on AFVN was "We Gotta Get Out of This Place" by the Animals.

A hugely popular and wildly comedic radio series on AFVN was *Chicken-Man*, a spoof on *Batman*. In each segment, Benton Harbor, a mild-mannered shoe salesman in real life, changes into his ChickenMan hero disguise to "strike terror into the hearts of criminals everywhere."

All across Vietnam, men imitated the throwaway lines of the "wonderful white-winged warrior." One of our helicopter companies even adopted CHICKEN MAN as its radio call sign.

AFVN Sports broadcast stateside games. I listened to a hotly contested baseball game while shaving one morning on LZ DOLLY, overlooking the enormous Michelin rubber plantation stretching off in the haze to the horizon.

We were twelve hours and a day ahead of the States. For a few magic moments, the crack of the bat against a fast pitch, the roar of the crowd, and the announcer's excited commentary as the batter rounded third brought me closer to home.

Popular stateside radio personalities like Wolfman Jack in Los Angeles, Bruce Morrow in New York, and many others recorded their radio programs, which were flown to Vietnam and broadcast on AFVN.

By far the most popular program of AFVN's television broadcast day was delivered by Bobbie Keith, an "Army brat" whose father was a Military Intelligence officer. As "Bobbie the Weather Girl," she was a bubbly, blue-eyed blonde. She gave the daily weather report in front of a backdrop with maps of the States and Vietnam. Her patter ran toward commentary like, "It's ninety-eight in Da Nang, a solid one hundred degrees at Hué, and tonight along the DMZ? Well, fellas, on the DMZ tonight it can get *very* hot!"

Occasionally when Bobbie predicted rain, she wore a swimsuit and was doused with a bucket of water delivered from above the backdrop. She reminded us all of "the girl back home."

20,000 MEN AND ME

We could expect to be on the LZ at base defense for about a week or two, then be combat assaulted back out to the field. While we maintained watch during the day and especially at night, it was a welcome pause and a chance for hot food, medical attention for some foot problems and jungle rashes for some of the troops, and a few warm beers, invariably Falstaff.

That stay on DOLLY started a bit differently. We had just finished getting the men to their assigned perimeter bunkers when I was called to the battalion TOC. Gene, the S-3, had a big smile. "We're getting a visitor, a VIP. You're designated as her escort officer."

"Her" escort? That was odd. "Who's visiting?"

"All I know is it's some airline stewardess. Division PIO is bringing her. You're going to show her around the LZ."

Just past noon, a Huey landed with our guest. Marilyn was a TWA stewardess, accompanied by the division's PIO, the public information officer, and a couple of photographers. She was a petite brunette with a big smile. She wore a light blue smock on which were pins and badges from all kinds of units and organizations in-country, given to her by men on her flights. They were an impressive collection.

Her group wasn't on the LZ more than an hour and a half. She told us she flew the Pacific on TWA's military charters, taking men to and from the war. We walked her around to a few bunkers and had pictures taken with some of our troops. She was serenaded by one of the soldiers, who had written a catchy song about the division. We showed her a few captured weapons and gave her a 5th Cavalry pin for her smock.

As I learned afterward, on one of her Pacific trips she had met Major General Elvy Roberts on his way to take command of the 1st Cavalry Division. She convinced him that a visit to the division in the field by a TWA stewardess would be a good public-relations idea. After a lot of back-and-forth between TWA and the Army, her visit was approved. Her charter was to visit as many of the division's units as possible.

In the several days she was in-country, she flew in helicopters to all kinds of units scattered over a huge area of jungle. She was allowed to pull the lanyard on a 105mm howitzer, landing a round on Nui Ba Den, the "Black Virgin" mountain. I wondered what the VC who had honeycombed the mountain with tunnels would have thought if they knew who was shooting at them.

What Marilyn did wasn't for the faint of heart; at all times while she was with the division in the field, she was at risk of injury, or death. After the war, she wrote *20,000 Men and Me*, about her visit. She attended almost every reunion of the 1st Air Cavalry Division, which "adopted" her. She passed away in the 1970s; her smock is in the division's museum at Fort Hood, Texas. She was a courageous young lady.

AN "UGLY AMERICAN"

At some point in their year in Vietnam, every soldier was allotted one week's leave out-of-country for "rest and recreation." Known as "R & R," it included air travel from Vietnam to and from a selected R & R destination, and hotel accommodation. R & R sites included Sydney, Bangkok, Tokyo, Hong Kong, Manila, Hawaii, Singapore, Taipei, and Penang and Kuala Lumpur in Malaysia.

My R & R came up at ten months in-country. I'd read a few novels by Nevil Shute: *On the Beach* and *A Town Like Alice*. I'd seen the movie version of *On the Beach* with Gregory Peck and Ava Gardner. I flew to Sydney.

I'd asked our admin people if I could have a change as to hotel accommodation. The usual hotels booked for R & R in Sydney were in the Kings Cross area, the equivalent of Times Square in New York City, with a lot of bars and raucous nightlife. I wasn't much of a hell-raiser then. I asked for a hotel away from Kings Cross. I was told they would make an exception and was switched to the Menzies Hotel, upscale and relatively new in 1969.

After an overnight flight from Vietnam, we landed in Sydney on a beautiful morning. The bus from the airport, loaded with eager troops headed for Kings Cross, dropped me at the Menzies. A few steps down from the entrance I entered a large, open lobby. Armchairs and tables, a palm here and there.

A stout man in a rumpled dark gray suit stood before the reception desk. His loud, unhappy voice carried through the room. He held a cigar in one hand, waving it as he spoke. I can't recall the precise dialogue, but this is close.

"My people assured me I would have a suite," exclaimed the man, "and now you're telling me there's been some kind of *mistake?*"

The middle-aged man in eyeglasses behind the reception desk looked apologetic. He held a phone to his ear and a pen on an open ledger before him.

The stout man continued, "Do you know how *long* a flight it is from LA? A very long flight; *very* long. Now, I'm damn tired, and I'd like to get freshened up." He drew on the cigar and blew out a cloud of smoke. "No suite! I can't believe this. I told my people explicitly: a suite!"

The clerk was contrite. "I'm very sorry, sir. There *does* seem to have been some mistake. But if you'd care to relax in the bar for a few minutes, we would be pleased to offer you a drink or coffee while we try to accommodate."

The stout man interrupted him. "I don't *want* to be 'accommodated.' I want the *suite* my people arranged." His voice grew louder. Heads were turning here and there. He was doing a good job of alienating everyone within earshot.

The back-and-forth went on for another minute or two as the clerk spoke into the phone, obviously trying to resolve the problem. The man shifted from one foot to the other. At last the clerk said, "Sir, again, I am very sorry, but it will take a bit to sort this out. If you would please just give us a few minutes."

The stout man glared at the clerk without saying a word, turned, and headed off to the bar, muttering and trailing cigar smoke.

Standing a few feet behind this scene, I was in the Army's short-sleeved khaki uniform. I hoped the R & R people hadn't screwed up *my* reservation. As another American, following that performance I could imagine where I might wind up. Likely in a room overlooking the hotel's service alley.

The desk clerk wrote in the ledger for a few moments, then looked up as though he hadn't noticed I'd been there. "Good morning, Captain, welcome to the Menzies. Just down from Vietnam?" He pronounced it "Veetnahm."

"Good morning. Yes." I handed him my R & R hotel voucher. He read it and nodded, held a hand up in a "wait a moment" gesture, and picked up the phone. He spoke a few words, then put it down.

"I remember many of your mates here in '43," he said. Happy to see them then, happy to have you with us now. Your reservation is confirmed, Captain." He made a notation in the ledger and looked up. "May I ask you something?"

"Yes, of course."

"It seems we've just had a suite open up," he smiled, "and we wonder if you would care for us to put you up in it during your stay with us. At no extra charge, of course."

FIGHTING THE ENEMY'S BIRTHRATE

One night in July, my company was on LZ DOLLY, taking our turn at base defense. At about 1 a.m., LZ GRANT, another battalion's firebase several kilometers to our southwest, was attacked by NVA sappers and infantry backed by mortars out in the jungle. From our ridgeline, we could clearly see the fireworks, and the surrounding terrain.

Sappers were enemy soldiers skilled in penetrating razor-wire and minefield defenses and attacking perimeter bunkers with satchel charges of high explosive. Once they breached the perimeter, assault troops were right behind them.

In 1968, I saw a demonstration, performed by a former NVA sapper who had voluntarily surrendered, or "*chieu-hoi'd*," to the South Vietnamese Army. The demonstration was in daylight, but it wasn't hard to imagine him performing the same thing at night. His body smeared with dirt, wearing only a strip of loincloth, he very slowly and carefully eased his way through barbed-wire entanglements, disarming trip flares and disconnecting claymore antipersonnel mines from their firing cables. Here and there he turned an armed claymore so that if it was detonated it would hit a defensive position. He didn't make a sound. An authentic ninja couldn't have been more impressive.

As the sappers, assault troops, and mortars worked on LZ GRANT, we watched like spectators at a football game. The sky was a tapestry of parachute flares, artillery illumination shells, rocket-firing Cobra attack helicopters, and the fiery breath of a rotary minigun on a twin-engine AC-47 aircraft droning in a circle above the chaos.

A cacophony of sounds came across to us: the slamming sound of artillery rounds exploding, the chainsaw scream of the minigun on the AC-47, the whoosh of the Cobras' rockets, the crump and smack of enemy mortars, and the chatter and crack of US and enemy small arms and machine guns. Our imaginations furnished the shouts and screams.

As the attack on GRANT started, we went to full alert, all bunkers manned, every man in full combat kit. We didn't know if the enemy would use the action "across the street" to launch an attack on us, too, under its diversion. As the five 105mm howitzers on our ridge banged away in support of GRANT, I went from bunker to bunker around the perimeter. Passing between two positions on the side away from GRANT, I looked out to the northeast, toward the Cambodian border. What I saw remains vivid now, as it was on that night over half a century ago.

Out in the blackness of the huge rubber plantation surrounding us, a string of lights was visible beneath the canopies of the rubber trees. Tiny, twinkling, but definite, they snaked in a long, long line that rounded a hill and stretched far back, toward the border.

The lights were small oil lamps carried by individual NVA soldiers; we found them on enemy dead after every contact. They were his flashlights. That night, every enemy soldier out there was using his. From the length of that long, long unbroken line of lights, I was seeing thousands of men on the move. They were passing our LZ a few thousand meters away, headed east, further into the III Corps area.

Within minutes, our artillery switched some of its fire out into the rubber, high explosive bursting on and around a portion of the lights. Huge sections of the light string were extinguished. The artillery stopped shooting. Within minutes, the lights came back on; the line re-formed, continuing its march eastward.

Those enemy soldiers had likely marched all the way down the trails from the North. They were headed into South Vietnam. We would hunt and fight and kill them in the jungle, but more would be coming. We were fighting the enemy's birthrate.

CLAUDE

"Unflappable and determined" described Claude, our battalion chaplain. He was a "circuit rider," spending most of the time in the field, walking with the men for days before flying on to another unit. He was respected by the men; his record of randomly choosing units that invariably made contact while he was with them earned him the tag "Combat Claude."

If anyone deserved the Combat Infantryman's Badge, he did. He'd joined the Army during the Korean War from East Tennessee, serving in Germany and in the last of the Military Police horse-mounted patrols. Leaving the Army in the late 1950s, he was ordained in the Mormon Church. He applied and was accepted as an Army chaplain. His two years in Vietnam were both with the 1st Air Cavalry Division.

Claude was steady, always with a smile and a good word. His easygoing approach let him fit right in. In that war, when death could be a step away, he was a great comfort to many of the men.

DOC

As our company senior medic, Lester was known simply as "Doc." Older than the rest of us, in our late teens or early twenties, he was a terrific professional and fearless soldier. He also packed a wicked sense of ironic humor and an irrepressible wit.

Doc's tales of his first assignment, as a young medical corpsman straight out of training at Fort Sam Houston, had the troops wide eyed. He was sent to the 64th US Army Hospital at Fontainebleau, just south of Paris. The duty, he said, was easy. He acquired a red sports car and access to great wines. A parade of gorgeous females pranced through his stories. I was impressed. Could that kind of duty have really existed?

Eventually, of course, the verity of Doc's tale spinning had to be confirmed. I was working on a map overlay one afternoon back on the LZ, getting set for the next combat assault. Looking at the map on the ground, I became aware of the toes of a pair of jungle boots covered in reddish-brown grime. The boots shifted a little.

I looked up. It was one of the older troops, a good soldier; solid, unflappable in the worst fights.

"Sir, got time for a question?"

"Sure," I said, sitting up. "What's on your mind?"

"Well, Sir, the boys and me, we were wondering . . . about Doc."

"Uh-huh. What about Doc?

"Doc's a great guy and all, Sir, but . . . um . . . do you think any of that stuff is for real?"

"What stuff?"

"You know, Sir. That stuff 'bout the girls and all?"

Whoa. This was going to be tricky. I had wondered myself, but the last thing I was going to do was put a pin in Doc's stories. And hey, if they *were* true, good on him; he was sure making up for all that fun sweating in the field with us.

I thought fast. "Hmm, OK. Let me ask you a question."

"Yes, Sir."

"Who has all the morphine and penicillin in this outfit?"

"Uh . . . Doc, Sir, I guess."

I smiled. "That's right. Do you think the man who has responsibility for that critical stuff, who is first on the scene if you're hit out there, and who takes care of any of you men if you stray off the patch with one of the local ladies, would be telling tall tales about girls?"

Of course this made very little sense, but it had the ring of authority, and it got the desired effect.

"Uh, no, Sir. No. I guess Doc's on the level. Thanks!"

I smiled. "I guess so, too. Don't mention it."

He nodded and walked off thoughtfully.

And that was that.

NIGHT EXTRACTION

0100, somewhere near the Cambodian border. The company was in its night defense position. I had chosen the site late the previous afternoon. During the hour it took to dig the positions, I had detailed and briefed two night ambushes, one from each designated platoon. Four or five men each, under an NCO, on this night they set up on trails we had passed during the day. As night fell, we settled into watch-on, watch-off.

My radio operator handed me the handset. The call from battalion wasn't the ordinary request for sitrep. Gene, the battalion S-3, was on the other end. "Prepare for soonest extraction of your family." "Family" was code for an infantry company. "Send your best estimate on time for availability for extraction. Situation brief will follow. Over." I acknowledged and signed off. We had never been tasked to do a night extraction before. Something big must be happening.

We recalled the ambushes. Very dangerous at night; they would be coming back into the company perimeter in total darkness. I ensured that everyone was aware the movement to their front was most likely friendly troops, but to be doubly cautious. We disarmed trip flares and claymore antipersonnel mines in front of the fighting positions. At the same time, we had to be on guard for any enemy activity taking advantage of the situation.

In the next hour, we broke down the perimeter, saddled up, and moved in a file to a big clearing we had passed about a hundred meters back the day before. I sent one platoon to the far side of the clearing to set up security. We configured the rest of the company into Huey loads. I estimated that the clearing could take five Hueys per lift in a trail formation and sent word to battalion that we were ready.

We set a strobe light in an upturned helmet at the touchdown point for the first aircraft. Its bright flashing white light could be seen from above but not on the ground.

At 0400, Hueys from KILLER SPADE touched down. My command group and I went out with the first lift; I still didn't know our mission and needed to be with our lead elements, wherever we were being landed. Over the next half hour, successive lifts took the rest of the company out. I was told on radio by our S-3 that we would be landed at the Special Forces airstrip at Loc Ninh. More details to follow.

Unknown to me while we were in the air, my company was passed to control of the 11th Armored Cavalry Regiment. A big fight was developing farther up in the division's area of tactical responsibility, at a place where 11th ACR needed help.

We landed at Loc Ninh just before dawn. The sky was clear, the temperature somewhere in the high seventies, almost no humidity. If there weren't a war on, it would be a beautiful day. By 0700 the whole company was on the assault airstrip. I was told by radio that another lift of Hueys would pick us up at 0730. We configured the company into Huey loads, spaced along both sides of the strip, and waited.

I was talking to battalion on the radio when an incoming, slow-velocity round sizzled overhead and detonated about fifty meters off the strip. It was likely a recoilless rifle, a Russian B10 or the Chinese Type 65. Both were 82mm. The Chinese version's eight-pound high-explosive round had a maximum range of 1,750 meters.

Several more rounds sailed overhead, all thankfully long, impacting in the forest. As I tried to get a good azimuth on the source of firing, I heard the *popopop!* of inbound helicopters. The lift birds were coming straight into an incoming enemy fire situation, in trail, stacked up one behind the other.

They hadn't contacted us yet. I told my RTOs to warn them off if they called, got up, and ran down the airstrip toward the incoming aircraft, waving my arms in *go away!* fashion. They kept coming. Finally the lead bird pilots saw everyone lying flat along the shallow drainage ditches lining the airstrip, and one man running toward them. They broke left and right like a flight of startled gooney birds and soared off over the tree canopies.

After several more rounds, the shelling ceased. We were shortly thereafter picked up and proceeded with the assault as planned. For us, it was just another day in the war.

COMBAT ASSAULTS

Gene, our S-3 Operations officer, was folksy, avuncular. "You and your tigers have a new job. In here." He tapped the acetate-covered map. We were in a corner of the battalion's TOC, the tactical operations center. In the center of the battalion's firebase, it was dug down into the ground about ten feet, roofed by heavy beams, metal mats, and layers of sandbags. Cyclone fence "standoff" arched over the roof to detonate incoming mortar rounds.

The wall was covered with maps. At the radio bench, the duty operators monitored battalion and brigade command nets and artillery and aviation frequencies. Conversation was muted and minimal. The hum of an outside generator served as background noise.

Sliding his finger in a circle over eight grid squares of green, heavily forested area, he said, "Your combat assault is 1000 tomorrow. Should be good hunting." Unsaid was, "Get in there, find the enemy, and kill him."

We'd been on "palace guard" at the battalion's firebase for two weeks of rest and refit as we manned the defensive perimeter. Tomorrow, one of the other companies would come in from the field, replacing us for their well-deserved break.

A combat assault was an airlift by helicopters of an infantry unit, usually a company of between 150 and 160 men, into a landing zone, or LZ, in a designated area. The LZ had to be large enough for several helicopters to land at a time.

The more helicopters possible in the first lift, the better. It was a matter of getting the maximum number of troops on the ground. If the enemy was on or near the LZ, the first lift, or group of helicopters in, would be at most risk. Men landing in that lift would fight with what they carried until more helicopters and more troops could come in.

In the 1st Air Cavalry Division, almost invariably UH1-D "Huey" helicopters were the troop lift for combat assaults. They came from the division's two assault helicopter battalions.

A combat assault of my company, which was usually understrength at around 140 men, needed eighteen to twenty aircraft. Ideally, the entire company could be airlifted in at once; we managed to do that several times. More commonly, a lift of only about six or seven birds was possible in each serial. I always went in with the first lift. With my radio operators, pace man, artillery forward observer, his radio operator, and my company senior medic, my command group was seven to eight men. That accounted for one Huey.

I huddled with my platoon leaders over my map. "We're going in here tomorrow morning. S-2 has reports of heavy traffic on these trails." I indicated two in our new area that were actually shown on the map sheet; experience proved that there were just as many that remained to be discovered. The enemy could use any of them.

The one "given" was that the enemy did use the trails. It was a percentages game: the border area was immense; his objective was to move men and equipment into South Vietnam from Cambodia as quickly as possible. Moving cross-country was wasted time and effort, so the trails were high-speed routes for his people.

Moving on trails in daylight, he risked being spotted by our hunter-killer helicopter teams: an OH-6 "low bird" and a rocket- and minigun-armed Cobra "high bird." So a lot of his movement was at night. Our ambushes were intended to catch him there.

Next morning we were picked up by KILLER SPADE birds. The LZ selected for the assault was big enough for six aircraft at a time. Four lifts to bring in the whole company.

The tightness of the flight formation kept by the pilots was always a bit unsettling. The tail rotor of the aircraft in front was so close it appeared to be moments from slicing through the canopy. The pilots were always unfazed.

We swung wide of the selected LZ, orbiting as artillery pounded the clearing's sides. Flashes and dirt flew until a pair of white phosphorus rounds detonated in the air on either side, signaling the end of the "artillery prep." As we began the slide down to land, a pair of escorting Cobras darted ahead, raking the forest on all sides with 40mm grenades and rocket fire.

As the lead troop-carrying Hueys flared for landing, the Cobras broke away. Our bird came in, individual plants and tall grasses zooming into focus. We jumped off and went to one knee as the entire serial lifted off. We'd done this many times; the men knew where to go and what to do. The company was at its most vulnerable with only the first lift on the ground. We had to secure and hold the LZ as the rest of the lifts came in.

On one combat assault, a scout helicopter saw something in the far tree line from our first serial of Hueys touching down. As we "unhorsed" the lift birds and began to move across the LZ, I was surprised as a pair of Cobras overflew us. Hovering down ahead of us a few feet off the ground, they opened up with rockets, chin turrets, and miniguns, raking the far tree line. The pilots did the same left-to-right-and-back-again pedal turn I recalled from that armed H-13 demonstration at Fort Rucker years before.

We watched the tracers and explosions of their grenades and rockets flashing all along the tree line. Then, as they both swooped up and to the right, one of the pilots, on our radio frequency, sang out the Lone Ranger's radio and TV signature line: "Hiyo, Silver! Away!"

It was a terrific demonstration of the firepower they could put down, and proof that helicopter pilots were a bit weird. Gifted, yes, but weird.

A RUMOR OF PACHYDERMS

Like the story about the Ontos, this came to me from "others who were there."

Our division's aviation units flew scout teams along the border. They looked for mainline NVA units and evidence of their movements. The two-helicopter team's low bird was a tiny light observation helicopter. Known as a "loach," it looked like a hard-boiled egg with rotors, and it carried a pilot and observer/gunner.

Keeping close watch on the loach from above was a Cobra attack helicopter, the team's high bird. Known as "snakes," the Cobras carried a pilot and copilot/gunner. Armed with two pods of 70mm rockets, a 7.62mm minigun, and a 40mm grenade launcher, they were killers.

The loaches trolled along just above the treetops, looking under the canopies if possible. At times they would drop down to weed height in clearings to look laterally under the trees. They were there to observe, and also to draw fire.

If this sounds dangerous, you're paying attention. Loaches were thin aluminum and Plexiglas; their only armor was a very light plate under each seat. They were flown by the sort of young warrant officers who would otherwise be right at home taming broncos at rodeos.

One of our brigade's loach crews on the border became a division legend. They had dropped below canopy level in a thin clearing. The pilot caught a fast glimpse of something unusual under the trees. Then it was gone. The observer got a quick look too.

"Damn! Was that an *elephant*!?" The pilot turned the bird slightly to get a better look, but whatever he'd seen was swallowed by the darkness beneath the canopy.

"Sure looked like it," the observer replied.

Back at Quan Loi, the loach crew reported their sighting. They were met with disbelief. Elephants? There hadn't been any in that area since the French had used them many years ago to haul teak. The French were long gone. The intelligence officer of their unit, the S-2, was particularly disbelieving.

A week later, another quick sighting, glimpsed from above. A pair of big, gray-brown animals moving beneath the canopy. Just as quickly gone.

The S-2 was still unconvinced. The loach crew was smoldering. Their eyesight was 20-20; they were observers, they'd seen the damn things. What was the problem?

That night, over a few beers at the club, a plan was hatched. Several days passed; they were now looking for anything less substantial. On the seventh day, *voila*!

The pilot did a fast descending pedal turn, calling the high bird—"Jackpot! Cover me!"—as he skidded the loach in over a trail across a clearing. Over the intercom to his observer, he said, "You see what I see?"

The observer chuckled. "Yeah. Let's make this real fast."

The pilot set the loach down on the trail. The observer unbuckled, hopped out, reached behind his seat, and ran a few quick steps.

They radioed ahead on the way back. A jeep waited beside the pad as they landed. At their unit headquarters, they lugged a sagging poncho between them into the Intelligence section. The S-2 was out. They spread the poncho, with its huge, matted ball of elephant dung, on his desk.

The S-2 hit the ceiling, of course, vowing eternal vengeance. But the aviation battalion commander, possibly appreciative of the imagination involved, gave both men a snap four-day leave to Bangkok. The S-2 was cooled down in the interim.

No one doubted elephants after that.

WILLY PETE

I've mentioned the necessity of knowing our location at all times, no matter whether in the rubber or the rainforest. In a contact, the ability of my artillery forward observer to call for precise fire support, usually from our 105mm howitzers, was critical. Seconds translated to effectiveness, and to potential friendly lives saved.

One afternoon in the rainforest, my focus on azimuth and pace count and my attention to the terrain, prompted a discussion with my artillery forward observer.

"I think something's wrong with this map sheet," I said as I looked up from a conversation with my pace man. He and I were in complete agreement that day on the pace count. I was keeping a close eye on our compass heading. The terrain was almost totally flat, with triple canopy and heavy underbrush. We had crossed an overgrown trail that was referenced on the map, and further on a dried-up stream course, also marked. But neither were where they should have appeared under the grid overprint on the map. It was as though a section of the grid print was off, or the terrain features had shifted. The former was far more likely. We had landed in this area a few days earlier and hadn't needed to call for artillery. Yet.

"What do you mean?" Paul was my FO, a good lieutenant out of ROTC at Clemson. He was a diligent forward observer and very good on the radio with our artillery.

"Doesn't seem to make sense," I said. "If I had to guess, I'd say it was a few hundred meters off."

"Shouldn't be." He looked dubious. "These are the best maps they can produce."

"Yeah, maybe." I thought about it. We stopped the company and dropped our rucksacks. I took off the sweat-soaked, olive-drab issue towel that, like almost every other man, I wore folded around the back of my neck. With the towel tucked under the shoulder straps of my rucksack, it cut down on chafing. Known as a "hump rag," mine was soaking wet with sweat; I laid it across the top of a low bush to air out as we talked.

"OK, let's shoot a marking round," he said. "I'll call it on this grid intersection." He pointed to it on the map: "Five hundred out and five hundred up." That meant it would be five hundred meters away from us, fused to explode five hundred feet high. That would give most of the white phosphorus flakes time to burn out before they reached the ground.

We used marking rounds occasionally; they were white phosphorus, "WP," known as "Willy Pete" by the troops. They detonated with a satisfying CRACK! and a highly visible burst of white smoke, out of which shot hundreds of white tendrils. They were also potentially lethal. WP comes down in a rain of flakes and particles, all white hot. Phosphorus burns on contact with air and keeps relentlessly burning until it burns though whatever it lands on, or until oxygen can somehow be denied it.

Because of the triple canopy above us, we wouldn't be able to see the WP marker round detonate. We'd be able to hear it and take a bearing on it with our compasses. As Paul got on the radio to the guns, I pulled my compass off my harness. I kept it clipped there by the little fold-up metal tab with the lens and sighting notch. I heard Paul say, "Shot out," acknowledging the "Shot over" alert from the guns. The marker round was on the way.

A few seconds later the sound of the incoming round was a short, high whistle that ended in a resounding CRACK!

Shit! It was right overhead! "Get down!" I yelled and hit the ground, trying to make myself very small. Seconds passed as sizzling bits of white phosphorus descended like a killer snowstorm all around us. We were in for severe, horrible casualties. I had seen what WP could do to the enemy.

"Check fire! Check fire!" Paul said on his radio to the guns.

Moments went by. The smell of burning leaves and foliage was in the air. No screams. No yells of "Medic!"

I turned to my company RTO. "Get the status." He called the platoon RTOs; the reports came back: no one was touched. Incredible. I stood up.

Paul was white faced. "Jesus!"

"Yeah," I said, "you and I better work out a deflection before we call in any more artillery." I was looking at my hump rag. It had a six-inch hole in it smoldering around its edges.

DANGER CLOSE!

We were in contact. Paul called the artillery inside fifty meters: "Danger close!" We kept our heads down as the rounds whined in and slammed into the jungle ahead of us with enormous flat CRUMP! detonations. The enemy's fire slowed, then ceased.

Two more rounds came in, the last of the mission. Remembering the demolitions instructor in Rangers warning us to stay well down after explosions, I did, as did the men.

Except for one of the new replacements, who stood up a second or two after the last round hit. A piece of delayed secondary frag moaned into a tree, tearing a chunk of wood off it, which hit him in the shoulder, knocking him backward and straight down on his ass.

It might have killed him, or at least torn a piece out of him. With the luck of the neophyte and a miracle of physics, it bled off enough energy that it didn't even break the skin. He couldn't move his arm for quite a while after a medic checked him over and taped him up. He had a hell of a Technicolor bruise for over a week, enduring enough ribbing for a lifetime. There was little slack given to dumb-assed, bad judgment calls.

ARCLITE

One very hot morning we suddenly found ourselves in near-fatal danger. We were operating against mainline North Vietnamese Army (NVA) units coming south down the Ho Chi Minh Trail network inside Laos and Cambodia.

For the enemy, it was a trip of hundreds of miles by truck and on foot. It took him months. Along the way, he was targeted by B-52 "ARCLITE" heavy bombing and tactical air strikes, a variety of nasty air-sown mines, and other devices. There were other hazards: malaria, amoebic dysentery, and a catalog of other diseases, in addition to floods, lightning, and even wild animals. But he kept coming.

Weapons, equipment, and munitions for enemy units in northern South Vietnam, across the border from Laos, came down the trail. But most supplies for enemy units operating in our III Corps Tactical Zone north of Saigon and those down in the Mekong Delta area arrived on Russian- or Warsaw Pact–flagged ships at Sihanoukville in Cambodia. From there they were trucked to big bunker complexes constructed just inside Cambodia. The truck convoys rolled on a heavy-duty highway built by the Cambodians using American US-AID money. War is full of ironies.

Enemy units arriving along the Cambodian border with South Vietnam rested in camps built around those bunker complexes. There they were supplied with their full combat loads. On any given night when moon and weather were advantageous, they slipped over the border and were well inside South Vietnam by first light. They could shelter in similar bunker complexes before deploying further.

Our mission was to find the enemy, "fix" him in place, and destroy him. It was a cat-and-mouse game; sometimes the mouse had very sharp fangs. The result was a vicious and deadly game of blindman's bluff.

We could bump into the enemy on the move, formally termed a "meeting engagement," or walk into one of his bunker complexes. Either resulted in a shoot-out at close range. Both were referred as a "contact."

The enemy was very good at building his bunkers with a thick overhead cover of earth and logs, emplaced in thick underbrush, well camouflaged in triple-canopy rainforest. He was expert at siting his bunkers so that he could shoot from slits just above ground level. He thinned the underbrush, providing "fire lanes" allowing good observation. He was careful to keep enough brush in the fire lanes so that we were unaware we were moving into a deadly kill zone of interlocking fire.

The enemy's objective was to let our point team and following troops in, then pin them down with crossfire. Once thoroughly "fixed" in those fields of fire, they could cut our troops to pieces.

Our challenge was to detect bunkers close enough to get an idea as to their positions but not allow ourselves to be immobilized. We would call for artillery and air to apply the firepower necessary to break the bunkers.

That day we were moving at a cautious rate through the jungle, stopping every few hundred meters to send out small patrols, which moved out fifty or a hundred meters on each side, then returned to the company.

At about 1400, my RTO carrying the radio on the battalion command frequency passed me the handset. Our battalion S-3, the operations officer, was on the line.

"DAY SIX, this is MOTORS THREE," he said. "This is a flash override message. I say again, flash override message. Send your location immediately. I say again: immediately. Over."

Flash override was the highest message priority, used only in the most critical situations.

"DAY SIX. Roger, stand by, over," I replied. Something serious was up, and an "immediate" request meant "like yesterday," so I used a previously prepared, one-time-only "shackle" code. They were arbitrary words or phrases of ten nonrepetitive letters, each representing a number, beginning with zero and going to nine. And they could only be used one time. I sent it.

"DAY SIX, ARCLITE strike is on the way to your location. I say again, ARCLITE strike is on the way to your location. Minutes away. Recommend you move on a ninety-degree azimuth. Move as fast as you can. Move now! MOTORS THREE out."

Holy shit! Each ARCLITE strike was delivered by a "cell" of three B-52 heavy bombers flying down across the Pacific and South China Sea to South Vietnam from Guam. It was a nine-hour round trip. They bombed by a combination of radar and inertial navigation in an "arrowhead" formation, from between twenty thousand and thirty thousand feet.

The weapons load of each B-52 could be up to sixty thousand pounds of 500- and 750-pound gravity or "dumb" bombs. A single strike was designed to absolutely devastate everything in the ARCLITE impact box about a thousand meters long by two to three hundred meters wide. We were just inside the edge of that box when the warning came.

On previous operations, we witnessed ARCLITE strikes going in from afar. The earth shook as in an earthquake; clouds from the explosions rose hundreds of feet in the air. To be on the receiving end of that kind of devastation would be certain destruction.

You would think death arrives with no warning whatever. But that isn't the case. I'll get to that in a moment. You can imagine our motivation was pretty high. We moved as fast as we could through the jungle on that ninety-degree, due-east azimuth.

What would we have done had we run into an enemy unit or a bunker complex, both of which we were carefully searching for? We would have handled it as best we could; the overwhelming urge was to get away from those bombs. We had seen what they could do from a distance; being an integral part of that process wasn't an option.

MOTORS THREE radioed, "Take cover immediately." No humor intended, but "cover" against a B-52 strike wasn't possible. We all hit the ground and tried to make ourselves as small as possible. I remember the sound of men panting, a couple of men praying, and the sounds of the jungle absolutely magnified. I could hear every leaf, every humming, buzzing, clicking insect. Their world, and mine, could change very much for the worse in just a few moments.

The sound of death, of the incoming sheaves of bombs, wasn't anything like the whistling sound in the war movies. It was at first a slight change in air pressure, followed by a discordant, moaning chorus like a thousand spirits, rising in volume.

The first bombs soared in over our heads, slamming into the jungle behind us with enormous force. We were heaved into the air by the jungle floor beneath us, literally jumping upward and back to the ground, up and down, as the earth bucked.

Air was forced out of our lungs by the concussion. The explosions were massive. Pieces of trees whizzed overhead. Bomb casing frag slashed enormous chunks out of the jungle canopy, followed by the raw-onion stink of high explosive and burned, shattered wood.

When it was over, our ears were ringing. We were practically lip-reading each other. Fortunately there were only a few nicks and dings from men bouncing off trees or the ground. Some were a bit stunned by concussion, but no one was injured by the strike.

My RTO handed me the battalion net handset. I could barely hear MOTORS THREE, who sounded anxious, and rightly so. I reported that we were OK, but it was as close as I'd want to come to another strike like it.

"MOTORS THREE. Move into the box, conduct a BDA, and report, over." He didn't sound a bit apologetic.

Moving into a freshly pounded ARCLITE target box to conduct a "bomb damage assessment" could turn out in a number of ways. We might find nothing; the immense amount of ordnance dropped by the Air Force didn't always connect with the enemy.

On the other hand, we might find that they had smacked an enemy base camp or other target, in which case we might find the remains of a lot of dead North Vietnamese.

A third scenario might find us fighting North Vietnamese the strike hadn't hit, madder than hornets and heavily armed.

What we did find was impressive in its scale. Huge, shattered trees piled like jackstraws. Enormous open spaces created by the blast. A stink of burning wood and human waste, mingled with the raw-onion smell of high explosive. Smoke curling up from massive craters. Scraps of cloth, bits of shattered weapons. A thin grime of dark grease filmed occasional shattered tree trunks. All that was left of the enemy.

One thing was almost certain; if the Air Force hadn't hit that outfit, we would have. We were headed right for it. How important it was could be assumed from why the strike was diverted. I learned later that a powerful radio transmitter was intercepted inside the coordinates of the box. A radio signal of that power indicated a major enemy unit or base area. A damn close call.

Next morning we were extracted and airlifted back to the battalion firebase for a stand-down and our turn on base defense. We'd been on continuous operation in the field for over three weeks.

When we landed at the LZ, we were greeted with warm cans of beer, mail from home, and a couple of the division "doughnut dollies," Red Cross girls with hot coffee and trays of pastries. The men were appreciative, but since it was "look but don't touch" where the girls were concerned, after a few admiring leers, they went for the beer and mail. Within an hour, most were fast asleep.

BADGES

In the Army of the 1960s, there were a few insignia that said you had done something noteworthy. Parachute wings and the Ranger tab, of course, showed that you had passed those hurdles. A lot of soldiers had jump wings; far fewer had the Ranger tab.

There were a few less common insignia that also merited: the Jungle Expert insignia, for example, from the school down in Panama, a combined survival and small-unit tactics course. It was a blue patch with a Spanish galleon in white. What that had to do with jungle warfare and survival, I had no idea.

There were two badges, however, that required actually being "out at the sharp end," in action, at the risk of your life. The Combat Infantryman's Badge, known simply as the "CIB," was the more numerous.

It was a long-barreled Revolutionary War musket on a blue rectangle against a silver wreath. To receive it, the soldier had to be an infantryman, assigned to an infantry unit for a specific period during which the unit was engaged in active ground combat against an armed and hostile enemy. Every man in my company earned the CIB in the minimum required period.

Less numerous, but in my mind dead even in terms of merit and risk, was the Combat Medical Badge. Like the CIB, it was awarded to medical personnel assigned to combat infantry units under hostile fire. It was a stretcher bearing a medical cross above the entwined serpents of the caduceus against a wreath, all in silver.

At the first bursts of fire in an opening fight, our medics were ready with their aid bags to leave whatever cover they had and run to the aid of a man down and in pain. To a man, they were simply terrific.

FEVER

Malaria rates among US units in Vietnam were so high some units were almost rendered combat ineffective. The antimalaria doctrine was a single dapsone tablet each morning six days a week and a chloroquine-primaquine tablet on the seventh day.

Late September out on the Cambodian border. Numbing heat and humidity. Day by day, humping rucks, weapons, water, rations, ammunition; my troops were wearing down. I saw it in slow motion. We were out on that operation almost three weeks. In a few days we were to be lifted back to the LZ for another turn at base defense.

I woke just before dawn feeling like the Tin Man in *The Wizard of Oz*. Every joint creaked. At twenty-three? That wasn't supposed to happen for four or five decades.

A chloroquine-primaquine malaria tab went down with instant powdered coffee. The stiffness didn't go away; my throat was really sore. Doc, our company senior medic, felt my forehead and stuck a thermometer under my tongue. "A couple degrees north of normal. Anything else?"

"Just stiff; kind of sore in the joints. I don't know." He shook out two APCs, the Army's superstrength "all-purpose capsules." I popped them down with more coffee.

We saddled up and moved out. Another heavy, hot day like a hundred others. But it felt all wrong. At midmorning my pace count didn't align with my pace man's. The map was fuzzy. I was lightheaded; I drank more water. Then I just sat down and couldn't get up.

Doc was saying, "104.5 and rising," and pouring water from my canteen over my face and head. One of the RTOs radioed a "pink team" that had passed over a few minutes earlier. The low bird, an OH-6 "loach," landed nearby. They shifted the observer to the rear and buckled me in the right seat. My vision was graying at the edges, like looking through a tube. I couldn't focus on the instruments in front of us.

I owe Doc and that scout pilot. Flying straight back to the medical unit, he radioed ahead. We barely touched down; two corpsmen picked me up, carried me to a canvas trough of water and chunks of ice, and dumped me in—harness, boots, and all. The relief was incredible, like a shot of adrenalin.

I woke late that night in a sweaty fever. A high school classmate stood by the cot in jungle fatigues and boots. I thought I was hallucinating.

"Priscilla. What are you doing here?"

"I work here," she said, touching the Army nurse insignia on her collar. "Saw your name on the admit list. You had a close call." I went back to sleep.

I had contracted *Plasmodium falciparum*. Ironic, since we had been assured that chloroquine-primaquine and dapsone were effective against malaria. I was experiencing the epidemiological equivalent of "Which do you trust? What they told you, or your own lying eyes?"

Ten days later and ten pounds lighter, I rejoined the battalion. When I was medevaced, my company command had gone to George—a good man, West Point. My field time was over.

My command OERs, signed by Colonel Pete and Colonel Ras', were terrific. Colonel Pete had written, "There is no doubt he will be a general officer someday." He must have seen something I did not.

FREEDOM BIRD

When my DROS date arrived, the end was an anticlimax. A bright morning upcountry, handshakes all around. "Say hello to the States," "Call my mom," "Send a postcard." Some smiled; a couple punched me in the chest, shook their heads. Their days would come.

The ride down to Bien Hoa on a Huey, watching the green-brown, mottled frog's back of the landscape slide by below. Nui Ba Den on the horizon, silent, keeping ancient counsel. All the trails under that canopy, all the fights; a division could be down there. Not my worry now.

At the DROS center at Long Binh, men in faded fatigues, dirty boots, thousand-yard stares. People running the center were efficient, distant. We were numbers to be batched into serials, loaded on planes, dispatched.

It was odd to be disarmed, relieved of responsibility. I met VMI classmates who had commanded companies. We sat over a pitcher of beer, getting our heads around going home.

Serials were numbered for transport to Tan Son Nhut, the big airfield outside Saigon. The PA system repeated, "Do not leave the center. Stay alert for your serial's number." They were posted on the board with times of departure. Mine was slated for 1000 the next morning.

I turned in but couldn't sleep. Many memories. Hard to believe I'd made it. The flight home in 1968 was on a medevac; this would be by chartered jet. Eventually I drifted off, unsettled.

The PA blared at 0200—2 a.m. My serial's number leaving for Tan Son Nhut in ten minutes. No explanation. We gathered in thick, steamy haze under overhead lights swarming with bugs. An idling, green Army bus with grenade wire on the windows. Answering as we were called, we climbed in. I sat directly behind the driver, a long-haired, unkempt soldier, his cap on the back of his head.

We ground off, passed the bunker at the perimeter gate, and turned onto the highway. No traffic. Pitch dark. Five or so minutes later the driver slowed, passed a side road, paused indecisively at another, turned at the third. It led to a street through a village bounded by shuttered shops and an empty open-air market. No one in sight.

The driver stopped. He was lost. The black windows of structures were so close they could be reached if we could stretch our arms from the steel-screened windows.

I almost couldn't believe it. But of course I could; we all could. Tension rose like steam in a boiler. We were disarmed, trapped in the bus with no escort, sitting ducks for any enemy out and about in the night. I believe we would have gladly killed the idiot driver, except we had no idea where we were either.

Eventually he ground the gears and moved on down the road. By some miracle we saw the lights of the field in the far distance. One of the men jumped up, stepped into the well beside the door, and guided him. "Right. Right! Now go straight. No, not there; keep straight, dammit!"

Finally, thankfully, there was the gate to the field, sandbagged bunkers on either side. We passed between soldiers with M16s in steel helmets and flak jackets. Snouts of machine guns showed black in the bunkers' firing slits. As we filed off, more than one man paused to verbally unload on the driver.

Sleek and clean, a Seaboard World DC-8 stood in a pool of light, something from another world. Boarding stairs led up to the warmly lighted door; a stewardess stood by in neat uniform and big smile. Several others were spotted in the aisle down long rows of seats. I dropped into a window seat on the port side. There was little chatter. Suspense hadn't abated; we expected some last-minute crisis or delay.

With a reassuring thump, the boarding door closed and locked. The engines started. Air flowed from the overheads, cooling the sweat on our faces and arms. The cabin crew gave the safety brief. The plane rolled down a taxiway, turning onto the main active, and stopped. The engines spooled up higher and higher. The pilot released the brakes. Slowly at first, then faster and faster, the blue lights beside the runway flickered by. In that first magic moment of flight, we lifted off. As the landing gear closed into the uplocks, a huge cheer broke from every man on board.

AFTERWORD

DREAM

For years after I came home from the war in 1970, the only dream I had of Vietnam was not of fighting or jungles at all. I still have it, though not as frequently as in the past.

It is always the same. It takes place not in the 1960s but in the present, and it begins in normal circumstances.

It starts on an ordinary day, a pleasant day from the looks of the sun and trees outside the window. I'm working in my study. I receive a phone call. On the other end is a voice I remember well from years ago, a particularly irritating major in the Infantry Officer Assignments Branch, Officer Personnel Directorate, at Headquarters, Department of the Army, in Washington, DC.

Assignment officers were known to all Infantry captains during Vietnam as being from OPO, or Branch. They held immense power over our lives. From them issued orders that would direct us to our next assignments. They could spell the difference between life and death, success or failure in a military career.

In the dream, I'm aware the war in Vietnam isn't over; it's very much still being fought. I know I'm no longer an active-duty Army officer and have no obligation to serve. I know, in short, that I don't have to listen to this guy from Branch at all.

But I do.

The major affirms that the war isn't going well. He tells me they're reaching out to the "old hands," asking us to go back. We'll be setting an example, "adding some steel," as he terms it, to the younger officers fighting in-country.

I listen patiently as he addresses me as "stud" and "tiger." He tells me my record shows that I was a "hard charger."

This is so much bullshit, and we both know it. "I don't want to go back to Vietnam," I finally spit out, my voice grating. "I've done my part. Get someone else. I'm not eligible, and you know it."

"You're absolutely right, absolutely right," he replies, emphasizing the second "*absolutely*." "But we've been in touch with a number of people you know. They've all gone back, and they're asking for you. Yes, asking for you. So what do you say?"

I ask him who's "gone back." He names them. Good men; I knew them in jump school and Ranger at Benning, served with a couple in the 82nd at Bragg and in the 1st Air Cavalry. The kind you'd trust your life to, or your wife and kids, if you had to be away.

That's the hook, of course: the guilt. And very skillfully played. So I'm thinking, if they've gone back, who am I to complain? "All right," I finally say, "I'll go."

That's when the dream switches to reality, and the door opens into the past. It's when I remember that all of them were killed in action long, long ago, in Vietnam.

EPILOGUE

For my combat service in Vietnam, I received the Silver Star "for Gallantry in Action," with Oak Leaf Cluster; the Bronze Star with a "V" device "for Valor"; the Purple Heart Medal with Oak Leaf Cluster for wounds; and the Vietnamese Cross of Gallantry with Palm. Each Oak Leaf Cluster represents the second award of the same decoration.

In 1970, I was sent to the Advanced Course at the Armor Center at Fort Knox, graduating a cross-trained tank-infantry combined arms officer. I received a secondary Armor officer MOS 1203, unique among my Infantry colleagues. I also received a "Prefix 5" to my primary MOS of 1543, infantry unit leader, qualifying me as a nuclear weapons target analyst. I'm grateful I never had to use it.

In 1971 I freed a woman trapped in a burning car in Washington, DC, for which I received the Soldiers Medal for saving human life while not in combat. General Westmoreland pinned it on me at the Pentagon, the only occasion I met him.

On active service, I completed a master's degree in the Graduate School of Foreign Service at Georgetown. There were opportunities to meet some of the diplomatic field's "greats." One Friday evening at a reception I asked a seasoned diplomat for any pointers I should keep in mind. "Certainly," he said, deftly snagging a canapé from a circulating tray. "Cultivate projecting the impression that you are intensely interested in what the other person is saying. Be able to stand on your feet for hours while drinking like a fish. Forget everything you've heard but the critical bits."

The Army was severely damaged in Vietnam. I could understand how the French Army was affected after its Indochina experience. In April 1975, I drove across the country to a new assignment in San Francisco. South Vietnam was being overrun by the North's army, with tanks and heavy artillery. Saigon was falling; intermittent reports on the car radio came from scratchy AM stations at Grand Island, North Platte, and Cheyenne, with long silent voids between.

Arriving at Presidio of San Francisco, I assisted in a huge building filled with pallets on which were Vietnamese "orphan" infants, "rescued" as Saigon fell and flown to the United States. Surreal.

Two years later I applied and was accepted to the Graduate School of Business at Stanford. At the same time, I was informed by the Army that I had made the early-selection list for promotion to major.

Acceptance of the promotion to major carried an obligation of two additional years of active service. I called my assignments officer at Infantry Branch in Washington, DC, and passed the news about Stanford.

He replied that the Army was severely contracting after Vietnam; there would be little need for officers with MBAs. He said the Army was in the process of being "built down," a term I have never heard anywhere else since.

At that time, in addition to being an Infantry officer, I was also a designated foreign area officer, or FAO. A parallel career-specialty track, FAO officers' overseas assignments should be in their particular foreign areas. As a FAO, I could go to any Infantry assignment among the then thousands in Europe. I could also serve as a military attaché in foreign postings or on joint Allied staffs.

I had passed the State Department language-fluency requirement in German. I held a master's degree with distinction from the Foreign Service School at Georgetown. My master's thesis at Georgetown was on "mutual and balanced force reduction" of tactical nuclear weapons between US and Soviet forces in Europe. Known as MBFR, it was a topic of great interest at the time. My thesis was later included as one of the reference documents in the SALT I negotiations on strategic arms reductions between the United States and the Soviets.

In spite of these qualifications and career orientation, I was informed my next assignment would be to Korea. Following that conversation, I weighed the situation, decided I had done what I could for my country, and resigned my Army commission. Four days after my resignation date, I entered Stanford Business School.

The rest has been a life lived on rational terms, acceptable rules. To paraphrase Major Alvin of the Florida Ranger camp so long ago, in business, very few die, though the risks and pressures of business can be as wearing as, though very different from, those experienced in combat.

My experiences after Stanford of working at Goldman Sachs and Morgan Stanley were interesting and challenging. For decades afterward, I worked in technology, serving as CEO of two companies, and founding two more.

I cofounded a partnership that for ten years served as technology acquisition and assessment consultants for major clients in the US intelligence community. Our largest intelligence agency client described us in an internal report as "the 'tip of the spear' in sourcing mission-critical technological information for the intelligence warfighter."

I live in suburban Marin County, California, and consider myself a supremely fortunate man. A wonderful wife, two great daughters, and the opportunity to serve my community twice as a councilman, and twice as mayor.

It has been quite a journey.

CODA

HOW THE UNITED STATES WENT TO WAR IN VIETNAM

The first US involvement in Vietnam was in 1945. In that last year of World War II, the United States armed and trained Ho Chi Minh's Vietminh, the forerunner of the Vietcong. They were communists, but as with my father's leadership of Italian communist partisan forces in Italy against the occupying Germans in World War II, the Vietminh were allies against Japan, a common enemy.

In 1945, the OSS's DEER mission parachuted into the jungle north of Hanoi to set up assistance to Ho. On arrival they found him near death, from severe "fever of unknown origin." The DEER team's American medic saved Ho's life.

When Japan surrendered in September 1945, Ho declared the foundation of the Democratic Republic of Vietnam. His OSS advisers were sympathetic with his "Vietnamese independence" movement, but their orders were to remain nonpolitical.

In the same month, twenty thousand British and Indian Army soldiers commanded by General Sir Douglas Gracey arrived in Vietnam from Burma to "secure and stabilize" the situation. The British operational name for this effort was MASTERDOM.

Gracey established his headquarters in Saigon. He found the city beset by rioting and looting. The Vietminh had entered the city in the vacuum between Japan's surrender and the arrival of his British and Indian Army forces. They were executing those accused or suspected of "counterrevolutionary tendencies." Japanese forces in Vietnam, meanwhile, remained armed and in protective enclaves.

Gracey declared a state of martial law. He refused a request by Ho to meet, and did not recognize Ho's new government. He freed French military and civilians imprisoned by the Japanese.

Unwilling to accept British authority or the prospect of a return of the French, the Vietminh began attacks on British outposts. The situation quickly escalated. Gracey deputized armed Japanese troops, including them in his efforts at restoring order.

A bloody, six-month anti-guerrilla campaign ensued. Hardened jungle-fighting veterans of the British and Indian armies, backed by the armed Japanese, made short work of Vietminh insurgents. By the time French military forces returned to Vietnam in late 1945, an estimated 2,500 Vietminh insurgents had been killed. The last British troops departed in May 1946. From then, the war in Indochina was a French affair, with significant assistance in weapons and equipment supplied by the United States.

In 1954, the day after the French garrison at Dienbienphu surrendered after an epic battle close to the Laotian border, an international conference then underway in Geneva called for a national plebiscite to be held in Vietnam within two years to determine the structure of its future government.

Determined that "Vietnam would not go communist," the US military and CIA instead supported the formation of the Republic of South Vietnam, installing Ngo Dinh Diem, a Catholic, as president of the predominantly Buddhist nation. The national plebiscite called for at Geneva was never held.

A state of queasy, low-level peace resulted until 1959 when accelerating Communist guerrilla warfare began anew in the South, opposed by the South Vietnamese Army, which was equipped, trained, and advised by Americans. With increasing American aid and equipment to the South Vietnamese, the low-level guerrilla war situation lasted until 1964, when Lyndon Johnson, as a result of the Tonkin Gulf Resolution, received blanket authority from Congress to manage the war in Vietnam.

In early 1965, US Marine combat forces landed in Vietnam. The "Second Indochina War," the American war, began.

Ironically, though few know of it to this day, in October 1963 President Kennedy had lost confidence in the Diem government, and issued National Security Action Memorandum (NSAM) 263. Classified TOP SECRET/EYES ONLY, it directed that the first one thousand US advisers were to be withdrawn from Vietnam by the end of 1963, with all US advisers withdrawn by 1965. NSAM 263 has since been declassified and can be found on the internet.

Kennedy determined that Vietnam was a losing proposition; it was certainly not the biggest issue the United States faced in those years. His intent, as detailed to then-senator Mike Mansfield, was to get through the 1964 election, then withdraw the remainder of the US military force presence in Vietnam.

Due to how close the United States had come to nuclear war with the Soviet Union during the Cuban Missile Crisis in October 1962, Kennedy's major concern in 1963 was nuclear disarmament. He made it the focus of the commencement speech he gave at the American University in Washington, DC, in the summer of 1963, and he reached out to Soviet premier Nikita Khrushchev on the issue.

Kennedy's murder in November 1963 changed everything. If he had lived, I am convinced there would have been no further US war in Vietnam.

I learned of Kennedy's October 1963 NSAM from McGeorge Bundy, who had served as Kennedy's national security adviser. Bundy was on my orals board when I was a graduate student in the School of Foreign Service at George-town University in the early 1970s.

At his first cabinet meeting as president, two days after Kennedy was killed, Lyndon Johnson withdrew Kennedy's NSAM 263. Two days later he issued NSAM 273, directing "increased covert action" against North Vietnam.

The CIA had been conducting covert actions against the North for years. The events resulting from NSAM 273 led to OPLAN 34-A, a program of land-ing South Vietnamese commando teams along the coast of North Vietnam and conducting nocturnal bombardments of the North's coastal installations from high-speed PT-type boats. These "increased covert actions" resulted in the naval engagement involving North Vietnamese patrol boats and US destroyers in the Tonkin Gulf in August 1964.

Johnson used the Tonkin Gulf confrontation as the rationale to request authorization, without a declaration of war, for the use of military forces in Southeast Asia. The "Tonkin Gulf Resolution" that he obtained from Congress marks the "official" start date of the US war in Vietnam.

AN OBSERVATION

The late Joe Galloway, war correspondent, veteran of the 1965 Battle of the Ia Drang, and chronicler of the Vietnam War, stated that once the United States put ground forces in Vietnam in 1965 to protect its air bases, the troops had to push out into the field, far enough to stop the enemy from hitting the bases with mortars and rockets. When we did that, he maintained, the United States began conducting combat operations. Galloway was correct.

LOST OPPORTUNITY FOR A SHORT WAR

In early 1965, the Joint Chiefs presented Johnson with what could have been a war-winning strategy, but it was contrary to the way the war was then being directed by Johnson and Secretary of Defense McNamara.

The Chiefs proposed an immediate and massive air-bombing campaign against the North's airfields, petroleum points, and targets in and around Hanoi, and Haiphong, the North's principal port. Code-named LINEBACKER, a fierce, short air campaign, they believed, would bring the North to discussion of terms for peace.

At the time, the North's air defenses were weak; chances of operational success were high. In four stages over thirteen weeks, the United States would deploy waves of B-52 heavy bombers and F-100, F-105, and F-4 fighter-bombers to destroy the North's air forces, mine its rivers and harbors, destroy its civil support infrastructure and power grid, isolate it from China, and annihilate as much of its political leadership as possible.

The first waves of B-52s were actually inbound to targets in Vietnam when the operation was canceled on recommendation of Secretary of Defense McNamara, who advocated a "graduated response" escalation of bombing against selected targets. Graduated response allowed the North to grow its air defenses, resulting in the loss of thousands of US aircraft and many hundreds of pilots and aircrew.

Ironically, the B-52 bombing campaign against North Vietnam authorized by President Nixon in 1972, which finally succeeded in bringing the North to discussion of terms for peace, was code-named LINEBACKER II.

WESTMORELAND'S WAR

General William Westmoreland's decision to fight a war of attrition using mostly American forces kept the Army of South Vietnam (ARVN) effectively sidelined. As General Creighton Abrams demonstrated by "Vietnamizing" the war after Westmoreland stepped down, if properly equipped and sustained by the United States, the ARVN could hold its own, even though organized as a "mini-US Army," which had been a major detriment from the beginning.

EROSION OF ETHICS

Deceitful reporting of progress by the American command in Vietnam was mirrored by a strong emphasis on inflating the "body count": numbers of enemy dead. The ethics of the Army suffered severely from such policies.

The massacre of civilians at My Lai by US forces in 1968 was suppressed by the Army chain of command until investigated and brought to light by the Peers Commission in 1970. As a result, the superintendent of West Point, who had commanded the 23rd ("American") Infantry Division responsible for the My Lai massacre at the time, was relieved, demoted from major general to brigadier general, and retired. Thirty-four other officers and men were recommended for courts-martial. Only one, Lieutenant William Calley, was convicted; he was paroled four years later.

THE DRAFT

In the beginning, the Joint Chiefs recommended using the active-duty Army with the National Guard and Reserve to fight the war, with minimal input from the draft. Johnson decided instead to conduct the war using the active-duty Army, with the draft as the manpower feeder, leaving the Guard and Reserve largely untouched.

The officers and men in the Guard and Reserve held civilian jobs, many of them in key industrial and commercial positions. Mobilizing them would have required the United States to provide a strategy for a relatively quick, clear victory in Vietnam in order to allow them to return to their jobs. In a war with no clear objective other than to somehow make North Vietnam desist in its operations in the South, that was politically infeasible.

The draft was a critical factor in fueling the antiwar movement on college campuses of the Sixties, "rock-and-roll" generation. The "immorality" of the war aside, the threat of disruption of their lives turned hundreds of thousands of college students out against the war. When Richard Nixon finally eliminated the draft, campus unrest evaporated.

TEN WARS, EACH ONE YEAR LONG

The "one-year tour" was a major error. To mollify domestic American sentiment on the issue of using draftees to fuel the war, the intent was to make the draftees' experiences short enough to be acceptable.

The one-year tour let the administration fight the war indefinitely, using the draft to fuel the war's manpower requirement with a steady stream of individual replacements.

The individual replacement policy created huge personnel turbulence in combat units in Vietnam. Just when men in the field were beginning to acquire "field knowledge," they were pulled out and sent to a base area to prepare to return to the United States.

The one-year tour created an environment in which officers in command at the battalion and company level were allowed an average of six months before being rotated out to allow for another officer to get "command time."

It is difficult to arrive at a rough number of casualties as a result of this policy of rotating officers into field commands. Clearly it was unfair to the troops, the majority of whom had to serve a full year in the field, while officers departed their field commands after roughly six months.

LOSS OF SUPPORT

Ironically, the media and public support for the war were almost "all in" at the beginning. Halberstam, Browne, Sheehan, and other correspondents who went to Vietnam in the early years of US involvement believed in the "mission": to help keep the South Vietnamese free.

They soon realized the South Vietnamese weren't making headway against communist incursion, yet the American "command" shelved accurate field reports from advisers like John Paul Vann, instead sending optimistic (and false) progress reports to Washington. By the time of the 1968 Tet Offensive, Walter Cronkite, who supported the war in the early years, felt that he and others in the media had been deceived, that we were not, in fact, "winning."

While World War II was anything but a short war, it was a global war, and we were "all in." Vietnam was a tiny war by comparison; by the time the public began to seriously turn against the war, the United States had half a million men incountry, and the steady flow of dead coming home was wearing the public down.

FAILED STRATEGIES

Vietnam at times seemed a war out of "Alice in Wonderland." We fought courageously and tenaciously in the field and in the air, but we ceded the enemy huge strategic advantages.

The Ho Chi Minh Trail, the enemy's major route of infiltration and supply, ran through Cambodia and Laos. Until May 1970, both countries were off limits to US ground forces. We bombed the trail incessantly, but the enemy's ability to move troops and equipment south was never successfully interdicted for long. Like Alice's White Rabbit, the enemy inside the South could disappear at will, into the sanctuaries of Cambodia and Laos; we could not follow until the limited "incursion" in 1970.

We used unilaterally declared "truce" periods and bombing halts to signal something never clearly defined: a willingness to talk, I imagined, which the enemy ignored. As demonstrated during Tet in 1968, the enemy could control the tempo of the war when he wished.

If there was truly a desire to enter into discussions, I assumed there had to be some channel to the leadership of North Vietnam, perhaps through neutral third-world governments. There evidently was none.

The men of the 1945 OSS DEER mission could have been approached as potential emissaries. Their American medicine saved Ho Chi Minh's life; surely they could be approached? It was never considered.

Years afterward, Bill Colby, the former World War II OSS officer who served as the CIA's chief of station in Vietnam, said we didn't have a single reliable source of intelligence in North Vietnam during the entire war. Astonishing.

If our strategy was intended to force the enemy to say "enough," resulting in a situation like that at the end of the Korean War, would the South Vietnamese be able to defend themselves independently? Unlikely. Would the United States be willing to commit and maintain American forces in South Vietnam indefinitely? Also unlikely.

THE REAL REASON WE WERE IN VIETNAM

The true history of the US conduct of the war is found in a 1967 internal Defense Department study. Commissioned by McNamara and headed by Dr. Leslie Gelb, then director of policy planning in the Pentagon, it chronicled all US military and political involvement in Vietnam from 1945 to 1967 and was classified TOP SECRET.

Leaked by Daniel Ellsberg in 1971, major extracts from the study were published by the *New York Times* as "the Pentagon Papers." They revealed that from Eisenhower to Johnson, successive administrations lied to the media and the public on the true status of US political and military involvement in Vietnam. Examples include the actual level of early US combat participation in-country; the active CIA encouragement of the 1963 coup resulting in the assassination of President Diem; OPLAN 34-A's clandestine commando raids along the coast of North Vietnam, which resulted in the "Tonkin Gulf" incidents of 1964; and the "secret" intensive air bombing of Cambodia and Laos.

The study further states that, in the words of Secretary of Defense McNamara, the true objective of US involvement in Vietnam was "not to aid an ally, but to contain China."

Ironically, when I was a graduate student and an active-service Army officer in the School of Foreign Service at Georgetown University in the early 1970s, Les Gelb was my master's thesis academic adviser. I never heard him mention McNamara's true rationale for our involvement.

THE COST OF THE WAR

The United States spent an estimated $116 billion directly attributable to the war in Vietnam. The increase in manufacturing of military products led to fewer consumer goods and lower domestic retail sales. That brought inflation, a weaker dollar, and higher interest rates. The US economy went from healthy growth in the 1960s to crisis by the early 1970s.

But those were only the financial costs. Of the 2.7 million American men and women sent to Vietnam, over fifty-eight thousand would die. Civilian Vietnamese deaths on both sides are estimated at more than 2 million, and 1.1 million North Vietnamese combatants and Vietcong were killed.

Domestically, the war toppled a US president, the antiwar effort caused great turmoil, and the release of the "Pentagon Papers" severely damaged the government's credibility. After the war, America's ability to continue as a trusted world leader was questioned.

One wonders what the world would look like today had John Kennedy lived to withdraw the United States from Vietnam.

COULD THE UNITED STATES HAVE "WON" IN VIETNAM?

After the war, Bui Tin, a former North Vietnamese Army staff colonel, stated that by cutting the Ho Chi Minh Trail network in Cambodia or Laos with ground forces, the United States could have brought the war to a rapid close. Although subjected to almost constant US air attack, the trail network for over ten years remained a strategic conduit for the North.

If the United States expanded the ground war in Southeast Asia, the great uncertainty was China's response. The Vietnamese and Chinese were historic enemies; would China have entered the war? No one could say, but one of Johnson's great fears was another war against Chinese forces, as we had fought in Korea.

The case could be made that, in the end, Johnson's irresolution might have been one of the North's key advantages.

With its amorphous objectives, shifting strategies, and lack of a defined, clearly stated goal, the United States paid little attention to the words of North Vietnamese general Vo Nguyen Giap: "The object of war is to win."

ABOUT THE AUTHOR

Phil Gioia served two combat tours in Vietnam between 1968 and 1970 and was awarded two Silver Stars, a Bronze Star with 'V' device, and two Purple Hearts. A graduate of the Virginia Military Institute, he went on to earn a master's in Foreign Service from Georgetown and an MBA from Stanford. He has lectured at West Point and Annapolis, published articles in the *Journal of Military History*, *World War II*, and *Armchair General*, and appeared in History Channel programs and in Ken Burns' Vietnam War documentary. He lives in Corte Madera, California.